Azure Data Engineer Associate Certification Guide

A hands-on reference guide to developing your data engineering skills and preparing for the DP-203 exam

Newton Alex

BIRMINGHAM—MUMBAI

Azure Data Engineer Associate Certification Guide

Publishing Product Manager: Reshma Raman

Senior Editor: David Sugarman

Content Development Editor: Priyanka Soam

Technical Editor: Devanshi Ayare

Copy Editor: Safis Editing

Project Coordinator: Aparna Ravikumar Nair

Proofreader: Safis Editing

Indexer: Pratik Shirodkar

Production Designer: Nilesh Mohite

Marketing Coordinator: Priyanka Mhatre

First published: March 2022

Production reference: 1310122

Published by Packt Publishing Ltd.

Livery Place

35 Livery Street

Birmingham

B3 2PB, UK.

ISBN 978-1-80181-606-9

www.packt.com

To my wife, Eshwari, and my children, Sarah and Ryan.

Without their constant support and motivation, this book would not have been possible.

Contributors

About the author

Newton Alex leads several Azure Data Analytics teams in Microsoft, India. His team contributes to technologies including Azure Synapse, Azure Databricks, Azure HDInsight, and many open source technologies, including Apache YARN, Apache Spark, and Apache Hive.

He started using Hadoop while at Yahoo, USA, where he helped build the first batch processing pipelines for Yahoo's ad serving team. After Yahoo, he became the leader of the big data team at Pivotal Inc., USA, where he was responsible for the entire open source stack of Pivotal Inc. He later moved to Microsoft and started the Azure Data team in India. He has worked with several Fortune 500 companies to help build their data systems on Azure.

About the reviewers

Hitesh Hinduja is an ardent AI enthusiast working as a Senior Manager in AI at Ola Electric, where he leads a team of 20+ people in the areas of ML, statistics, CV, NLP, and reinforcement learning. He has filed 14+ patents in India and the US and has numerous research publications to his name. Hitesh has been involved in research roles at India's top business schools: the Indian School of Business, Hyderabad, and the Indian Institute of Management, Ahmedabad. He is also actively involved in training and mentoring and has been invited to be a guest speaker by various corporations and associations across the globe.

Ajay Agarwal was born and brought up in India. He completed his master's of technology at BITS. He has significant experience in product management in the analytics domain. For years, he has managed and evolved multiple cloud capabilities and analytics products in the data science and machine learning domains. He is known for his passion for technology and leadership.

Anindita Basak is a cloud architect who has been working on Microsoft Azure from its inception. Over the last 12 years, she has worked on Azure in cloud migration, app modernization, and cloud advisory assignments. She has been working in IT for the last 14 years and has worked on 12 books on Azure/AWS as a technical reviewer and author. She has also published multiple video courses on Azure Data Analytics from Packt Publishing.

I would like to thank my family and the entire Packt team.

Joseph Gnanaprakasam is a data architect, husband, and father living in Virginia. He has over a decade of experience in building data engineering and business intelligence solutions. Recently, he has started sharing his musings on data at joegnan.com. He is an avid photographer and enjoys traveling.

Table of Contents

Part 2: Data Storage

2

Designing a Data Storage Structure

3

Designing a Partition Strategy

4
Designing the Serving Layer

5
Implementing Physical Data Storage Structures

6
Implementing Logical Data Structures

7

Implementing the Serving Layer

Part 3: Design and Develop Data Processing (25-30%)

8

Ingesting and Transforming Data

9

Designing and Developing a Batch Processing Solution

10
Designing and Developing a Stream Processing Solution

11

Managing Batches and Pipelines

Part 4: Design and Implement Data Security (10-15%)

12

Designing Security for Data Policies and Standards

Part 5: Monitor and Optimize Data Storage and Data Processing (10-15%)

13

Monitoring Data Storage and Data Processing

14

Optimizing and Troubleshooting Data Storage and Data Processing

Part 6: Practice Exercises

15

Sample Questions with Solutions

Preface

Azure is one of the leading cloud providers in the world, providing numerous services for data hosting and data processing. Most of the companies today are either cloud-native or are migrating to the cloud much faster than ever. This has led to an explosion of data engineering jobs, with aspiring and experienced data engineers trying to outshine each other.

Gaining the DP-203: Azure Data Engineer Associate certification is a sure-fire way of showing future employers that you have what it takes to become an Azure Data Engineer. This book will help you prepare for the DP-203 examination in a structured way, covering all the topics specified in the syllabus with detailed explanations and exam tips.

The book starts by covering the fundamentals of Azure, and then takes the example of a hypothetical company and walks you through the various stages of building data engineering solutions. Throughout the chapters, you'll learn about the various Azure components involved in building the data systems and will explore them using a wide range of real-world use cases. Finally, you'll work on sample questions and answers to familiarize yourself with the pattern of the exam.

By the end of this Azure book, you'll have gained the confidence you need to pass the DP-203 exam with ease and land your dream job in data engineering.

Who this book is for

This book is intended for data engineers who want to pass the DP-203: Azure Data Engineer Associate exam and are looking to gain more in-depth knowledge of the Azure cloud stack.

This book will also help engineers and product managers who are new to Azure or who will be interviewed by companies working on Azure technologies so as to acquire good hands-on experience of the Azure data technologies.

A basic understanding of cloud technologies, extract, **transform, and load (ETL)**, and databases is expected to help you get the most out of this book.

What this book covers

The chapters in this book are designed around the skill sets listed by Microsoft for the coursework:

> **Exam DP-203: Data Engineering on Microsoft Azure – Skills Measured**
> `https://query.prod.cms.rt.microsoft.com/cms/api/`
> `am/binary/RE4MbYT`

Chapter 1, *Introducing Azure Basics*, introduces the audience to Azure and explains its general capabilities. This is a refresher chapter designed to renew our understanding of some of the core Azure concepts, including VMs, data storage, compute options, the Azure portal, accounts, and subscriptions. We will be building on top of these technologies in future chapters.

Chapter 2, *Designing a Data Storage Structure*, focuses on the various storage solutions available in Azure. We will cover topics such as Azure Data Lake Storage, Blob storage, and SQL- and NoSQL-based storage. We will also get into the details of when to choose what storage and how to optimize this storage using techniques such as data pruning, data distribution, and data archiving.

Chapter 3, *Designing a Partition Strategy*, explores the different partition strategies available. We will focus on how to efficiently split and store the data for different types of workloads and will see some recommendations on when and how to partition the data for different use cases, including analytics and batch processing.

Chapter 4, *Designing the Serving Layer*, is dedicated to the design of the different types of schemas, such as the Star and Snowflake schemas. We will focus on designing slowly-changing dimensions, building a dimensional hierarchy, temporal solutions, and other such advanced topics. We will also focus on sharing data between the different compute technologies, including Azure Databricks and Azure Synapse, using metastores.

Chapter 5, *Implementing Physical Data Storage Structures*, focuses on the implementation of lower-level aspects of data storage, including compression, sharding, data distribution, indexing, data redundancy, archiving, storage tiers, and replication, with the help of examples.

Chapter 6, *Implementing Logical Data Structures*, focuses on the implementation of temporal data structures and slowly-changing dimensions using **Azure Data Factory** (**ADF**), building folder structures for analytics, as well as streaming and other data to improve query performance and to assist with data pruning.

Chapter 7, *Implementing the Serving Layer*, focuses on implementing a relational star schema, storing files in different formats, such as Parquet and ORC, and building and using a metastore between Synapse and Azure Databricks.

Chapter 8, Ingesting and Transforming Data, introduces the various Azure data processing technologies, including Synapse Analytics, ADF, Azure Databricks, and Stream Analytics. We will focus on the various data transformations that can be performed using T-SQL, Spark, and ADF. We will also look into aspects of data pipelines, such as cleansing the data, parsing data, encoding and decoding data, normalizing and denormalizing values, error handling, and basic data exploration techniques.

Chapter 9, Designing and Developing a Batch Processing Solution, focuses on building an end-to-end batch processing system. We will cover techniques for handling incremental data, slowly-changing dimensions, missing data, late-arriving data, duplicate data, and more. We will also cover security and compliance aspects, along with techniques to debug issues in data pipelines.

Chapter 10, Designing and Developing a Stream Processing Solution, is dedicated to stream processing. We will build end-to-end streaming systems using Stream Analytics, Event Hubs, and Azure Databricks. We will explore the various windowed aggregation options available and learn how to handle schema drifts, along with time series data, partitions, checkpointing, replaying data, and so on. We will also cover techniques to handle interruptions, scale the resources, error handling, and so on.

Chapter 11, Managing Batches and Pipelines, is dedicated to managing and debugging the batch and streaming pipelines. We will look into the techniques to configure and trigger jobs, and to debug failed jobs. We will dive deeper into the features available in the data factory and Synapse pipelines to schedule the pipelines. We will also look at implementing version control in ADF.

Chapter 12, Designing Security for Data Policies and Standards, focuses on how to design and implement data encryption, both at rest and in transit, data auditing, data masking, data retention, data purging, and so on. In addition, we will also learn about the RBAC features of ADLS Gen2 storage and explore the row- and column-level security in Azure SQL and Synapse Analytics. We will deep dive into techniques for handling managed identities, keys, secrets, resource tokens, and so on and learn how to handle sensitive information.

Chapter 13, Monitoring Data Storage and Data Processing, focuses on logging, configuring monitoring services, measuring performance, integrating with CI/CD systems, custom logging and monitoring options, querying using Kusto, and finally, tips on debugging Spark jobs.

Chapter 14, Optimizing and Troubleshooting Data Storage and Data Processing, focuses on tuning and debugging Spark or Synapse queries. We will dive deeper into query-level debugging, including how to handle shuffles, UDFs, data skews, indexing, and cache management. We will also spend some time troubleshooting Spark and Synapse pipelines.

Chapter 15, *Sample Questions with Solutions*, is where we put everything we have learned into practice. We will explore a bunch of real-world problems and learn how to use the information we learned in this book to answer the certification questions. This will help you prepare for both the exam and real-world problems.

> **Note**
> All the information provided in this book is based on public Azure documents. The author is neither associated with the Azure Certification team nor has access to any of the Azure Certification questions, other than what is publicly made available by Microsoft.

Download the example code files

You can download the example code files for this book from GitHub at `https://github.com/PacktPublishing/DP-203-Azure-Data-Engineer-Associate-Certification-Guide`. If there's an update to the code, it will be updated in the GitHub repository.

We also have other code bundles from our rich catalog of books and videos available at `https://github.com/PacktPublishing/`. Check them out!

Download the color images

We also provide a PDF file that has color images of the screenshots and diagrams used in this book. You can download it here: `https://static.packt-cdn.com/downloads/9781801816069_ColorImages.pdf`.

Conventions used

There are a number of text conventions used throughout this book.

`Code in text`: Indicates code words in the text, database table names, folder names, filenames, file extensions, pathnames, dummy URLs, user input, and Twitter handles. Here is an example: "And, finally, query from the star schema tables. Here is a sample query to get a list of all those customers whose end location was `'San Jose'`."

A block of code is set as follows:

```
SELECT trip.[tripId], customer.[name] FROM
dbo.FactTrips AS trip
JOIN dbo.DimCustomer AS customer
```

```
ON trip.[customerId] = customer.[customerId]
WHERE trip.[endLocation] = 'San Jose';
```

When we wish to draw your attention to a particular part of a code block, the relevant lines or items are set in bold:

```
df = spark.createDataFrame(data= driverData, schema =
columnNames)
df.write.partitionBy("gender","salary")..parquet("abfss://path/
to/output/")
```

Any command-line input or output is written as follows:

```
az vm extension set \
   --resource-group <YOUR_RESOURCE_GROUP> \
   --vm-name <VM_NAME> \
   --name OmsAgentForLinux \
   --publisher Microsoft.EnterpriseCloud.Monitoring \
   --protected-settings '{"workspaceKey":"<YOUR_WORKSPACE_
KEY>"}' \
   --settings '{"workspaceId":"<YOUR_WORKSPACE_ID>"}'
```

Bold: Indicates a new term, an important word, or words that you see on screen. For instance, words in menus or dialog boxes appear in **bold**. Here is an example: "You can see that the data in the top table is distributed horizontally based on the **Trip ID** range."

> Tips or Important Notes
> Appear like this.

Get in touch

Feedback from our readers is always welcome.

General feedback: If you have questions about any aspect of this book, email us at customercare@packtpub.com and mention the book title in the subject of your message.

Errata: Although we have taken every care to ensure the accuracy of our content, mistakes do happen. If you have found a mistake in this book, we would be grateful if you would report this to us. Please visit www.packtpub.com/support/errata and fill in the form.

Piracy: If you come across any illegal copies of our works in any form on the internet, we would be grateful if you would provide us with the location address or website name. Please contact us at copyright@packt.com with a link to the material.

If you are interested in becoming an author: If there is a topic that you have expertise in and you are interested in either writing or contributing to a book, please visit authors.packtpub.com.

Reviews

Please leave a review. Once you have read and used this book, why not leave a review on the site that you purchased it from? Potential readers can then see and use your unbiased opinion to make purchase decisions, we at Packt can understand what you think about our products, and our authors can see your feedback on their book. Thank you!

For more information about Packt, please visit packt.com.

Share Your Thoughts

Once you've read *DP-203: Azure Data Engineer Associate Certification Guide*, we'd love to hear your thoughts! Scan the QR code below to go straight to the Amazon review page for this book and share your feedback.

https://packt.link/r/1-801-81606-9

Your review is important to us and the tech community and will help us make sure we're delivering excellent quality content.

Part 1:
Azure Basics

In this part, we focus on brushing up on the basics of Azure, including the IaaS, PaaS, and SaaS services that are available in Azure. We will cover topics including VMs, VNets, app services, Service Fabric, storage, managing services using the Azure portal, APIs, and command-line options.

This section comprises the following chapter:

- *Chapter 1, Introducing Azure Basics*

1
Introducing Azure Basics

With all the initial formalities now behind us, let's start our journey in Azure. Our journey starts here: `https://azure.microsoft.com`.

Azure is one of the most important cloud platform providers on the market today. It provides several cloud, hybrid, and on-premises services such as VMs, networks, compute, databases, messaging, **machine learning** (**ML**), artificial intelligence, **Internet of Things** (**IoT**), and many more services while focusing on security and compliance. You could use these services to build anything from web pages and mobile apps, from data analytics solutions to IoT solutions and more.

In Azure, users have the flexibility to choose from completely hosted no-code solutions to completely build their solutions ground up using the basic building blocks like VMs and VNets, where the users have full control over each and every aspect of the system. And most of these technologies come prebaked with the cloud advantages, such as geo-replication, high availability, data redundancy, scalability, and elasticity.

Let's quickly review the basics of Azure. The following sections will focus on brushing up on the fundamentals of Azure. If you already have a working knowledge of Azure and know how to spin up resources in Azure, then you can safely skip this chapter and go directly to the next one.

In this first chapter, we'll provide an overview of Azure, including introducing some common Azure services. We'll get a good grounding in the basics, such as Accounts, **virtual machines** (**VMs**), storage, compute, and networking. We'll also walk through how to spin up services using both the Azure portal and the CLI.

In this chapter, we will cover the following topics:

- Introducing the Azure portal
- Exploring Azure accounts, subscriptions, and resource groups
- Introducing Azure services
- Exploring Azure VMs
- Exploring Azure storage
- Exploring Azure networking (VNet)
- Exploring Azure compute

Let's get started!

Technical requirements

To follow along with this chapter, you will need the following:

- An Azure account (free or paid)
- The Azure CLI installed on your workstation

Introducing the Azure portal

The **Azure portal** is the starting page for all Azure developers. You can think of it as an index page that contains links to all the services provided by Azure. The following screenshot shows what the Azure portal looks like:

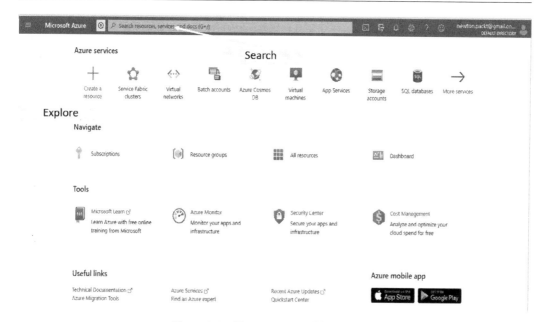

Figure 1.1 – The Azure portal home page

You can browse through all the services available in Azure or quickly search for them using the search box. Once you click on a service, the corresponding service web page will appear (also known as **blades** in Azure). Azure maintains strong consistency in terms of blade design. All the service blades will look very similar. So, if you are familiar with one, you should be able to easily navigate the others. We will be exploring a few of the service blades in this chapter.

Exploring Azure accounts, subscriptions, and resource groups

You can explore Azure with or without an account. If you are just exploring Azure and are planning to run a few Sandbox experiments, you don't need to create an Azure account. But if you are planning on investing more time in Azure, then it is recommended to create an account. Azure provides USD 200 worth of free credits for the first 30 days for you to play around. This USD 200 should get you fairly good mileage for the practice exercises for this certification. You can enroll for a free account here: `https://azure.microsoft.com/free`.

> **Note**
>
> Azure requires a valid credit card number to create the account, but it doesn't charge the credit card for free accounts. Once the USD 200 credit is exhausted, it will notify you and then delete the resources.

Let us start with Azure accounts.

Azure account

An **Azure account** refers to the Azure Billing account. It is mapped to the email id that you used to sign up for Azure. An account can contain multiple subscriptions; each of these subscriptions can have multiple resource groups and the resource groups, in turn, can have multiple resources. The billing is done at the level of subscriptions. So, one account could have multiple invoices raised per subscription.

Next, let us look at Azure subscription.

Azure subscription

Every resource (VMs, VNets, databases, and so on) that you create in Azure is tied to a **subscription**. A subscription is a container for all the resources that are created for applications and solutions under that subscription. A subscription contains the details of all the VMs, networks, storage, and other services that were used during that month that will be used for billing purposes. Azure creates a default subscription when you create an account. But you could choose to have multiple subscriptions based on your teams (dev, test, sales, marketing, finance, and so on), regions (North America, EMEA, Asia Pacific, and so on), or other logical divisions that you feel are appropriate for your use case.

Next, let us look at Resource groups.

Resource groups

Resource groups are logical groups of resources belonging to an application or a team. You can think of them as tags associated with the resources so that you can easily query, monitor, and manage the collection of resources as one. For example, you could create a resource group called Sandbox for the Azure practice sessions. At the end of the day, you can delete all the resources that were created under that resource group in one go, instead of going through every resource and deleting them. You can have multiple resource groups under a Subscription.

Resources

Resources refer to all the VMs, stores, databases, functions, and so on that can be created in Azure.

Before we move on to the next topic, let us set up an example use case of an imaginary company. We will use this imaginary company as a real-world use case across all the chapters and will try to build our data solutions for it.

Establishing a use case

Let's pretend that there is a company called **Imaginary Airport Cabs** (**IAC**). IAC wants to build a cab booking portal. They have an engineering team and a marketing team that needs applications to be hosted on Azure. The engineering team is planning to build a scalable web server with an Azure SQL backend. The frontend and the backend are segregated using two different virtual networks for isolation and security reasons. The marketing team, on the other hand, has a simpler requirement of just an Azure SQL database to store their customer information.

If we plot this requirement against the accounts, subscriptions, resource groups, and resources, it might look something like this:

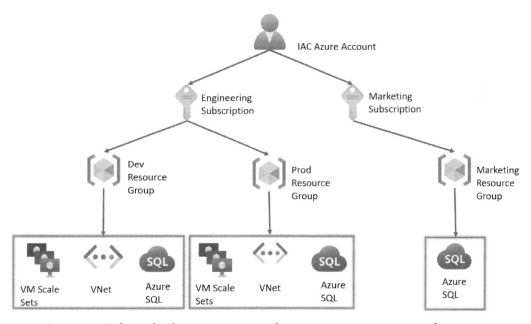

Figure 1.2 – Relationship between accounts, subscriptions, resource groups, and resources

We'll be returning to IAC and using Azure to solve their IT needs throughout this book. We will solve more complicated use cases for IAC in the following chapters so that you can understand the Azure concepts with real examples for your certification exam. Azure offers a variety of services that might be useful to IAC. We'll look at some of them in the following section.

Introducing Azure Services

Azure provides a wide array of services and technologies that can easily fulfill most real-world use cases. The services provided by Azure can be categorized like so.

Infrastructure as a Service (IaaS)

In **IaaS**, you get the bare infrastructure such as VMs, VNets, and storage, and you need to build the rest of the application stack yourself. This option gives the most flexibility for the developers in terms of OS versions, library versions, custom patches, and so on.

Platform as a Service (PaaS)

In **PaaS**, the software platforms are pre-installed and pre-configured. These are managed services in the sense that Azure manages the life cycle of this software for you. Examples include Azure SQL Server, Azure Databricks, and Azure Kubernetes Service. You will still be able to tune the software to some level, but you might not have the flexibility of choosing particular versions, patches, and so on.

Software as a Service (SaaS), also known as Function as a Service (FaaS)

What other platforms call **Software as a Service** (**SaaS**), Azure refers to as **Function as a Service** (**FaaS**). In SaaS or FaaS, you don't get to see any of the software installation details. You usually have a notebook-like user interface or an API interface for directly submitting your jobs; the cloud service provider takes care of instantiating the service, scaling the service and running the jobs for you. This is the easiest and quickest way to get started but the most restrictive in terms of software setup. Examples include Azure Functions, Azure Synapse SQL Serverless, and so on.

For those of you who are not very familiar with the IaaS, PaaS, and SaaS services, here is a diagram that explains these concepts:

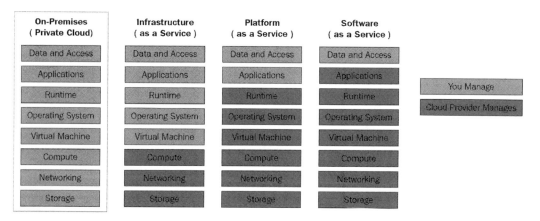

Figure 1.3 – Breakdown of Azure services

Let us next look at Azure VMs.

Exploring Azure VMs

Virtual machines (**VMs**) are software abstractions of the physical hardware. They can emulate the computer hardware for the applications running on it. We can have multiple VMs running on a single machine. Each VM will have a portion of the host machine's CPU, memory, and storage allocated to it.

Azure VMs are the most common resources that are spun up in Azure. You can use VMs to set up virtually any application that you want. They are like plain vanilla servers that can be used to install any software that you need, except the OS upgrades and security patches, which are taken care of by Azure. Azure VMs provide the advantage of faster deployments, scalability, security isolation, and elasticity. Azure provides both Windows and Linux VMs. There is a huge collection of OS flavors and versions available in the Azure Marketplace that can be used to spin up the VMs. Here are some of the VM types available at the time of writing this book. You can look for more up-to-date information at `https://docs.microsoft.com/en-us/azure/virtual-machines/sizes`:

- General-purpose
- Compute-optimized
- Memory-optimized
- Storage-optimized
- GPU
- High performance

In the following subsections, we'll walk through the process of creating a VM.

Creating a VM using the Azure portal

First, let's learn how to create a virtual machine using the Azure portal and then using the CLI. The following is a screenshot of the **Create a virtual machine** page:

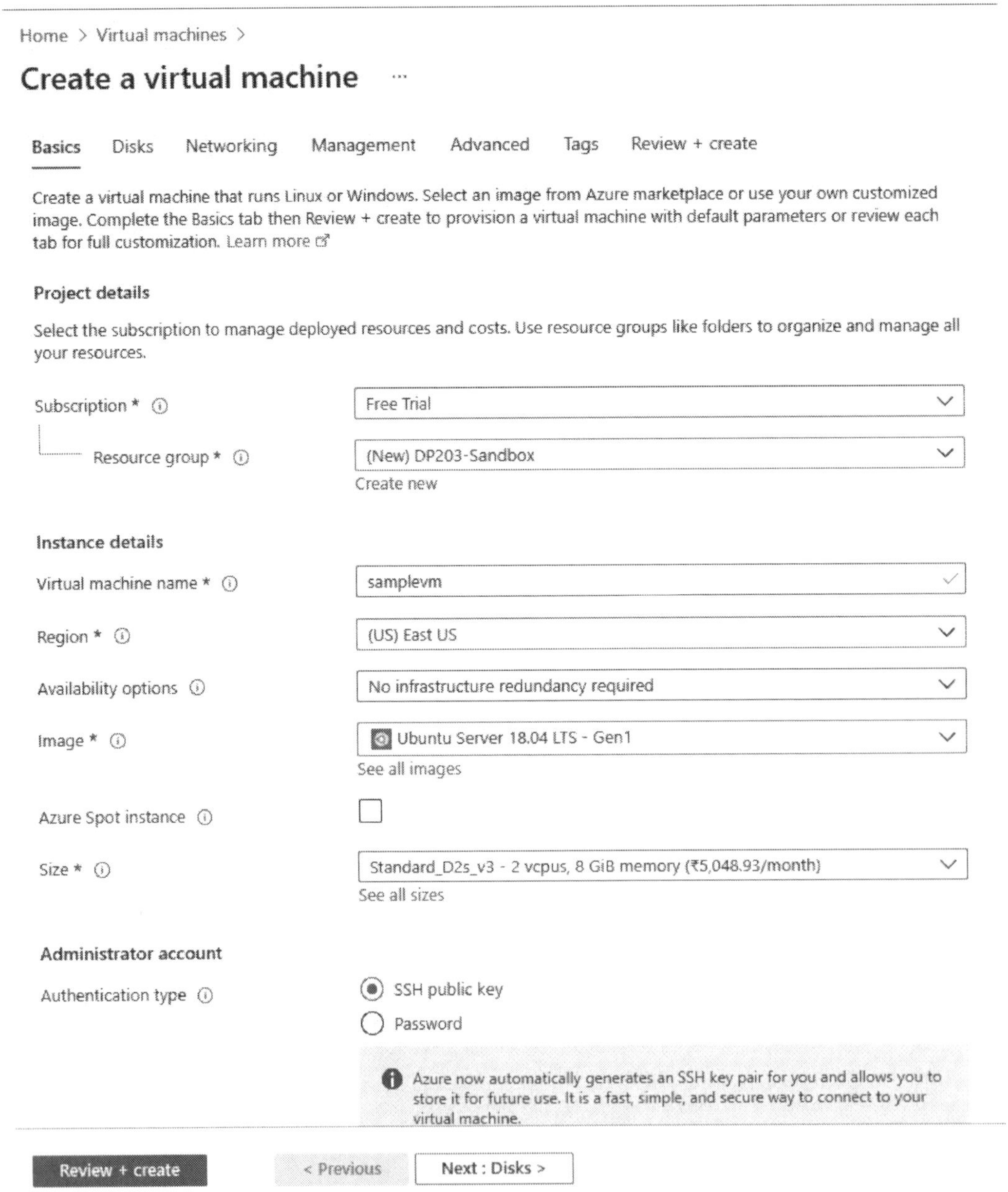

Home > Virtual machines >

Create a virtual machine   ...

Basics   Disks   Networking   Management   Advanced   Tags   Review + create

Create a virtual machine that runs Linux or Windows. Select an image from Azure marketplace or use your own customized image. Complete the Basics tab then Review + create to provision a virtual machine with default parameters or review each tab for full customization. Learn more ☐

Project details

Select the subscription to manage deployed resources and costs. Use resource groups like folders to organize and manage all your resources.

Subscription * ⓘ	Free Trial ⌄
⌐ Resource group * ⓘ	(New) DP203-Sandbox ⌄
	Create new

Instance details

Virtual machine name * ⓘ	samplevm ✓
Region * ⓘ	(US) East US ⌄
Availability options ⓘ	No infrastructure redundancy required ⌄
Image * ⓘ	⦿ Ubuntu Server 18.04 LTS - Gen1 ⌄
	See all images
Azure Spot instance ⓘ	☐
Size * ⓘ	Standard_D2s_v3 - 2 vcpus, 8 GiB memory (₹5,048.93/month) ⌄
	See all sizes

Administrator account

Authentication type ⓘ	⦿ SSH public key
	◯ Password
	❶ Azure now automatically generates an SSH key pair for you and allows you to store it for future use. It is a fast, simple, and secure way to connect to your virtual machine.

Review + create   < Previous   Next : Disks >

Figure 1.4 – Creating VMs using the Azure portal

Here are the steps to create the VM using the portal:

1. From the portal, choose **Virtual Machines** (using the search bar or **Explorer**).

2. Click on the **+ Create** sign and select **Virtual Machines**.

3. Enter a **Virtual machine name**, select a **Resource group**, select a **VM image**, select the **Size** of VM property, and an **Authentication type**.

4. Click **Review + Create** and then **Submit**.

5. You should see a pop-up with the option to **Download private key and create resource**. Click on the **Download** button and save the private key in a safe location. You will need this key to log in to your VM.

6. You can also configure **Advanced** options such as **Disks**, **Networking**, **Management**, and **Tags**, as shown in the preceding screenshot.

Now, let's learn how to create a VM using the Azure CLI.

Creating a VM using the Azure CLI

Since this is the first time we are using the CLI, we'll learn how to get started.

Installing the CLI

There are two ways to use the CLI. First, you can use the Azure CLI option directly from the Azure portal, as shown here:

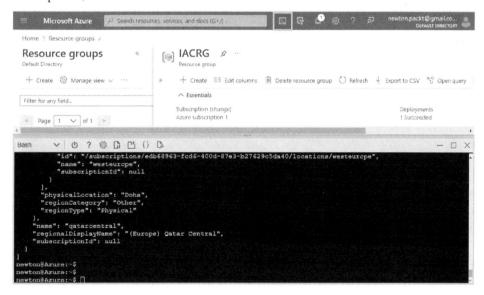

Figure 1.5 – Using the CLI directly from the Azure portal

Alternatively, you can choose to install the Azure CLI client on your local machine and run the commands from there. You can learn how to download and install the Azure CLI client here: `https://docs.microsoft.com/en-us/cli/azure/install-azure-cli-windows`.

Now, let's look at an example of creating a VM using the Azure CLI.

To create a VM using the CLI, we will have to follow a sequence of steps. For this example, we'll create an Ubuntu VM:

1. First, we have to find all the Ubuntu images that are available using the `vm image list` option:

    ```
    az vm image list --all --offer Ubuntu --all
    ```

2. Next, we need to find the Azure regions where we want to deploy. We can use `account list-locations` for this. You can choose a region that is closest to you:

    ```
    az account list-locations --output table
    ```

3. Once we've done this, we can either create a new resource group or use an existing one to associate this VM with. Let us create a new resource group called `IACRG` using the `group create` option, as shown here:

    ```
    az group create --name 'IACRG' --location 'eastus'
    ```

4. Finally, let us create a VM using the information from the preceding commands. In this example, I've chosen the `eastus` location to deploy this VM to. All the non-mandatory fields will default to the Azure default values:

    ```
    az vm create --resource-group 'IACRG' --name 'sampleVM'
    --image 'UbuntuLTS' --admin-username '<your username>'
    --admin-password '<your password>' --location 'eastus'
    ```

The previous command will create a VM named `sampleVM` under the resource group named `IACRG`.

That should have given you a good idea of how the CLI works in Azure. You can learn more about Azure VMs here: `https://azure.microsoft.com/en-in/services/virtual-machines/`.

Next, let's check out the storage options that are available in Azure.

Exploring Azure Storage

Azure has multiple storage options that suit a wide range of applications and domains. We will explore the most common ones here.

Azure Blob storage

Blob storage is the most common storage type in Azure. It can be used to store unstructured data such as videos, audio, metadata, log files, text, and binary. It is a highly scalable and very cost-effective storage solution. It provides support for tiered storage, so the data can be stored at different tiers based on their access pattern and usage frequency. Highly used data can be kept at hot tiers, the not-so-used data in cold tiers, and historical data can be archived. The data in Blob storage can be easily accessed via REST endpoints, as well as client libraries available in a wide set of languages, such as .NET, Java, Python, Ruby, PHP, Node.js, and more.

> **Blob Storage**
>
> You can access your Blob Storage at `https://<storage-account>.blob.core.windows.net`.

The following screenshot shows the creation of a storage account from the Azure portal:

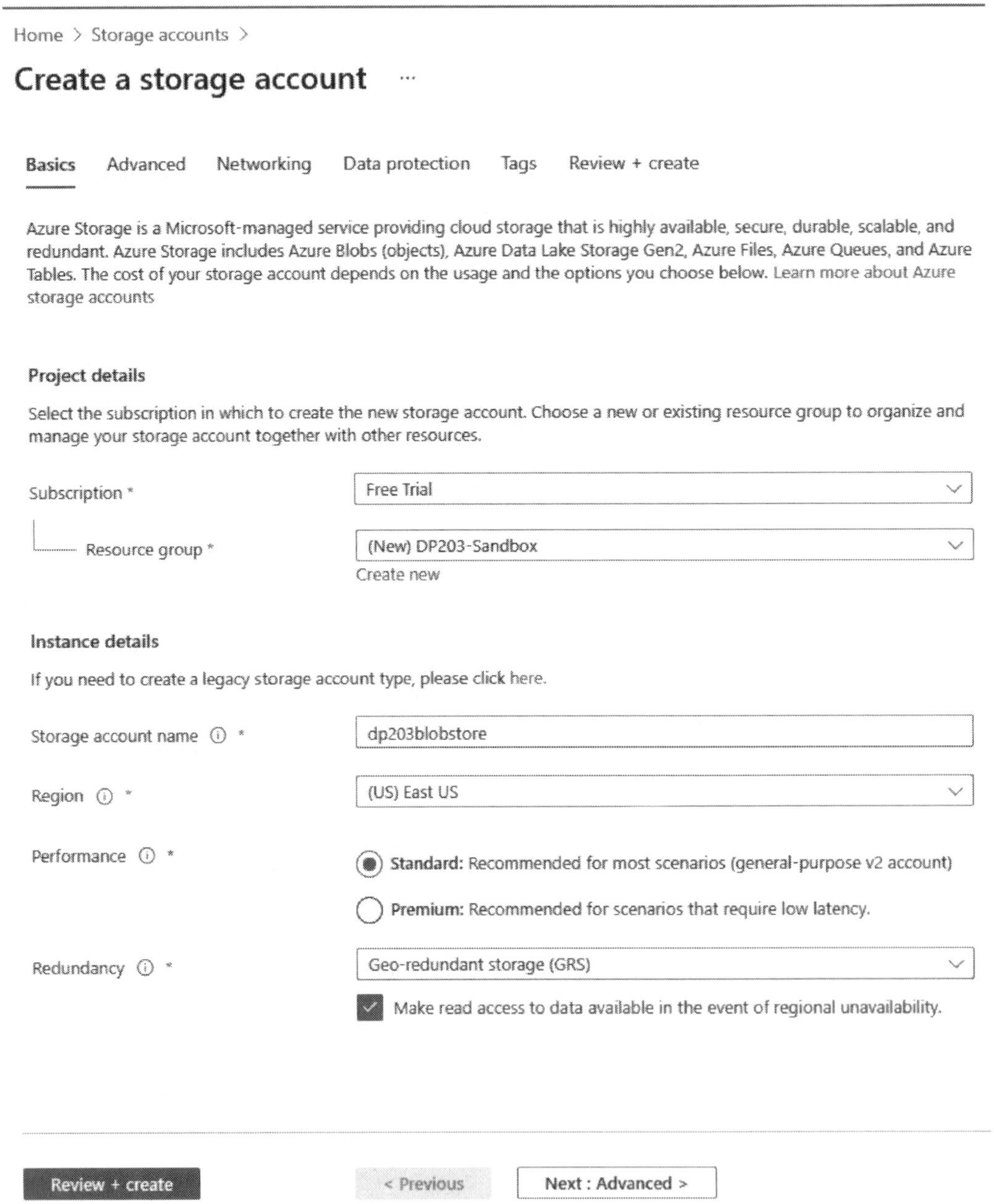

Home > Storage accounts >

Create a storage account   ...

Basics   Advanced   Networking   Data protection   Tags   Review + create

Azure Storage is a Microsoft-managed service providing cloud storage that is highly available, secure, durable, scalable, and redundant. Azure Storage includes Azure Blobs (objects), Azure Data Lake Storage Gen2, Azure Files, Azure Queues, and Azure Tables. The cost of your storage account depends on the usage and the options you choose below. Learn more about Azure storage accounts

Project details

Select the subscription in which to create the new storage account. Choose a new or existing resource group to organize and manage your storage account together with other resources.

Subscription *	Free Trial

Resource group *	(New) DP203-Sandbox

Create new

Instance details

If you need to create a legacy storage account type, please click here.

Storage account name ⓘ *	dp203blobstore

Region ⓘ *	(US) East US

Performance ⓘ *	● **Standard:** Recommended for most scenarios (general-purpose v2 account)
	○ **Premium:** Recommended for scenarios that require low latency.

Redundancy ⓘ *	Geo-redundant storage (GRS)

☑ Make read access to data available in the event of regional unavailability.

Review + create   < Previous   Next : Advanced >

Figure 1.6 – Creating a storage account using the Azure portal

Go ahead and create a storage account now, if you don't already have one. You will need this storage account throughout this book to store all the sample data, scripts, and more.

Now, let's look at another important storage option provided by Azure that will be used extensively for data lakes: Azure Data Lake Gen2.

Azure Data Lake Gen 2

Azure Data Lake Gen2 or **Azure Data Lake Storage Gen 2** (**ADLS Gen2**) is a superset of Blob storage that is optimized for **big data analytics**. ADLS Gen2 is the preferred option for data lake solutions in Azure. It provides hierarchical namespace support on top of Blob storage. Hierarchical namespace support just means that directories are supported. Unlike Blob storage, which provides pseudo directory operations via namespaces, ADLS Gen2 provides real support for directories with POSIX compliance and **Access Control List** (**ACL**) support. This makes operations such as renaming and deleting directories atomic and quick. For example, if you have 100 files under a directory in Blob storage, renaming that directory would require hundreds of metadata operations. But, in ADLS Gen2, just one metadata operation will need to be performed at the directory level. ADLS Gen2 also supports **role-based access controls** (**RBACs**), just like Blob storage does.

Another important feature of ADL Gen2 is that it is a **Hadoop-compatible filesystem**. So, building any open source analytics pipeline on top of ADL Gen2 is a breeze.

Since we are talking about ADL Gen2, you might be curious to learn about what happened to ADL Gen1.

ADL Gen1, as its name suggests, was the first generation of highly scalable and high-performing data lake storage that was built for data analytics. It is still available but will be deprecated in February 2024. ADLS Gen1 is optimized for large files, so it works best for file sizes of 256 MB and above. The features of Gen1 are available in Gen2 now. Gen2 also has some additional advantages, such as better regional availability, meaning that it is available in all Azure regions, compared to a select few regions where Gen1 is available. Gen2 also supports **Locally Redundant Storage** (**LRS**), **Zone Redundant Storage** (**ZRD**), and **Geo Redundant Storage** (**GRS**) for data redundancy and recovery, while Gen1 only supports LRS.

ADLS Gen2

You can access ADLS Gen2 at `https://<storage-account>.dfs.core.windows.net`.

To create an ADLS Gen2 account, you need to select the **Enable hierarchical namespace** checkbox on the **Create a storage account** screen:

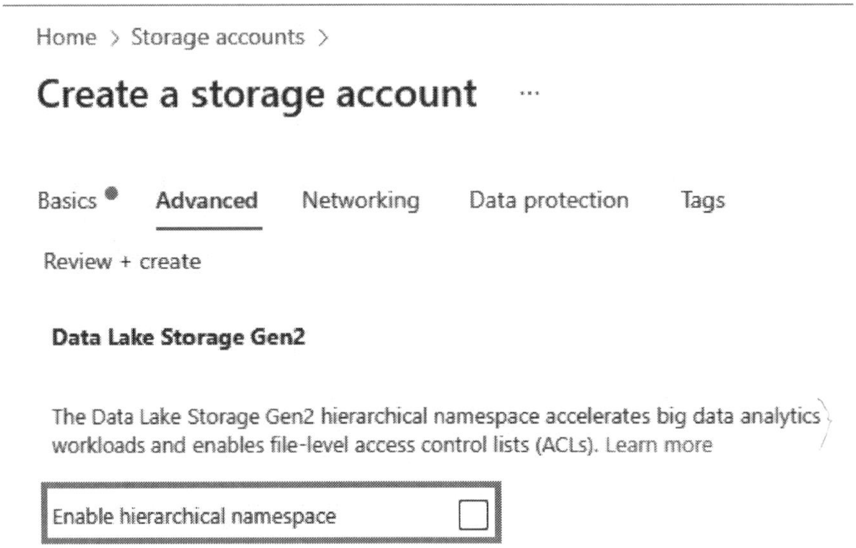

Figure 1.7 – Selecting Data Lake Storage Gen2 (Enable hierarchical namespace) while creating an Azure Storage instance

Next, let's learn about another Azure storage technology called Azure Files.

Azure Files

Azure Files provides remote file shares that can be mounted using **Server Message Block (SMB)** or **Network File Share (NFS)** protocols. These are great storage options for anyone planning to migrate on-premises workloads to the cloud with a lift and shift model, for instance, without having to invest in redevelopment for the cloud-based model. Azure files can easily be mounted both from cloud servers and on-premises servers. Azure Files is particularly useful for cases that need shared data, shared configurations, shared applications, and more across multiple users, teams, or regions. Let's look at some example commands for how to create file shares in Azure.

Creating Azure file shares with the Azure CLI

As we have already seen a few prior examples of using the Azure portal, let's explore this one using the Azure CLI so that we become familiar with the command-line options too. We will continue to use the IAC example here so that you get a good understanding of how to use the CLI with real examples. You can just glance through these examples to get an idea of how the Azure File commands are structured.

All the following examples assume that you have already created a storage account named `IACStorageAcct`. Let's get started:

1. You can create a new Azure file share for IAC using the `share create` option. The following command will create a file share named `IACFileShare` under the `IACStorageAcct`.

    ```
    az storage share-rm create --resource-group IACRG
    --storage-account IACStorageAcct --name IACFileShare
    ```

2. You can list the file shares using the `share list` option:

    ```
    az storage share list --account-name IACStorageAcct
    ```

3. You can put a file into our file share using the `file upload` option:

    ```
    az storage file upload --share-name IACFileShare --source
    ./testfile.txt
    ```

4. You can view the files in your file share using `file list`:

    ```
    az storage file list --share-name IACFileShare
    ```

5. Finally, you can download the file that we previously uploaded using the `file download` option:

    ```
    az storage file download --share-name IACFileShare -p
    testfile.txt --dest ./testfile.txt
    ```

As you can see, Azure provides a very easy and intuitive set of commands for interfacing with the various Azure services that are available.

Let us next look at Azure Queues.

Azure Queues

Azure queues are used to store a large number of messages that can be accessed asynchronously between the source and the destination. This helps in decoupling applications so that they can scale independently. Azure queues can be used across applications that are running in the cloud, on-premises, on mobile devices, and more. There are two types of queues: **Storage queues** and **Service Bus**.

Storage queues can be used for simple asynchronous message processing. They can store up to 500 TB of data (per storage account) and each message can be up to 64 KB in size. If your application needs more than a simple async queue and needs advanced features such as pub-sub models, strict ordering of messages, and blocking and non-blocking APIs, then Service Bus is a better option. With Service Bus, the message sizes can be up to 1 MB but the overall size is capped at 80 GB.

> **Azure Queues**
>
> Azure queues URL: `https://<storage account>.queue.core.windows.net/<queue>`.

Now, let's look at some example commands for creating queues in Azure.

Creating Azure Queues using the CLI

Let's look at some sample CLI commands for creating and using an Azure Queue. Again, we will assume that the `IACStorageAcct` storage account has already been created:

1. You can create a new Azure queue using the `storage queue create` command. The following command will create a queue named `IACqueue` under the `IACStorageAcct`.

    ```
    az storage queue create --name IACqueue --account-name
    IACStorageAcct
    ```

2. You can easily list the queues under a storage account using the `storage queue list` term:

    ```
    az storage queue list --account-name IACStorageAcct
    ```

3. You can add a new message to the newly created queue using the `storage message put` option:

    ```
    az storage message put --queue-name IACqueue --content
    "test"
    ```

4. Finally, use the `storage message peek` command to view the message. This command retrieves one or more messages from the front of the queue but does not alter the visibility of the message:

    ```
    az storage message peek --queue-name IACqueue
    ```

Now that you understand the basics of Azure queues, let's look at Azure tables.

Azure tables

Azure tables are key-value stores provided by Azure. They are good for storing structured non-relational data. There are two solutions available in Azure for Table stores: **Azure Table Storage** and **Cosmos DB**.

Both these features provide the same table model and **Create**, **Read**, **Update**, **and Delete** (**CRUD**) features, but the difference lies in their scale, SLAs, and availability. Cosmos DB is the premium version of Table store and can provide more than 10 million operations per second, whereas Azure Table storage has a scaling limit of 20K operations per second.

Cosmos DB also provides several additional advantages, such as five flexible levels of consistency, up to 99.999% read availability on multi-region databases, serverless mode, global presence, and more. CosmosDB deserves a complete chapter on its own. We will explore CosmosDB in more detail later in this book.

> **Azure Table**
>
> Azure Table URL: `http://<storage account>.table.core.windows.net/<table>`.

Like the other storage options we looked at, let's look at some example CLI commands to become familiar with this technology. You can just glance through these examples for now. We will provide detailed steps for implementing the examples required for the certification later in this book.

Creating Azure tables using the CLI

Let's learn how to use the Azure CLI to create and use an Azure Table:

1. We can create a new Azure Table for our example company, IAC, by using the `storage table create` option. The following command will create a table named `IACtable` under the `IACStorageAcct`.

    ```
    az storage table create --name IACtable --account-name
    IACStorageAcct
    ```

2. We can easily list the Tables under a storage account using the `storage table list` option:

    ```
    az storage table list --account-name IACStorageAcct
    ```

3. We can insert an entity into the newly created Table using the `storage entity insert` option:

```
az storage entity insert --table-name IACtable
--entity PartitionKey=testPartKey RowKey=testRowKey
Content=testContent
```

4. Finally, we can use the `storage entity show` command to view the entry:

```
az storage entity show --table-name IACtable --partition-
key testPartKey --row-key testRowKey
```

With that, we have covered the core storage options provided by Azure. Next, we'll look at Azure Managed Disks, which are required for managing disk/SSD storage for VMs.

Azure Managed disks

Azure managed disks are the virtual hard disks that are mounted to an Azure VM. As the name suggests, these disks are completely managed by Azure. So, you don't need to worry about OS upgrades, security patches, and so on. Unlike physical disks, Azure Managed Disks offer 99.999% availability. They achieve such a high availability score by storing three different replicas of the data on different servers. Managed VMs can also be allocated to availability sets and availability zones (distributed across racks and data centers) to increase their survivability in cases of server, rack (stamp), or data center outages. The managed disks also provide options for data encryption at rest and disk-level encryptions. There are different types of managed disks available, such as standard HDD, standard SSD, premium SSD, and ultra disks.

Creating and attaching Managed Disks to a VM using the CLI

Let's learn how to use the CLI to create and attach Managed Disks to `sampleVM`, which we created earlier:

```
az vm disk attach --resource-group IACRG --vm-name sampleVM
--name IACmgdisk --size-gb 64 -new
```

This is a simple one-line command for creating a new disk and attaching it to an existing VM. Please do remember that you also have the option to specify more advanced configuration parameters as part of the CLI command itself that, when not specified, would assume default values.

You can learn more about Azure storage technologies here: `https://docs.` `microsoft.com/en-us/azure/storage/common/storage-introduction`.

Now, let's explore another core Azure technology, known as Azure Networking.

Exploring Azure Networking (VNet)

Like Azure VMs, **Azure VNet** is another core component of Azure that we should be aware of. A VNet ties all resources, such as VMs, stores, and databases, together securely in a private network. It is used to encapsulate the cloud or on-premises services together within a secure boundary by controlling who can access these services and from which endpoints.

Azure Networking provides the following four main services:

- Secure connectivity within Azure resources using the basic VNet, VNet Peering, and Service Endpoints.

- Networking beyond the Azure Cloud and into the internet and hybrid clouds using Express Routers, Private Endpoints, and Point-to-Site and Site-to-Site VPNs.

- Network filtering or, in other words, Firewall Rules that can be implemented either via the Network or App Security Groups. There are options to implement the same using network appliances, which are ready-made VMs available for specialized networking scenarios.

- Network routing abilities that allow you to configure network routes using Route Tables and Border Gateway Protocols.

Now, let's learn how to create a VNet using the Azure CLI.

Creating an Azure VNet using the CLI

Let's look at a simple example of how to create a VNet and assign a VM to it. We will reuse the IACRG resource group that we used in the examples earlier in this chapter:

1. First, we need to create a VNET by specifying the necessary IP ranges and subnet prefixes. The following command creates a VNET named IACvnet under the IACRG resource group.

```
az network vnet create --address-prefixes 10.20.0.0/16
  --name IACvnet --resource-group IACRG --subnet-name
  IACsubnet --subnet-prefixes 10.20.0.0/24
```

2. Then, we need to create a public IP so that we can access our VM from the internet:

```
az network public-ip create --resource-group IACRG --name
IACpubip --allocation-method dynamic
```

3. Next, we must create a **network interface card** (**NIC**), which will be the network interface between the VM and the outside world, with the previously created VNet and public IP:

```
az network nic create --resource-group IACRG --vnet-name
IACvnet --subnet IACsubnet --name IACnic --public-ip-
address IACpubip
```

4. We now have all the components required to create a VM within our new VNet, IACVnet. We can reuse the UbuntuLTS image that we used in the earlier virtual machine creation example to create a new VM within the new VNet:

```
az vm create --resource-group IACRG --name sampleVM
--nics IACnic --image UbuntuLTS --generate-ssh-keys
```

We hope that has given you a good understanding of how to create networking components such as VNets, public IPs, and more.

You can learn more about Azure networking here: https://azure.microsoft.com/en-in/product-categories/networking/.

Next, we'll look at Azure Compute.

Exploring Azure Compute

Azure Compute is a generic term for all the compute-focused technologies in Azure. Let's explore some of the common *Compute Services* provided by Azure. Each of these technologies is worthy of a book, so we will just be focusing on introducing these technologies in this chapter. We will dive deeper into some of the technologies that are required for the certification later in this book.

VM Scale Sets

VM Scale Sets is a collection of load-balanced VMs that can be used to build highly scalable services. For example, we can have a set of web servers that can scale horizontally based on the load. The advantage of using VM Scale Sets as opposed to manually setting up VMs is that VM Scale Sets can be launched and managed using centralized templates. It comes with a load balancer by default, so we don't have to set it up manually. It also takes care of automatic scale out and scale in based on the load. In addition, VM Scale Sets have higher reliability as the workload is spread across multiple servers. Even if a few nodes fail, VM Scale Sets can quickly bring up additional nodes to replace the capacity. VM Scale Sets can be configured across availability zones to improve the availability even more.

You can learn more about VM Scale Sets here: `https://azure.microsoft.com/en-in/services/virtual-machine-scale-sets/`.

Azure App Service

Azure App Service allows you to develop and host web apps, mobile apps, and APIs using a wide selection of languages such as .NET, Java, Node.js, Python, ASP.NET, and more. These are fully managed services that provide support for the entire life cycle of apps such as development, CI/CD, releases, maintenance, debugging, and scaling. Azure App Service is backed by enterprise-grade security and compliance. There are very detailed examples, tutorials, and support available in Azure for building complete web and mobile solutions using Azure App Service.

You can learn more about Azure App Service here: `https://azure.microsoft.com/en-in/services/app-service/`.

Azure Kubernetes Service

Kubernetes is an open source container orchestration software. **Azure Kubernetes Service** (**AKS**) is a PaaS version of Kubernetes that's hosted on Azure. AKS provides a complete life cycle management for containerized apps, starting from development (using Visual Studio, code, and other Kubernetes tools), through to CI/CD (integration with GitHub), deployment, scaling, telemetry, logging, monitoring, and more. AKS also supports Docker images, which are widely used for containerization.

You can learn more about AKS here: `https://azure.microsoft.com/en-in/services/kubernetes-service/`.

Azure Functions

Azure Functions is a perfect example of a serverless technology and is a SaaS. Serverless doesn't mean that there are *no* servers, it just means that you don't have to deploy, maintain, or upgrade your servers (VMs); someone else is doing it for you in the background and abstracting the details from you. You can use functions to write your processing logic based on event triggers and bindings such as a transaction in a database, an IoT event, and a REST call. The blocks of code you write are called functions (no points for guessing that). All you need to do is open the Azure Functions Notebook Interface and write your logic (code) directly in it. There are function extensions available in the many languages that support integration with Development, CI/CD, and DevOps tools.

You can learn more about Azure Functions here: `https://azure.microsoft.com/en-in/services/functions/`.

Azure Service Fabric

Service Fabric is a very powerful cluster technology that takes care of app deployment, scaling, upgrades, and maintenance for microservice-based applications. It can take care of the entire life cycle management process for applications. This is similar to AKS but for non-containerized applications. Many of the core Azure services themselves run on top of Service Fabric. Service Fabric is an open source project and has very high reliability and availability.

You can learn more about Azure Service Fabric here: `https://azure.microsoft.com/en-in/services/service-fabric/`.

Azure Batch

Azure Batch is used to run large parallel processing applications or high-performance computing applications. Batch provides the necessary resource management, scheduling, and scaling support to run any traditional MPP programs. It spins up the VMs and deploys and runs your programs in a parallel manner. It can dynamically scale up and down as required to optimize the cost. Azure Batch can be used for high volume batch processing, financial modeling, video rendering, weather prediction model generation, and so on.

You can learn more about Azure Batch here: `https://azure.microsoft.com/en-in/services/batch/`.

Summary

With that, we have completed our first chapter. If it was too overwhelming for you, don't worry – this chapter was just meant to provide an overview of Azure. By the time you complete the next few chapters, your confidence will increase. On the other hand, if this chapter was easy for you, then you are probably already aware of some level of cloud technologies, and the next set of chapters should also be easy for you.

Now that you have completed this chapter, you should know how to navigate the Azure portal. You now understand the relationship between Azure accounts, subscriptions, resource groups, and resources. You also know how to create new VMs, Storage instances, VNets, and so on using both the Azure portal and the CLI. You are also aware of the major compute services that are available in Azure. With this foundational knowledge in place, we can move on to more interesting and certification-oriented topics.

We will be exploring Azure storage technologies in the next chapter.

Part 2: Data Storage

This part dives into the details of the different types of storage, data partition strategies, schemas, file types, high availability, redundancy, and more.

This section comprises the following chapters:

2

Designing a Data Storage Structure

Welcome to Chapter 2. We will be focusing on **Azure data storage technologies** in this chapter. Azure provides several storage technologies that can cater to a wide range of **cloud** and **hybrid** use cases. Some of the important Azure storage technologies includes: **Blobs**, **Files**, **Queues**, **Tables**, **SQL Database**, **Cosmos DB**, **Synapse SQL Warehouse**, and **Azure Data Lake Storage** (**ADLS**). Azure bundles the four fundamental storage technologies, namely:—Blobs, Files, Queues, and Tables—as Azure Storage. Other advanced services such as Cosmos DB, SQL Database, ADLS, and so on are provided as independent Azure services.

From this chapter onward, we will be following the exact sequence of the *DP-203* syllabus.

We will mostly be focusing on the design aspects of storage structures in this chapter. The corresponding implementation details will be covered in the later chapters.

This chapter will cover the following topics:

- Designing an Azure data lake
- Selecting the right file types for storage
- Choosing the right file types for analytical queries
- Designing storage for efficient querying
- Designing storage for data pruning

- Designing folder structures for data transformation
- Designing a distribution strategy
- Designing a data archiving solution

Let's get started.

Technical requirements

For this chapter, you will need the following:

- An Azure account (free or paid)
- The **Azure command-line interface** (**Azure CLI**) installed on your workstation. Please refer to the section, in *Creating a VM using Azure CLI* in *Chapter 1, Introducing Azure Basics* for instructions on installing the Azure CLI.

Designing an Azure data lake

If you have been following the big data technologies domain, you would have definitely come across the term *data lake*. Data lakes are distributed data stores that can hold very large volumes of diverse data. They can be used to store different types of data such as structured, semi-structured, unstructured, streaming data, and so on.

A data lake solution usually comprises a storage layer, a compute layer, and a serving layer. The compute layers could include **Extract, Transform, Load** (**ETL**); **Batch**; or **Stream** processing. There are no fixed templates for creating data lakes. Every data lake could be unique and optimized as per the owning organization's requirements. However, there are few general guidelines available to build effective data lakes, and we will be learning about them in this chapter.

How is a data lake different from a data warehouse?

The main difference between a data lake and a **data warehouse** is that a data warehouse stores structured data, whereas a data lake can be used to store different formats and types of data. Data lakes are usually the landing zones for different sources and types of data. This raw data gets processed and the eventual curated data is loaded into structured data stores such as data warehouses. The other main differentiating factor is the scale. Data lakes can easily store data in the range of **Petabytes** (**PB**), **Exabytes** (**EB**), or even higher, while data warehouses might start choking at the PB range.

When should you use a data lake?

We can consider using data lakes for the following scenarios:

- If you have data that is too big to be stored in structured storage systems like data warehouses or SQL databases

- When you have raw data that needs to be stored for further processing, such as an ETL system or a batch processing system

- Storing continuous data such as **Internet of Things (IoT)** data, sensor data, tweets, and so on for low latency, high throughput streaming scenarios

- As the staging zone before uploading the processed data into an SQL database or data warehouse

- Storing videos, audios, binary blob files, log files, and other semi-structured data such as **JavaScript Object Notation (JSON)**, **Extensible Markup Language (XML)**, or **YAML Ain't Markup Language (YAML)** files for short-term or long-term storage.

- Storing processed data for advanced tasks such as ad hoc querying, **machine learning (ML)**, data exploration, and so on.

Let's next look at the different zones or regions in a data lake.

Data lake zones

A data lake can be broadly segregated into three zones where different stages of the processing take place, outlined as follows:

1. **Landing Zone** or **Raw Zone**: This is where the raw data is ingested from different input sources.

2. **Transformation Zone**: This is where the batch or stream processing happens. The raw data gets converted into a more structured and **business intelligence (BI)**-friendly format.

3. **Serving Zone**: This is where the curated data that can be used to generate insights and reports are stored and served to BI tools. The data in this zone usually adheres to well-defined schemas.

> **Tip**
>
> In the Landing zones, data gets accumulated from various input sources. If the source is a streaming input or an IoT input, then the files tend to be smaller. Large numbers of small files are known to cause performance issues with data lakes. For example, ADLS Gen2 recommends file sizes of 256 **Megabytes** (**MB**) to 100 **Gigabytes** (**GB**) for optimal performance. If there are too many small files, then it is recommended to merge them into larger files.

Let's now explore a few standard data lake models.

Data lake architecture

The following image shows a data lake architecture for both batch and stream processing. The diagram also includes examples of the Azure technologies that can be used for each of the data lake zones. The names of the services listed by the icons are presented in the image after this:

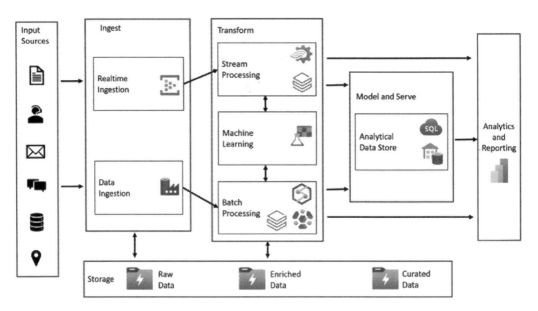

Figure 2.1 – Data lake architecture using Azure services

Here are the names of the services represented by the icons in the preceding diagram:

Figure 2.2 – Icon legends

We will be learning more about these technologies throughout this book. Next, let's look at batch processing.

Batch processing

In a batch processing framework, the data usually lands into the Landing Zone (or Raw Zone) from various input sources. Once the data lands in the Landing Zone, the orchestration framework triggers the data processing pipelines. The pipelines usually have multiple stages that will take the data through various processing stages such as data cleansing, filtering, aggregating the data from various tables and files, and finally generating curated data for BI and exploration. The stages in the pipeline could be run in parallel or in a sequential fashion. Azure provides a service called Data Factory that can be used for building such pipelines. **Azure Data Factory** (**ADF**) is a very versatile tool that also provides the ability to ingest data from a variety of sources and perform simple data processing activities such as joins, filtering, and so on.

Batch processing can be used for ETL jobs, data preparation jobs, periodic report generation, and more. From a certification standpoint, you should be aware of the Azure technologies that can be used for building the batch components of a data lake. The following table lists some of the commonly used Azure technologies for building batch processing pipelines:

Storage Technologies	Azure Data Lake Gen2 Azure Blob Storage Azure CosmosDB Azure SQL Database
Data Transformation Technologies	Spark (via Azure Synapse, Azure HDInsight or Azure Databricks) Apache Hive (via Azure HDInsight) Apache Pig (via Azure HDInsight)
Analytical Datastore	Synapse SQL Warehouse (via Azure HDInsight) Apache HBase (via Azure HDInsight) Apache Hive (via Azure HDInsight)

Figure 2.3 – Azure technologies available for building a batch processing system

Let's next learn about stream processing.

Stream processing or real-time processing

Stream processing refers to the near-real-time processing of data. Unlike batch processing, which processes data at rest, stream processing deals with data as and when it arrives. As such, these systems need to be low-latency and high-throughput systems.

For example, consider our **Imaginary Airport Cabs (IAC)** example that we used in *Chapter 1, Basics of Azure*. We might want to perform surge pricing based on a demand for taxis, so the system needs to process requests for taxis coming from a particular geographical area in near real time. This data can then be aggregated and used to decide the dynamic pricing.

Generally, in stream processing scenarios, data arrives in small files in quick succession. We refer to these small data files as messages. The streaming system usually does some quick checks for the correct format of data, processes the data, and writes the data to a store. So, we need to ensure that the stores used for real-time processing support high-volume writes with low latency.

The following table lists some of the Azure technologies that can be used to build a stream processing pipeline for a data lake:

Ingestion Tools	Azure Event Hub Azure IoT Hub Apache Kafka (via Azure HDInsight)
Stream Processing Tools	Azure Stream Analytics Spark Streaming (via Azure HDInsight or Azure Databricks) Apache Storm (via Azure HDInsight)
Analytical Datastore	Synapse SQL Warehouse Apache HBase (via Azure HDInsight) Apache Hive (via Azure HDInsight)

Figure 2.4 – Azure technologies available for building a stream processing system

Let's next learn about two of the common architectures used in data lakes.

Lambda architecture

One of the shortcomings of batch processing systems is the time it takes for them to process the data. Usually, a batch pipeline that processes a day or a month's worth of data might run for several hours—or sometimes even days—to generate the results. In order to overcome this shortcoming, we can use a hybrid architecture called **Lambda architecture** that uses a combination of fast and slow pipelines. The slow path processes a larger volume of data and produces accurate results but takes more time. The fast path, on the other hand, works on a much smaller dataset (usually sampled data) and gives an approximate result much quicker. The fast path could also use different technologies such as streaming technologies to speed up the processing. Both these pipelines feed into a Serving layer that updates the incremental updates from the fast path into the baseline data from the slow path. Any analytics client or reporting tool can then access the curated data from the Serving layer.

You can see an overview of Lambda architecture in the following diagram:

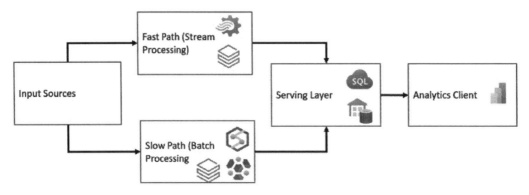

Figure 2.5 – Lambda architecture

This Lambda model will help us make informed decisions more quickly, compared to batch-only models.

Kappa architecture

Kappa is an alternative architecture to Lambda architecture and focuses only on the fast path or the streaming path. It is built on the assumption that the data under consideration can be represented as an immutable data stream and that such streams can be stored for long periods of time in a data storage solution with the same streaming format. If we need to recalculate some historical data, the corresponding input data from the data store can be replayed through the same Streaming layer to recalculate the results.

The main advantage of Kappa architecture is reduced complexity, as compared to Lambda architecture, where we implement two pipelines. It thus avoids the dual processing of the same data, as happens in Lambda architecture.

In Kappa architecture, the input component is a message queue such as an **Apache Kafka** or **Azure Event Hubs** queue, and all the processing is usually done through **Azure Stream Analytics**, **Spark**, or **Apache Storm**.

You can see an overview of Kappa architecture in the following diagram:

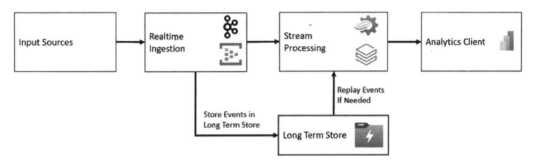

Figure 2.6 – Kappa architecture

Kappa architecture can be used for applications such as real-time ML and applications where the baseline data doesn't change very often.

Exploring Azure technologies that can be used to build a data lake

Now that we understand some of the recommended ways to build a data lake, let's explore Azure technologies that can be used to build data lakes.

ADLS Gen2 or Blob storage

The most important component of a data lake is the storage component. Choosing the right storage could be the difference between the success or failure of a data lake. Azure provides a specialized storage technology for building data lakes, called ADLS Gen2. ADLS Gen2 is usually a good choice for most data lake storage requirements, but we can also choose to use regular Blob storage for the data lake if our requirements are mostly for just storing unstructured data and if we don't need **access-control lists** (**ACLs**) on the files and folders. ACLs provide control on which users have read, write, or execute permissions on the files and folders.

Azure Data Factory (ADF)

Once we have the store decided, we need a way to automatically move the data around. This functionality is fulfilled by ADF. ADF is a very powerful tool that can be used for the following:

- Data ingestion from a wide array of inputs, such as Azure Storage, Amazon Redshift, Google BigQuery, SAP HANA, Sybase, Teradata, generic **HyperText Transfer Protocol** (**HTTP**), **File Transfer Protocol** (**FTP**), and so on

- Simple data transformations such as joins, aggregations, filtering, and cleanup

- Scheduling pipelines to move the data from one stage to another

Compute and data processing components

Now that we have figured out where to store the data, how to get the data, and how to move it around, we need to decide on how to process the data for advanced analytics. This can be achieved using a variety of technologies available in Azure. Some of them are listed here:

- **Azure Synapse Analytics** for its SQL and Spark pools

- **Azure Databricks** for Spark

- **Azure HDInsight** for Hive, Spark, and other **open source software** (**OSS**) technologies

- **Azure Stream Analytics** for streaming requirements

You might be wondering: *Why does Azure have so many options for Spark?* Well, Spark has been gaining a lot of traction of late as one of the most popular analytical tools for data engineers. Spark provides something for every developer, be it batch processing, streaming, ML, interactive notebooks, and so on, and Spark makes it very easy to switch between the different use cases by providing very consistent coding interfaces. Once you know how to write a batch program, writing a streaming program is very similar, with a very shallow learning curve. It is this ease of use and support for a wide variety of analytical tools that make Spark the preferred choice for the latest generation of data engineers. Azure understands this trend and provides multiple Spark options. It provides the Azure Databricks version for customers who love the features of Databricks Spark. It provides HDInsight Spark for customers who prefer OSS technologies, and it also provides Synapse Spark, which is a performance-boosted version of the OSS Spark for those customers who prefer an integrated single-pane experience within Azure Synapse Analytics.

Let's explore these compute technologies a little bit more.

Azure Synapse Analytics

Azure Synapse Analytics is the premium analytics service that Azure is investing in quite heavily. When we hear *Azure Synapse Analytics*, we usually think of it as an SQL data warehouse but, in reality, Synapse Analytics is a complete suite of integrated analytical services. Synapse Analytics has integrated support for several Azure stores, compute technologies such as **SQL Data Warehouse** and **Synapse Spark**, orchestration engines such as **ADF**, specialized stores such as **Cosmos DB**, cloud-based **identity and access management** (**IAM**) services such as **Azure Active Directory** (**Azure AD**), data governance support via **Azure Purview**, and more.

Azure Synapse Analytics also doubles up as the analytics store for the Serving layer as it has a highly scalable SQL Warehouse store in its core. This can be used to store the processed data that is reduced in size to be used for analytical queries, data insights, reporting, and so on.

Azure Databricks

Azure Databricks is the Databricks version of Spark hosted on Azure. Azure Databricks provides a very feature-rich Notebook experience and is well connected with the other Azure services, including Storage, ADF, Power BI, Authentication, and other Azure features. We can use Azure Databricks to write Spark code or scripts to do the data processing for us. For example, we can use Azure Databricks Spark to clean up the input data, condense it via filtration, aggregation, or sampling, and add a structure to the data so that it can be used for analytics by SQL-like systems.

Azure HDInsight

Azure also provides an option to use open-source versions of **Apache Spark**, **Apache Hive**, **Apache HBase**, and more via the **HDInsight** product. Similar to Azure Databricks, we can use the open source version of Spark or Hive to accomplish the data processing for our data lake. The HDInsight version of Spark uses Jupyter Notebooks. This is one of the commonly used open source Notebooks. Hive, on the other hand, has been the preferred data processing technology till Spark took over the limelight. Hive is still one of the most widely deployed services in enterprise big data platforms.

Azure Stream Analytics

Stream processing refers to the quick processing of data as and when it comes in. So, we need technologies that provide high throughput and near-real-time processing capabilities. Azure provides both proprietary and open source options for such stream processing requirements. Azure's native streaming technology is called **Azure Stream Analytics** (**ASA**). ASA works natively with all Azure Storage services and can directly connect to reporting tools such as Power BI without an intermediate data store. But, if you prefer to use an open-source service for streaming, we can use services such as **Apache Kafka** and **Apache Storm**, available via HDInsight.

Reporting and Power BI

Now that we know the components that can be used to transform raw data from the data lake store into more curated forms, we need to decide how to present this data. The final step in data analytics is presenting the data in a manner that drives business insights or generates reports to indicate the state of the business. In either case, we need tooling such as **Power BI** to display interactive reports. Power BI is a collection of tools that can operate on big data and provide visual insights into the data. Power BI has built-in connectivity with Azure to seamlessly integrate with services such as Cosmos DB, Synapse Analytics, Azure Storage, and more.

Azure ML

Azure also provides some advanced services such as **Azure ML** for advanced analytics and prediction. ML is usually the next step in the progression of an analytics pipeline. Once you start generating insights from the data, the next step is to predict future trends. Azure ML provides support for a wide range of algorithms and models for data analytics. Since ML is not in the syllabus for this book, we will not be going deeper into it, but if you would like to explore the topic, you can check out the details at the following link: `https://azure.microsoft.com/en-in/services/machine-learning/`.

You should now have a fairly good understanding of how to build a data lake and which technologies to use from Azure. That was a lot of keywords and technologies to remember. If you feel overwhelmed by all the technologies and the keywords, don't worry—we will be revisiting these technologies throughout the book. By the time we are halfway through the book, you will have a good grasp of these technologies.

Selecting the right file types for storage

Now that we understand the components required to build a data lake in Azure, we need to decide on the file formats that will be required for efficient storage and retrieval of data from the data lake. Data often arrives in formats such as text files, log files, **comma-separated values** (CSV), JSON, XML, and so on. Though these file formats are easier for humans to read and understand, they might not be the best formats for data analytics. A file format that cannot be compressed will soon end up filling up the storage capacities; a non-optimized file format for read operations might end up slowing analytics or ETLs; a file that cannot be easily split efficiently cannot be processed in parallel. In order to overcome such deficiencies, the big data community recommends three important data formats: **Avro**, **Parquet**, and **Optimized Row Columnar** (ORC). These file formats are also important from a certification perspective, so we will be exploring these three file formats in depth in this chapter.

Choosing the right file type is critical, as it will not be easy to change this later once data starts pouring in. Each of the file formats has its own advantages and disadvantages, but there is rarely one file format that will fit all the requirements. So, based on our requirements, we can even choose to have more than one file format within the data lake. Azure calls this **polyglot persistence**.

> **Tip**
> Try to stick with just one or two file formats, ideally one file format per zone of the data lake. Too many file formats might become a management nightmare, with several duplicate copies of data getting generated over time.

There are multiple factors to be considered while choosing a file format. The most important ones are listed here:

- **Type of workload**: Some file formats perform better with some tools than others— for example, ORC performs better with Hive, while ORC and Parquet both perform well with Spark. So, the data processing technology that we plan to adopt will have a say in deciding the file format too.

- **Cost**: This is going to be the primary concern for any organization. How do we keep the cost low? The more we store in the data lake, the more we will end up paying for it. So, file formats that support better compression ratios become important here.

- **Compression**: If we know that our data lake is not going to ever get into PB or EB ranges, then we can decide on data formats that have a good balance of compression versus performance. And, similarly, if our storage size is going to be huge, we definitely need a format that supports higher compression levels.

- **Performance**: Aspects such as read speed, write speed, the ability to split files for parallel processing, and fast access to relevant data will impact the performance of the analytical tools. So, the performance requirement is another key point when deciding on the file format.

> **Tip**
> If you still need to store the data in any of the semi-structured formats such as CSV, JSON, XML, and so on, consider compressing them using Snappy compression.

Let's now explore the file formats in detail.

Avro

Avro is a row-based storage format. That means it stores each complete row one after the other in its file storage. For example, imagine we have a table like this:

Driver ID	Name	License Number
111	Annie	A1234
222	Brian	B5678
333	Charlie	C3456

Figure 2.7 – A table showing Avro format

Avro will store it logically, as shown in the following screenshot. In reality, it would be adding the metadata required for decoding the file together in the same file:

111	Annie	A1234	222	Brian	B5678	333	Charlie	C3456

Figure 2.8 – An example Avro row, including metadata

This format is good for write-intensive transactional workloads such as ETL jobs that need to read entire files to process data.

> **Avro information**
>
> More information about Avro can be found at the following link:
> `https://avro.apache.org`.

Parquet

Parquet, on the other hand, is a column-based format. That means it stores data from each related column together one after the other in its file. For example, if we consider the same table in the Avro example, Parquet will logically store it as shown in the following screenshot. As with Avro, Parquet will also store some metadata along with the actual data in its file:

111	222	333	Annie	Brian	Charlie	A1234	B5678	C3456

Figure 2.9 – An example Parquet row

Such column-based storage makes Parquet exceptionally good for read-intensive jobs such as analytical workloads, as they generally query only a subset of columns for processing. This ensures that we don't have to read entire rows just to process a small sub-section of those rows, unlike with row-oriented data formats. Projects such as Apache Spark and Apache Drill are most compatible with Parquet and can take advantage of query optimization features such as **Predicate Pushdowns** while working with Parquet.

> **Parquet information**
>
> More information about Parquet can be found at the following link:
> `https://parquet.apache.org.`

ORC

ORC is also a column-based format similar to Parquet and works really well with analytical workloads for that reason. Projects such as Apache Hive are most compatible with ORC, as ORC natively supports some of the Hive data types and enables features such as **atomicity, consistency, isolation, and durability** (**ACID**) support and predicate pushdowns in Hive.

> **ORC information**
>
> More information about ORC can be found at the following link:
> `https://orc.apache.org.`

Comparing Avro, Parquet, and ORC

Let's compare the three file formats from the perspective of the core evaluation parameters required for data lake storage, as follows:

Features	AVRO	Parquet	ORC
READ Performance	Low	High	High
WRITE Performance	High	Low	Low
Ability to Split files for Parallel Processing	Yes	Yes	Yes (Best)
Schema Evolution Support	Yes (Best)	Yes	Yes

Figure 2.10 – File format comparisons

Now that we understand the basics of the file formats, here are some tips for choosing the file format for each of the zones described in the *Data lake zones* section:

Landing Zone or Raw Zone

- If the data size is going to be huge (in **terabytes** (**TB**), PB, or higher), you would need good compression, so go with Avro or compressed text using technologies such as **Snappy compression**.
- If you plan to have a lot of ETL jobs, go with Avro.
- If you plan to have just one file format for ease of maintenance, then Parquet would be a good compromise from both a compression and performance perspective.

Transformation Zone

- If you are primarily going to use Hive, go with ORC.
- If you are primarily going to use Spark, go with Parquet.

Choosing the right file types for analytical queries

In the previous section, we discussed the three file formats—Avro, Parquet, and ORC—in detail. Any format that supports fast reads is better for analytics workloads. So, naturally, column-based formats such as Parquet and ORC fit the bill.

Based on the five core areas that we compared before (read, write, compression, schema evolution, and the ability to split files for parallel processing) and your choice of processing technologies, such as Hive or Spark, you could select ORC or Parquet.

For example, consider the following:

- If you have Hive- or Presto-based workloads, go with ORC.
- If you have Spark- or Drill-based workloads, go with Parquet.

Now that you understand the different types of file formats available and the ones to use for analytical workloads, let's move on to the next topic: designing for efficient querying.

Designing storage for efficient querying

In order to design for efficient querying, we will have to understand the different querying technologies that are available in Azure. Even though this chapter is primarily focused on storage technologies, a small diversion into the world of querying will help us understand the process of designing for efficient querying better. There are two types of querying services available: SQL-based ones such as **Azure SQL**, **Synapse Serverless/Dedicated Pools** (previously known as SQL Warehouse), and big data analytical engines such as **Spark** and **Hive**. Let's explore the important design techniques for both these groups of query engines.

We can broadly group the techniques available for efficient querying into the following three layers:

- **Storage layer**—Using techniques such as **partitioning**, **data pruning**, and **eventual consistency**

- **Application layer**—Using techniques such as **data caching** and **application tuning** (such as varying the sizes of containers, increasing parallelism)

- **Query layer**—Using specialized techniques such as **indexing** and **materialized views** that are available within some of the services

Don't worry about all the new keywords in this section. We will be all exploring these technologies in detail in the following sections. Let's start with the Storage layer.

Storage layer

Designing a partition strategy correctly early on is important because once we implement the partitions, it will be difficult to change these at a later point. Changing partitions at a later stage will require data transfers, query modifications, changes to applications, and so on. A partition strategy for one type of query might not work for another query, so we should focus on designing a partition strategy for our most critical queries. Let's look at the important points to consider while designing partitions.

Partitions

A partition just refers to the way we split the data and store it. The best partitions are those that can run parallel queries without requiring too many inter-partition data transfers. So, we divide the data in such a way that the data is spread out evenly and the related data is grouped together within the same partitions. Partitions are a very important concept from a certification perspective and, as such, there is a whole chapter dedicated to partitions (*Chapter 3, Designing a Partition Strategy*). So, let's just focus on a high-level overview here.

Some important partition concepts that can help accelerate query performance are discussed next.

Replicating data

Smaller, more frequently used static data such as lookup data or catalog data can be replicated across partitions. This will help reduce the data access time and, in turn, will speed up the queries considerably.

Reducing cross-partition operations and joins

Minimizing cross-partition joins by running jobs in parallel within each partition and aggregating only the final results will help in cross-partition data access. Any cross-partition access is an expensive operation, so trying to perform as much data processing within the same partition before exporting only the required filtered data will help improve the overall performance of queries.

Data pruning

Data pruning or data exclusion refers to the process of ignoring unnecessary data during querying and thereby reducing **input/output** (**I/O**) operations. This is also an important topic for certification, so, we have a complete section dedicated to data pruning later in this chapter.

Eventual consistency

Storage systems support different levels of consistency. Cloud stores usually keep redundant copies of your data in multiple servers. Consistency refers to how soon all the internal copies of your data will reflect a change that was made to the primary copy. Data stores usually support strong consistency or eventual consistency, but some stores such as Cosmos DB even support multiple levels in between strong and eventual consistency. If the storage system is strongly consistent, then it ensures that all the data copies are updated before the user can perform any other operation. On the other hand, if the storage system is eventually consistent, then the storage lets the data in each of the copies get updated gradually over time. Queries running on strongly consistent data stores tend to be slower as the storage system will ensure that all the writes (to all the copies) are complete before the query can return. But in eventually consistent systems, the query will return immediately after the first copy is done, and the rest of the updates to all the other copies happen asynchronously. Hence, if your system can tolerate eventual consistency, then it will tend to be faster.

Next, let's look at the components of the Application Layer.

Application Layer

Application layer optimizations deal with how efficiently we use the core components such as the **central processing unit** (**CPU**), memory, network, and so on. Let's look at some of the ways to improve performance at the application layer.

Tuning applications

Big data analytical services such as Spark and Hive can be optimized by configuring the number of parallel executions and other attributes such as memory, CPU, networking bandwidth, and the size of the containers. Here are some points to consider for tuning such services:

- Consider the right **virtual machine** (**VM**) sizes. Select VMs that have enough memory, CPU, disk, and network bandwidth for your applications.

- Larger VMs can support more containers and hence increase parallelization, but this is subject to the application's ability to scale with the increased parallelization. Find the sweet spot between the application's ability to scale and the VM sizes.

  For example, let's consider Spark. Each of Spark's worker containers is called an executor. You can consider experimenting with the following configurations for executors:

- Num-executors—How many executors you want to run in each machine.

- Executor-memory—How much memory you want to allocate to each executor so that they don't run out of memory. This usually depends on the size and skew of your data. Based on how much data will get processed by each executor, you need to configure the memory.

- Executor-cores—How many CPU cores you want to allocate to each executor. If your job is more compute-intensive, then adding more cores to each executor could speed up the processing.

Let's next look at how caching data can help speed up queries.

Caching

Caching refers to storing intermediate data in faster storage layers to speed up queries. We can use external services such as **Redis cache** to store frequently accessed data by queries to save on read latencies. We can also enable inbuilt caching options like **Resultset** caching available in technologies like Synapse SQL to speed up query performance.

Next, let's look a bit closer at the query layer.

Query layer

The query layer is also technically part of the application layer, but query optimization is an entire area of interest in itself. There are thousands of academic papers dedicated to the area of query optimization. Hence, we look at the options available for query optimizations as a separate section in itself in *chapter 14, Optimizing and Troubleshooting Data Storage and Data Processing.*

Indexing

One of the important techniques to use for efficient querying is indexing. If you have used any SQL technologies before, you might have heard about indexing tables based on certain key columns. Indexes are like the keys in a **HashMap** that can be used to directly access a particular row without having to scan the entire table.

In SQL-based systems, you might be required to access rows using values other than the primary key. In such cases, the query engine needs to scan all the rows to find the value we are looking for. Instead, if we can define a secondary index based on frequently searched column values, we could avoid the complete table scans and speed up the query. The secondary index tables are calculated separately from the primary indexes of the table, but this is done by the same SQL engine.

In Azure, we have technologies that can perform indexing on huge volumes of data. These indexes can then be used by analytical engines such as Spark to speed up the queries. One such technology that Azure offers is called **Hyperspace**.

Hyperspace lets us create indexes on input datasets such as Parquet, CSV, and so on, which can be used for query optimization. The Hyperspace indexing needs to be run separately to create an initial index. After that, it can be incrementally updated for the new data. Once we have the Hyperspace index, any Spark query can leverage the index, similar to how we use indexes in SQL.

Materialized views

Views are logical projections of data from multiple tables. Materialized views are just pre-populated versions of such views. If a query needs to do complex merges and joins of multiple tables or multiple partitions, it might be beneficial to perform such merges and joins beforehand and keep the data ready for the query to consume. Materialized views can be generated at regular intervals and kept ready before the actual query runs.

For all practical purposes, materialized views are just specialized caches for the queries. The data in materialized views is read-only data and can be regenerated at any time. It is not persisted permanently in the storage.

Now that we have considered how efficient querying needs might influence our designs, let's extend that consideration to data pruning.

Designing storage for data pruning

Data pruning, as the name suggests, refers to *pruning* or *snipping* out the unnecessary data so that the queries need not read the entire input dataset. I/O is a major bottleneck for any analytical engine, so the idea here is that by reducing the amount of data read, we can improve the query performance. Data pruning usually requires some kind of user input to the analytical engine so that it can decide on which data can be safely ignored for a particular query.

Technologies such as Synapse Dedicated Pools, Azure SQL, Spark, and Hive provide the ability to partition data based on user-defined criteria. If we can organize the input data into physical folders that correspond to the partitions, we can effectively skip reading entire folders of data that are not required for such queries.

Let's consider the examples of Synapse Dedicated Pool and Spark as they are important from a certification point of view.

Dedicated SQL pool example with pruning

Let's consider a very simple example that anyone with a simple SQL background will understand. Once we get into the implementation details in the later chapters, we will explore many of the advanced features provided by Dedicated SQL Pool.

Here, we create a trip table for our IAC scenario. Just to refresh your memory, IAC is our sample customer scenario that we are running throughout this book.

The table has been partitioned using the `PARTITION` keyword on `tripDate`, as illustrated in the following code snippet:

```
CREATE TABLE dbo.TripTable
(
    [tripId] INT NOT NULL,
    [driverId] INT NOT NULL,
    [customerID] INT NOT NULL,
    [tripDate] INT,
    [startLocation] VARCHAR(40),
    [endLocation] VARCHAR(40)
)
```

```
WITH
(
    PARTITION ([tripDate] RANGE RIGHT FOR VALUES
        ( 20220101, 20220201, 20220301 )
    )
)
```

The `RANGE RIGHT` syntax specified just ensures that the values specified in the `PARTITION` syntax will each belong to the right side of the range. In this example, the partitions will look like this:

```
Partition 1: All dates < 20220101
Partition 2: 20220101 to 20220131
Partition 3: 20220201 to 20220228
Partition 4: 20220301 to 20220331
```

If we had given `RANGE LEFT`, it would have ended up creating partitions like this:

```
Partition 1:  All dates < 20220102
Partition 2: 20220102 to 20220201
Partition 3: 20220202 to 20220301
Partition 4: All dates > 20220301
```

Now, let's say we need to find all the customers who traveled with IAC in the month of January. All you need to do is use a simple filter, such as in the following example:

```
SELECT customerID FROM TripTable
WHERE tripDate BETWEEN '20220101' AND '20220131'
```

If it were not for the partition, the query would have to scan through all the records in the table to find the dates within the range of `'20220101'` AND `'20220131'`. But with the partition in place, the query will only scan through the records in the `'20220101'` partition. This makes the query more efficient.

Spark example with pruning

Let's see how we can implement data pruning for Spark. In this example, let's create a simple Spark Data Frame and write it into date partitions such as `"year/month/day"`. Then, we will see how to read only from a required partition of data. We'll proceed as follows:

1. Let's create some sample data using a simple array, as follows:

```
columnNames = ["tripID","driverID","customerID","cabID",
"date","startLocation","endLocation"]
tripData = [
    ('100', '200', '300', '400', '20220101', 'New York',
'New Jersey'),
    ('101', '201', '301', '401', '20220102', 'Tempe',
'Phoenix') ]
```

2. Create a DataFrame using the previous data, like this:

```
df = spark.createDataFrame(data= tripData, schema =
columnNames)
```

3. Since the `tripDate` is in simple date format, let's split it into year, month, and day, as follows:

```
dfDate = df.withColumn("date", to_timestamp(col("date"),
'yyyyMMdd')) \
        .withColumn("year", date_format(col("date"),
"yyyy")) \
        .withColumn("month", date_format(col("date"),
"MM")) \
        .withColumn("day", date_format(col("date"),
"dd"))
```

4. Now, repartition the data in memory, like this:

```
dfDate = dfDate.repartition("year", "month", "day")
```

5. And, finally, write it to different files under the `abfs://IAC/Trips/Out` output directory. Here, `abfss` refers to the **Azure Blob File System** driver. The code is illustrated in the following snippet:

```
dfDate.write.partitionBy("year", "month", "day").
parquet("abfss://IAC/Trips/Out"))
```

6. At this point, our output directory will be created with the following structure:

```
abfss://IAC/Trips/Out/
                year=2022/
                            day=01/
                                        part*.parquet
```

7. Now, let's see how pruning works. For example, if we run the following query, Spark will intelligently read only the `year="2022/month=01/day=03"` folder without requiring us to scan all the data under the `IAC/Trips/Out` folder:

```
readDF = spark.read.parquet("abfss://IAC/Trips/Out/
year=2022").filter("month=01", "day=03")
```

As you will have observed, partitioning data via good folder structures can help improve the efficiency of queries. This is a good segue into our next topic, which explains how to design folder structures for data lakes.

Designing folder structures for data transformation

Considering the variety and volume of data that will land in a data lake, it is very important to design a flexible, but a maintainable, folder structure. Badly designed or ad hoc folder structures will become a management nightmare and will render the data lake unusable. Some points to keep in mind while designing the folder structure are given here:

- **Human readability**—Human-readable folder structures will help improve data exploration and navigation.

- **Representation of organizational structure**—Aligning the folder structure according to the organizational structure helps segregate the data for billing and access control. Such a folder structure will help restrict cross-team data access.

- **Distinguish sensitive data**—The folder structure should be such that it can separate sensitive data from general data. Sensitive data will require higher levels of audit, privacy, and security policies, so keeping it separate makes it easy to apply the required policies.

- **Manageability of ACLs**—If you remember from earlier in the chapter, ACLs are used to provide control on which users have read, write, or execute permissions on files and folders. We should design the folders such that we need to apply ACLs only at the top levels of the folders and not at the leaf folders. We should not end up in a situation whereby we need to update the ACLs every time a subfolder is automatically created, such as new timestamp folders for streaming inputs.

- **Optimize for faster and evenly distributed reads**—If we can distribute the data evenly, then workloads can access the data in parallel. This will improve query performance. Also, think of support for pruning, which we discussed in an earlier section.

- **Consider subscription limits**—Azure has per-subscription limits on the size of data, the network ingress/egress, parallelism, and so on. So, if the data is going to be huge, we need to plan to split it at a subscription level.

With the preceding guidelines in mind, let's explore the folder structures for three different use cases.

Streaming and IoT Scenarios

Streaming and IoT scenarios are complicated as there will be thousands of files streaming in from different sources such as tweets, sensors, telemetry data, and so on. We need an efficient way to track and organize the data.

The layout template recommended by Microsoft is given here:

```
{Region}/{SubjectMatter(s)}/{yyyy}/{mm}/{dd}/{hh}/
```

Let's consider the IAC example. If we want to store all the trips made by a particular cab, the folder structure could be something like this:

```
New York/cabs/cab1234/trips/2021/12/01
```

Or, if we want to collect the customer details for each of the cabs each day, it could be something like this:

```
New York/cabs/cab1234/customers/2021/12/01
```

But what if the customer details are considered sensitive information that needs to adhere to higher levels of security and privacy policies? In such cases, the preceding folder structure becomes inconvenient because we need to iterate each cab and then apply ACLs for each of the customer folders under it. So, a better structure would look like this:

```
New York/sensitive/customers/cab1234/2021/12/01
```

In the preceding folder structure, we can easily apply all the security policies and ACLs at the `sensitive` folder itself. The restrictions will automatically be inherited by all subfolders under it.

So, if you have data categorized as sensitive, then you could consider the following templates:

```
{Region}/Sensitive/{SubjectMatter(s)}/{yyyy}/{mm}/{dd}/{hh}/
{Region}/General/{SubjectMatter(s)}/{yyyy}/{mm}/{dd}/{hh}/
```

Let's next look at batch scenarios.

Batch scenarios

In batch processing systems, we read the input data and write processed data into output directories, so it is intuitive to maintain separate input and output directories in the folder paths. In addition to the I/O directories, it would also be beneficial to have a directory for all bad files such as corrupt files, incomplete files, and so on so that they can be checked at regular intervals by the data administrators.

The layout template recommended by Microsoft is given here:

```
{Region}/{SubjectMatter(s)}/In/{yyyy}/{mm}/{dd}/{hh}/
{Region}/{SubjectMatter(s)}/Out/{yyyy}/{mm}/{dd}/{hh}/
{Region}/{SubjectMatter(s)}/Bad/{yyyy}/{mm}/{dd}/{hh}/
```

Continuing our IAC example, let's assume we want to generate daily reports for the cab trips. So, our input directory could look like this:

```
New York/trips/In/cab1234/2021/12/01/*
```

Our output directory could look like this:

```
New York/trips/Out/reports/cab1234/2021/12/01
```

And finally, the bad files directory could look like this:

```
New York/trips/Bad/cab1234/2021/12/01
```

Here again, if you have data categorized as sensitive, you could consider the following templates:

```
{Region}/General/{SubjectMatter(s)}/In/{yyyy}/{mm}/{dd}/{hh}/
```
```
{Region}/Sensitive/{/{SubjectMatter(s)}/Out/{yyyy}/{mm}/{dd}/
{hh}/
```
```
{Region}/General/{/{SubjectMatter(s)}/Bad/{yyyy}/{mm}/{dd}/
{hh}/
```

> **Tip**
>
> Do not put date folders at the beginning as it makes applying ACLs to every subfolder more tedious. Also, there are limits on the number of ACLs that can be applied, so there are chances of you running out of ACLs as time progresses.

Now that we have learned some of the best practices for creating folder structures in a data lake, let's move ahead to explore some optimization strategies involving Azure Synapse Analytics, as required by our certification syllabus.

Designing a distribution strategy

Distribution strategies are techniques that are used in **Synapse Dedicated SQL Pools**. Synapse Dedicated SQL Pools are **massively parallel processing** (**MPP**) systems that split the queries *into 60 parallel queries* and execute them in parallel. Each of these smaller queries runs on something called a **distribution**. A distribution is a basic unit of processing and storage for a dedicated SQL pool.

Dedicated SQL uses Azure Storage to store the data, and it provides three different ways to distribute (shard) the data among the distributions. They are listed as follows:

- Round-robin tables
- Hash tables
- Replicated tables

Based on our requirements, we need to decide on which of these distribution techniques should be used for creating our tables. To choose the right distribution strategy, you should understand your application, the data layout, and the data access patterns by using query plans. We will be learning how to generate and read query plans and data patterns in later chapters. Right now, let's try to understand the high-level difference in each of the distribution techniques and how to choose the right option.

Round-robin tables

In a **round-robin table**, the data is serially distributed among all the distributions. It is the simplest of the distributions and is the default when the distribution type is not specified. This option is the quickest to load data but is not the best for queries that include joins. Use round-robin tables for staging data or temporary data, where the data is mostly going to be read.

Here is a simple example of creating a round-robin distributed table in Dedicated SQL Pool:

```
CREATE TABLE dbo.CabTable
(
    [cabId] INT NOT NULL,
    [driverName] VARCHAR(20),
    [driverLicense] VARCHAR(20)
)
```

There is no need to specify any attribute for round-robin tables; it is the default distribution.

Hash tables

In a **hash table**, the rows are distributed to different *distributions* based on a hash function. The hash key is usually one of the columns in the table. Hash tables are best for queries with joins and aggregations. They are ideal for large tables.

Here is a simple example of creating a hash distributed table in Dedicated SQL Pool:

```
CREATE TABLE dbo.CabTable
(
    [cabId] INT NOT NULL,
    [driverName] VARCHAR(20),
    [driverLicense] VARCHAR(20)
)
```

```
WITH
(
    DISTRIBUTION = HASH (cabId)
)
```

> **Tip**
> Choose a column key that is distinct and static as this can balance the data distribution among the partitions.

Replicated tables

With **replicated tables**, the table data is copied over to all the *distributions*. These are ideal for small tables where the cost of copying the data over for the query joins outweighs the storage costs for these small tables. Use replicated tables for storing quick **lookup tables (LUTs)**.

Here is a simple example of creating a replicated table in Dedicated SQL Pool:

```
CREATE TABLE dbo.CabTable
(
    [cabId] INT NOT NULL,
    [driverName] VARCHAR(20),
    [driverLicense] VARCHAR(20)
)
WITH
(
    DISTRIBUTION = REPLICATE
)
```

We will be revisiting these concepts in detail when we learn how to implement them for practical problems in the following chapters. Let's now move on to the last topic of our chapter, which appropriately deals with the end of life for our data.

Designing a data archiving solution

Now that we have learned how to design a data lake and optimize the storage for our analytical queries, there is one final component that remains to be designed. How do we archive or clean up the old data? Without a proper archiving and/or deletion solution, the data will grow and fill up the storage very soon.

Azure provides three tiers of storage: **Hot Access Tier**, **Cold Access Tier**, and **Archive Access Tier**.

Hot Access Tier

The Hot Access Tier is ideal for data that is accessed frequently. It provides the lowest access cost but at a higher storage cost.

Cold Access Tier

The Cold Access Tier is ideal for data that is accessed occasionally, such as slightly older data that is probably used for backups or monthly reports. It provides lower storage costs but at higher access costs. Azure expects the cold access tier data to be stored for at least 30 days. Early deletion or tier change might result in extra charges.

Archive Access Tier

The Archive Access Tier is ideal for storing data for long durations. It could be for compliance reasons, long-term backups, data archival, and so on. The Archive Access Tier is an offline storage solution, which means you will not be able to access the data unless you rehydrate that data from Archive to an Online tier. This is the cheapest storage option among all the tiers. Azure expects the Archive Tier data to be stored for at least 180 days. Early deletion or tier change might result in extra charges.

Data life cycle management

Azure Blob storage provides tools for data life cycle management. Using these tools, we can define policies such as how long a particular data needs to be in the Hot Access Tier, when to move the data between the different access tiers, when to delete blobs, and so on. Azure runs these policies on a daily basis.

Let's see an example of how to create a data life cycle policy.

Azure portal

Let's explore how to create a data life cycle policy using the Azure portal, as follows:

1. In the Azure portal, select your storage account.
2. Go to the **Data Management** tab and select **Life Cycle Management**.
3. Click on the + sign to add a new rule.
4. In the **Details** page, add a name for your rule and select which storage blobs this rule needs to apply.
5. Click **Next**, and on the **Base blobs** page, you can specify the actual rule. An example is shown in *Figure 2.11*.
6. Once done, click on the **Add** button.

You can see an overview of this in the following screenshot:

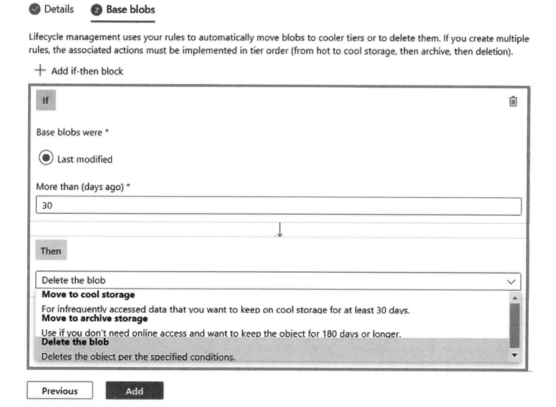

Figure 2.11 – How to specify data life cycle management rules in Azure Storage

> **Note**
>
> Azure runs data life cycle policies only once a day, so it could take up to 24 hours for your policies to kick in.

Summary

With that, we have come to the end of our second chapter. We explored the various data lake designs in detail and learned good practices for designing one. You should now be comfortable answering questions related to data lake architectures and the storage, compute, and other technologies involved in creating a data lake. You should also be familiar with common file formats such as Avro, Parquet, and ORC and know when to choose which file formats. We also explored different optimization techniques such as data pruning, partitioning, caching, indexing, and more. We also learned about folder structures, data distribution, and finally, designing a data life cycle by using policies to archive or delete data. This covers the syllabus for *DP-203* exam, *Design a Data Storage Structure* chapter. We will be reinforcing the learnings from this chapter via implementation details and tips in the following chapters.

Let's explore the concept of partitioning in more detail in the next chapter.

3
Designing a Partition Strategy

Data partitioning refers to the process of dividing data and storing it in physically different locations. We partition data mainly for performance, scalability, manageability, and security reasons. Partitioning itself is a generic term, but the methods and techniques of partitioning vary from service to service—for example, the partitioning techniques used for Azure Blob storage might not be the same as those applied for database services such as **Azure SQL** or **Azure Synapse Dedicated SQL pool**. Similarly, document databases such as **Cosmos DB** have different partitioning techniques from **Azure Queues** or **Azure Tables**. In this chapter, we will explore some of the important partitioning techniques and when to use them.

As in the previous chapter, we will again be focusing more on the design aspects, as per the syllabus. The implementation details will be covered in *Chapter 5, Implementing Physical Data Storage Structures*.

This chapter will cover the following topics:

- Understanding the basics of partitioning
- Designing a partition strategy for files
- Designing a partition strategy for analytical workloads
- Designing a partition strategy for efficiency/performance
- Designing a partition strategy for Azure Synapse Analytics
- Identifying when partitioning is needed in **Azure Data Lake Storage Gen2 (ADLS Gen2)**

Almost all of the major Azure Storage and Azure Analytics services support partitioning in one way or another, but in the interest of the certification, we will be covering only those services that are relevant to the certification. If you are interested in learning about partitioning in the other Azure services, you can refer to the following link: `https://docs.microsoft.com/en-us/azure/architecture/best-practices/data-partitioning-strategies`.

Let's dive into the world of partitioning!

Understanding the basics of partitioning

In the previous chapter, we briefly introduced the concept of partitioning as part of the *Designing storage for efficient querying* section. We explored storage-side partitioning concepts such as replicating data, reducing cross-partition operations such as joins, and eventual consistency to improve query performance. In this chapter, we will deep dive more systematically into both storage and analytical partitioning techniques. Let's start with the benefits of partitioning.

Benefits of partitioning

Partitioning has several benefits apart from just query performance. Let's take a look at a few important ones.

Improving performance

As we discussed in the previous chapter, partitioning helps improve the parallelization of queries by splitting massive monolithic data into smaller, easily consumable chunks.

Apart from parallelization, partitioning also improves performance via **data pruning**, another concept that we already discussed in the previous chapter. Using data pruning queries can ignore non-relevant partitions, thereby reducing the **input/output (I/O)** required for queries.

Partitions also help with the archiving or deletion of older data. For example, let's assume we need to delete all data older than 12 months. If we partition the data into units of monthly data, we can delete a full month's data with just a single `DELETE` command, instead of deleting all the files one by one or all the entries of a table row by row.

Let's next look at how partitioning helps with scalability.

Improving scalability

In the world of big data processing, there are two types of scaling: vertical and horizontal.

Vertical scaling refers to the technique of increasing the capacity of individual machines by adding more memory, CPU, storage, or network to improve performance. This usually helps in the short term, but eventually hits a limit beyond which we cannot scale.

The second type of scaling is called **horizontal scaling**. This refers to the technique of increasing processing and storage capacity by adding more and more machines to a cluster, with regular hardware specifications that are easily available in the market (commodity hardware). As and when the data grows, we just need to add more machines and redirect the new data to the new machines. This method theoretically has no upper bounds and can grow forever. Data lakes are based on the concept of horizontal scaling.

Data partitioning helps naturally with horizontal scaling. For example, let's assume that we store data at a per-day interval in partitions, so we will have about 30 partitions per month. Now, if we need to generate a monthly report, we can configure the cluster to have 30 nodes so that each node can process one day's worth of data. If the requirement increases to process quarterly reports (that is, reports every 3 months), we can just add more nodes—say, 60 more nodes to our original cluster size of 30 to process 90 days of data in parallel. Hence, if we can design our data partition strategy in such a way that we can split the data easily across new machines, this will help us scale faster.

Let's next look at how partitioning helps with data management.

Improving manageability

In many analytical systems, we will have to deal with data from a wide variety of sources, and each of these sources might have different data governance policies assigned to them. For example, some data might be confidential, so we need to restrict access to that; some might be transient data that can be regenerated at will; some might be logging data that can be deleted after a few months; some might be transaction data that needs to be archived for years; and so on. Similarly, there might be data that needs faster access, so we might choose to persist it on premium **solid-state drive (SSD)** stores and other data on a **hard disk drive (HDD)** to save on cost.

If we store such different sets of data in their own storage partitions, then applying separate rules—such as access restrictions, or configuring different data life cycle management activities such as deleting or archiving data, and so on—for the individual partitions becomes easy. Hence, partitioning reduces the management overhead, especially when dealing with multiple different types of data such as in a data lake.

Let's next look at how data partitioning helps with security.

Improving security

As we saw in the previous section about improving manageability, confidential datasets can have different access and privacy levels. Customer data will usually have the highest security and privacy levels. On the other hand, product catalogs might not need very high levels of security and privacy.

So, by partitioning the data based on security requirements, we can isolate the secure data and apply independent access-control and audit rules to those partitions, thereby allowing only privileged users to access such data.

Let's next look at how we can improve data availability using partitioning.

Improving availability

If our data is split into multiple partitions that are stored in different machines, applications can continue to serve at least partial data even if a few partitions are down. Only a subset of customers whose partitions went down might get impacted, while the rest of the customers will not see any impact. This is better than the entire application going down. Hence, physically partitioning the data helps improve the availability of services.

In general, if we plan our partition strategy correctly, the returns could be significant. I hope you have now understood the benefits of partitioning data. Let's next look at some partition strategies from a storage/files perspective.

Designing a partition strategy for files

In this section, we will look at the partitioning techniques available for Azure Storage, which should also cover files. The Azure Storage services are generic and very flexible when it comes to partitioning. We can implement whatever partition logic we want, using the same **Create, Read, Update, Delete (CRUD) application programming interfaces (APIs)** that are publicly available. There are no special APIs or features available for partitioning. With that background, let's now explore the partitioning options available in **Azure Blob storage** and **ADLS Gen2**.

Azure Blob storage

In Azure Blob storage, we first create Azure accounts; then, within accounts, we create containers; and within containers, we create actual storage blobs. These containers are logical entities, so even when we create data blobs within containers, there is no guarantee that the data will land within the same partition. But there is a trick to enhance our chances of storing the blobs in the same partition.

Azure uses something called **range partitioning** for storing blobs. In a range partition, files that are in a *lexical sequence* end up together in a partition.

For example, if we have filenames such as `Cab1-20211220`, `Cab1-20211221`, `Cab1-20211222`, and `Cab1-20211223`, these files will mostly end up in the same partition.

Similarly, filenames such as `IAC-Cabs`, `IAC-Routes`, `IAC-Customers`, and `IAC-Drivers` will mostly end up within the same partition.

Azure Storage uses <account name + container name + blob name> as the partition key. It continues to store blobs in the same partition until it reaches the partition's internal limit. At that point, Azure Storage repartitions and rebalances the data and spreads it evenly among the partitions. This entire process of repartitioning and rebalancing will be taken care of automatically by Azure Storage, without intervention from the user.

If the amount of data stored is large and Azure Storage starts repartitioning and rebalancing the data, the latency of the CRUD APIs will get impacted. You can avoid or delay such repartitions by adding a three-digit hash value (random value) to your filenames. This will cause the data to be distributed across multiple partitions.

For example, your filenames could use the following format:

```
New York/cabs/cab1234/customers/{XYZYYYYMMDD}
```

Here, `XYZ` could be the random hash value.

ADLS Gen2

The solution to file partitioning in a data lake is the same as *designing the folder structure*, which we already discussed in the previous chapter. We can apply different security policies or different data life cycle management configurations to individual folders in ADLS Gen2. Since we have already explored the folder structure topic in detail, we will not be covering it again here.

Apart from the folder structure, we can also partition data for the benefits we discussed earlier in this chapter, such as performance, scalability, manageability, security, availability, and so on. The process of segregating the data into partitions could either be done manually or it could be automated using **Azure Data Factory** (**ADF**). We will be looking deeper into automation using ADF in the later implementation-oriented chapters.

Now that we have a fairly good idea about storage- and file-based partitioning optimizations, let's explore partitioning from an analytical workload standpoint.

Designing a partition strategy for analytical workloads

There are three main types of partition strategies for analytical workloads. These are listed here:

- Horizontal partitioning, which is also known as sharding
- Vertical partitioning
- Functional partitioning

Let's explore each of them in detail.

Horizontal partitioning

In a **horizontal partition**, we divide the table data horizontally, and *subsets of rows* are stored in different data stores. Each of these subsets of rows (with the same schema as the parent table) are called **shards**. Essentially, each of these shards is stored in different database instances.

You can see an example of a horizontal partition here:

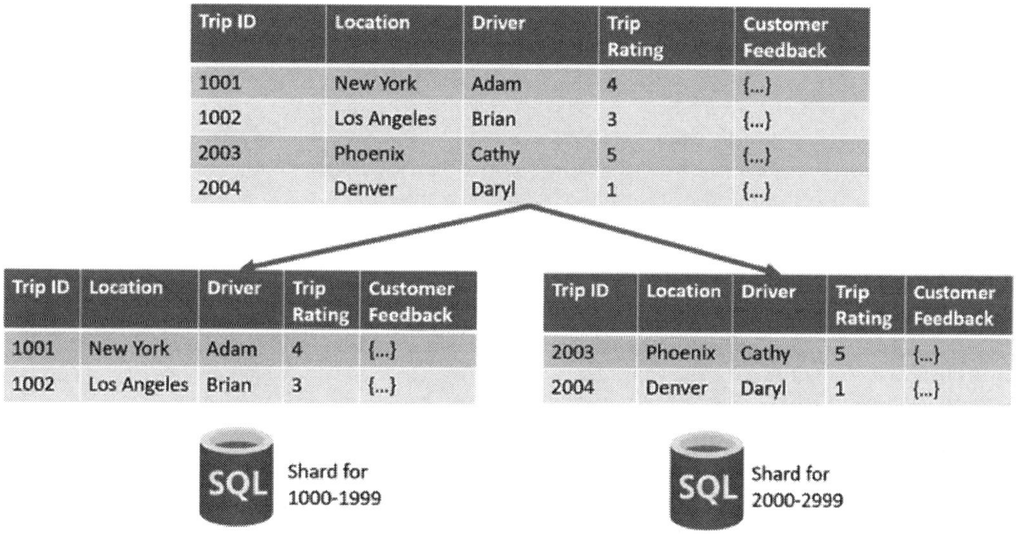

Figure 3.1 – Example of a horizontal partition

In the preceding example, you can see that the data in the top table is distributed horizontally based on the **Trip ID** range.

Selecting the right shard key

It is very important we select the right **shard key** (also called **partition key**) for partitioning the data, as changing it later will be a very expensive operation. The following guidelines will help us with this:

- Select a key that spreads the data in such a way that the application traffic to the data partitions is evenly distributed.

- Select a key that doesn't change too often. Good keys are static and are widespread—in other words, the range of that key should neither be too small nor too large. As a general rule, a key that can generate hundreds of partitions is good. Avoid keys that generate too few partitions (tens of partitions) or too many partitions (thousands of partitions).

> **Note**
>
> Don't try to balance the data to be evenly distributed across partitions unless specifically required by your use case because usually, the most recent data will get accessed more than older data. Thus, the partitions with recent data will end up becoming bottlenecks due to high data access.

We will be covering the sharding pattern in depth in the next section when we talk about partitioning for efficiency and performance.

Vertical partitioning

In a **vertical partition**, we divide the data vertically, and each *subset of the columns* is stored separately in a different data store. In the case of vertical partitioning, we partially normalize the table to break it into smaller tables (fewer columns). This type of partitioning is ideal in cases where a table might have a subset of data that is accessed more frequently than the rest. Vertical partitioning can help speed up queries as only the required subset of data can be selectively retrieved, instead of reading entire rows. This is ideal for column-oriented data stores such as HBase, Cosmos DB, and so on.

You can see an example of a vertical partition here:

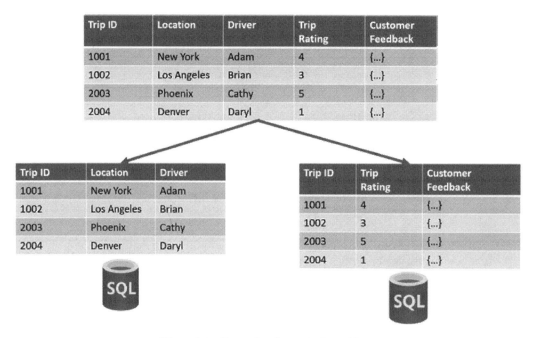

Figure 3.2 – Example of a vertical partition

In the preceding example, you can see that columns such as **Trip Rating** and **Customer Feedback** that might not be used frequently are split into separate partitions. This will help reduce the amount of data being read for queries.

Functional partitioning

Functional partitions are similar to vertical partitions, except that here, we store entire tables or entities in different data stores. They can be used to segregate data belonging to different organizations, frequently used tables from infrequently used ones, read-write tables from read-only ones, sensitive data from general data, and so on.

You can see an example of a functional partition here:

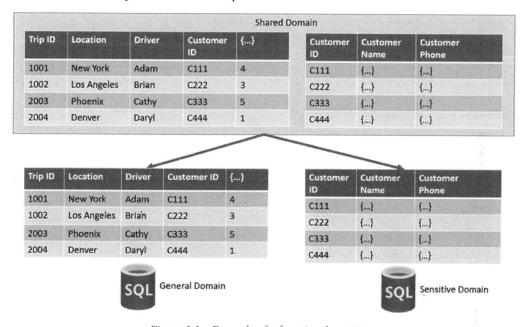

Figure 3.3 – Example of a functional partition

In this example, you can see how the customer data is moved into its own partition. This segregation will help us apply different privacy and security rules for the different partitions.

Azure services such as Azure SQL and Azure Synapse Dedicated pool support all the partitioning formats discussed in this section.

Designing a partition strategy for efficiency/ performance

In the last few sections, we explored the various storage and analytical partitioning options and learned about how partitioning helps with performance, scale, security, availability, and so on. In this section, we will recap the points we learned about performance and efficiency and learn about some additional performance patterns.

Here are some strategies to keep in mind while designing for efficiency and performance:

- Partition datasets into smaller chunks that can be run with optimal parallelism for multiple queries.

- Partition the data such that queries don't end up requiring too much data from other partitions. Minimize cross-partition data transfers.

- Design effective folder structures to improve the efficiency of data reads and writes.

- Partition data such that a significant amount of data can be pruned while running queries.

- Partition in units of data that can be easily added, deleted, swapped, or archived. This helps improve the efficiency of data life cycle management.

- File sizes in the range of 256 **megabytes** (**MB**) to 100 **gigabytes** (**GB**) perform really well with analytical engines such as HDInsight and Azure Synapse. So, aggregate the files to these ranges before running the analytical engines on them.

- For I/O-intensive jobs, try to keep the optimal I/O buffer sizes in the range of 4 to 16 MB; anything too big or too small will become inefficient.

- Run more containers or executors per **virtual machine** (**VM**) (such as Apache Spark executors or Apache **Yet Another Resource Negotiator** (**YARN**) containers).

Try to remember the preceding good practices when you design your next partition strategy. Let's next try to understand how to actually find the right data to partition and how much data to partition.

Iterative query performance improvement process

Here is a high-level iterative process to improve query performance:

1. List business-critical queries, the most frequently run queries, and the slowest queries.

2. Check the query plans for each of these queries using the EXPLAIN keyword and see the amount of data being used at each stage (we will be learning about how to view query plans in the later chapters).

3. Identify the joins or filters that are taking the most time. Identify the corresponding data partitions.

4. Try to split the corresponding input data partitions into smaller partitions, or change the application logic to perform isolated processing on top of each partition and later merge only the filtered data.

5. You could also try to see if other partitioning keys would work better and if you need to repartition the data to get better job performance for each partition.

6. If any particular partitioning technology doesn't work, you can explore having more than one piece of partitioning logic—for example, you could apply horizontal partitioning within functional partitioning, and so on.

7. Monitor the partitioning regularly to check if the application access patterns are balanced and well distributed. Try to identify hot spots early on.

8. Iterate this process until you hit the preferred query execution time.

We will be using these guidelines in our examples in future chapters too. Let's next explore the specifics of partitioning in Azure Synapse Analytics.

Designing a partition strategy for Azure Synapse Analytics

We learned about Azure Synapse Analytics in *Chapter 2*, *Designing a Data Storage Structure*. Synapse Analytics contains two compute engines, outlined here:

- A **Structured Query Language** (**SQL**) pool that consists of serverless and dedicated SQL pools (previously known as SQL Data Warehouse)
- A Spark pool that consists of Synapse Spark pools

But when people refer to Azure Synapse Analytics, they usually refer to the Dedicated SQL pool option. In this section, we will look at the partition strategy available for Synapse Dedicated SQL pool.

> **Note**
> We have already briefly covered partitioning in Spark as part of the *Data pruning* section in the previous chapter. The same concepts apply to Synapse Spark, too.

Before we explore partitioning options, let's recap the data distribution techniques of a Synapse dedicated pool from the previous chapter as this will play an important role in our partition strategy, as follows:

A dedicated SQL pool is a massively parallel processing (MPP) system that splits the queries into 60 parallel queries and executes them in parallel. Each of these smaller queries runs on something called a distribution. A distribution is a basic unit of processing and storage for a dedicated SQL pool. There are three different ways to distribute (shard) data among distributions, as listed here:

- *Round-robin tables*
- *Hash tables*
- *Replicated tables*

Partitioning is supported on all the distribution types in the preceding list. Apart from the distribution types, Dedicated SQL pool also supports three types of tables: **clustered columnstore**, **clustered index**, and **heap** tables. We will be exploring these table options in detail in the upcoming chapters. Partitioning is supported in all of these types of tables, too.

In a dedicated SQL pool, data is already distributed across its 60 distributions, so we need to be careful in deciding if we need to further partition the data. The clustered columnstore tables work optimally when the number of rows per table in a distribution is around 1 million.

For example, if we plan to partition the data further by the months of a year, we are talking about 12 partitions x 60 distributions = 720 sub-divisions. Each of these divisions needs to have at least 1 million rows; in other words, the table (usually a fact table) will need to have more than 720 million rows. So, we will have to be careful to not over-partition the data when it comes to dedicated SQL pools.

That said, partitioning in Synapse dedicated pools has two distinct advantages, as we'll see now.

Performance improvement while loading data

Partitioning helps while loading data for queries in dedicated SQL pools. This is a technique that we already discussed in the *Benefits of partitioning* section of this chapter. If we can group the data belonging to a particular time frame together in a partition, then adding or removing that data becomes as simple as running a simple ADD or DELETE command. For example, let's assume that we need to generate a rolling 12-month report. At the end of every month, we remove the oldest month and add a new month to the report. If we have partitioned the data with the granularity of months, then we can easily delete the old data and add the new data using a partition-switching technique in a dedicated SQL pool.

Performance improvement for filtering queries

Partitioning can also help improve query performance by being able to filter the data based on partitions. In particular, partitions help with the WHERE clause in queries. For example, if we have partitioned the data based on the months of a year, we can specify which exact month to look for in our queries, thereby skipping the rest of the months.

I hope you have understood the features and restrictions for partitioning in Azure Synapse dedicated pools. Let's move to our next section, which talks about when to start partitioning data in ADLS Gen2.

Identifying when partitioning is needed in ADLS Gen2

As we have learned in the previous chapter, we can partition data according to our requirements—such as performance, scalability, security, operational overhead, and so on—but there is another reason why we might end up partitioning our data, and that is the various I/O bandwidth limits that are imposed at subscription levels by Azure. These limits apply to both Blob storage and ADLS Gen2.

The rate at which we ingest data into an Azure Storage system is called the **ingress** rate, and the rate at which we move the data out of the Azure Storage system is called the **egress** rate.

The following table shows a snapshot of some of the limits enforced by Azure Blob storage. This table is just to give you an idea of the limits that Azure Storage imposes. When we design our data lake applications, we need to take care of such restrictions as part of our design itself:

Resource	Limit
Number of storage accounts per region per subscription, including standard, and premium storage accounts.	250
Maximum storage account capacity	5 PiB (can be increased by calling Azure Support)
Maximum request rate[1] per storage account	20,000 requests per second
Maximum ingress[1] per storage account (US, Europe regions)	10 Gbps
Maximum ingress[1] per storage account (regions other than US and Europe)	5 Gbps if RA-GRS/GRS is enabled, 10 Gbps for LRS/ZRS
Maximum egress for general-purpose v2 and Blob storage accounts (all regions)	50 Gbps
Maximum number of IP address rules per storage account	200
Maximum number of virtual network rules per storage account	200

Figure 3.4 – Some of the limits for Azure Blob storage as of the time this book was published

So, for example, if your egress rate is beyond 50 **gigabits per second** (**Gbps**) for your data lake, you will have to create multiple accounts and partition your data among those accounts.

> Tip
> If you are using a hybrid setup of on-prem and on-cloud systems and if you transfer data between such systems often, then ensure that your source/destination machines and the actual public network can support the level of ingress and egress data transfer rates provided by Azure Storage. If you are moving data from on-prem sources, consider using **Azure ExpressRoute**.

For complete and up-to-date Azure Storage limits, please refer to the following documentation: `https://docs.microsoft.com/en-us/azure/storage/common/scalability-targets-standard-account`.

Note that some of the limits in the table (such as ingress rates and storage capacity limits) are soft limits, which means you can reach out to Azure Support to increase those limits to some extent; however, you will eventually hit the hard limits for each option. Other resources such as **Internet Protocol (IP)**, addresses, **virtual networks (VNets)**, and so on are hard limits, so you need to plan the partitions with these numbers in mind.

> **Note**
>
> The higher ingress/egress requirements could also come from the applications running on top of Azure Storage and not just via direct data uploads and downloads into the Azure store. For example, if we have an Azure SQL or Azure Synapse dedicated pool (data warehouse) that has a very busy shard, it might exceed the read (egress) limits of that storage account. In such cases, we will have to repartition that shard to divide the data among multiple accounts.

In general, for any Azure service, do keep an eye on the resource limits so that it doesn't come as a surprise when your product is deployed to production.

Summary

With that, we have come to the end of our third chapter. I hope you enjoyed learning about the different partitioning techniques available in Azure! We started with the basics of partitioning, where you learned about the benefits of partitioning; we then moved on to partitioning techniques for storage and analytical workloads. We explored the best practices to improve partitioning efficiency and performance. We understood the concept of distribution tables and how they impact the partitioning of Azure Synapse Analytics, and finally, we learned about storage limitations, which play an important role in deciding when to partition for ADLS Gen2. This covers the syllabus for the *DP-203* exam, *Designing a Partition Strategy*. We will be reinforcing the learnings from this chapter via implementation details and tips in the following chapters.

Let's explore the serving layer in the next chapter.

4
Designing the Serving Layer

In this chapter, we will be learning about the techniques and technologies involved in designing a data serving layer. As we have seen previously in the **data lake** design, data passes through several zones. It starts from a **Landing Zone**, from where it gets processed into more useful formats in the **Transformation Zone**, and finally, the derived data insights land in the **Serving Zone** (also called the **Serving layer**). The Serving Zone serves the processed data and insights to the end users. The Landing Zone and Transformation Zone of a data lake focus on aspects such as efficient storage of data, processing huge volumes of data, optimizing queries, and so on. The **Serving layer**, on the other hand, focuses mainly on how to serve the data in a fast and efficient way to the **business intelligence** (**BI**) tools.

Serving layers are usually built using relational data stores (**Structured Query Language** (**SQL**)-based stores). This is done for two reasons: relational data stores can store data in efficient normalized tables and perform queries faster than big data analytical services. This works well because the amount of data in the Serving Zone is usually magnitudes of order smaller than in the Transformation Zone; also, SQL is the preferred language for a majority of data analysts, and it is universally supported by BI tools.

Azure provides us with a variety of services that can be used to build the Serving layer, such as Azure Synapse Analytics, Azure SQL, Cosmos DB, Apache Hive, Apache HBase, and so on. We will be exploring the important ones for the certification in this chapter.

In this chapter, we will be focusing on the following topics:

- Learning the basics of data modeling and schemas
- Designing Star and Snowflake schemas
- Designing **slowly changing dimensions (SCDs)**
- Designing a solution for temporal data
- Designing a dimensional hierarchy
- Designing for incremental loading
- Designing analytical stores
- Designing metastores in Azure Synapse Analytics and Azure Databricks

This is the last of the design-focused chapters. The next three chapters will be dedicated to the implementation details of what we have learned so far.

Let's get started!

Technical requirements

For this chapter, you will need an Azure account (free or paid).

Learning the basics of data modeling and schemas

Data modeling is a process of designing how data will be represented in data stores. Many data modeling techniques were originally designed for databases and warehouses. Since the Serving layers are usually built with relational data stores such as data warehouses, some of the data modeling techniques can be applied for the Serving layer design too. But do remember that the Serving layer could be built using other storage technologies such as document databases, key-value stores, and so on, based on the customer requirements.

Unlike data lakes, in databases or data warehouses we don't have the luxury of storing huge volumes of data in the format we like. Databases and data warehouses can perform querying exceptionally fast, provided the data is stored in predetermined formats and is limited in size. Hence, while designing the Serving layer, we need to identify the specifics of which data needs to be stored, which format to store it in, and how much data to store. To be specific, we need to decide on which SQL tables are required, what would be the relationship between these tables, and which restrictions need to be imposed on these tables.

There are different data-modeling methods such as **entity-relationship** (**ER**) modeling, hierarchical modeling, dimensional data modeling, relational data modeling, **object-oriented** (**OO**) data modeling, and so on. Among these, dimensional modeling is the most relevant to data warehousing, so we will be focusing only on dimensional modeling techniques in this chapter.

Dimensional models

Dimensional modeling focuses on easier and faster information retrieval, whereas other models usually focus on storage optimization. The most commonly used dimensional data models are **Star schemas** and **Snowflake schemas**. We will be focusing on these two schemas in the following sections.

Designing Star and Snowflake schemas

Schemas are guidelines for arranging data entities such as SQL tables in a data store. Designing a schema refers to the process of designing the various tables and the relationships among them. Star and Snowflake schemas are two of the most commonly used schemas in the data analytics and BI world. In fact, Star schemas are used more frequently than Snowflake schemas. Both have their own advantages and disadvantages, so let's explore them in detail.

Star schemas

A Star schema is the simplest of the data warehouse schemas. It has two sets of tables: one that stores quantitative information such as transactions happening at a retail outlet or trips happening at a cab company, and another that stores the context or descriptions of events that are stored in the quantitative table.

The quantitative tables are called **fact tables** and the descriptive or context tables are called **dimension tables**.

The following diagram shows an example of a Star schema:

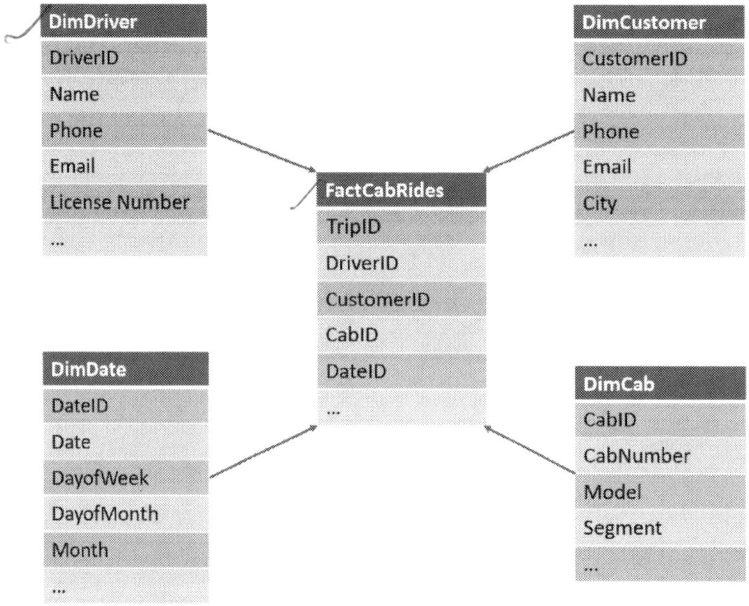

Figure 4.1 – Example of a Star schema

As it might be obvious by the names of the tables, `FactTrips` is our fact table, and all the other ones—such as `DimDriver`, `DimCustomer`, `DimDate`, and `DimCab`—are dimension tables.

Since the relationship diagram of the Star schema is in the shape of a star, it is called a Star schema. The fact table at the middle is the center of the star, and the dimension tables are the arms of the star.

Let's look at some important points about Star schemas, as follows:

- Fact tables are usually of much higher volume than dimension tables.

- Dimension tables are not connected; they are independent of each other.

- Data is not normalized in a Star schema. It is very common to find data replicated in multiple tables. The tables are designed for speed and ease of use.

- They are optimized for **BI** queries. The queries are usually very simple as it just has one level of joins.

- Queries are usually much faster too due to the lesser number of joins.

Now, let's see how Snowflake schemas are different.

Snowflake schemas

A snowflake schema is an extension of the Star schema. In this model, the fact table remains the same, but the dimension tables are further split into their normalized forms, which are referenced using **foreign keys**. There could be multiple levels of hierarchy among the dimension tables.

The following diagram shows how the same example used for a Star schema can be extended to a Snowflake schema:

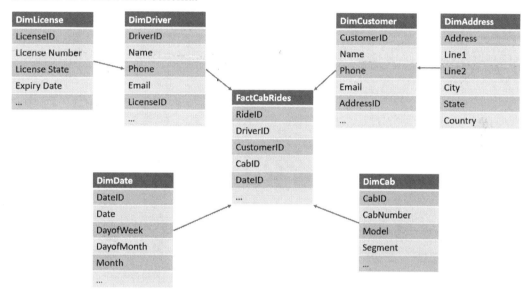

Figure 4.2 – Example of a Snowflake schema

As you will notice from the preceding diagram, the DimDriver table has been normalized to have the license details separately. Similarly, we have normalized the address details away from the DimCustomer table.

You can choose a Snowflake schema if you have both BI and non-BI applications sharing the same data warehouse. In such cases, from an overall perspective, it might be better to have normalized data.

Let's look at some important points about Snowflake schemas, as follows:

- Fact tables, here again, are similar to Star schemas and are of much higher volume than dimension tables.

- Dimension data is normalized, thereby avoiding any redundant data.

- Dimensions could be connected to each other.

- The data is optimized for storage and integrity, but not speed.

- The schema is more complex than a Star schema, so this might not be the most preferred option for BI and reporting use cases.

- Queries are usually slower compared to Star schemas due to the multi-level joins required.

I hope you now have a good idea about Star and Snowflake schemas. There is one more type of schema called a **Fact Constellation schema** or a **Galaxy schema**. With this type of schema, there could be more than one fact table, and the dimension tables are shared. This schema is not as important as Star and Snowflake schemas from a certification perspective, but if you would like to learn more about this schema, you could start from here: `https://www.javatpoint.com/data-warehouse-what-is-fact-constellation-schema`.

Let's next look at how to handle slowly changing data in dimension tables.

Designing SCDs

SCDs refer to data in dimension tables that changes slowly over time and not at a regular cadence. A common example for SCDs is customer profiles—for example, an email address or the phone number of a customer doesn't change that often, and these are perfect candidates for SCD. In this section, we will look at how to design for such changes.

Services such as Azure SQL provide inbuilt support for SCD, but in data warehouses such as Synapse dedicated pools, we will have to implement them ourselves.

Here are some of the main aspects we will need to consider while designing an SCD:

- Should we keep track of the changes? If yes, how much of the history should we maintain?

- Or, should we just overwrite the changes and ignore the history?

Based on our requirements for maintaining the history, there are about seven ways in which we can accomplish keeping track of changes. They are named SCD1, SCD2, SCD3, and so on, up to SCD7.

Among these, SCD1, SCD2, SCD3, SCD4, and SCD6 are the most important ones, and we will be focusing only on those in this chapter. These are also the important ones from a certification perspective.

Designing SCD1

In SCD type 1, the values are overwritten and no history is maintained, so once the data is updated, there is no way to find out what the previous value was. The new queries will always return the most recent value. Here is an example of an SCD1 table:

CustomerID	Name	City	Email	...
1	Adam	New York	adam@....	...

CustomerID	Name	City	Email	...
1	Adam	New Jersey	adam@....	...

Figure 4.3 – Example of SCD type 1

In this example, the value of the **City** column is changing from **New York** to **New Jersey**. The value just gets overwritten.

Designing SCD2

In SCD2, we maintain a complete history of changes. Every time there is a change, we add a new row with all the details without deleting the previous values. There are multiple ways in which we can accomplish this. Let's take a look at the most common approaches.

Using a flag

In this approach, we use a flag to indicate if a particular value is active or if it is current. Here is an example of this:

SurrogateID	CustomerID	Name	City	isActive	...
1	1	Adam	New York	True	...

SurrogateID	CustomerID	Name	City	isActive	...
1	1	Adam	New York	False	...
2	1	Adam	New Jersey	False	...
3	1	Adam	Miami	True	...

Figure 4.4 – Example of SCD type 2: flag

In the second table, every time there is a change, we add a new row and update the isActive column of the previous rows to False. That way, we can easily query the active values by filtering on the isActive=True criteria.

> **Note**
> Surrogate keys are secondary row identification keys. They are added in all SCD2 cases because the primary identification key will not be unique anymore with newly added rows.

Using version numbers

In this approach, we use version numbers to keep track of changes. The row with the highest version is the most current value. Here is an example of this:

SurrogateID	CustomerID	Name	City	Version	...
1	1	Adam	New York	0	...

SurrogateID	CustomerID	Name	City	Version	...
1	1	Adam	New York	0	...
2	1	Adam	New Jersey	1	...
3	1	Adam	Miami	2	...

Figure 4.5 – Example of SCD type 2: version numbers

In the previous example, we need to filter on the **MAX(Version)** column to get the current values.

Using date ranges

In this approach, we use date ranges to show the period a particular record (row) was active, as illustrated in the following example:

SurrogateID	CustomerID	Name	City	StartDate	EndDate
1	1	Adam	New York	01-Jan-2020	NULL

SurrogateID	CustomerID	Name	City	StartDate	EndDate
1	1	Adam	New York	01-Jan-2020	25-Mar-2020
2	1	Adam	New Jersey	25-Mar-2020	01-Dec-2020
3	1	Adam	Miami	01-Dec-2020	NULL

Figure 4.6 – Example of SCD type 2: date ranges

In the previous example, every time we change a field, we add a new record to the table. Along with that, we update the **EndDate** column of the previous record and the **StartDate** column for the new record with today's date. In order to fetch the current record, we have to filter on the `EndDate=NULL` criteria, or, instead, we could just fill in a very futuristic date instead of `NULL`—something such as `31-Dec-2100`.

As a variation to the date-range approach, we could also add a flag column to easily identify active or current records. The following example shows this approach:

SurrogateID	CustomerID	Name	City	StartDate	EndDate	isActive
1	1	Adam	New York	01-Jan-2020	25-Mar-2020	False
2	1	Adam	New Jersey	25-Mar-2020	01-Dec-2020	False
3	1	Adam	Miami	01-Dec-2020	NULL	True

Figure 4.7 – Example of SCD type 2: date ranges and flag

Let's now look at designing SCD3.

Designing SCD3

In SCD3, we maintain only a partial history and not a complete history. Instead of adding additional rows, we add an extra column that stores the previous value, so only one version of historic data will be preserved. As with the SCD2 option, here again, we can choose to add date columns to keep track of modified dates, but we don't need surrogate keys in this case as the identification key of the record doesn't change. Here is an example of this:

CustomerID	Name	City	PrevCity	...
1	Adam	New York	NULL	

CustomerID	Name	City	PrevCity	...
1	Adam	New Jersey	New York	

Figure 4.8 – Example of SCD type 3

In the previous example, we have added a new column called **PrevCity**. Every time the value of **City** changes, we add the previous value to **PrevCity** and update the **City** column with the current city.

Designing SCD4

SCD4 was introduced for dimension attributes that change relatively frequently. In type 4, we split the fast-changing attributes of the dimension table into another smaller dimension table and also reference the new dimension table directly from the fact table.

For example, in the following diagram, if we assume that the carpool (also known as *High occupancy vehicles*) pass needs to be purchased every month, we can move that field to a smaller mini-dimension and reference it directly from the fact table:

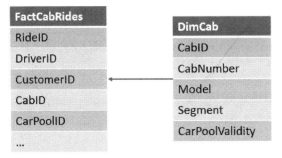

Figure 4.9 – Example of SCD4: before split

We can split the table into a mini **DimCarPool** dimension, as in the following diagram:

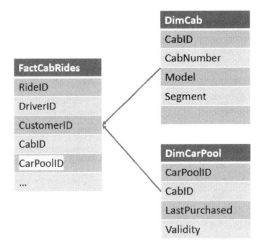

Figure 4.10 – Example of SCD type 4: after split

This sub-division helps in modifying only a smaller amount of data frequently instead of the complete row.

Designing SCD5, SCD6, and SCD7

The rest of the SCDs—SCD5, SCD6, and SCD7—are derivatives of the previous four SCDs. Among these derived ones, SCD6 is a relatively important one, so we will be exploring that as part of the next sub-section.

Designing SCD6

Type 6 is a combination of 1, 2, and 3. In this type, along with the addition of new rows, we also update the latest value in all the rows, as illustrated in the following screenshot:

Surrogate ID	Customer ID	Name	CurrCity	PrevCity	StartDate	EndDate	isActive
1	1	Adam	Miami	NULL	01-Jan-2020	25-Mar-2020	False
2	1	Adam	Miami	New York	25-Mar-2020	01-Dec-2020	False
3	1	Adam	Miami	New Jersey	01-Dec-2020	NULL	True

Figure 4.11 – Example of SCD type 6

In the previous example, you would have noticed that the CurrCity value for all the records belonging to customer Adam has been updated. This is just another benefit of extracting the latest values.

That explains SCD type 6. If you are interested in learning about SCDs 5 and 7, you can find more information at the following links:

SCD5: https://www.kimballgroup.com/data-warehouse-business-intelligence-resources/kimball-techniques/dimensional-modeling-techniques/type-5/

SCD7: https://www.kimballgroup.com/data-warehouse-business-intelligence-resources/kimball-techniques/dimensional-modeling-techniques/type-7

Now that you have a fair idea about SCDs, let's explore how to handle temporal.

Designing a solution for temporal data

Temporal data refers to data at specific points in time. Storing temporal data is required in situations like data auditing, forensic investigations, maintaining SCDs, point in time recoveries and so on. Azure SQL and SQL server provides a mechanism called Temporal tables to store temporal data.

Temporal tables are specialized tables that keep track of data changes over time. They track the history of data changes like what we had already seen in SCD tables, but in this case the system takes care of managing the time validity period of each row, instead of we having to do it manually. Hence these tables are also called as System-versioned temporal tables.

> **Note**
>
> Temporal table is a concept of Azure SQL database and SQL server. It was not available in Azure Synapse pools as of writing this book.

Let us look at an example of how to create Temporal tables in Azure SQL:

```
CREATE TABLE Customer
(
    [customerId] INT NOT NULL PRIMARY KEY CLUSTERED,
    [name] VARCHAR(100) NOT NULL,
    [address] VARCHAR(100) NOT NULL,
    [email] VARCHAR (100) NOT NULL,
    [phone] VARCHAR(12) NOT NULL,
    [validFrom] DATETIME2 GENERATED ALWAYS AS ROW START,
    [validTo] DATETIME2 GENERATED ALWAYS AS ROW END,
    PERIOD FOR SYSTEM_TIME (validFrom, validTo),
)
WITH (SYSTEM_VERSIONING = ON);
```

If you notice, there are three statements that would stand out:

```
[validFrom] DATETIME2 GENERATED ALWAYS AS ROW START,

[validTo] DATETIME2 GENERATED ALWAYS AS ROW END,

PERIOD FOR SYSTEM_TIME (validFrom, validTo),
```

For a temporal table, we need to define the Period Start Column and the Period End Column. In our example, the Period Start Column is `validFrom` and the Period End Column is the `validTo`. And we tell the Database engine that these are our start and end time indicators using the `PERIOD FOR SYSTEM_TIME (validFrom, validTo)` line.

> **Note**
>
> There should be only one `PERIOD FOR SYSTEM_TIME` defined with two datetime2 columns. These two datetime2 columns should be declared as `GENERATED ALWAYS AS ROW START / END`.

Now, let us update one of the table entries and see how the temporal table keeps track of the changes.

```
UPDATE [dbo].[Customer] SET [address] = '111 Updated Lane, LA'
WHERE [customerId] = 101;
```

Let us query the table based on the two time boundaries and see all the changes that have happened to the customer with customerId=101.

```
33    SELECT [customerId]
34       , [name]
35       , [address]
36       , [validFrom]
37       , [validTo]
38       , IIF (YEAR(validTo) = 9999, 1, 0) AS IsActual
39    FROM [dbo].[Customer]
40    FOR SYSTEM_TIME BETWEEN '2022-01-22' AND '2022-01-24'
41    WHERE CustomerId = 101
42    ORDER BY validFrom DESC;
43
```

Results   Messages

customerId	name	address	validFrom	validTo	IsActual
101	Alan Li	111 Updated Lane, LA	2022-01-23T07:38:32....	9999-12-31T23:59:59....	1
101	Alan Li	101 Test Lane, LA	2022-01-23T07:36:26....	2022-01-23T07:38:32....	0

Figure 4.12 – Sample result of a Temporal query

As you can see, the Temporal table has kept track of the change along with the timestamps. We have derived the `IsActual` based on the value of the `validTo` column.

When we create a Temporal table, behind the scenes two tables get created. One is called the Temporal table (the one we defined) and another table with the exact schema called the history table. Whenever data changes, the current values get persisted in the Temporal table and the old values get moved into the history table with the end time updated to the current time stamp, indicating that that row is no longer active. There are also options to define our own History tables with additional indexing, distributions and so on and provide that to Azure SQL to use as the history table.

All you need to do is define the History table and provide the name as shown during the Temporal table creation.

```
WITH (SYSTEM_VERSIONING = ON (HISTORY_TABLE = dbo.
CustomerHistory));
```

Now you know how to can leverage Temporal tables support in Azure SQL for building applications that need to record changes over time.

You can learn more about Temporal tables here: https://docs.microsoft.com/en-us/sql/relational-databases/tables/temporal-tables?view=sql-server-ver15

Let's next look at how to design a dimensional hierarchy.

Designing a dimensional hierarchy

Dimensional hierarchy refers to the way we group and organize the dimensional data at multiple levels. In a hierarchical structure, there are usually one-to-many or many-to-many parent-child relationship. Examples of hierarchical structures could be organizational structures, product categories in an online store, a file system and so on. The main characteristic of the hierarchical structure is that all the nodes are identical, and they include pointers to their parent or children's nodes.

In order to achieve a dimensional hierarchy, we can use a technique called as the *self-referencing relationship* or *self-joins* within the dimension table. Let us take an example of an Employee dimension.

```
CREATE TABLE DimEmployee (
    [employeeId] VARCHAR(20) NOT NULL,
    [name] VARCHAR(100),
    [department] VARCHAR(50),
    [title] VARCHAR(50),
    [parentEmployeeId] VARCHAR(20)
)
```

Here, we have a column called `parentEmployeeID` referencing the `employeeID` column. If the Database supports *Foreign key* constraint then the `parentEmployeeID` would be defined as the Foreign Key to `employeeID`. Synapse SQL doesn't yet support Foreign Keys, so we need to ensure correctness at the application level.

> **Note**
>
> The Parent Key should allow NULL entries as the root elements of the hierarchy will not have a parent.

A sample hierarchical table with entries would look like this:

```
5   CREATE TABLE DimEmployee (
6       [employeeId] VARCHAR(20) NOT NULL,
7       [name] VARCHAR(100),
8       [department] VARCHAR(50),
9       [title] VARCHAR(50),
10      [parentEmployeeId] VARCHAR(20)
11  )
12
```

Results   Messages

🔍 Search to filter items...

employeeId	name	department	title	parentEmployeeId
100	Alan Li	Manufacturing	Manager	
200	Brenda Jackman	Manufacturing	Supervisor	100
300	David Hood	Manufacturing	Machine operator	200

Figure 4.13 – Sample Hierarchical dimension table

We can see that David reports to Brenda and Brenda reports to Alan. We have effectively created a hierarchy using the same table.

> **Tip**
> If you are using Dimensional Hierarchy as part of an SCD, always add the
> Parent key pointing to the Surrogate Key instead of the Business primary key.
> Because surrogate keys will be unique, and it will ensure that the dimensional
> hierarchy doesn't break when changes to the business key happens.

I hope you got a clear idea about dimensional hierarchies. Let's next look at designing an incremental loading solution for the Serving layer.

Designing for incremental loading

Incremental loading or delta loading refers to the process of loading smaller increments of data into a storage solution—for example, we could have daily data that is being loaded into a data lake or hourly data flowing into an **extract, transform, load** (ETL) pipeline, and so on. During data-ingestion scenarios, it is very common to do a bulk upload followed by scheduled incremental loads.

Azure has a very versatile service called **Azure Data Factory** (**ADF**) which can help with incremental loading. Since this is the first time we are using ADF in this book, let's learn a little more about it now as the information will come in handy in future chapters.

ADF is a managed cloud service that can be used to coordinate and orchestrate complex cloud- or hybrid- (on-premises)-based pipelines. ADF provides the ability to build ETL and **extract, load, transform** (**ELT**) pipelines. With ADF, you can do the following:

- Ingest data from a wide variety of sources such as databases, file shares, **Internet of Things** (**IoT**) hubs, **Amazon Web Services** (**AWS**), **Google Cloud Platform** (**GCP**), and more.

- Build complex pipelines using variables, parameters, branches, and so on.

- Transform data by using compute services such as Synapse, HDInsight, Cosmos DB, and so on.

- Schedule and monitor ingestions, control flow, and data flow operations.

Here is how the ADF workspace looks like:

Figure 4.14 – Data Factory Workspace landing screen

ADF is built of some basic set of components. The important ones are listed here:

- **Pipelines**—A pipeline is a collection of activities that are linked together to perform some control flow or data transformation.

- **Activities**—Activities in ADF refer to the steps in the pipeline such as copying data, running a Spark job, and so on.

- **Datasets**—This is the data that your pipelines or activities operate on.

- **Linked Services**—Linked services are connections that ADF uses to connect to a variety of data stores and computes in Azure. They are like connection strings that let you access data from external sources.

- **Triggers**—Triggers are events that are used to start pipelines or start an activity.

We will be using a lot of the preceding terminologies while using ADF, so it's good to understand them.

Now that we know what ADF is, let's explore the different ways in which we can design incremental loading using ADF. Based on the type of data source, we can have different techniques to implement incremental loading. Some of them are listed here:

- **Using watermarks**—If the data source is a database or relational table-based system
- **Using file timestamps**—If the source is a filesystem or blob storage
- **Using partition data**—If the source is partitioned based on time
- **Using folder structure**—If the source is divided based on time

Let's explore each of these techniques in detail.

Watermarks

Watermarking is a very simple technique whereby we just keep track of the last record loaded (our watermark) and load all the new records beyond the watermark in the next incremental run.

In relational storage technologies such as SQL databases, we can store the watermark details as just another simple table and automatically update the watermark with stored procedures. Every time a new record is loaded, the stored procedure should get triggered, which will update our watermark table. The next incremental copy pipeline can use this watermark information to identify the new set of records that need to be copied. Let's look at how we can implement a watermark design with ADF using Azure SQL as a source. Let's assume we have a simple table named `FactTrips` that needs to be incrementally loaded into an Azure SQL table. Proceed as follows:

1. Select the **Azure SQL** service from the Azure dashboard and create a new Azure SQL instance if you don't already have one. Create a simple `FactTrips` table as shown in the following screenshot and insert some dummy values into it using the **Query editor (preview)** option:

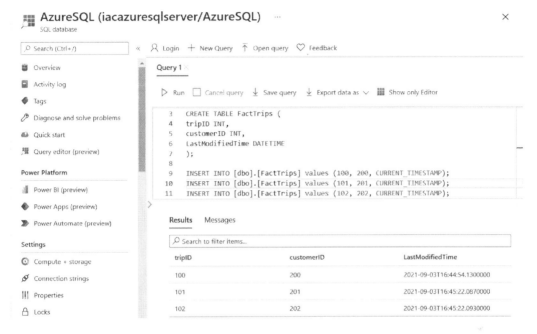

Figure 4.15 – Creating a simple table in Azure SQL

2. Create a watermark table, like this:

```
CREATE TABLE WatermarkTable
(
    [TableName] VARCHAR(100),
    [WatermarkValue] DATETIME,
);
```

3. Create a stored procedure to automatically update the watermark table whenever there is new data.

```
CREATE PROCEDURE [dbo].uspUpdateWatermark @
LastModifiedtime DATETIME, @TableName VARCHAR(100)
AS
BEGIN
UPDATE [dbo].[WatermarkTable] SET [WatermarkValue] = @
LastModifiedtime WHERE [TableName] = @TableName
END
```

4. Now, on the ADF side, we need to create a new pipeline for finding the delta between the old and new watermarks and then initiate an incremental copy.

5. From the **Pipeline** page in ADF, create two **Lookup** activities. They can be found at **Activities** -> **General** -> **Lookup**. Here is a sample ADF screen:

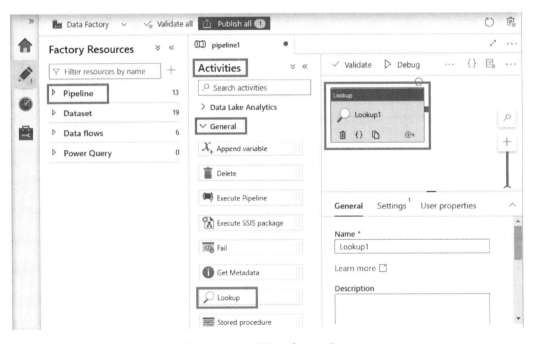

Figure 4.16 – ADF Authoring Page

6. Configure the first one to look up the previous watermark table entry, as shown in the following screenshot. The **Watermark** dataset has been configured to point to the Azure `WatermarkTable`.

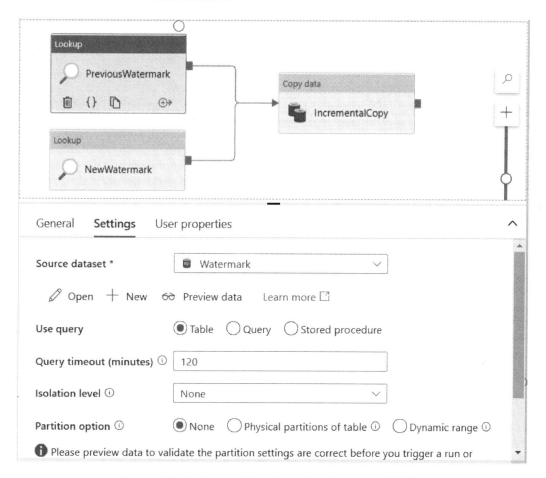

Figure 4.17 – lookup configuration using the watermark table

7. Configure the next **Lookup** activity to look at the latest file modified time in the source table, which in our case would be the `FactTrips` table:

```
SELECT MAX(LastModifiedTime) AS NewWatermarkValue FROM
FactTrips;
```

You will have to enter the following query in the **Query** textbox under the **Settings** tab:

Figure 4.18 – New watermark lookup configuration using LastModifiedTime

8. Finally, add a new **Copy** activity from **Activities** -> **Move and Transform** -> **Copy Data** and configure it as follows:

```
SELECT * FROM FactTrips WHERE
LastModifiedTime > '@{activity('PreviousWatermark').
output.firstRow.WatermarkValue}'
AND
LastModifiedTime <= '@{activity('NewWatermark').output.
firstRow.WatermarkValue}';
```

In the **Query** section under the **Source** tab, enter the following query:

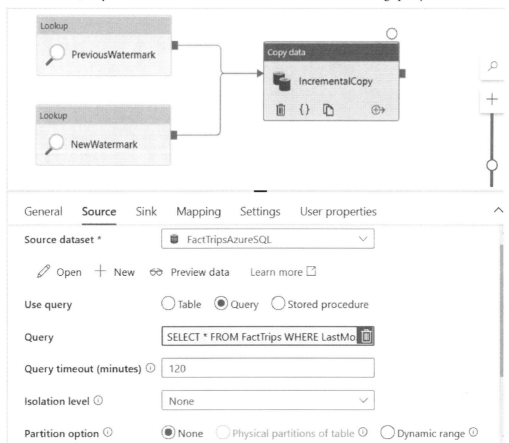

Figure 4.19 – ADF Copy activity with watermark-based delta generation

9. Save (publish) the preceding pipeline and set up a scheduled trigger using the **Add Trigger** button in the **Pipeline** screen. Now, every time there are changes to the FactTrips table, it will get copied into our destination table at regular intervals.

Let's next learn how to do incremental copying using file timestamps.

File timestamps

There's another technique available to incrementally load only the new files from a source to a destination: ADF's **Copy Data tool** functionality. This tool provides an option to scan the files at the source based on the LastModifiedDate attribute. So, all we need to do is to specify the source and destination folders and select the **Incremental load: LastModifiedDate** option for the **File loading behavior** field.

You can launch the **Copy Data tool** functionality from the ADF main screen, as shown in the following screenshot:

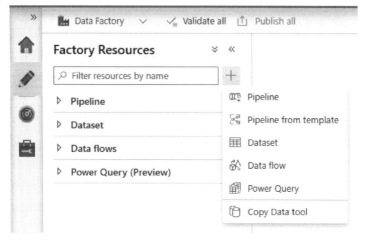

Figure 4.20 – ADF Copy Data tool launch screen

Once you click **Copy Data tool**, it launches a wizard screen where you can specify the incremental load details, as illustrated in the following screenshot:

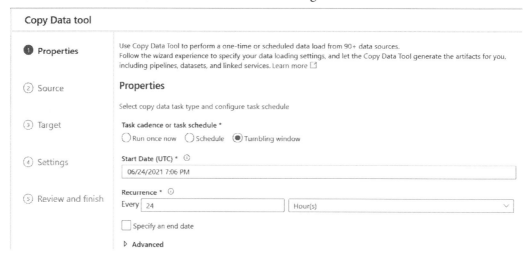

Figure 4.21 – Selecting Tumbling window for incremental load based on file modified time

> **Note**
>
> In the **Properties** tab shown in the previous screenshot, you need to select **Tumbling window** for the **Task Cadence or task schedule** setting; otherwise, the incremental load option won't show up.

In the **Source** window, select the **Incremental load: LastModified Date** option, as shown in the following screenshot:

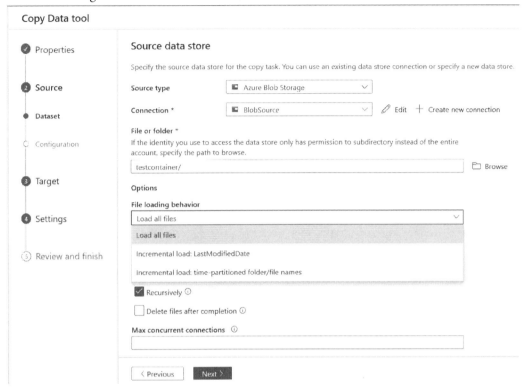

Figure 4.22 – ADF incremental load option with LastModifiedDate timestamps

Fill in the rest of the fields and select **Next** at the **Summary** screen to create an incremental copy pipeline using file modified dates.

Let's next learn how to do incremental copying using folder structures.

File partitions and folder structures

For both the options of file partitioning and data organized in date-based folder structures, we can use the ADF **Copy Data tool** functionality to perform incremental loading. The files and folders in both approaches will have a similar folder hierarchy based on date/time. If you recall the section on folder structure in *Chapter 2, Designing a Data Storage Structure*, we designed a folder structure using a date hierarchy. Let's assume that our input data is landing in a date-structured folder, as shown here:

```
New York/Trips/In/2022/01/01
```

Let's try to incrementally upload this data to another location in the blob storage on a regular basis. ADF's **Copy Data tool** has support for incremental copying for files and folders that are partitioned using date/time. Similar to how we instantiated a **Copy** activity in the previous section for the incremental copy based on file modified date timestamps, we need to instantiate the **Copy Data tool** functionality with the **File Loading behavior** field set to **Incremental load: time-partitioned folder/file names**. In this screen, once you start typing the input format using date variables such as {year}/{month}/ {day}, the **Options** section expands to show the year format, month format, and day format fields. You can select your preferred folder structure format using the dropdowns and complete the rest of the flow. The following screenshot shows an example of this:

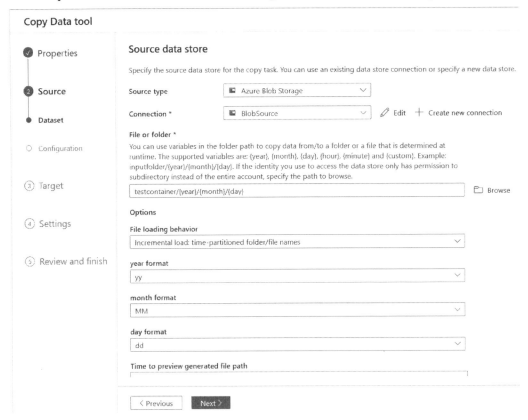

Figure 4.23 – ADF incremental load option with time-partitioned folders

Once you review the details and click **Next** on the **Summary** screen, the incremental pipeline for partitioned data/folder structures will get deployed.

We have now learned three different methods to perform incremental copying. Let's next explore how to select the right analytical data store for our Serving layer.

Designing analytical stores

Analytical stores could either be SQL or NoSQL data stores deployed in the data lake Serving Zone. The main job of an analytical data store is to serve the data generated by the data transformation pipelines to the BI tools in a fast and simple manner. Analytical stores are usually subjected to ad hoc querying from business analysts and other end users. As such, these stores need to perform really well with random reads. Azure provides a variety of storage technologies that can cater to these requirements. Here are some of the most important ones:

- **Azure Synapse Analytics (Serverless/dedicated SQL pools and Spark pools)**—Synapse Analytics provides both SQL pools and Spark pools. Among these, the SQL dedicated pools are **massively parallel processing (MPP)** data warehouses and are usually ideal for a majority of analytical store situations. Serverless SQL pools can be used for ad hoc querying. Spark pools, on the other hand, can support analytical workloads through their in-memory store and wide columnstore support. Both support SQL/SQL-like interfaces.

- **Azure Databricks**—Azure Databricks is another Spark distribution that can provide limited analytical store capabilities via its in-memory stores and wide columnstore support. It also supports SQL-like interfaces.

- **Azure Cosmos DB**—Cosmos DB provides support for document databases, key-value stores, graph stores, wide columnstores, and more. It also supports SQL/SQL-like interfaces.

- **Azure SQL Database/SQL Database on custom virtual machines (VMs)**—Azure SQL provides relational database support and, of course, supports the SQL interface.

- **HBase/Phoenix on HDInsight**—Provides analytical store support through the in-memory store and wide columnstore support. It also supports SQL/SQL-like interfaces.

- **Hive LLAP on HDInsight**—Provides analytical store support through the in-memory store. It also supports SQL/SQL-like interfaces.

- **Azure Data Explorer**—Provides relational store and time-series support. It also supports SQL/SQL-like interfaces.

There are other criteria such as security and scalability that you might want to consider.

Security considerations

Here is a high-level security comparison table reproduced from the Azure documentation that can help you decide on the right analytical store for you:

Service	Authentication options	Supports data encryption at rest	Supports row-level security	Supports dynamic data masking	Supports firewalls
Synapse Analytics	SQL/**Azure Active Directory** (**Azure AD**)	Yes	Yes	Yes	Yes
Cosmos DB	Azure AD	Yes	No	No	Yes
Azure SQL	SQL/Azure AD	Yes	Yes	Yes	Yes
HBase/Phoenix	Local/Azure AD	Yes	Yes	Yes	Yes (with Azure **virtual networks** (**VNets**))
Hive LLAP	Local/Azure AD	Yes	Yes	Yes	Yes (with Azure VNets)
Azure Data Explorer	Azure AD	Yes	No	Yes	Yes
Azure Analysis Services	Azure AD	Yes	Yes	No	Yes

Figure 4.24 – Security comparison of the different Azure analytical stores

Let's look at the scalability comparison next.

Scalability considerations

Here is another comparison table that can help you decide on an analytical store based on your data size and speed considerations:

Service	Supports redundant regional servers for high availability (HA)	Supports query scale-out	Supports scale-up	Supports in-memory caching
Synapse Analytics	No	Yes	Yes	Yes
Cosmos DB	Yes	Yes	Yes	No
Azure SQL	Yes	No	Yes	Yes
HBase/Phoenix	Yes	Yes	No	No
Hive LLAP	No	Yes	No	Yes
Azure Data Explorer	Yes	Yes	Yes	Yes
Azure Analysis Services	No	Yes	Yes	Yes

Figure 4.25 – Scalability comparison of the different Azure analytical stores

You can learn more about analytical store selection criteria here: `https://docs.microsoft.com/en-us/azure/architecture/data-guide/technology-choices/analytical-data-stores`

We are almost at the end of this chapter. In the last section, let's explore what metastores are and how to set them up in Azure Synapse Analytics and Azure Databricks.

Designing metastores in Azure Synapse Analytics and Azure Databricks

Metastores store the metadata of data in services such as **Spark** or **Hive**. Think of a metastore as a data catalog that can tell you which tables you have, what the table schemas are, what the relationships among the tables are, where they are stored, and so on. Spark supports two metastore options: an **in-memory version** and an **external version**.

In-memory metastores are limited in accessibility and scale. They can help jobs running on the same **Java virtual machine** (**JVM**) but not much further than this. Also, the metadata is lost once the cluster is shut down.

For all practical purposes, Spark uses an external metastore, and the only supported external metastore at the time of writing this book was Hive Metastore. Hive's metastore is mature and provides generic **application programming interfaces** (**APIs**) to access it. Hence, instead of rebuilding a new metastore, Spark just uses the mature and well-designed Hive metastore for its own cataloging.

Let's explore the metastore features available in both Azure Synapse Analytics and Azure Databricks.

Azure Synapse Analytics

Synapse Analytics supports metadata sharing among its computational pools such as Spark and SQL. Spark databases and external tables that are created using **Parquet** format can be easily accessed from the SQL pools.

Two main metadata components can be shared in the current version of Synapse: databases and tables. Let's look at them in detail.

Databases

Any database you create using Spark SQL can be directly accessed by the dedicated or serverless SQL pools in Synapse, provided both these pools have storage-level access to the newly created database.

For example, create a `FactTrips` table in Spark by running the following code:

```
spark.Sql("CREATE DATABASE FactTrips")
```

Then, read it from SQL, like this:

```
SELECT * FROM sys.databases;
```

You don't have to do any configuration; Synapse automatically makes the databases visible across its compute pools. Now, let's look at the other metadata component that can be shared in the current version of Synapse: tables.

Tables

Any Parquet-based table that Spark stores in the `warehouse` directory is automatically shared to the SQL pools.

Any Parquet-based external tables created by Spark can also be shared with the SQL pools, by providing the location of the table.

Azure Databricks (and Azure Synapse Spark)

As we briefly saw in *Chapter 2, Designing a Data Storage Structure*, **Azure Databricks** is the Databricks version of Spark hosted on Azure. It is available as an independent Azure service and is well connected to most of the Azure services. Azure Databricks and Azure Synapse Spark both use **Hive Metastore** as their external metastore. Such external metastores enable data access between different Spark clusters and also between other computes such as Hive. Theoretically, any service that can talk to the Hive metastore and has the right access levels can read the Spark catalogs persisted in the metastore. The Hive metastore itself is usually deployed on top of a SQL database such as Azure SQL. Setting up an external Hive metastore is a manual procedure for both Databricks and Synapse Spark. There are two sets of configurations that you will have to set up, one for Spark and one for Hive.

On the Spark side, while creating a cluster, you just need to add the following parameters into the Spark configuration options field. Here, we assume that you already have a Hive cluster and an **Azure SQL database** (to be used as the metastore) up and running. You can choose to use any SQL database, not necessarily Azure SQL for the metastore. Proceed as follows:

1. Specify the **Java Database Connectivity (JDBC)** connect string for a JDBC metastore, as follows:

```
spark.hadoop.javax.jdo.option.ConnectionURL <mssql-
connection-string>
```

2. Specify the username to be used for the metastore, as follows:

```
spark.hadoop.javax.jdo.option.ConnectionUserName <mssql-
username>
```

3. Specify the password to be used for the metastore, as follows:

```
spark.hadoop.javax.jdo.option.ConnectionPassword <mssql-
password>
```

4. Specify the driver class name for a JDBC metastore, as follows:

```
spark.hadoop.javax.jdo.option.ConnectionDriverName com.
microsoft.sqlserver.jdbc.SQLServerDriver
```

5. Specify the Hive metastore version, as follows:

```
spark.sql.hive.metastore.version <hive-version>
```

6. Specify the location of the metastore jars, **Java ARchive (JAR)** files, as follows:

```
spark.sql.hive.metastore.jars <hive-jar-source>
```

> **Note**
>
> A spark.hadoop prefix is added to make sure these Hive-specific options
> propagate to the metastore client.

And on the Hive server, please update the following configurations with the right values:

1. Specify the JDBC connect string for a JDBC metastore, as follows:

```
javax.jdo.option.ConnectionURL <mssql-connection-string>
```

2. Specify the username for the metastore database, as follows:

```
javax.jdo.option.ConnectionUserName <mssql-username>
```

3. Specify the password metastore database, as follows:

```
javax.jdo.option.ConnectionPassword <mssql-password>
```

4. Specify the connection driver class name for the JDBC metastore, as follows:

```
javax.jdo.option.ConnectionDriverName com.microsoft.
sqlserver.jdbc.SQLServerDriver
```

If your versions of Spark/Hive don't match the default ones provided by Azure, then you will have to download the right version of the JAR files and upload them into the workspace. The following link has more details on this: `https://docs.microsoft.com/en-us/azure/databricks/data/metastores/external-hive-metastore`.

Summary

That brings a close to our fourth chapter. Congratulations on making it this far.

Just to recap, we started off with the basics of data modeling and learned about Star and Snowflake schemas. We then learned about designing for SCDs, the different sub-types of SCDs, dimensional hierarchies, handling temporal data by using time dimensions, loading data incrementally using ADF, and selecting the right analytical store based on the customer's requirements. Finally, we learned about creating metastores for Synapse and Azure Databricks. All these topics complete the syllabus for *DP203 – Design the Serving Layer*. You have now learned how to design your own Serving layer in Azure.

We have now come to the end of our design chapters. We will be focusing on the implementation details from the next chapter onward. Yay!

5
Implementing Physical Data Storage Structures

Hope you have had a good learning experience up till now. Let's continue our journey toward certification with more interesting topics in this chapter. Till the previous chapter, we have been focusing on the design aspects, but from now on, we will be focusing on the implementation details. We will learn how to implement the storage-level concepts that we learned in the previous chapters. Once you complete this chapter, you should be able to decide on and implement the following: what kind of data sharding is required, when to compress your data, how many partitions to create, what kind of data redundancy to maintain, and so on.

We will cover the following topics in this chapter:

- Getting started with Azure Synapse Analytics
- Implementing compression
- Implementing partitioning

- Implementing horizontal partitioning or sharding
- Implementing distributions
- Implementing different table geometries with Azure Synapse Analytics pools
- Implementing data redundancy
- Implementing data archiving

Technical requirements

For this chapter, you will need the following:

- An Azure account (free or paid)
- An active Synapse workspace

Let's start implementing!

Getting started with Azure Synapse Analytics

Most of the examples in this chapter will be executed in an **Azure Synapse Analytics** workspace, so let's look at how to create one. Proceed as follows:

1. From the Azure portal, search for Synapse. From the results, select **Azure Synapse Analytics**.

2. Once inside, click on **+ Create** and enter the details for a new workspace. The **Create Synapse workspace** screen is shown in the following screenshot:

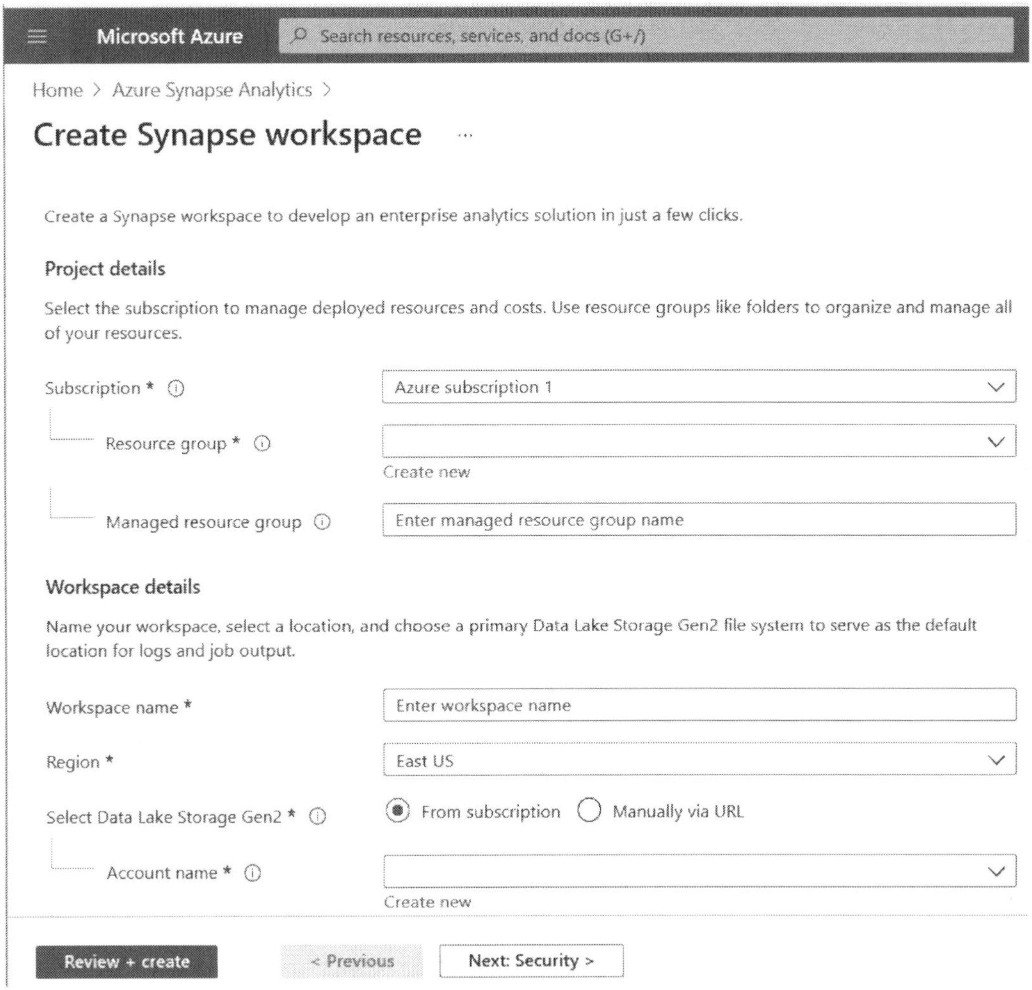

Figure 5.1 – Azure Synapse workspace creation

3. Once done, click on the **Review + create** button and, finally, the **Create** button on that screen to create a new Synapse workspace.

This workspace will provide us with **Structured Query Language** (**SQL**) and Spark pools, required to experiment with the various concepts that we learned in the previous chapters. Let's start by implementing compression in the next section.

Implementing compression

In the previous chapters, we learned about the importance of data **compression** in data lakes. As the size of the data in data lakes grows, it becomes important that we store the data in a compressed format in order to save on cost. There are numerous ways in which we can implement compression in Azure. There are a lot of compression libraries available in the market and technically, all we need to do is write some scripts to call those libraries to compress data. But writing ad hoc scripts brings its own maintenance complexity, so let's look at some easy-to-maintain ways of implementing compression in Azure using Azure Synapse Pipelines. The same can be achieved using **Azure Data Factory** too. Azure Synapse Pipelines is just the same Azure Data Factory implementation within Synapse Analytics.

Compressing files using Synapse Pipelines or ADF

In the previous chapter, we learned about ADF. Like ADF, Synapse Pipelines can be used to create pipelines to do a wide range of activities such as **extract, transform, load** (**ETL**), **extract, load, transform** (**ELT**), **copying data**, and so on. ADF and Synapse Pipelines supports several dozens of services as data sources and sinks, both within Azure and outside Azure. Among them, services such as Azure Blob Storage or **Azure Data Lake Storage Gen2** (**ADLS Gen2**) support the option of compressing the data before copying. Let's see an example of reading uncompressed files and compressing them before writing them back into ADLS Gen2 using Synapse Pipelines.

Proceed as follows:

1. Create a **Copy Data tool** instance by clicking on the + sign, as shown in the following screenshot:

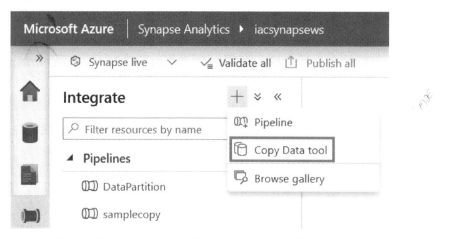

Figure 5.2 – Selecting Copy Data tool in Synapse Pipelines

2. In the **Copy Data tool** instance, enter the **Source** and **Destination** folders on your Azure data store.

3. On the **Configuration** page, you can specify a **Compression type** option, as shown in the following screenshot:

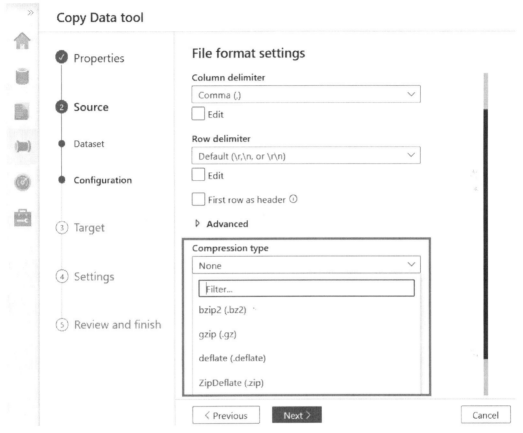

Figure 5.3 – Compression type options in the destination data store page of Copy Data tool

4. Select one of the **Compression type** options, fill in the other mandatory fields in the other tabs, then finally click **Publish** on the **Review and finish** page to save this **Copy Data tool** instance.

5. You can then trigger this **Copy Data tool** instance on demand or set up a recurring trigger to perform the compression at regular intervals from the ADF pipeline screen.

That is how simple it is to set up a regular compression job using Synapse Pipelines (similarly in ADF). Next, let's explore how to compress files using **Spark**, which is one of the compute pools available in **Synapse**. You can also choose to use **Azure Databricks Spark**. The examples provided here will work fine with any flavor of Spark.

Compressing files using Spark

Spark provides libraries that can directly write the outputs in compressed formats such as **Parquet**, **ORC**, and so on. On top of this, we can specify the compression algorithms to be used. For example, the following Python script stores the data in Parquet format using `gzip` compression:

```
columnNames = ["name","license","gender","salary"]
driverData = [
    ('Alice', 'A224455', 'Female', 3000),
    ('Bryan','B992244','Male',4000),
    ('Catherine','C887733','Female',4000)
]
df = spark.createDataFrame(data= driverData, schema =
columnNames)


df.write.option("compression", "gzip"). parquet("abfss://path/
to/output")
```

> **Note**
>
> Spark supports these compression options: `snappy`, `gzip`, `lzo`, `brotli`, `lz4`, and `zstd`. You can learn more about Spark compression options at `https://spark.apache.org/docs/latest/configuration.html`.

Now that we have learned how to compress data using ADF and Spark, let's look at the different ways to partition data in Azure Synapse.

Implementing partitioning

In *Chapter 3*, *Designing a Partition Strategy*, we covered the basics of **partitioning**. In this section, we will be learning how to implement the different types of partitioning. We will start with partitioning on Azure data stores and then look into partitioning for analytical workloads.

For storage-based partitioning, the main technique is to partition the data into the correct folder structure. In the previous chapters, we learned about how to store the data in a date-based format. The recommendation from Azure is to use the following pattern:

```
{Region}/{SubjectMatter(s)}/{yyyy}/{mm}/{dd}/{hh}/
```

Let's learn how to implement folder creation in an automated manner using ADF.

Using ADF/Synapse pipelines to create data partitions

You can use ADF or Synapse Pipelines, as both use the same ADF technology. In this example, I'm using Synapse Pipelines. Let's look at the steps to partition data in an automated fashion:

1. In your **Synapse** workspace, select the **Pipelines** tab and select a **Data flow** activity, as illustrated in the following screenshot:

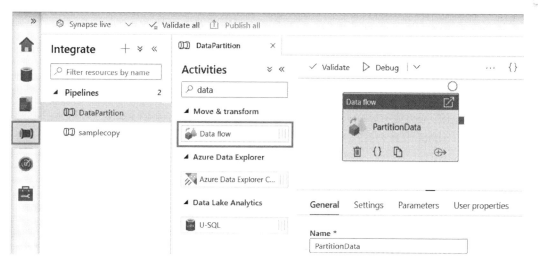

Figure 5.4 – Selecting the Data flow activity in Synapse Pipelines

2. Double-click on the **Data flow** activity to reveal the **Source** and **Destination** nodes.

3. Configure the **Source** details. Under the **Source options** tab, fill in the **Wildcard paths** field, similar to the example shown in the following screenshot:

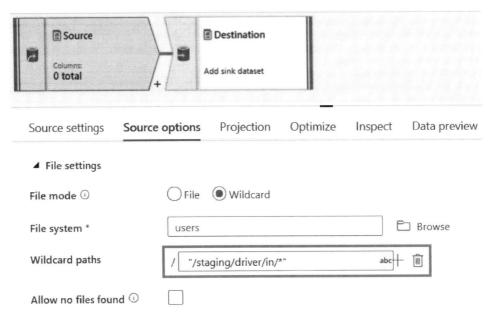

Figure 5.5 – Entering source information in the Data flow activity

4. Now, click on the **Destination** node and fill in the destination folder details, as illustrated in the following screenshot:

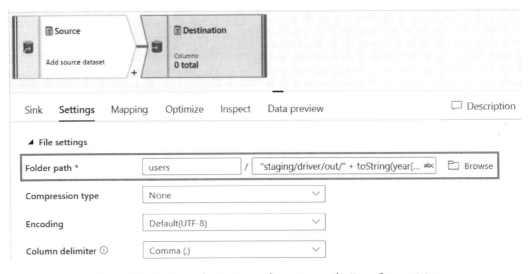

Figure 5.6 – Entering destination information in the Data flow activity

5. The important field here is **Folder path**. This field accepts dynamic expressions. If you click on the folder path text box, it pops up an **Expression Builder** tool that can be used to build complex expressions denoting the file format that we need.

6. Here is a sample expression that can be used to create date directories:

```
"staging/driver/out/" + toString(year(currentDate()))
+ "/" + toString(month(currentDate())) + "/" +
toString(dayOfMonth(currentDate()))
```

7. If the current date is January 1, 2022, the previous expression would generate a folder such as this:

```
staging/driver/out/2022/01/01
```

8. And the next day, a new folder with the date 02 would get created, and so on.

9. Once you are done adding the folder path, publish the pipeline and trigger it.

This is how we can automatically partition and store incoming data. Let's next look at the partitioning options available for analytical workloads.

Partitioning for analytical workloads

In *Chapter 3, Designing a Partition Strategy*, we learned about the three types of partitioning for analytical workloads, which are listed again here:

- Horizontal partitioning or sharding
- Vertical partitioning
- Functional partitioning

Among these, **horizontal partitioning** or **sharding** techniques are dynamic in nature and are done after schemas are created. They are usually performed regularly during data loading or during the data transformation phase. Synapse dedicated pools and Spark pools provide several options to perform sharding. We will be dedicating a full section to sharding next.

Vertical or functional partitioning, on the other hand, is done at the time of schema build-out. These types of partitioning involve figuring out the right set of tables based on the queries and the data distribution. Once we figure out the required tables based on our business needs, the implementation just involves creating multiple tables using the CREATE TABLE command and linking the tables using a constraint such as a FOREIGN KEY constraint.

> **Note**
> As of writing this book, the `FOREIGN KEY` constraint is not yet supported in dedicated SQL pools.

From a certification perspective, sharding is more important, so let's focus on that next.

Implementing horizontal partitioning or sharding

Let's explore sharding from two different perspectives: a dedicated SQL pool and Spark. Just note that we will be using the terminologies **horizontal partitioning** and **sharding** interchangeably throughout the book, but they mean the same thing.

Sharding in Synapse dedicated pools

Synapse SQL dedicated pools have three different types of tables based on how the data is stored, outlined as follows:

- Clustered columnstore
- Clustered index
- Heap

We will be learning more about these table types later in this chapter. Synapse dedicated pools support sharding for all these table types. They provide three different ways to shard the data, as follows:

- Hash
- Round-robin
- Replicated

These methods through which a SQL dedicated pool distributes data among its tables are also called **distribution** techniques. Sharding and distribution techniques are overlapping technologies that are always specified together in SQL `CREATE TABLE` statements.

> **Note**
> The dedicated SQL pool by default partitions the data into 60 distributions. The partitions that we specify explicitly add to the partitions that the SQL dedicated pool already creates. So, ensure that you don't end up over-partitioning the data, as this can negatively affect the query performance.

Let's now take a look at examples of how to shard data in a dedicated SQL pool.

Using dedicated SQL pools to create sharding

Dedicated SQL pools have an option called PARTITION that can be used during the table creation process to define how the data has to be partitioned. Let's use the same base example that we used in *Chapter 2, Designing a Data Storage Structure*, to try the partitioning. We'll proceed as follows:

1. Let's create a simple table that partitions on the tripDate field, as follows:

```
CREATE TABLE dbo.TripTable
(
    [tripId] INT NOT NULL,
    [driverId] INT NOT NULL,
    [customerId] INT NOT NULL,
    [tripDate] INT,
    [startLocation] VARCHAR(40),
    [endLocation] VARCHAR (40)
)
WITH
(
    CLUSTERED COLUMNSTORE INDEX,
    DISTRIBUTION = HASH ([tripId]),
    PARTITION ([tripDate] RANGE RIGHT FOR VALUES
        ( 20220101, 20220201, 20220301 )
    )
)
```

2. Insert some sample data into the table, as shown in the following code block:

```
INSERT INTO dbo.TripTable VALUES (100, 200, 300,
20220101, 'New York', 'New Jersey');
INSERT INTO dbo.TripTable VALUES (101, 201, 301,
20220101, 'Miami', 'Dallas');
INSERT INTO dbo.TripTable VALUES (102, 202, 302,
20220102, 'Phoenix', 'Tempe');
. . .
```

3. Now, let's run the query as shown in the following screenshot. Don't worry if you don't understand the details of the query—it is just trying to get the partition details in an easy-to-read format. This query can be found in the Synapse documentation:

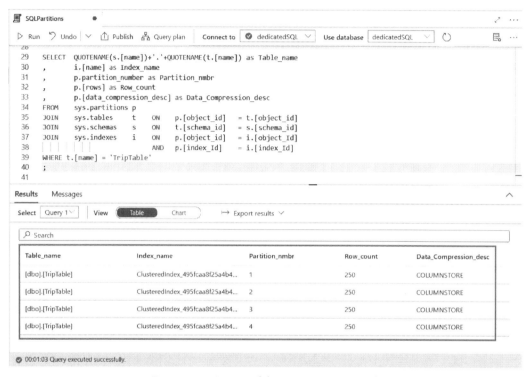

Figure 5.7 – Output of the partition command

4. As you can see in the **Results** section, four partitions have been created.

Two of the attributes used while defining the partition are RANGE RIGHT and RANGE LEFT. We learned about these keywords in *Chapter 2, Designing a Data Storage Structure*, while learning about data pruning. Just to recap, RANGE RIGHT ensures that the value specified in the PARTITION syntax will belong to the right-side partition and vice versa for the RANGE LEFT keyword.

Next, let's look at the options Spark provides for sharding.

Sharding using Spark

Spark by default partitions data based on the number of cores available or the number of **Hadoop Distributed File System (HDFS)** blocks (if it is running on HDFS). If we need to partition the data in any other custom format, then Spark provides options for that too. Spark supports two types of partitioning: **in-memory partitioning** and **on-disk partitioning**. Let's look at both these types of partitioning in detail.

In-memory partitioning

Spark provides the following three methods to perform in-memory partitioning:

- `repartition()`—To increase the number of partitions.
- `coalesce()`—To decrease the number of partitions.
- `repartitionByRange()`—This is a specialization of the `repartition` command where you can specify the ranges.

Let's consider an example Spark snippet to understand these three partition types, as follows:

```
columnNames = ["name","license","gender","salary"]
driverData = [
    ('Alice', 'A224455', 'Female', 3000),
    ('Bryan','B992244','Male',4000),
    ('Catherine','C887733','Female',2000),
    ('Daryl','D229988','Male',3000),
    ('Jenny','J663300','Female', 6000)
]
df = spark.
createDataFrame(data= driverData, schema = columnNames)
print("Default Partitions: " + str(df.rdd.getNumPartitions()))
repartitionDF = df.repartition(3)
print("Repartition Partitions: " + str(repartitionDF.rdd.
getNumPartitions()))
coalesceDF=df.coalesce(2)
print("Coalesce Partitions: " + str(coalesceDF.rdd.
getNumPartitions()))
repartitionRangeDF = df.repartitionByRange(1,'salary')
print("Range Partitions: " + str(repartitionRangeDF.rdd.
getNumPartitions()))
```

The output of the previous code snippet would look something like this:

```
Default Partitions: 8
Repartition Partitions: 3
Coalesce Partitions: 2
Range Partitions: 1
```

As you can see, with each of the partition commands, the number of partitions gets updated.

Now that we have explored in-memory partitions in Spark, let's next look into on-disk partitioning methods.

On-disk partitioning

Spark provides the `partitionBy()` operator, which can be used to partition the data and store it in different files while writing the output. Here is a sample code snippet to perform `partitionBy()`. This example continues the example from the *In-memory partitioning* section:

```
df = spark.
createDataFrame(data= driverData, schema = columnNames)
df.write.partitionBy("gender","salary")..parquet("abfss://path/
to/output/")
```

The preceding code snippet will create two separate folders, one for `Female` and one for `Male`. The output will be as shown here:

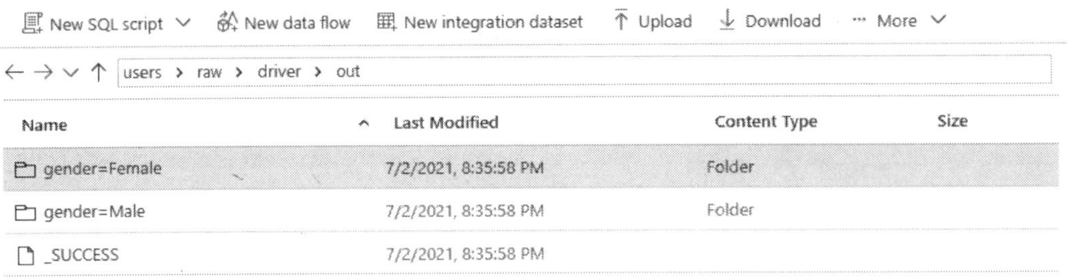

Figure 5.8 – Output of the PartitionBy command

With that, we have covered how we can perform partitioning using Spark. Now, let's move on to distributions, which is a concept related to partitions in dedicated SQL pools.

Implementing distributions

A dedicated SQL pool **massively parallel processing** (**MPP**) engine splits the data into **60 parallel partitions** and executes them in parallel. Each of these smaller partitions, along with the compute resources to run the queries, is called a **distribution**. A distribution is a basic unit of processing and storage for a dedicated SQL pool.

Dedicated SQL pools provide three options for distribution. Let's look at each of them in detail.

Hash distribution

This type of distribution distributes the data based on a hash function. Rows with the same values for the hashed column will always move to the same partition. This can be implemented by providing the DISTRIBUTION = HASH (COLUMN_ID) value in the WITH clause of CREATE TABLE. Here is an example:

```
CREATE TABLE dbo.TripTable
(
    [tripId] INT NOT NULL,
    [driverId] INT NOT NULL,
    [customerID] INT NOT NULL,
    [tripDate] INT,
    [startLocation] VARCHAR(40),
    [endLocation] VARCHAR(40)
)
WITH
(
    CLUSTERED COLUMNSTORE INDEX,
    DISTRIBUTION = HASH ([tripId]),
    PARTITION ([tripDate] RANGE RIGHT FOR VALUES
        ( 20220101, 20220201, 20220301 )
    )
)
```

> **Tip**
> Use hash distribution if the table size is greater than 2 **gigabytes** (**GB**) or if the table has very frequent updates.

Round-robin distribution

This type of distribution just distributes the data randomly across nodes in a round-robin fashion. It can be implemented by providing the `DISTRIBUTION = ROUND_ROBIN` value in the `WITH` clause of `CREATE TABLE`. Here is an example:

```
WITH
(
    CLUSTERED COLUMNSTORE INDEX,
    DISTRIBUTION = ROUND_ROBIN
    PARTITION (...)
)
```

Choose round-robin distributions while loading data into staging tables or when there is no good indexing to choose from.

Replicated distribution

This type of distribution just copies the complete table across all the nodes. It can be implemented by providing the `DISTRIBUTION = REPLICATE` value in the `WITH` clause of `CREATE TABLE`. Here is an example:

```
WITH
(
    CLUSTERED COLUMNSTORE INDEX,
    DISTRIBUTION = REPLICATE
    PARTITION (...)
)
```

Use `REPLICATE` to copy small but frequently accessed data such as retail catalog tables, price chart tables, and so on.

I hope you got a good grasp of sharding and distributions in a Synapse SQL pool. Now that we know how to implement distributions, let's learn about the other attributes of Synapse tables.

Implementing different table geometries with Azure Synapse Analytics pools

The term *table geometry* is not standard database terminology, so I'm taking an educated guess that the certification team meant the different features of Azure Synapse dedicated pool tables.

The main features of Synapse dedicated pool tables are **partitions**, **indexes**, and **distributions**. We have already covered partitions and distributions in detail, so we will focus on the remaining feature, which is indexing.

SQL dedicated pools provide the following three types of indexing:

- Clustered columnstore indexing
- Heap indexing
- Clustered indexing

Let's look at them in detail.

Clustered columnstore indexing

Clustered columnstore is the default indexing option of a dedicated SQL pool table. This type of indexing works best for large fact tables. It is a column-based data storage and provides very high levels of compression and better query performance than row-based indexes.

Here is an example of how to create a table with clustered columnstore indexing:

```
CREATE TABLE dbo.Driver
(
    [driverId] INT NOT NULL,
        [name] VARCHAR(40),
    . . .
)
WITH ( CLUSTERED COLUMNSTORE INDEX );
```

Heap indexing

Heap tables are used as temporary data-loading tables as they provide faster loading times. They are usually used for staging data before loading it into other refined tables. Heap indexing works better for smaller tables.

Here is an example of how to create a table with heap indexing:

```
CREATE TABLE dbo.Driver
(
    [driverId] INT NOT NULL,
    [name] VARCHAR(40),
    . . .
)
WITH ( HEAP );
```

Clustered indexing

Clustered index tables are row-based storage tables. They are usually faster for queries that need row lookups with highly selective filters on the clustered index column.

Here is an example of how to create a table with clustered indexing:

```
CREATE TABLE dbo.Driver
(
    [driverId] INT NOT NULL,
    [name] VARCHAR(40),
    . . .
)
WITH ( CLUSTERED INDEX (driverId) );
```

> **Note**
> If your table size is less than the recommended 60 million rows for clustered columnstore indexing, consider using heap or clustered index tables.

You have now learned some of the important features of SQL dedicated pool tables, such as partitioning, indexing, and distributions. Now, let's look into our next topic: data redundancy.

Implementing data redundancy

Data redundancy is the process of storing multiple copies of data at different locations, in order to protect the data from events such as power failures, disk failures, network failures, and even major catastrophes such as entire data center outages. Azure Storage provides multiple options for data redundancy both at local data center levels and across data centers. We can broadly group the options into these two categories:

- Primary region redundancy
- Secondary region redundancy

Let's look at these options in detail.

Azure storage redundancy in the primary region

This type of redundancy covers localized failures such as disk failures, machine failures, and rack failures. There are two types of primary region redundancy, as detailed next.

Locally redundant storage (LRS)

With this type of redundancy, the data is copied three times across multiple machines in the same physical region within a data center. This option provides protection against local failures such as disk, machine, or local network failures. If all three data copies end up residing on the same rack and if the rack loses power, we might then end up losing the data. This is the cheapest of all the redundant-storage options.

Zone-redundant storage (ZRS)

This type of redundancy is similar to LRS, but the data is intelligently copied across multiple **Availability Zones (AZs)**. AZs are local regions within a data center that have different power and networking supplies and non-overlapping maintenance periods. This ensures that even if one of the zones is down, the other zones can continue serving the data. This option is more expensive than LRS.

Azure storage redundancy in secondary regions

This type of redundancy provides data protection against major geographical region failures such as total data center outages caused due to massive power outages, earthquakes, hurricanes, and so on. With this type of redundancy, along with the local copies, a copy of the data is stored in a data center at a different geological location. If the primary region goes down, the applications would be able to either automatically or manually fail over to the secondary region. There are two options for secondary region redundancy, as detailed next.

Geo-redundant storage (GRS)

GRS is basically an LRS setup at both the primary and secondary regions. The data is first written in an LRS fashion synchronously at the primary region, and then a remote copy happens asynchronously at the secondary region. At the remote site, the data is again replicated three times using local LRS.

Azure also provides a read-only extension to GRS called **read-access GRS** (**RA-GRS**). The only difference is that the remote copy is a read-only copy in this case.

Geo ZRS (GZRS)

GZRS is ZRS at the primary region and LRS at the secondary region. Similar to GRS, the local copies are synchronously copied, and the remote ones are asynchronously copied. The remote location still keeps an LRS copy, but not a ZRS one. This is the highest data-redundancy option provided by Azure and, not surprisingly, the most expensive one too. As with GRS, GZRS also provides a read-only remote copy option called RA-GZRS.

Similar to the storage data redundancy options, there are some additional specialized data redundancy options available for services like Azure SQL, Synapse SQL, CosmosDB and other similar services. Let us briefly look at them too.

Azure SQL Geo Replication

Azure SQL provides a feature called Active Geo replication. This is a data redundancy feature that replicates the complete Azure SQL server instance to the secondary servers configured in a different geographical back up region. The secondary servers serve as read only servers and can be switched to read-write during failovers. The failovers can be initiated programmatically, thereby reducing the time to switch over during failures.

You can learn more about Azure SQL Active Geo Replication here: `https://docs.microsoft.com/en-us/azure/azure-sql/database/active-geo-replication-overview`

Azure Synapse SQL Data Replication

Azure Synapse does geo-backups to its paired data centres (usually geographically distributed) every 24 hours unless you have opted out of this feature. You can restore from your geo-backups to any Synapse SQL pool in any region if that region has support for Synapse SQL pools.

You can learn more about Azure SQL Pool data redundancy here:

```
https://docs.microsoft.com/en-us/azure/synapse-analytics/
sql-data-warehouse/backup-and-restore#geo-backups-and-
disaster-recovery
```

CosmosDB Data Replication

CosmosDB is a globally distributed database that transparently replicates your data to the configured geographical locations. It provides very low latencies by allowing read and write from the local replicas of the data base. Hence, just by configuring CosmosDB in multiple geo-locations you get data redundancy.

CosmosDB also automatically backs up your data periodically. You can use the automatic backups to recover in case of accidental deletes, updating of your CosmosDB account and so on.

You can learn more about CosmosDB global data replication here:

```
https://docs.microsoft.com/en-us/azure/cosmos-db/distribute-
data-globally.
```

> **Note**
>
> Not all Azure services or regions support all four redundancies, so please read about the redundancy support available for each service and plan for your product deployment accordingly.

Now, let's see how to implement redundancy in Azure Storage.

Example of setting up redundancy in Azure Storage

While creating a new storage account, you can choose among the four data-redundancy options, as shown in the following screenshot:

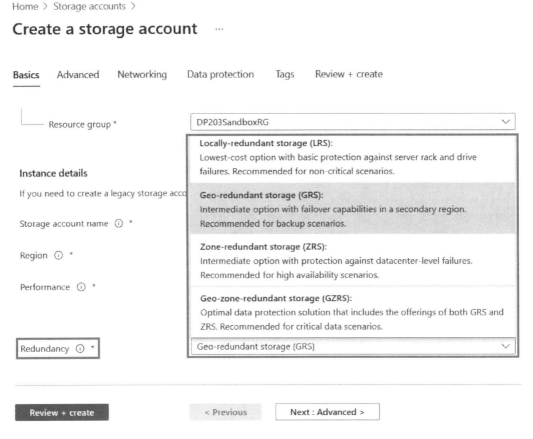

Figure 5.9 – Choosing data redundancy option during storage account creation

If you wish to change the redundancy after the storage has been created, you can still do that from the following **Configuration** screen:

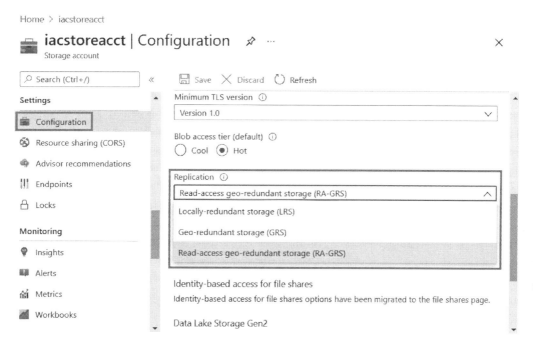

Figure 5.10 – Choosing data redundancy option after storage account creation

However, changing the redundancy after creation will require you to do manual or live migration. Manual migration refers to the process of either copying the data over to the new storage manually or automating it using ADF. This will usually result in application downtime.

On the other hand, if you need your applications to be up during the migration, you can request a live migration with Microsoft Support. This might result in some support charges.

Implementing data archiving

In *Chapter 2*, *Designing a Data Storage Structure*, we already explored how to design and implement **data archiving**. We learned about the Hot, Cold, and Archive tiers of data storage and how to build data life cycle management policies. As we have covered the details already, we will not be repeating them here. Please refer to the *Designing a data archiving solution* section of *Chapter 2*, *Designing a Data Storage Structure*, again if you have forgotten about archiving.

Summary

That brings us to the end of this chapter. I hope you enjoyed it as much as I enjoyed writing it. We started with learning how to compress data in a clean way using Synaspe Pipelines and ADF, and natively using Spark. Then, we focused on learning about implementing partitioning, sharding, and distributions in SQL dedicated pools and Spark. After that, we learned about the different types of tables and indexing available in SQL dedicated pools, and finally, we concluded with learning how to set up data redundancy and archiving.

All the preceding topics should cover the syllabus of *DP203 – Implement Physical Data Storage Structures*. We will focus on implementing logical data storage structures in the next chapter.

6
Implementing Logical Data Structures

I hope you enjoyed learning about the implementation details of storage structures. In this chapter, we will be covering the implementation details of logical data structures. You will learn to implement advanced data loading concepts like slowly changing dimensions, storage based solutions for optimizing query performance and techniques to read external data without having to copy them over to local storage.

We will cover the following topics in this chapter:

- Building a temporal data solution
- Building a slowly changing dimension
- Building a logical folder structure
- Implementing file and folder structures for efficient querying and data pruning
- Building external tables

Technical requirements

For this chapter, you will need the following:

- An Azure account (free or paid)
- The Azure CLI installed on your workstation
- An active Synapse workspace

Let's get started!

Building a temporal data solution

Temporal data refers to data at specific points in time. Building a temporal solution deals with building systems that can handle and store such time based data. We have already seen how to use the **Azure SQL Temporal tables** feature to build such a system in *Chapter 4, Designing the Serving Layer* under the section: *Designing a solution for temporal data*. Since we have already explored this topic in detail there, we will not be repeating it again. Please refer to Chapter 4 to refresh your memory about Temporal tables.

Let us next learn how to implement a slowly changing dimension.

Building a slowly changing dimension

In *Chapter 4, Designing the Serving Layer*, we learned about the different ways to build **Slowly Changing Dimensions** (**SCDs**). In this section, we will learn to implement a few of them using **ADF/Synapse Pipelines Mapping** flows. We will implement the Type 2 SCD as it involves a slightly more complicated workflow. Once you know how to implement one of the SCDs, implementing the others will be similar.

Let's consider the following example scenario:

- We have a `DimDriver` dimension table in a Synapse SQL dedicated pool that contains the driver's data. This data doesn't change very often, so it is a good choice for an SCD.
- Let us assume that the changes to the driver data appears periodically as a CSV file in a folder in **Azure Data Lake Gen2**.
- We have to build an ADF pipeline to take the data from the CSV file and apply it to the `DimDriver` table while maintaining its history.
- We will build the **Flag-based SCD** option in this example.

Creating a pipeline in ADF is like building the steps of a flow chart. We will have to take the data through various steps to reach the final desired result. The following SCD example is going to be slightly lengthier. I have tried to explain each and every step so that it will be easy for you to understand. But, if you find it difficult to follow, I'd recommend you to first look at *Chapter 8, Ingesting and Transforming Data* section: *Transforming data by using ADF* to get a good understanding of the ADF activities. That section has a lot of smaller ADF examples which can help you understand the following ADF example better.

Let's look at the steps that are required for the SCD2 example. On a high level, we are going to perform the following steps:

1. If the incoming data is for new drivers, we just add them directly to the Synapse SQL `DimDriver` table with `isActive` column set to 1.

2. If the incoming data is an update to an existing row in the `DimDriver` table, then we need to take care of two conditions:

    a. The first condition updates the latest rows from the CSV file as the active row for the corresponding `DriverIds` by setting the `isActive` column to 1.

    b. The second condition updates all the previous rows for those `DriverIds` as inactive, by setting the `isActive` column to 0.

The preceding logic can be executed using three separate flows within a Data flow, one for the new rows and two for the modified rows. Let us look at the new rows case first.

Updating new rows

Here are the steps to build the flow to update the new rows:

1. The first step is to create a new Data flow, which can be used to chain the transformation steps, also called as **Activities** together. Click on the + sign and choose **Data flow** option from the ADF or Synapse Studio, as shown:

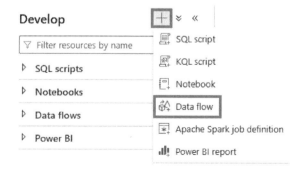

Figure 6.1 – Creating a new Data flow in Synapse Pipelines

2. The next step is to create a source dataset for our CSV file. Click on the **Add Source** link in the Data flow canvas region, as shown in the following image.

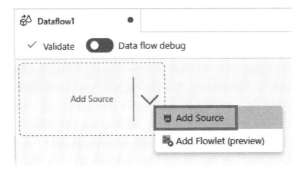

Figure 6.2 – Creating a new data source

3. When you click on the **Add Source** a new Source dataset screen pops up. In that screen, you can create a new dataset using the **+ New** link, to point to the input driver CSV folder, as shown next:

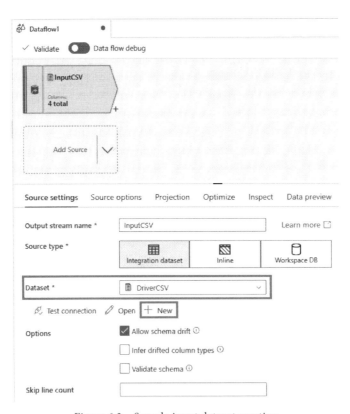

Figure 6.3 – Sample input dataset creation

4. We have to create a similar Source dataset to find the `MaxSurrogateID` from the Synapse SQL `DimDriver` table. While creating a new Dataset pointing to Synapse SQL, we have to specify the query to be run to fetch the max `surrogateId`. We will use this value later to distinguish the newly added rows from the existing rows in the `DimDriver` table. Here is a screen shot of how to specify the query.

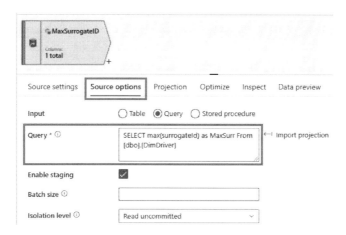

Figure 6.4 – Finding the max value of the surrogate keys

5. Now, let us add the newly calculated `maxSurrogate` value to the incoming CSV driver dataset as a new column using the **Join** activity, as shown in the following screenshot:

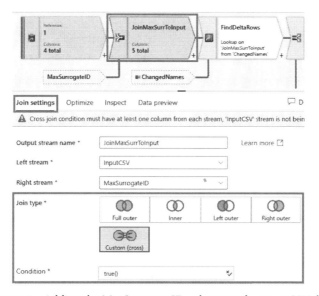

Figure 6.5 – Adding the MaxSurrogateID column to the input CSV data

6. Now that we have the `MaxSurrogateID` along with our CSV Driver data, we need to find the list of all the modified rows vs newly added rows. We can use a **Lookup** activity with `LEFT OUTER JOIN` between the Driver CSV and the Synapse SQL `DimDriver` table to achieve this. Here is a screen shot of how to achieve this:

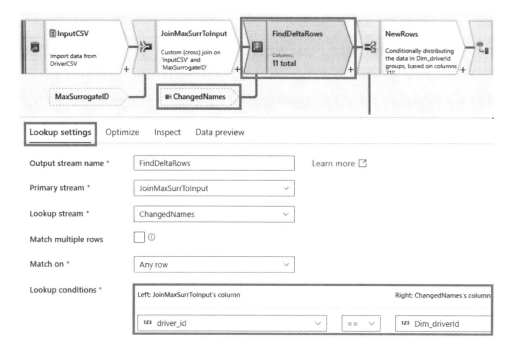

Figure 6.6 – Using LEFT OUTER JOIN to get the updated rows

7. In the preceding Lookup setting, I'd have used a slightly modified `DimDriver` table called **ChangedNames** for joining. This table is obtained by renaming the column names of the Synapse SQL `DimDriver` table. This is required as both the left and right tables for the join will otherwise have the exact same column names. Here is how we can rename the column names using a **Select** activity.

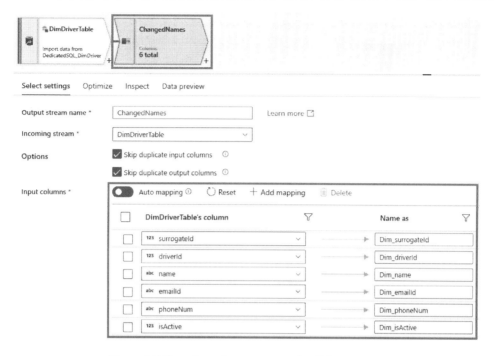

Figure 6.7 Changing column names using Select activity

8. Now that we have identified the rows to be updates, let us split the data flow into two branches using **Conditional split**: one that takes care of the newly added values and another that updates the modified rows:

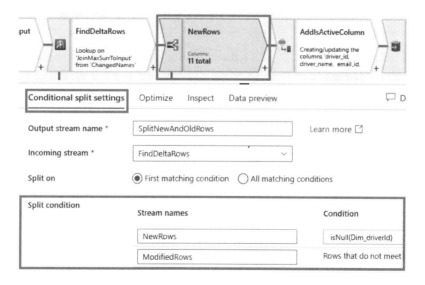

Figure 6.8 – Splitting the flow into two branches – new and modified rows

9. In the NewRows branch, just add a column (`isNewActive=1`), using the Derived Column activity. We will change this name to `isActive` just before updating it to the Synapse SQL tables at the last Sink activity.

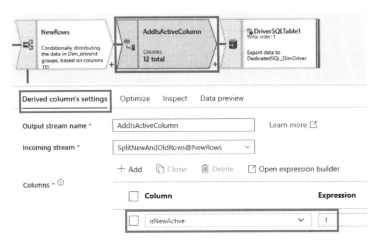

Figure 6.9 – Adding isActive column to the input rows

10. Now send all these new rows with the `isNewActive` column renamed as `isActive`, to the destination using a Sink activity. We are using a temporary `isNewActive` flag to avoid column name collisions. You will have to disable **Auto mapping** and ensure that the field mapping is done correctly at the SQL Sink, as shown in the following image:

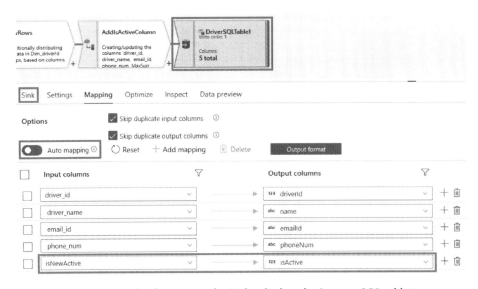

Figure 6.10 – An example of writing to the Sink, which is the Synapse SQL table in our case

With this we have completed the flow for the newly added rows. Now let us look at the steps for the modified rows branch, the one where we conditionally split the branch based on NewRows vs ModifiedRows (*Figure 6.8*).

Updating the modified rows

Here are the steps to update the modified rows.

1. For the modified rows branch, there are two sub tasks. The newly updated rows can be directly added with isActive=1 and the old rows for the corresponding DriverIds need to be updated with isActive=0. So, we need to split the **ModifiedRows** data set into two branches using the **New branch** option. Click on the little + sign after the activity box to get the **New branch option**, as shown:

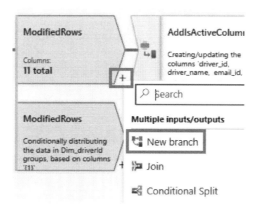

Figure 6.11 creating a new branch

2. In one of these branches, just add the isActive column with value of 1 and write it to the Synapse DimDriver table Sink, similar to what we did earlier for the new rows (refer *Figure 6.9*) . This should take care of the first sub-task of modified rows.

3. Now, we have to make `isActive=0` for the previous rows with the same `driverID`. For this, we can add a **Derived column** activity to add an isActive column to all the rows, followed by a Filter activity to filter only the old rows before writing to the sink. That way the latest row for that `DriverId`, which was updated in the previous step doesn't get changed. Here also, I use a temporary column called `isOldRowActive` to avoid column name conflict. This will be changed to isActive just before writing it to the SQL `DimDriver` sink.

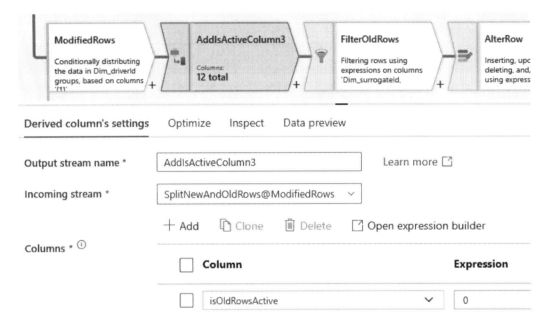

Figure 6.12 Adding an extra column using Derived Column

4. Now filter the old rows out, by using the `Dim_surrogateId <= MaxSurr` condition, as shown:

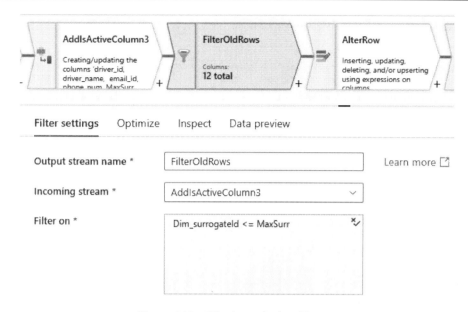

Figure 6.13 – Filtering only the old rows

5. Use an `Alter  row` step to update only the rows whose surrogate IDs are smaller than the max surrogate value into the Synapse SQL using a Sink activity:

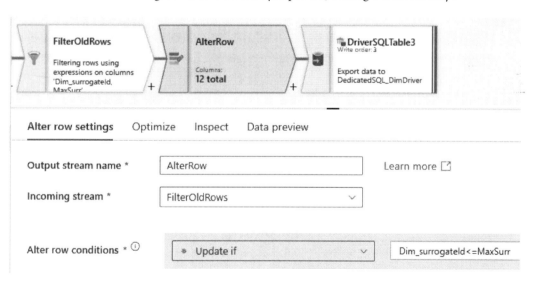

Figure 6.14 – Altering the number of rows while using the MaxSurr value as a reference

6.   Here is how the Sink configuration will look:

Figure 6.15 Synapse SQL Sink configuration

7.   Finally, set up a pipeline and trigger it to run the data flow periodically. Your ADF pipeline should look similar to the following:

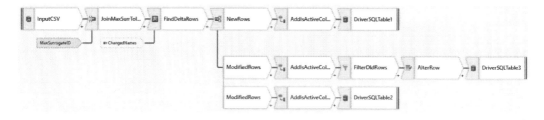

Figure 6.16 – Sample ADF pipeline for SCD 2

That is how we build SCDs using Synapse Pipelines (or ADF). You might find it difficult to follow all the steps the first time. So try reading this section again after you complete *Chapter 8, Ingesting and Transforming Data*, which has more ADF/Synapse Pipelines examples.

Now, let's learn how to implement logical folder structures.

Building a logical folder structure

We learned about efficient folder structures in *Chapter 2, Designing a Data Storage Structure*, where we explored the best practices for storing data for batch processing and streaming scenarios. The rule of thumb is to store the data in a hierarchical date folder structure, with the date part added toward the end, as shown here:

```
{Region}/{SubjectMatter(s)}/{yyyy}/{mm}/{dd}/{hh}/
```

We can have more intermediate folders in the folder path based on our business requirements. Please refer to *Chapter 2, Designing a Data Storage Structure*, to refresh your memory on designing efficient folder structures.

To create a container on Azure Data Lake Gen 2, you can use the following command via the Azure CLI:

```
az storage fs create -n <container name> --account-name
<account name> --auth-mode login
```

Once you have created a container, you can easily create folders in it by using the following command:

```
az storage fs directory create -n <folder path> -f <container
name> --account-name <account name> --auth-mode login
```

You can also use UI tools like the Azure Storage portal or Azure Storage Explorer to create the folder structure.

Since we have already covered this topic in detail in the previous chapters, let's move on and look at what data structures we can use for effective querying and pruning.

Implementing file and folder structures for efficient querying and data pruning

The concepts we explored in the previous section applies here too. Once we have a date-based hierarchical folder structure, query performance can be improved via data partitioning. If we divide the data into partitions and if we ensure that the partitions are stored in different folder structures, then the queries can skip scanning the irrelevant partitions altogether. This concept, as we already know, is called **data pruning**.

Another benefit of partitioning is the increased efficiency of data loading and deletion by performing **partition switching** and **partition deletion**. Here, instead of reading each row and updating it, huge partitions of data can be added or deleted with simple metadata operations. *Chapter 2, Designing a Data Storage Structure*, already covered examples of how queries can benefit from data pruning by skipping reading from unnecessary partitions. In this section, we'll learn how to improve data load and unload performance via partition switching.

> **Note**
> Partitions have to be aligned perfectly on the boundaries for partition switching.

Let's consider the same example Fact table that we have been using so far:

```
CREATE TABLE dbo.TripTable
(
    [tripId] INT NOT NULL,
    [driverId] INT NOT NULL,
    [customerId] INT NOT NULL,
    [tripDate] INT,
    [startLocation] VARCHAR (40),
    [endLocation] VARCHAR (40)
)
WITH
(
    CLUSTERED COLUMNSTORE INDEX,
    DISTRIBUTION = HASH ([tripId]),
    PARTITION ([tripDate] RANGE RIGHT FOR VALUES
        ( 20220101, 20220201, 20220301 )
    )
)
```

Let's assume that we need to store only 3 months' worth of data. Our Fact table, dbo.TripTable, contains the data for 20220101, 20220201, and 20220301. Now, let's learn how to delete the first month's data and add the latest month's data, 20220401, to the table.

Deleting an old partition

To delete a partition, we need to create a dummy table that has the same structure as the original table and then swap out the partition for the dummy table. This section will show you how to switch out the 20220101 partition.

Create a dummy table that contains the partition that needs to be switched out, as follows:

```
CREATE TABLE dbo.TripTable_20220101
WITH
(
    CLUSTERED COLUMNSTORE INDEX,
    DISTRIBUTION = HASH ([tripId]),
    PARTITION ([tripDate] RANGE RIGHT FOR VALUES (20220101) )
)
AS
SELECT * FROM dbo.TripTable WHERE 1=2 ;
```

Note that to switch out temporary tables, we can just have the one partition that we are planning to switch out. 20220101 is the second partition since the first partition will correspond to all the values before 20220101, which, in our case, would be empty. Run the ALTER TABLE command, as shown in the following code block, to swap the partition out:

```
ALTER TABLE dbo.TripTable SWITCH PARTITION 2 TO dbo.
TripTable_20220101 PARTITION 2 WITH (TRUNCATE_TARGET = ON);
```

Now, dbo.TripTable will contain 0 rows for partition 2, which corresponds to 20220101.

Next, let's add a new partition, 20220401, to the table.

Adding a new partition

To add our new partition, we need to split the last partition into two partitions. We can use the following SPLIT command to do this:

```
ALTER TABLE dbo.TripTable SPLIT RANGE (20220401);
```

This will split the last partition into `20220301` and `20220401`.

> **Note**
>
> The split will not work if the partition contains data. So, we will have to temporarily swap out the last partition to a dummy table, as we did earlier in the *Deleting an old partition* section. Once the last partition is empty, split that partition using the `split` command and then add the temporarily swapped-out partition back to the original table.

Once we have created the new partition for `20220401`, we must create a dummy table with the same partition alignment to load the `20220401` data. The following code snippet does this:

```
CREATE TABLE dbo.TripTable_new
WITH
(
    CLUSTERED COLUMNSTORE INDEX,
    DISTRIBUTION = HASH ([tripId]),
    PARTITION ([tripDate] RANGE RIGHT FOR VALUES
        (20220101, 20220201, 20220301, 20220401)
)
)
AS
SELECT * FROM dbo.TripTable WHERE 1 = 2;
```

For the sake of this example, let's add some values to the new partition:

```
INSERT INTO dbo.TripTable_new
VALUES (333, 444, 555, 20220401, "New York", "New Jersey");
```

Once we have loaded the partition data into the dummy table, we can switch the partition into our Fact table using the `ALTER` command, as shown in the following code block. This command will switch the last partition for April (`20220401`) into the original `TripTable`:

```
ALTER TABLE dbo.TripTable_new SWITCH PARTITION 5 TO dbo.
TripTable PARTITION 5 WITH (TRUNCATE_TARGET = ON);
```

These ALTER TABLE commands will return almost immediately as they are metadata operations and don't involve copying rows from one partition to another. And that is how we can increase the efficiency of the data load and delete operations. You can refer to the complete example in the GitHub repository of this book.

Let us next look at accessing data using external tables.

Building external tables

External tables are similar to regular tables except that the data is stored in external storage locations such as Azure Data Lake, Azure Blob storage, and HDFS. With external tables, you don't need to copy data into internal tables for processing. They can directly read the data from external sources, which saves on the data transfer cost. In Synapse, both dedicated SQL and serverless SQL support external tables. We have to define the following three constructs to access data via external tables:

- **EXTERNAL DATA SOURCE**

  Here is an example of how we can create an external data source named users_iacstoreacct:

  ```
  CREATE EXTERNAL DATA SOURCE [Dp203DataSource]
      WITH ( LOCATION  = 'abfss://path/to/data')
  ```

- **EXTERNAL FILE FORMAT**

  Here is an example of how to create an external file format named SynapseParquetFormat:

  ```
  CREATE EXTERNAL FILE FORMAT [Dp203ParquetFormat]
      WITH ( FORMAT_TYPE = PARQUET )
  ```

- **EXTERNAL TABLE**

  We can use the external data source and the external file format to create the external table:

  ```
  CREATE EXTERNAL TABLE TestExtTable (
      [tripId] INT,
      [driverId] INT,
      . . .
      [endLocation] VARCHAR (50)
  )
  ```

```
WITH (
        LOCATION = '/path/to/*.parquet',
        DATA_SOURCE = [Dp203DataSource],
        FILE_FORMAT = [Dp203ParquetFormat]
)
```

You can also easily create external tables from Synapse UI, as shown in the following screenshot:

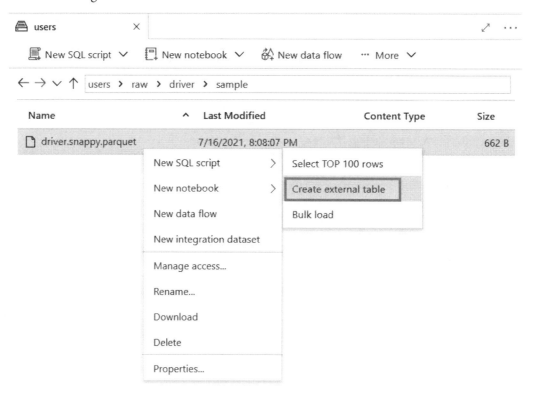

Figure 6.17 – An example of creating an external table from Synapse UI

On the screen that appears, you need to do the following:

1. Select **SQL Pool**.

2. Enter a name for the database to be created.

3. Enter a name for the external table to be created.

New external table

Select target database
Learn more ☐

Select SQL pool* ⓘ

✅ Built-in	⌄

Select a database* ⓘ

SQLExternalTable	⌄

External table name

[schema].[tableName]

Create external table

◯ Automatically   ⦿ Using SQL script

ⓘ This will generate a SQL script and you will be required to run the SQL script.

Open script	Back		Cancel

Figure 6.18 – Specifying the details for external table

Once you click on **Open script**, Synapse will autogenerate the SQL script for creating external tables.

Summary

That brings us to the end of this chapter. This was a smaller chapter but it had some very important concepts from the certification's perspective. We started by looking at building SCDs, which was a lengthy but relatively easy process as we mostly had to just drag and drop the components into Synapse pipelines and configure them. Then, we revisited the general rule of thumb for building an efficient folder structure. We also learned how to quickly switch partitions in and out using Synapse SQL. Finally, we learned how easy it is to create external tables in Synapse.

All the topics that were covered in this chapter should cover the syllabus for *DP203 – Implementing the logical data structures*. In the next chapter, we will focus on implementing the serving layer.

7
Implementing the Serving Layer

I hope you enjoyed learning about the implementation details of the logical data structures in the previous chapter. In this chapter, we will learn about implementing the serving layer, which involves implementing star schemas, techniques to read and write different data formats, sharing data between services such as SQL and Spark, and more. Once you complete this chapter, you should be able to understand the differences between a Synapse dedicated SQL pool versus traditional SQL systems for implementing the Star schema, the various ways of accessing Parquet data using technologies such as Spark and SQL, and the details involved in storing metadata across services. All this knowledge should help you build a practical and maintainable serving layer in a data lake and, of course, clear the certification too.

We will cover the following topics in this chapter:

- Delivering data in a relational star schema
- Implementing a dimensional hierarchy
- Delivering data in Parquet files
- Maintaining metadata

Technical requirements

For this chapter, you will need the following:

- An Azure account (free or paid)

- An active Synapse workspace

Let's get started.

Delivering data in a relational star schema

We had learned about star schema in *Chapter 4, Designing the Serving Layer*. We will take the same example here and show how to implement a star schema in Synapse SQL and deliver data from it.

Star schemas have two types of tables, **fact tables** and **dimensional tables**. Fact tables are usually much higher in volume than the dimension tables and hence would benefit from using a **hash distribution** with **clustered columnstore indexing**. On the other hand, dimension tables are smaller and can benefit from using **replicated tables**.

> **Important Note**
> Synapse dedicated SQL pools didn't support **foreign key** constraints at the time of writing this book. Hence, the responsibility of maintaining data integrity falls on the applications.

Let's consider the same **Imaginary Airport Cabs (IAC)** cab rides example for our star schema from *Chapter 4, Designing the Serving Layer*. We had the following tables in that design:

- **FactTrips**

- **DimDriver**

- **DimCustomer**

- **DimCab**

- **DimDate**

Let's see how to implement these tables.

1. In the Synapse screen, create a new SQL pool from the **Manage** tab, as shown in the following screenshot. Click on the **+New** symbol and fill in the details to create a new dedicated SQL pool.

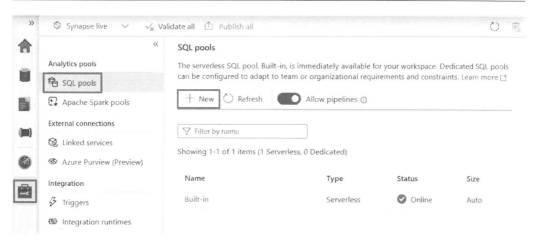

Figure 7.1 – Creating a new dedicated SQL Pool

2. Next, create a new SQL script from the **Editor** tab by clicking on the + sign, as shown in the next screenshot:

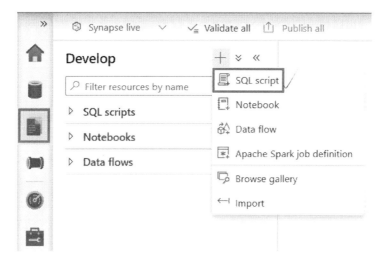

Figure 7.2 – Creating a new SQL script

3. In the SQL editor, you can enter SQL commands to create tables representing the star schema. Here is an example of how to create a sample fact table, FactTrips:

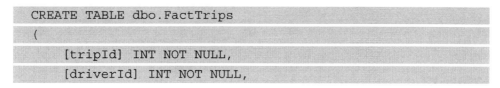

```
CREATE TABLE dbo.FactTrips
(
    [tripId] INT NOT NULL,
    [driverId] INT NOT NULL,
```

```
    [customerId] INT NOT NULL,
    [tripdate] INT,
    [startLocation] VARCHAR(40),
    [endLocation] VARCHAR(40)
)
WITH
(
    CLUSTERED COLUMNSTORE INDEX,
    DISTRIBUTION = HASH ([tripId])
)
```

Here is an example of a sample customer dimension table:

```
CREATE TABLE dbo.DimCustomer
(
    [customerId] INT NOT NULL,
    [name] VARCHAR(40) NOT NULL,
    [emailId] VARCHAR(40),
    . . .
    [city] VARCHAR(40)
)
WITH
(
    CLUSTERED COLUMNSTORE INDEX,
    DISTRIBUTION = REPLICATE
)
```

Here is an example of a date dimension table:

```
CREATE TABLE dbo.DimDate
(
    [dateId] INT NOT NULL,
    [date] DATETIME NOT NULL,
    [dayOfWeek] VARCHAR(40),
    [fiscalQuarter] VARCHAR(40)
)
WITH
(
```

```
        CLUSTERED COLUMNSTORE INDEX,
        DISTRIBUTION = REPLICATE
)
```

4. Now, let's look at how to load data into these tables. You can use the COPY INTO statement to populate the tables. The fact and dimension tables will have the same syntax for loading information:

```
COPY INTO dbo.DimCustomer
FROM 'https://path/to/customer.csv'
WITH (
    FILE_TYPE='CSV',
    FIELDTERMINATOR=',',
    FIELDQUOTE='',
    ROWTERMINATOR='\n',
    ENCODING = 'UTF8',
    FIRSTROW = 2 // To skip the header line
)
```

5. And, finally, query from the star schema tables. Here is a sample query to get the list of all customers whose end location was 'San Jose':

```
SELECT trip.[tripId], customer.[name] FROM
dbo.FactTrips AS trip
JOIN dbo.DimCustomer AS customer
ON trip.[customerId] = customer.[customerId]
WHERE trip.[endLocation] = 'San Jose';
```

As you can see, once we understand the concept of star schemas, creating them is as simple as creating tables in Synapse SQL.

You can learn more about Synapse SQL and schemas here: https://docs. microsoft.com/en-us/azure/synapse-analytics/sql-data-warehouse/ sql-data-warehouse-tables-overview.

Let's next look at implementing a dimensional hierarchy.

Implementing a dimensional hierarchy

As we have already explored dimensional hierarchy in *Chapter 4*, *Designing the Serving Layer* under the *Designing a dimensional hierarchy* section we will not be repeating it here. Please have a look at *Chapter 4* to refresh your understanding of dimensional hierarchy.

Let's next look at the techniques available for reading and writing data in Parquet files.

Delivering data in Parquet files

In this section, we will learn to deliver data that is present in Parquet files via both Synapse SQL and Spark. We will use the concept of external tables that we learned in the previous chapter to accomplish this.

Let's consider an example where we have the `trips` data stored as Parquet files. We will use Synapse SQL serverless pools and Spark to access the data and run some sample queries on it.

Synapse SQL serverless

Let's create an external table from within the Synapse SQL query editor that points to the Parquet files on the Azure storage. The following screenshot shows an example:

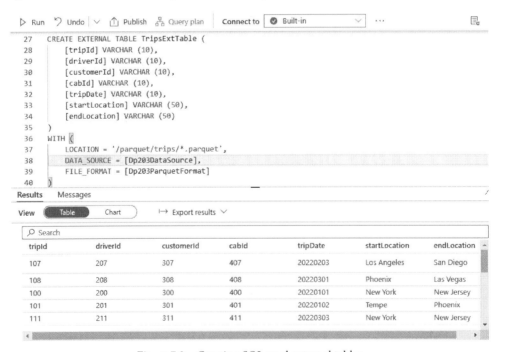

Figure 7.3 – Creating SQL pool external tables

Now, let's run a sample query, like how a BI tool would access this data. Let's try to find the number of trips per location from the data loaded in the previous step and view it as a chart:

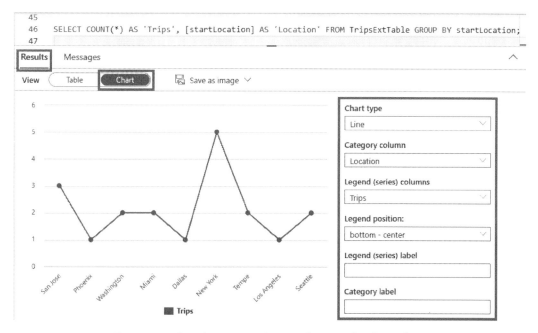

Figure 7.4 – Sample query on Parquet data visualized as a chart

You have to select the **Chart** option in the **Results** screen to view the charts. Synapse SQL provides several options to configure the charts, as shown on the right-hand side of the previous image.

As you can see, reading and serving data from Parquet files is as simple as defining an external table and querying it.

You can learn more about using external tables in Synapse SQL here: `https://docs.microsoft.com/en-us/azure/synapse-analytics/sql/develop-tables-external-tables`.

Now, let's try the same exercise using Spark.

Synapse Spark

In a Synapse Spark Notebook, you can read Parquet files using the `spark.read.load('path/to/parquet/files', format='Parquet')` command. The following screenshot shows an example:

Figure 7.5 – Using Spark to query Parquet files

Spark also provides charting options as shown in the previous image.

Let's next explore how we can accomplish the same using Azure Databricks.

Azure Databricks

Azure Databricks' Spark examples are similar to the Synapse Spark examples. In the case of Azure Databricks, you will need to define a **service principal** for Azure Databricks to talk to Azure Data Lake Storage Gen2.

You can find detailed information on setting up the service principal here: `https://docs.microsoft.com/en-us/azure/databricks/scenarios/databricks-extract-load-sql-data-warehouse`.

Once you have the session configured, you can use the exact same Spark syntax that we saw in the Synapse Spark use case here too. The following is an example to view the contents of all the Parquet files in the `parquet/trips` folder:

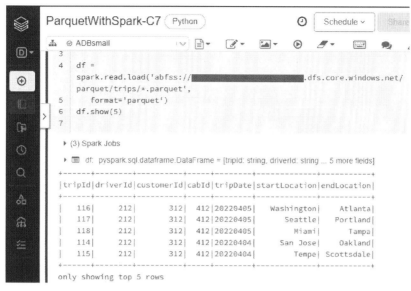

Figure 7.6 – Azure Databricks notebook with the Azure Data Lake Storage Gen2 access example

Here is an example of the same transformation query that we ran earlier in Synapse Spark, in Databricks:

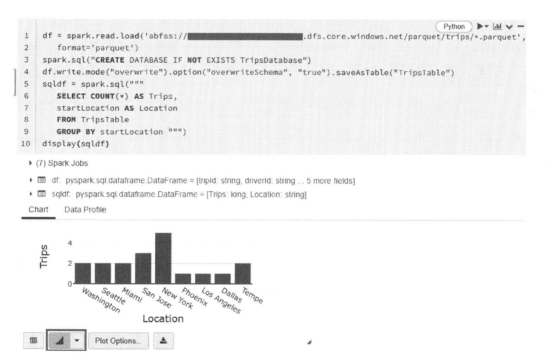

Figure 7.7 – Simple Spark query on Parquet data

Azure Databricks also provides a rich set of charting options that can be used to visualize the data. You can access the charting options by clicking on the **Chart** icon below the results.

You can learn more about using Spark and Parquet here: `https://spark.apache.org/docs/latest/sql-data-sources-parquet.html`.

I hope you now have an idea of how to serve Parquet data using both SQL and Spark services in Azure. Let's next look at the metadata options available in Azure.

Maintaining metadata

As we have seen in *Chapter 4*, *Designing a Partition Strategy*, metastores are like data catalogs that contain information about all the tables you have, the table schemas, the relationships among them, where they are stored, and so on. In that chapter, we learned at a high level about how to access the metadata in Synapse and Databricks. Now, let's learn the details of implementing them.

Metadata using Synapse SQL and Spark pools

Synapse supports a shared metadata model. The databases and tables that use Parquet or CSV storage formats are automatically shared between the compute pools, such as SQL and Spark.

> **Important Note**
> Data created from Spark can only be read and queried by SQL pools but cannot be modified at the time of writing this book.

Let's look at an example of creating a database and a table using Spark and accessing it via SQL:

1. In the Synapse Spark notebook, create a sample table, as shown in the following screenshot:

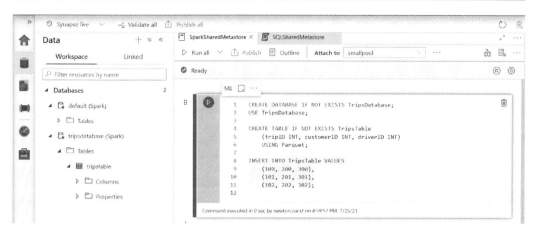

Figure 7.8 – Creating a sample table in Spark

2. Now, let's query the contents of the table from the SQL serverless pool.

> **Important Note**
> This database will be synced asynchronously, so there might be a slight delay before you see the databases and tables in the SQL pool.

3. SQL serverless pool is an on-demand service, so all you need to do is just click on the + sign in the Synapse workspace page and select **SQL script** to create a new SQL editor, as shown in the following screenshot:

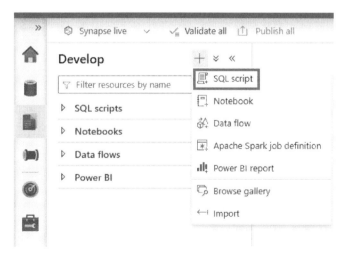

Figure 7.9 – Creating a new SQL script

4. Then, in the **Connect to** field, select the **Built-in** pool, as shown in the following screenshot:

Figure 7.10 – Connecting to serverless SQL pool

5. Now, just run a simple script to query the shared table; in the example, the shared table would be the `tripID` table:

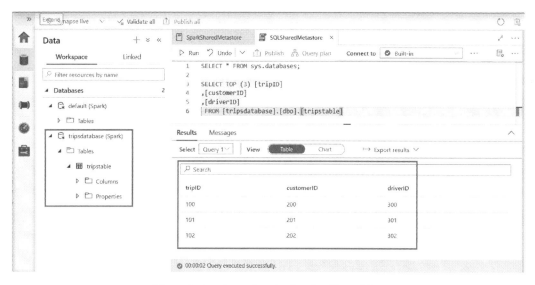

Figure 7.11 – Accessing the Spark table in SQL

As you just noticed, the shared data model of Synapse makes it very easy to share data between SQL and Spark pools. Everything is already taken care of by Synapse and the data is readily made available to us.

You can learn more about maintaining metadata in Synapse here: `https://docs.microsoft.com/en-us/azure/synapse-analytics/metadata/overview`.

Let's next explore how to work with metastores in Azure Databricks.

Metadata using Azure Databricks

In order to share data between Spark and other services outside of Synapse, we have to make use of the Hive metastore. Spark uses the Hive metastore to share information with other services. Let's look at an example of sharing data between Azure Databricks Spark and Azure HDInsight Hive. The logic and steps for using an external Hive metastore would be similar for Synapse Spark too. Here are the steps:

1. We will need a standalone database that can be used by Spark to store the metadata. Let's use Azure SQL for this purpose. Create an Azure SQL database from the Azure portal. Search for **Azure SQL** from the portal search box and select it. Click on the **+ Create** option. You will see a screen, as shown in the following screenshot:

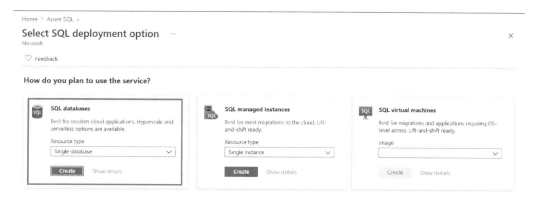

Figure 7.12 – Azure SQL plans

2. Select the **SQL databases** box and click the **Single database** option from the dropdown.

3. You can create the database with pre-populated sample data so that we have ready-made data for experimentation. Select the **Sample** option for the **Use existing data** field, as shown in the following screenshot:

Figure 7.13 – Populating the database with sample data

4. Fill up the rest of the tabs and click on **Review + create** to create the Azure SQL database.

5. Retrieve the JDBC connection string from the **Connection Strings** tab, as shown in the following screenshot, and save it in Notepad. We will need this information later:

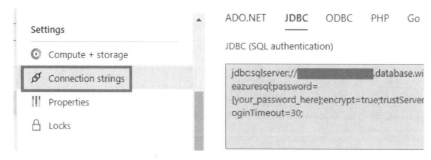

Figure 7.14 – Getting the connection strings for Azure SQL

6. Next, we have to create an **HDInsight** Hive cluster. By now, you might already know the process to instantiate any Azure service. Just search for **HDInsight** in the portal search bar and click on it. On the HDInsight portal home page, click on the **+ Create** link to open the create form and fill in the details.

7. On the **Create HDInsight cluster** screen, you can choose either the **Hadoop** option or the **Interactive Query** option for **cluster type**, as both will install Hive. Refer to the next screenshot for the options available:

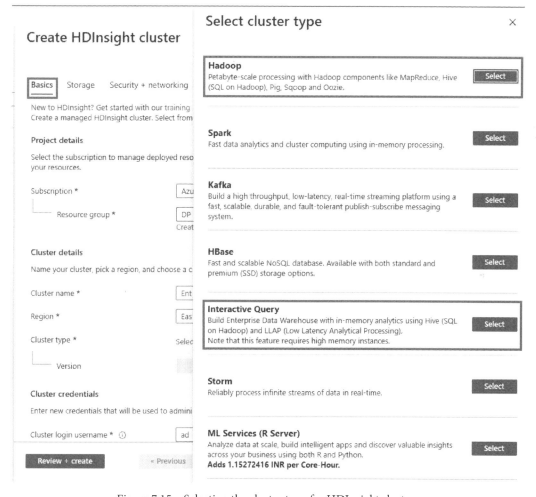

Figure 7.15 – Selecting the cluster type for HDInsight clusters

8. Once you have selected the type of cluster, fill up the rest of the fields on the **Basics** screen.

9. In the **Storage** tab, under the **External metadata stores** section, provide the Azure SQL database that we created in the earlier steps as **SQL database for Hive**. The following screenshot shows the location:

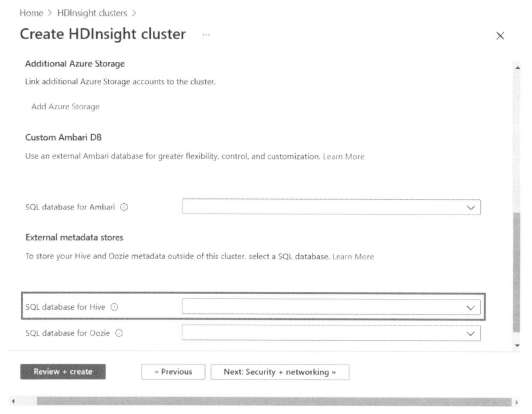

Figure 7.16 – Creating a Hive cluster in HDInsight with Azure SQL as the metastore

10. Complete the rest of the fields and then click on **Review + Create** to create the HDInsight cluster.

11. Once the cluster is created, go to the Ambari home page from the HDInsight portal by clicking on the **Ambari home** link, as shown in the following screenshot:

Figure 7.17 – Link to Ambari home from the HDInsight portal home page

12. From the Ambari dashboard, click on **Hive view 2.0**, as shown in the following screenshot:

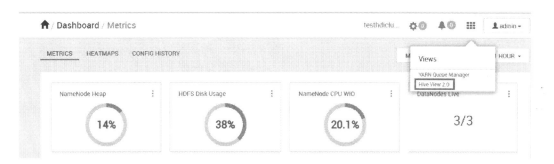

Figure 7.18 – Hive view 2.0 from the Ambari dashboard

13. Now, you should be able to see the `Hivesampletable` database in the Hive dashboard, as shown in the following screenshot:

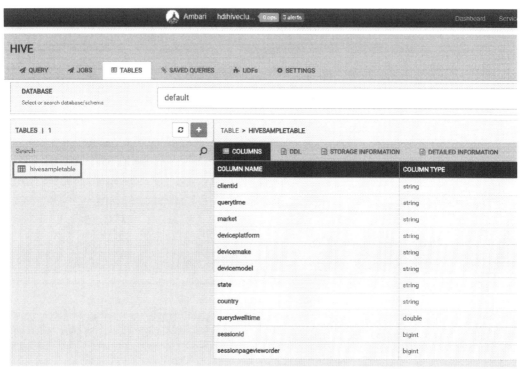

Figure 7.19 – Hive query view of the sample table

14. Now that we have the HDInsight cluster, we have to next create an Azure Databricks cluster. We have to create a new cluster with the following configurations. Let's see how to enter these configurations in the Spark create screen in the next step:

```
spark.sql.hive.metastore.version 2.1.1 // For HDInsight
Interactive 2.1 version
```

```
spark.hadoop.javax.jdo.option.ConnectionUserName <Your
Azure SQL Database Username>
```

```
spark.hadoop.javax.jdo.option.ConnectionURL <Your Azure
SQL Database JDBC connection string>
```

```
spark.hadoop.javax.jdo.option.ConnectionPassword <Your
Azure SQL Database Password>
```

```
spark.hadoop.javax.jdo.option.ConnectionDriverName com.
microsoft.sqlserver.jdbc.SQLServerDriver
```

```
spark.sql.hive.metastore.jars <Location where you have
copied the Hive Metastore Jars>
datanucleus.autoCreateSchema true
datanucleus.fixedDatastore false
```

Note that you will have to use the JDBC link that you had saved earlier, for the config that says `spark.hadoop.javax.jdo.option.ConnectionURL`.

15. You will have to enter the configs in the **Spark Config** field on the **Create Cluster** page, as shown in the following screenshot:

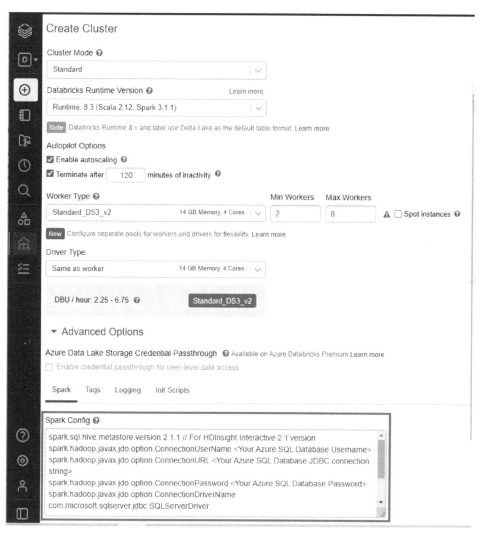

Figure 7.20 – Adding custom configuration while creating the Azure Databricks cluster

> **Important Note**
>
> Apart from the config fields, you will also have to download the Hive metastore JAR files and provide them a location where the Azure Databricks clusters can access them. Azure provides step-by-step instructions along with readymade scripts to easily download the JAR files here: `https://docs.microsoft.com/en-us/azure/databricks/_static/notebooks/setup-metastore-jars.html`.

16. Once you have created the Spark cluster, you will be able to access the Hive Metastore tables directly from a Spark notebook. In the following screenshot, you can see how the Databricks Spark cluster is able to access the `HiveSampletable` table that we saw earlier using the Hive query view:

Figure 7.21 – Spark's able to access data from the Hive external metastore

Hurray! Now you know how to access metadata between Spark and Hive clusters using an external Hive metastore.

You can learn more about Azure Databricks metastores here: `https://docs.microsoft.com/en-us/azure/databricks/data/metastores/external-hive-metastore`. With that, we have come to the end of this section and the chapter. You should now be familiar with the different ways in which metadata can be shared across the SQL, Spark, and Hive services in Azure.

Summary

This was another small but interesting chapter. We started with implementing the star schema, then learned about delivering data in Parquet format, and, finally, looked at how we can share data between the SQL-Spark and Spark-Hive services in Azure. With all this knowledge, you should now be able to design and implement a basic serving layer for a data lake architecture using Azure services. To learn more, please follow the links that I have provided at the end of important topics.

With this, we have reached the end of the first major section of the *DP-203 syllabus, Designing and Implementing Data Storage*. This covers about 40–45% of the certification examination. We are getting closer to the halfway mark. Good going!

In the next section, we will learn about designing and developing data processing systems and, more specifically, about ingesting and transforming data in data lakes.

Part 3: Design and Develop Data Processing (25-30%)

The third part of this book focuses on the next level of the stack, which is the data processing layer.

This section comprises the following chapters:

- *Chapter 8, Ingesting and Transforming Data*
- *Chapter 9, Designing and Developing a Batch Processing Solution*
- *Chapter 10, Designing and Developing a Stream Processing Solution*
- *Chapter 11, Managing Batches and Pipelines*

8
Ingesting and Transforming Data

Welcome to the next major section of the book. In this section, we will focus on designing and developing data processing systems.

In the last chapter, we learned about implementing the serving layer and saw how to share data between services such as **Synapse SQL** and Spark using metastores. In this chapter, we will focus on data transformation—the process of transforming your data from its raw format to a more useful format that can be used by downstream tools and projects. Once you complete this chapter, you will be able to read data using different file formats and encodings, perform data cleansing, and run transformations using services such as Spark, SQL, and **Azure Data Factory** (**ADF**).

We will cover the following topics in this chapter:

- Transforming data by using Apache Spark
- Transforming data by using **Transact-SQL** (**T-SQL**)
- Transforming data by using ADF
- Transforming data by using Azure Synapse pipelines
- Transforming data by using Stream Analytics

- Cleansing data

- Splitting data

- Shredding **JavaScript Object Notation** (**JSON**)

- Encoding and decoding data

- Configuring error handling for the transformation

- Normalizing and denormalizing values

- Transforming data by using Scala

- Performing **exploratory data analysis** (**EDA**)

Technical requirements

For this chapter, you will need the following:

- An Azure account (free or paid)

- An active Synapse workspace

- An active ADF workspace

Let's get started.

Transforming data by using Apache Spark

Apache Spark supports transformations with three different **Application Programming Interfaces** (**APIs**): **Resilient Distributed Datasets** (**RDDs**), **DataFrames**, and **Datasets**. We will learn about RDDs and DataFrame transformations in this chapter. Datasets are just extensions of DataFrames, with additional features like being type-safe (where the compiler will strictly check for data types) and providing an **object-oriented** (**OO**) interface.

The information in this section applies to all flavors of Spark available on Azure: Synapse Spark, Azure Databricks Spark, and HDInsight Spark.

What are RDDs?

RDDs are an immutable fault-tolerant collection of data objects that can be operated on in parallel by Spark. These are the most fundamental data structures that Spark operates on. RDDs support a wide variety of data formats such as JSON, **comma-separated values** (**CSV**), Parquet, and so on.

Creating RDDs

There are many ways to create an RDD. Here is an easy way using the `parallelize()` function:

```
val cities = Seq("New York", "Austin")
val rdd=spark.sparkContext.parallelize(cities)
```

Once we have created an RDD, we can run different kinds of transformations on them. Let's explore the most common ones.

RDD transformations

Here are some of the most commonly used RDD transformations in Spark:

- `map()` —Applies the function provided as a parameter to all the elements of the source and returns a new RDD. Here is an example to do a word count:

```
val maprdd=rdd.map(word => (word,1))
maprdd.collect.foreach(println)
```

- `flatMap()` —Similar to `map()`, but can apply the function provided to more than one element, as illustrated here:

```
val fmrdd = rdd.flatMap(word => word.split(" "))
fmrdd.collect.foreach(println)
```

- `filter()` —Returns a new RDD that satisfies the filter condition, as illustrated here:

```
val emptystrfilterrdd = rdd.filter(_.nonEmpty)
emptystrfilterrdd.collect.foreach(println)
```

- `groupByKey()` —Collects identical data into groups and can perform aggregate actions on top of it, as illustrated here:

```
val groupbyrdd = rdd.groupBy(word => word.charAt(0))
groupbyrdd.collect.foreach(println)
```

- union()—Returns a new RDD that is a union of the two datasets, as illustrated here:

```
val rdd1 = spark.sparkContext.parallelize(List(1, 2, 3))
val rdd2 = spark.sparkContext.parallelize(List(4, 5, 6))
val unionrdd = rdd1.union(rdd2)
unionrdd.collect().foreach(println)
```

- distinct()—Returns a new dataset that contains only the unique elements from the input dataset, as illustrated here:

```
val distrinctrdd = rdd.distinct()
distrinctrdd.collect.foreach(println)
```

Spark supports a huge list of transformations. If you would like to view the complete list, please refer to the Apache Spark documentation here: https://spark.apache.org/docs/latest/rdd-programming-guide.html.

Let's next look at DataFrames.

What are DataFrames?

DataFrames are similar to tables in relational databases. They are like RDDs in that they are also immutable, redundant, and distributed, but they represent a higher form of data abstraction. DataFrames contain schemas, columns, and rows, just as in relational tables, and are useful in processing large volumes of data while using relational table-like operations.

Creating DataFrames

Let's look at the options available to create DataFrames. They're set out here:

- Converting an RDD to a DataFrame, as follows:

```
val df = rdd.toDF()
```

- Creating a DataFrame from a CSV file, as follows:

```
csvDf = spark.read.csv("/path/to/file.csv")
```

- Creating a DataFrame from a JSON file, as follows:

```
jsonDf = spark.read.json("/path/to/file.json")
```

- Creating a DataFrame with a schema, as follows:

```
data = [("Adam","Smith","Male","CA"),
        ("Brenda","Jones","Female","FL")]
schema = ["firstname","lastname","gender","state"]
df = spark.createDataFrame(data = data, schema = schema)
```

Next, let's look at DataFrame transformations.

DataFrame transformations

For data analytics, DataFrame transformations are more relevant than RDD transformations as they deal with table-like abstractions, which makes it easier for data analysts.

> **Note**
>
> A DataFrame transformation is eventually converted into an RDD transformation within Spark:

Let's look at some important DataFrame transformations. Let's assume that df, df1, and df2 are valid DataFrames.

- `select()`—To select data from a subset of columns, as follows:

```
df.select("firstname","lastname").show()
```

- `filter()`—To filter rows based on condition, as follows:

```
df.filter('location === "Florida").show()
```

- `distinct()`—To select unique rows from the input, as follows:

```
df.distinct().show()
```

- `orderBy()`—To sort rows by a particular column, as follows:

```
df.orderBy("location").show()
```

- `join()`—To join two tables based on the provided conditions, as follows:

```
df1.join(df2, df1("id") === df2("id"),"inner")
```

- groupBy() and avg()—Can be used in combination to aggregate values that are grouped together on some column values, such as location in the following case:

```
df.groupBy("location").avg("salary").show()
```

The preceding examples should give you a good sense of the types of transformations available in Spark. You can learn more about DataFrames here: https://spark. apache.org/docs/latest/sql-programming-guide.html.

Now, let's see the transformations available in T-SQL.

Transforming data by using T-SQL

T-SQL is a procedural language that is used by both dedicated and serverless SQL pools in Synapse. Similar to the transformations that we have seen in Spark, T-SQL also provides a rich set of transformations. Let's look at some of the important ones here:

- SELECT—To select data from a subset of columns, as follows:

```
[firstName], [lastName] from dbo.Driver WHERE [city] =
'New York';
```

- ORDER BY—To sort rows by a particular column, as follows:

```
SELECT [firstName], [lastName] from dbo.Driver ORDER BY
[firstName];
```

- DISTINCT—To select unique rows from the input, as follows:

```
SELECT DISTINCT [firstName], [lastName] from dbo.Driver;
```

- GROUP BY—To group rows by columns so that aggregate operations can be performed on them, as follows:

```
SELECT [gender], AVG([salary]) AS 'AVG salary' from dbo.
Driver GROUP BY [gender];
```

- UNION—To combine rows from two tables containing the same schema, as follows:

```
SELECT [firstName], [lastName] FROM
dbo.Driver
WHERE [city] = 'New York'
UNION
```

```
select [firstName], [lastName] FROM
dbo.TempDriver
WHERE [city] = 'New York';
```

- JOIN—To join two tables based on the provided conditions, as follows:

```
SELECT driver.[firstName], driver.[lastName], feedback.
[rating], Feedback.[comment] FROM
dbo.Driver AS driver
INNER JOIN dbo.Feedback AS feedback
ON driver.[driverId] = feedback.[driverId]
WHERE driver.[city] = 'New York';
```

- VIEW—Apart from the standard transformations, T-SQL also provides a VIEW transformation, which can help in reporting and ad hoc querying. We'll now look at a simple example of how to create and use a VIEW transformation, as follows:

```
CREATE VIEW CompleteDriverView
AS
SELECT driver.[firstName], driver.[lastName], feedback.
[rating], feedback.[comment] FROM
dbo.Driver AS driver
INNER JOIN dbo.Feedback AS feedback
ON driver.[driverId] = feedback.[driverId]
WHERE driver.[city] = 'New York';
```

Here is how you can use a VIEW transformation:

```
SELECT DISTINCT * from CompleteDriverView;
```

That covers some of the important transformations in T-SQL. For a more comprehensive list, please refer to the T-SQL documentation available here: https://docs.microsoft.com/en-us/sql/t-sql/language-reference.

Let's next learn about the transformation options available in ADF.

Transforming data by using ADF

We have already seen a few examples of ADF in the previous chapters. Just to refresh, search for `Azure Data Factory` from the Azure portal and create a new Azure data factory. Once created, you can launch the Azure data factory, as shown in the following screenshot:

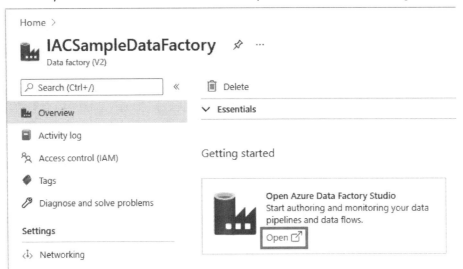

Figure 8.1 – Launching the Azure data factory

This will open up the ADF workspace where you can build your pipelines, as shown in the following screenshot:

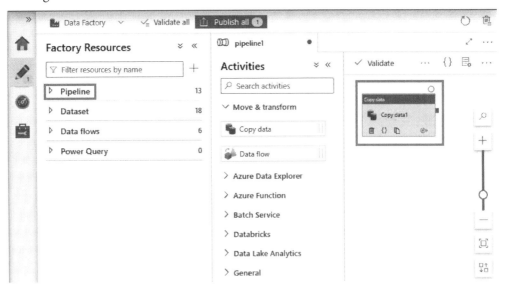

Figure 8.2 – ADF Studio

All ADF transformations happen on datasets. So, before we can do any transformation, we will have to create datasets of the source data. You can click on the + symbol to create a new dataset, as shown in the following screenshot:

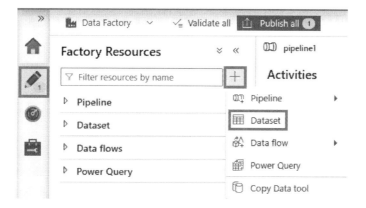

Figure 8.3 – Creating a new dataset in ADF

ADF provides a wide range of Azure and non-Azure data sources, as shown in the following screenshot.

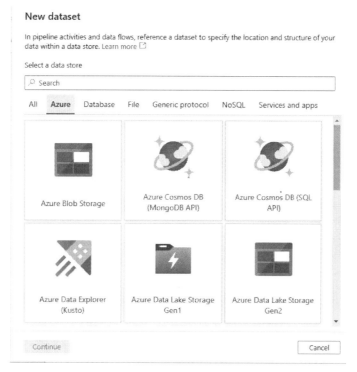

Figure 8.4 – Dataset source options in ADF

You can select the appropriate data source, click on **Continue**, and add the location of the source data files or folders that need to be transformed. This will create source datasets.

ADF provides convenient code-free transformation options called mapping data flows. Mapping data flows provide three types of transformations, as outlined here:

- **Schema transformations**—Such as adding new columns.

- **Row transformations**—Such as updating rows, creating views, and so on.

- **Multi-input/output (I/O) transformations**—Such as splitting rows, merging rows, and so on.

Let's look in detail at some of the important options available under these three transformation types.

Schema transformations

Schema transformations refer to the actions that result in changing the schema of the table or DataFrames. Let's look at some commonly used schema transformations, as follows:

- **Aggregate**—To perform Min, Max, Sum, Count, and so on the incoming data. Here is a screenshot of how to find the average of the Salary column:

Figure 8.5 – Aggregate transformation in ADF

> **Note**
>
> Aggregate transforms will only output the columns used in the aggregation. So, perform a self-join with the source data after this stage if you want the other columns to be present for further stages.

- **Derived column**—Use this transformation to add any new columns to existing data. In the following screenshot, we are adding a simple `isActive` column to the `Driver` table extracted from a CSV file:

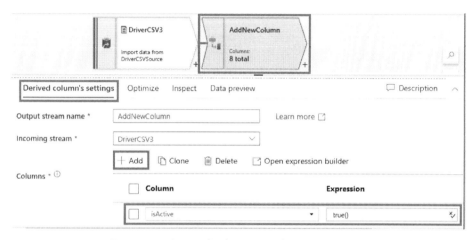

Figure 8.6 – Derived column transformation in ADF

- **Select**—You can use this transformation to select only the required columns from the input or to change the name of the columns before storing them in a data store, as demonstrated in the following screenshot. You can click on the trash can icon to delete the columns that are not needed:

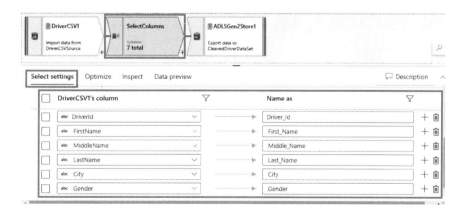

Figure 8.7 – Select transformation in ADF

Next, let's look at some row transformations.

Row transformations

These are transformations that apply to the rows of the table, and are outlined here:

- **Alter row**—Used to insert, delete, update, and upsert (insert or update) rows into a database or data warehouse. In the following screenshot, we insert the rows into a database only if the DriverId value is not NULL:

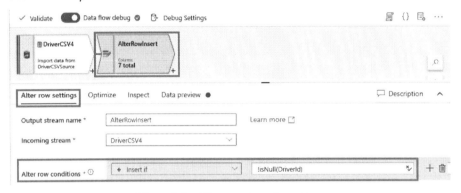

Figure 8.8 – Alter row transformation

> **Note**
>
> Alter row works only on databases, Cosmos DB, or **REpresentational State Transfer** (**REST**) endpoint sinks.

- **Filter**—To filter rows based on conditions. In the following screenshot, we are filtering the rows where the City value is New York:

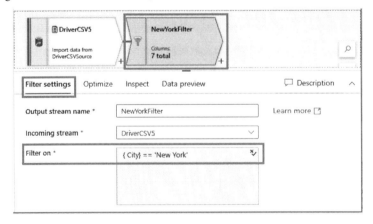

Figure 8.9 – Filter transformation in ADF

- **Sort**—To sort rows based on any column or group of columns, as illustrated in the following screenshot:

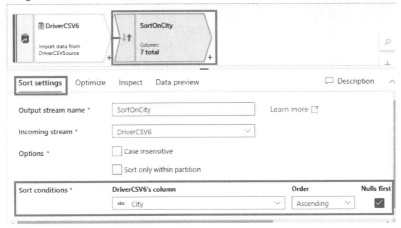

Figure 8.10 – Sort transformation

Next, let's look at multi-I/O transformations.

Multi-I/O transformations

These are transformations that operate on more than one input or, conversely, split the input into more than one output. They are outlined here:

- **Conditional split**—This can be used to split the input into two output streams based on conditions. In the following screenshot, we split the input based on `Rating`:

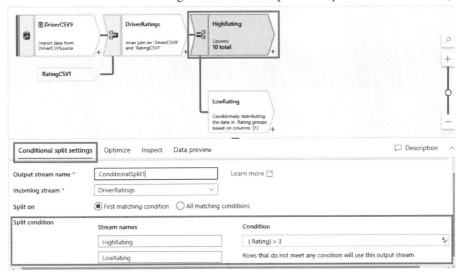

Figure 8.11 – Conditional split transformation in ADF

- **Join**—This is used to join two streams based on one or more join conditions. The following screenshot shows how to merge the `DriverCSV` and `RatingsCSV` datasets by using the `DriverId` value:

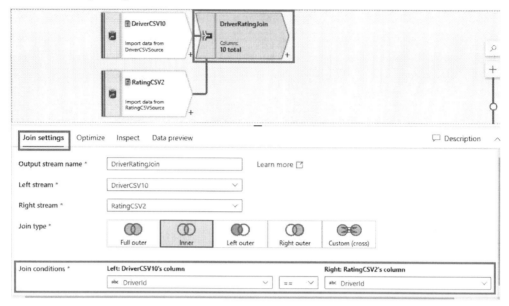

Figure 8.12 – Join transformation in ADF

- **Union**—This merges two input datasets with the same schema into one, as illustrated in the following screenshot:

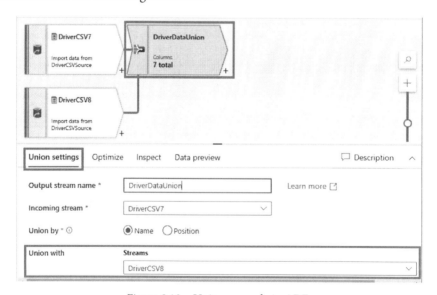

Figure 8.13 – Union example in ADF

For a complete list of transformations, you can refer to the Azure ADF documentation available here: `https://docs.microsoft.com/en-us/azure/data-factory/data-flow-transformation-overview`.

ADF provides convenient templates that can accomplish a lot of the standard pipeline activities. Let's look at these next.

ADF templates

ADF provides standard templates that you can use for various data copy and transformation activities. You can explore the templates under the **Pipeline templates** link on the ADF Studio home page, as shown in the following screenshot:

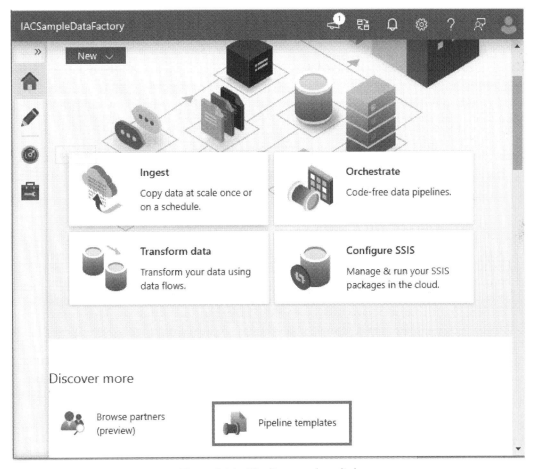

Figure 8.14 – Pipeline templates link

Here is a sample of the template gallery:

↑ Import pipeline template

Bulk Copy from Database to Azure Data Explorer

Use this template to copy large amount of data in bulk from database like SQL Server, Google BigQuery, etc to Azure Data Explorer (ADX), using...

by Microsoft

Bulk Copy from Database

Use this template to copy data in bulk from database using external control table to store partition list of source tables.

...

by Microsoft

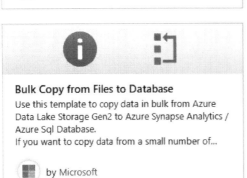

Bulk Copy from Files to Database

Use this template to copy data in bulk from Azure Data Lake Storage Gen2 to Azure Synapse Analytics / Azure Sql Database.

If you want to copy data from a small number of...

by Microsoft

Copy and convert data from Office 365 into Common Data Model for Open Data...

Use this template to copy data from your Office 365 organization and convert it into Common Data Model format to be included in the Open Data...

by Microsoft

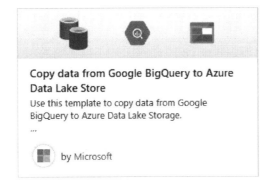

Copy data from Google BigQuery to Azure Data Lake Store

Use this template to copy data from Google BigQuery to Azure Data Lake Storage.

...

by Microsoft

Copy data from HDFS to Azure Data Lake Store

Use this template to copy data from HDFS (Hadoop Distributed File System) to Azure Data Lake Storage.

...

by Microsoft

Figure 8.15 – ADF template gallery sample

Please use the templates wherever possible instead of reinventing the procedures, as this will save you a lot of time and prevent common pitfalls.

Let's next look at transformations using Synapse pipelines.

Transforming data by using Azure Synapse pipelines

Azure Synapse pipelines is just ADF implemented inside Azure Synapse Analytics, so the transformation examples that we saw in the ADF section apply here too. The only difference is the launching page. You can launch Synapse pipelines from the **Synapse Analytics** tab, as shown in the following screenshot:

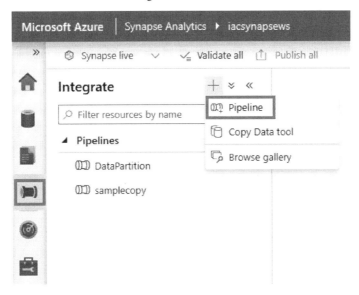

Figure 8.16 – Launching Synapse pipelines

Hope you got a grasp of the transformations available in ADF and Synapse pipelines. Let's next look at the transformation options available in Stream Analytics.

Transforming data by using Stream Analytics

Stream Analytics setup, concepts, and other details will be covered in *Chapter 10, Designing and Developing a Stream Processing Solution*. Since we need streaming background before we can talk about the transformations, we will cover Stream Analytics transformations as part of *Chapter 10, Designing and Developing a Stream Processing Solution*.

Let us next look at the concept of Cleansing data.

Cleansing data

Cleansing data is an important activity in any data pipeline. As data flows in from various sources, there are chances that the data won't adhere to the schemas and there might be missing values, non-standard entries, duplicates, and so on. During the cleansing phase, we try to correct such anomalies. Let's look at a few common data cleansing techniques.

Handling missing/null values

We can handle missing or `Null` values in multiple ways. We can choose to filter out such rows, substitute missing values with default values, or substitute them with some meaningful values such as mean, median, average, and so on. Let's look at an example of how we can replace missing values with some default string such as `'NA'`.

Substituting with default values

Substituting with default values can be achieved using the **Derived columns** transformation, as shown in the following screenshot:

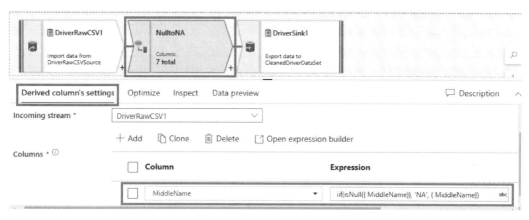

Figure 8.17 – Substituting with default values

Let's next look at filtering out null values.

Filtering out null values

You can filter out null values using the **Alter row** transformation, as we have already seen in *Figure 8.8*.

Let's next look at how to trim input values.

Trimming inputs

Values with trailing whitespace are a common problem. You can easily trim such values using the `trim()` method from within a **Derived column** transformation. Here is an example of this:

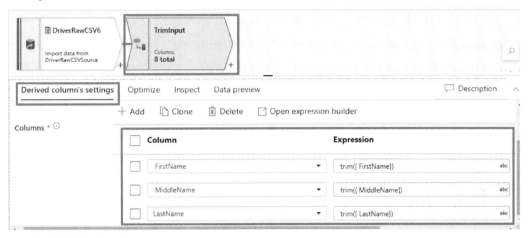

Figure 8.18 – Trimming whitespace

Let's next look at standardizing input values.

Standardizing values

Different input sources might use different conventions for the data. For example, say one of the input sources uses the $ symbol to represent the dollar value and another input stream uses USD, we might want to standardize the inputs before sending them downstream for further processing. In the following screenshot, we can see how to replace the $ symbol in the `Salary` column with USD. You just have to use the `replace({` `Salary}, '$', 'USD')` script in the **Expression** field:

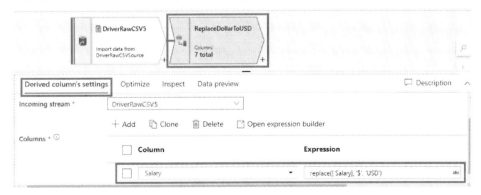

Figure 8.19 – Replacing values using the Derived column

Let's next see how to handle outlier values.

Handling outliers

If the values of some of the fields look abnormal, you could replace them with averages or median values. Let's see an example of how to do this, as follows:

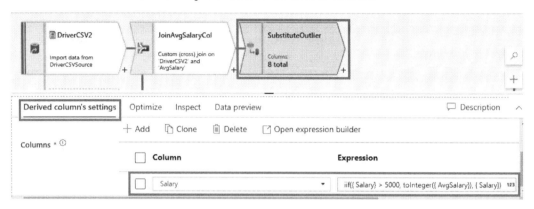

Figure 8.20 – Using the Derived column to substitute values

In the preceding screenshot, in the **Expression** field, we are substituting any value > 5000 with the average salary.

> **Note**
>
> You can use the **Aggregate** transformation to find the average, median, min, max, and other mathematical grouping functions.

Let's next look at how to remove duplicates.

Removing duplicates/deduping

You can remove duplicate rows using the **Aggregate** transformation. Here is an example of this:

Figure 8.21 – Deduping using Aggregate transformation

Aggregates by default emit only the column that is operated upon. In this case, since I've grouped it on `DriverId`, so it would just emit the `DriverId` column. In order to overcome this, under the **Column** field, for the **Each column that matches** option, I've specified `name != DriverId` so that all the other columns also show up in the output.

> **Note**
>
> You can accomplish any of this cleansing and data preparation work using the Spark or SQL transformations that we discussed earlier in the chapter. Those would work perfectly fine too.

We have now covered the details of the most commonly used cleansing operations. With the variety of transformations available in ADF, Spark, and SQL, you can get creative on how to accomplish your tasks in an efficient manner. Let's next look at how to split data in data pipelines.

Splitting data

ADF provides multiple ways to split data in a pipeline. The important ones are **Conditional Split** and cloning (**New branch**). While **Conditional Split** is used to split data based on certain conditions, the **New branch** option is used to just copy the entire dataset for a new execution flow. We have already seen an example of **Conditional Split** in *Figure 8.11*. Let's see how we can create a new branch in the data pipeline.

In order to create a new branch, just click on the + icon next to any data source artifact (such as the `DriverCSV11` block shown in the following screenshot). From there, you can choose the **New branch** option:

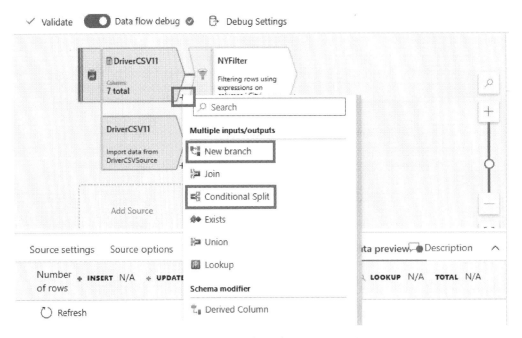

Figure 8.22 – New branch option in ADF

Apart from these two options, ADF also provides the ability to split the input files into multiple sub-files using partitions. Let's see how to accomplish that next.

File splits

In order to use file splits, create a new **Sink** artifact, and in the **Optimize** tab, just specify the number of partitions required. The following screenshot shows how this can be done:

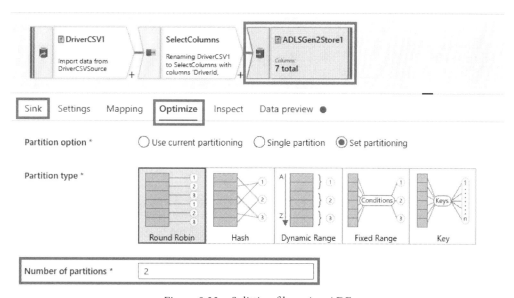

Figure 8.23 – Splitting files using ADF

Now that we know how to split the data for processing, let's look next at how to extract data from JSON files.

Shredding JSON

Shredding refers to the process of extracting data from JSON files into tables. Spark, Synapse SQL pools, and ADF provide native support to extract data from JSON. Let's look at examples for each of the services.

Extracting values from JSON using Spark

Spark can directly read JSON files and extract the schema from them. Here is a simple code snippet that can accomplish the JSON read:

```
val dfJSON = spark.read.json("abfss://path/to/json/*.json")
dfJSON.printSchema()
dfJSON.show(false)
```

Here is how the output looks:

```
root
 |-- firstname: string (nullable = true)
 |-- gender: string (nullable = true)
 |-- id: string (nullable = true)
 |-- lastname: string (nullable = true)
 |-- location: string (nullable = true)
 |-- middlename: string (nullable = true)
 |-- salary: long (nullable = true)
```

```
+---------+------+---+--------+----------+----------+------+
|firstname|gender|id |lastname|location  |middlename|salary|
+---------+------+---+--------+----------+----------+------+
|Catherine|Female|102|        |California|Goodwin   |4300  |
|Jenny    |Female|104|Simons  |Arizona   |Anne      |3400  |
|Bryan    |Male  |101|Williams|New York  |M         |4000  |
|Alice    |Female|100|Hood    |New York  |          |4100  |
|Daryl    |Male  |103|Jones   |Florida   |          |5500  |
|Daryl    |Male  |103|Jones   |Florida   |          |5500  |
+---------+------+---+--------+----------+----------+------+
```

Figure 8.24 – Output of JSON operation

You can also manually specify the schema, as shown in the following example:

```
val driverSchema = new StructType()
.add("firstname", StringType)
.add("middlename", StringType)
. . .
.add("salary",IntegerType)
val dfJSON = spark.read.schema(driverSchema).json("abfss://
path/to/json/*.json")
```

Once you have the data in the DataFrame, you can use any of the transformations available in Spark on it to extract and modify data.

Next, let's look at how to extract values from JSON using SQL.

Extracting values from JSON using SQL

T-SQL provides the OPENROWSET function to query remote data stores. We can use this function to bulk load data into dedicated or serverless SQL instances. Here is an example of how we can load and parse JSON files from remote storage using serverless SQL:

```
SELECT
    JSON_VALUE(doc, '$.firstname') AS firstname,
    JSON_VALUE(doc, '$.lastname') AS lastname,
    CAST(JSON_VALUE(doc, '$.id') AS INT) as driverid,
    CAST(JSON_VALUE(doc, '$.salary') AS INT) as salary
FROM openrowset(
        BULK 'abfss://path/to/json/*.json',
        FORMAT = 'csv',
        FIELDTERMINATOR ='0x0b',
        FIELDQUOTE = '0x0b'
    ) WITH (doc nvarchar(max)) AS ROWS
GO
```

The results for the preceding query would look something like this:

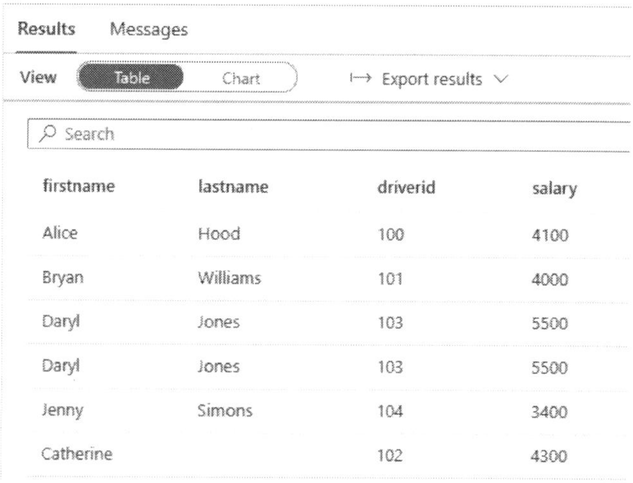

firstname	lastname	driverid	salary
Alice	Hood	100	4100
Bryan	Williams	101	4000
Daryl	Jones	103	5500
Daryl	Jones	103	5500
Jenny	Simons	104	3400
Catherine		102	4300

Figure 8.25 – Sample output of parsing JSON using OPENROWSET

> **Note**
>
> You need to specify the FORMAT value as CSV for JSON, as highlighted in the previous code snippet.

Extracting values from JSON using ADF

ADF provides **Flatten transformation** to convert hierarchical data structures such as JSON into flat structures such as tables. There is another similar denormalization transformation called **Pivot**, which you will learn about later in this chapter.

Let's assume that you have a source dataset with the following JSON:

```
{
  "firstname": "Alice",
  "middlename": "",
  "lastname": "Hood",
  "id": "100",
  "locations": [{"city": "San Francisco","state": "CA"},
    {"city": "San Jose","state": "CA"},
    {"city": "Miami", "state": "FL"}
  ],
  "gender": "Female"
}
```

Select **Flatten transformation** from ADF and specify the column mapping as shown in the following figure:

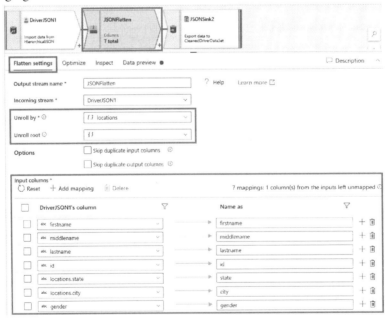

Figure 8.26 – Flatten transformation in ADF

For complex structures such as arrays within JSON, you can use **Unroll by** to split them into multiple rows. In our example, you can see that the Location field, which was an array, has been denormalized into separate lines in the **Input columns** section.

You can learn more about **Flatten transformation** here: `https://docs.microsoft.com/en-us/azure/data-factory/data-flow-flatten`.

Let's next look at how to encode and decode data.

Encoding and decoding data

In this section, we will see how to take care of encoding and decoding values such as **American Standard Code for Information Interchange (ASCII)**, **Unicode Transformation Format 8 (UTF-8)**, UTF-16, and so on while reading or writing data from different sources. We will see examples using Spark, SQL, and ADF here again.

Encoding and decoding using SQL

In Synapse SQL, **collation** defines the encoding type, sorting type, and so on in SQL strings. Collation can be set at both the database and table level. At the database level, you can set the collation, as shown here:

```
CREATE DATABASE TripsDB COLLATE Latin1_General_100_BIN2_UTF8;
```

At the table level, you can set it as shown here:

```
CREATE EXTERNAL TABLE FactTrips (
    [tripId] VARCHAR (40) COLLATE Latin1_General_100_BIN2_UTF8,
    . . .
)
```

Once you define the right collation, Synapse SQL takes care of storing the data in the right format and using the right set of encoding for further operations on that dataset.

Let's next look at how to accomplish coding/decoding in Spark.

Encoding and decoding using Spark

Spark supports methods called `encode` and `decode`, which can be used to accomplish conversion. The following Spark SQL example shows a simple `encode` and `decode` operation. We convert the data to **hexadecimal** (**hex**) format to display the results in a compact and readable format, but you can also directly use the `encode` and `decode` methods without the `hex()` function:

```
>SELECT hex(encode('Azure', 'UTF-16'));
FEFF0041007A007500720065
>SELECT decode(X'FEFF0041007A007500720065', 'UTF-16')
Azure
```

The `encode` and `decode` methods are also available in the Python and Scala versions of Spark.

Encoding and decoding using ADF

ADF provides the ability to specify the right encoding in the dataset artifacts. If you click on the **Connection** tab, you can see the **Encoding** field, as shown in the following screenshot:

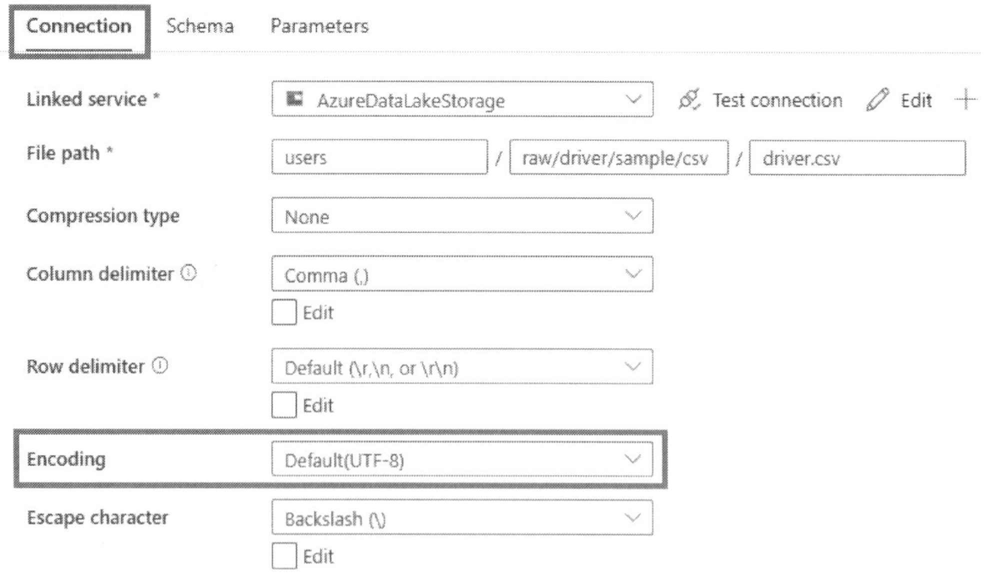

Figure 8.27 – Encoding function in ADF source datasets

Apart from the dataset encoding option, ADF also provides functions to encode and decode **Uniform Resource Identifiers (URIs)**, Base64, and so on using its conversion commands. I've shared a few conversion commands from the ADF documentation, as follows:

`base64ToBinary()`	Return the binary version for a Base64-encoded string.
`base64ToString()`	Return the string version for a Base64-encoded string.
`decodeBase64()`	Return the string version for a Base64-encoded string.
`dataUriToBinary()`	Return the binary version for a data URI.
`dataUriToString()`	Return the string version for a data URI.
`decodeDataUri()`	Return the binary version for a data URI.

Figure 8.28 – Table of encoding/decoding functions available in ADF

You can find a detailed list of conversion functions in ADF here: `https://docs.microsoft.com/en-us/azure/data-factory/control-flow-expression-language-functions#conversion-functions`.

Let's next look at how to configure error handling in ADF transformations.

Configuring error handling for the transformation

In all our examples of ADF pipelines till now, we have seen only success cases. ADF also provides a separate flow to handle errors and failures. In fact, ADF supports four different flows, as shown in the following screenshot:

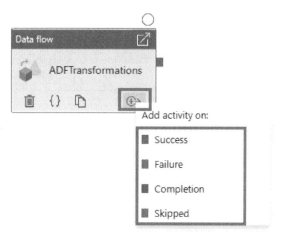

Figure 8.29 – ADF activity flows

In case of any errors in any step of the pipeline, we can build an error-handling branch that can be used to either fix the errors or store them for future actions. The following screenshot shows one such pipeline. You will have to connect the orange line to the error-handling activity:

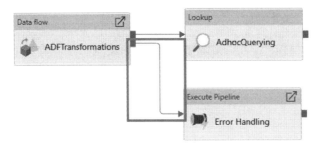

Figure 8.30 – Creating an error-handling pipeline

Select the **Execute Pipeline** activity and link the **Failure** flow (the orange line) from any of the other activities to it. This new **Execute Pipeline** activity could be a full-fledged pipeline in itself, as with the transformation pipelines that we saw earlier in the chapter, or it could be a simple standalone activity to just record the error logs. It can also be configured to insert the error details into a database so that we can analyze the errors later using the familiar SQL scripts.

ADF **Sink** also provides options to automatically write error lines to an external data store such as a blob store. This is another convenient option that helps analyze errors asynchronously. It can be configured using the **Error row handling settings** option under the **Settings** tab of the **Sink** activity, as shown in the following image.

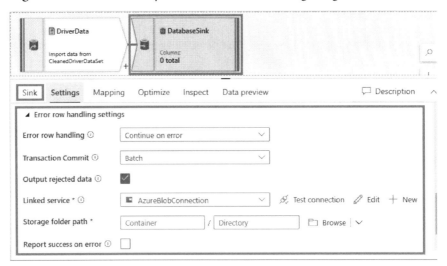

Figure 8.31 – Redirecting error lines to blob storage

Let's next look at the **Pivot** and **Unpivot** features, which are used to normalize and denormalize tables.

Normalizing and denormalizing values

We have already seen the ADF **Flatten** activity, which helps to denormalize data. There are two more such transformations to help normalize and denormalize datasets—**Pivot** and **Unpivot**. Let's look at them in detail.

Denormalizing values using Pivot

Let's assume that you have a table with a normalized column to store `City` values, but for reporting purposes, you want to have one column per city in your tables. In such a case, you can use the **Pivot** function to denormalize the table. The **Pivot** function takes the unique row values and converts them into table columns. Here is an example of how to pivot the tables:

1. Let's consider the following sample table:

DriverId 123	FirstName abc	MiddleName abc	LastName abc	City abc	Gender abc	Salary 123
200	Alice	NULL	Hood	New York	Female	4100
201	Bryan	M	Williams	New York	Male	4000
202	Catherine	Goodwin	NULL	California	Female	4300
203	Daryl	NULL	Jones	Florida	Male	5500
204	Jenny	Anne	Simons	Arizona	Female	3400
203	Daryl	NULL	Jones	Florida	Male	5500

Figure 8.32 – Sample table before pivoting

2. Select the **Pivot** activity from the ADF **Data Flow** tile, and in the **Group by** tab, specify Gender, as illustrated in the following screenshot:

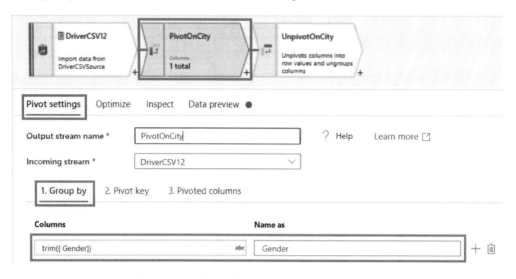

Figure 8.33 – Group by settings for pivot operation

3. In the **Pivot key** tab, specify City as the pivot key, as illustrated in the following screenshot:

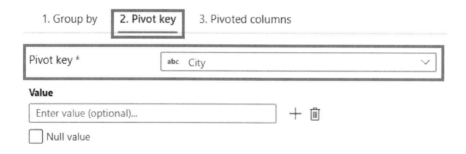

Figure 8.34 – Pivot key tab of the Pivot function

4. And finally, specify any aggregation that you need, along with the prefix to be used for the column names, as shown in the following screenshot:

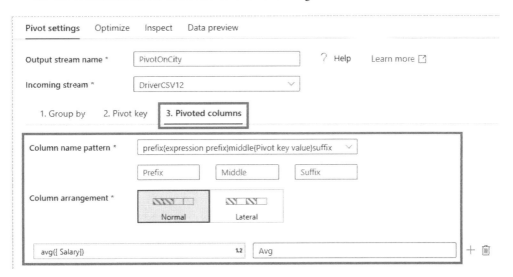

Figure 8.35 – Specifying the column name pattern and aggregation for the Pivot function

5. After the pivot operation, the table would look like this:

Figure 8.36 – Post-Pivot table

You can see that the rows of the table have been converted to columns here. Next, let's look at the **Unpivot** operation.

Normalizing values using Unpivot

Unpivot is the reverse of **Pivot**. This can be used to normalize the data—for example, if we have a column each for multiple cities, then we can unpivot them into a single column called City. Follow these next steps:

1. For this example, specify Gender under the **Ungroup by** column, as illustrated in the following screenshot:

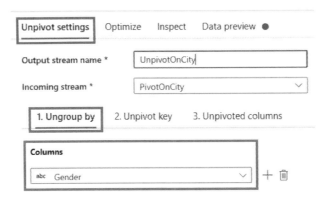

Figure 8.37 – Ungroup By tab for Unpivot operation

2. Add a new name and type for the unpivoted column under the **Unpivot key** tab, as illustrated in the following screenshot:

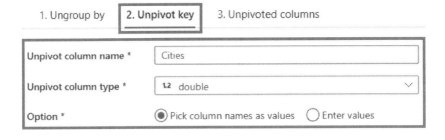

Figure 8.38 – Specifying Unpivot key for the Unpivot operation

3. In the **Unpivoted columns** tab, you can specify aggregate operations, as illustrated in the following screenshot:

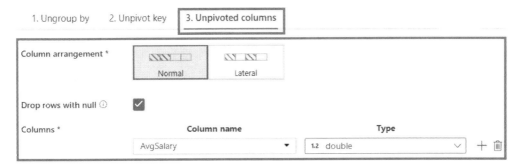

Figure 8.39 – Unpivoted columns tab of Unpivot operation

4. After the **Unpivot** operation, the output table will look like this:

Gender abc	Cities abc	AvgSalary 1.2
Female	AvgArizona	3400.0
Female	AvgCalifornia	4300.0
Female	AvgNew York	4100.0
Male	AvgFlorida	5500.0
Male	AvgNew York	4000.0

Figure 8.40 – Unpivoted table

Now that you have learned how to denormalize and normalize using the **Pivot** and **Unpivot** operations, let's next look at Scala transformations.

Transforming data by using Scala

All the Spark transformation examples that we saw in the initial sections of this chapter were in Scala, so you already know how to transform data using Scala. Since learning Scala is not in the scope of this book, we will not go deeper into the language aspects of Scala. If you are interested in learning Scala, then you can find some good resources here: https://www.scala-lang.org/.

Performing Exploratory Data Analysis (EDA)

Data exploration is much easier from inside Synapse Studio as it provides easy one-click options to look into various formats of data. Let's look at some of the options available for data exploration using Spark, SQL, and ADF/Synapse pipelines.

Data exploration using Spark

From within Synapse Studio, you can just right-click on the data file and select **Load to DataFrame**, as shown in the following screenshot:

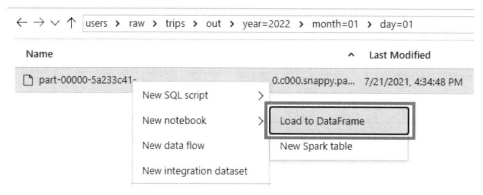

Figure 8.41 – Launching a DataFrame from the Synapse data file

Once you click on **Load to DataFrame**, Synapse creates a new notebook, as shown in the following screenshot. After that, all you have to do is just click on the **Run** icon (the little triangle symbol) to see the contents of the file, which are displayed in the following screenshot:

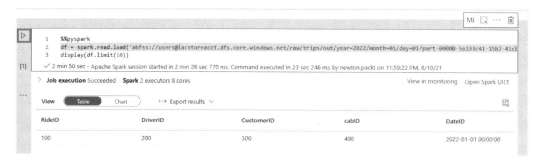

Figure 8.42 – Exploration using Spark Load to DataFrame

This is one easy way to explore the contents of a file. Let's next look at how to do the same via SQL.

Data exploration using SQL

Synapse SQL also provides similar options to explore data. You can select the file, click on **New SQL script**, and then choose **Select TOP 100 rows**, as shown in the following screenshot:

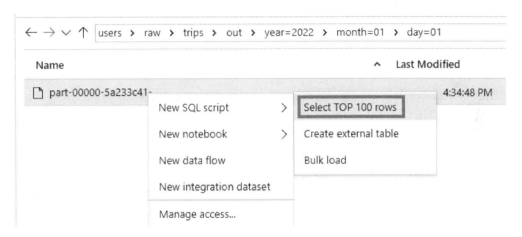

Figure 8.43 – Launching a SQL script to explore data from the Synapse data file

Once you click the **Select TOP 100 rows** option, Synapse opens a new SQL script, as shown in the following screenshot. Now, just click **Run** to get the top 100 rows:

Figure 8.44 – Sample of the SQL script that Synapse auto launches to help us explore data

Next, let's look at how to accomplish this in ADF.

Data exploration using ADF

ADF provides a **Data preview** tab that works when we have the **Data flow debug** setting turned on. Once we have the debug turned on, a small Azure Databricks cluster (called the ADF **Integration Runtime**) runs behind the scenes and fetches real data so that we can quickly explore and fine-tune our transformations and pipelines. An example is shown in the following screenshot:

Figure 8.45 – Data exploration using the ADF Data preview tab

As you can see, Synapse and ADF make it very easy to explore data without having to leave the studio.

Summary

With that, we have come to the end of this interesting chapter. There were lots of examples and screenshots to help you understand the concepts. It might be overwhelming at times, but the easiest way to follow is to open a live Spark, SQL, or ADF session and try to execute the examples in parallel.

We covered a lot of details in this chapter, such as performing transformations in Spark, SQL, and ADF; data cleansing techniques; reading and parsing JSON data; encoding and decoding; error handling during transformations; normalizing and denormalizing datasets; and, finally, a bunch of data exploration techniques. This is one of the important chapters in the syllabus. You should now be able to comfortably build data pipelines with transformations involving Spark, SQL, and ADF. Hope you had fun reading this chapter. We will explore designing and developing a batch processing solution in the next chapter.

9
Designing and Developing a Batch Processing Solution

Welcome to the next chapter in the data transformation series. If you have come this far, then you are really serious about the certification. Good job! You have already crossed the halfway mark, with only a few more chapters to go.

In the previous chapter, we learned about a lot of technologies, such as **Spark**, **Azure Data Factory** (**ADF**), and **Synapse SQL**. We will continue the streak here and learn about a few more batch processing related technologies. We will learn how to build end-to-end batch pipelines, how to use Spark Notebooks in data pipelines, how to use technologies like PolyBase to speed up data copy, and more. We will also learn techniques to handle late-arriving data, scaling clusters, debugging pipeline issues, and handling security and compliance of pipelines. After completing this chapter, you should be able to design and implement ADF-based end-to-end batch pipelines using technologies such as Synapse SQL, Azure Databricks Spark, PolyBase, and Azure Batch in the ADF pipelines.

This chapter is going to be slightly lengthier as we need to cover a lot of important concepts. I've taken the liberty of rearranging the syllabus topics for this chapter by grouping the related ones together. This will help in creating a better flow for the chapter. We will be covering the following topics:

- Designing a batch processing solution
- Developing batch processing solutions using Data Factory, Data Lake, Spark, Azure Synapse Pipelines, PolyBase, and Azure Databricks
- Creating data pipelines
- Integrating Jupyter/Python notebooks into a data pipeline
- Designing and implementing incremental data loads
- Designing and developing slowly changing dimensions
- Handling duplicate data
- Handling missing data
- Handling late-arriving data
- Upserting data
- Regressing to a previous state
- Introducing Azure Batch
- Configuring the batch size
- Scaling resources
- Configuring batch retention
- Designing and configuring exception handling
- Designing and creating tests for data pipelines
- Debugging Spark jobs using the Spark UI
- Handling security and compliance requirements

Technical requirements

For this chapter, you will need the following:

- An Azure account (free or paid)
- An active Synapse workspace
- An active Azure Data Factory workspace

Let's get started!

Designing a batch processing solution

In *Chapter 2*, *Designing a Data Storage Structure*, we learned about the data lake architecture. I've presented the diagram here again for convenience. In the following diagram, there are two branches, one for batch processing and the other for real-time processing. The part highlighted in green is the *batch processing* solution for a data lake. Batch processing usually deals with larger amounts of data and takes more time to process compared to *stream processing*.

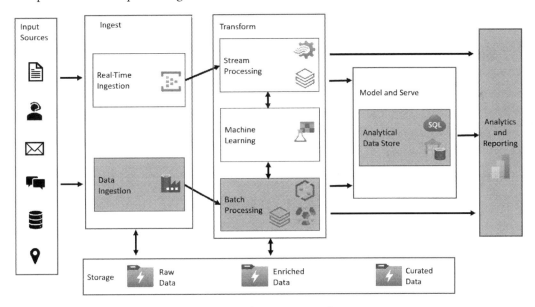

Figure 9.1 – Batch processing architecture

A batch processing solution typically consists of five major components:

- Storage systems such as Azure Blob storage, ADLS Gen2, HDFS, or similar

- Transformation/batch processing systems such as Spark, SQL, or Hive (via Azure HDInsight)

- Analytical data stores such as Synapse Dedicated SQL pool, Cosmos DB, and HBase (via Azure HDInsight)

- Orchestration systems such as ADF and Oozie (via Azure HDInsight)

- **Business Intelligence** (**BI**) reporting systems such as Power BI

We have already explored many of these technologies independently in the previous chapters. In the upcoming sections, we will see how to link them up to create a pipeline for a batch processing system.

But before we get into the details, I want to introduce you to another technology with the same name – **Azure Batch**. Azure Batch is a general-purpose batch processing system that can be used to run **High-Performance Computing** (**HPC**). Azure Batch takes care of running your applications in parallel on multiple **Virtual Machines** (**VMs**) or containers. Azure Batch is an independent service in Azure whereas the batch pipeline we are discussing is a collection of services put together as a pipeline to derive insights from data. We will explore more about Azure Batch later in this chapter.

Let's now look at how to build a batch processing system using ADF, Spark, Synapse, PolyBase, and Azure Databricks.

Developing batch processing solutions by using Data Factory, Data Lake, Spark, Azure Synapse Pipelines, PolyBase, and Azure Databricks

Let's try to build an end-to-end batch pipeline using all the technologies listed in the topic header. We will use our **Imaginary Airport Cab** (**IAC**) example from the previous chapters to create a sample requirement for our batch processing pipeline. Let's assume that we are continuously getting trip data from different regions (zip codes), which is stored in Azure Blob storage, and the trip fares are stored in an Azure SQL Server. We have a requirement to merge these two datasets and generate daily revenue reports for each region.

In order to take care of this requirement, we can build a pipeline as shown in the following diagram:

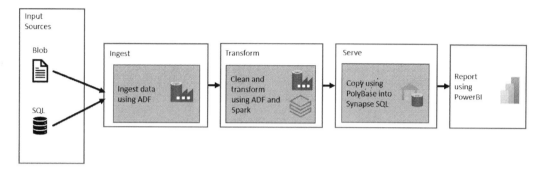

Figure 9.2 – High-level architecture of the batch use case

The preceding pipeline, when translated into an ADF pipeline, would look like the following figure:

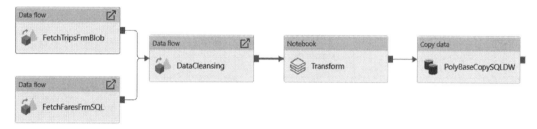

Figure 9.3 – Sample data pipeline

As you can see, the pipeline has four stages:

- **Data ingestion**: The first two stages, **FetchTripsFrmBlob** and **FetchFaresFrmSQL** get the data into the data lake.

- **Data cleansing**: The **DataCleansing** stage in the diagram cleans up the data.

- **Transformation**: The Spark Notebook **Transform** stage in the diagram transforms the data.

- **Loading into an analytical database**: The **PolyBaseCopySQLDW** stage to copies the data into a Synapse SQL pool.

The last stage would be BI tools reading from the analytical database and generating reports (which is not shown in the diagram as that is not an ADF activity).

Before we start looking into each of these stages, let's define what our storage is going to be.

Storage

Let's consider ADLS Gen2 as our data lake storage. We can create the following folder structure to handle our batch pipeline:

- The `raw trips` data can be stored here:

```
iac/raw/trips/2022/01/01
```

- The cleaned-up data can be copied over to the `transform/in` folder:

```
iac/transform/in/2022/01/01
```

- The output of the transformed data can move into the `transform/out` folder:

```
iac/transform/out/2022/01/01
```

- Finally, we can import the data from `transform/out` into Synapse SQL Dedicated pool using **PolyBase**.

Note that tools such as **ADF** and **PolyBase** also provide the ability to directly move data between Spark and Synapse SQL Dedicated pool. You can choose this direct approach instead of storing the intermediate data in the data lake if that works better for you in terms of performance and cost. But in most data lakes, more than one tool might access the intermediate data from the data lake and it will be useful to keep historical datasets for future analysis. Hence it might make sense to keep a copy in the data lake also.

Now let's look into each of the batch pipeline stages in detail.

Data ingestion

This is the process of getting all the raw data into the data lake. Data from various sources lands in the raw zone of the data lake. Based on where the data is coming from, such as on-premise systems, other cloud systems, and so on, we could use different ingestion tools. Let's look at some of the options available in Azure:

- **Azure Data Factory** – You are already familiar with this technology. It provides data ingestion support from hundreds of data sources, and even from other clouds such as AWS, GCP, Oracle, and so on. We will be using this again to build our pipeline as recommended in the syllabus.

- **Azure Copy (AzCopy)** – This is a command-line tool that can be used to copy data over the internet and is ideally suited for smaller data sizes (preferably in the 10–15 TB range). You can learn more about AzCopy here: `https://docs.microsoft.com/en-us/azure/storage/common/storage-use-azcopy-v10`.

- **Azure ExpressRoute** – If you need a secure way to transfer data into Azure, then use ExpressRoute. It routes your data through dedicated private connections to Azure instead of the public internet. This is also the preferred option if you want to have a dedicated pipeline with a faster data transfer speed. You can learn more about Azure ExpressRoute here: `https://docs.microsoft.com/en-us/azure/expressroute/expressroute-introduction`.

Let's consider an ingestion example using ADF to read from the Blob store:

1. In order to first connect to the Blob store, you will have to create a **linked service** in ADF. You can create one from the **Manage** tab of ADF as shown in the following screenshot.

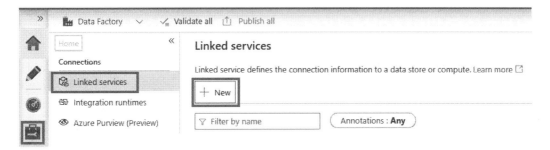

Figure 9.4 – Configuring a linked service in ADF

2. Click on the **+ New** symbol and choose **Azure Blob storage** from the list. You will get a page as shown in the following screenshot. Once you fill it up and create the linked service, you will be able to access the data in your Blob storage directly from ADF.

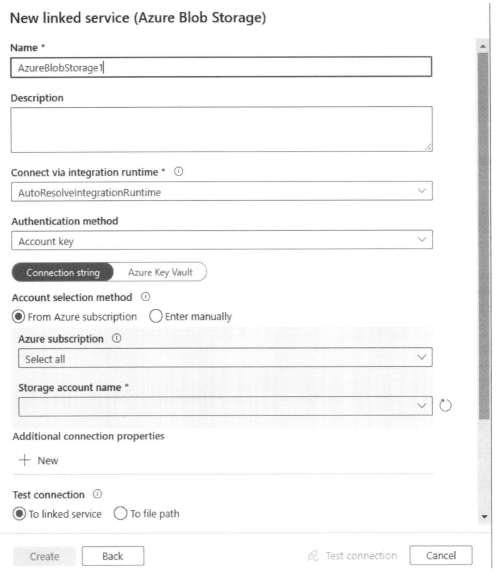

Figure 9.5 – Creating an Azure blob storage linked service

3. The next step is to create a data flow in ADF.

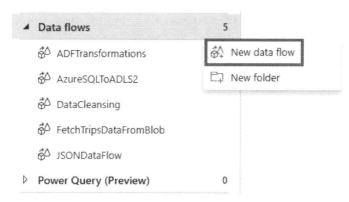

Figure 9.6 – Creating a new data flow in ADF

4. In the data flow, you will have to specify the source and destination. For **Source type**, select the **Dataset** option and define a new dataset using the Blob storage linked service that you created earlier.

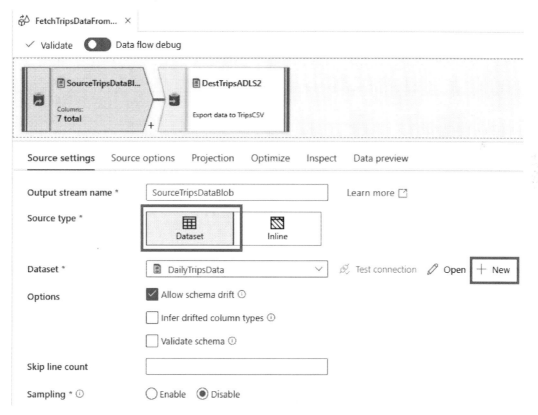

Figure 9.7 – Creating source and destination datasets in a data flow

Here is how the dataset creation screen looks when you click on **+ New** for the **Dataset** option.

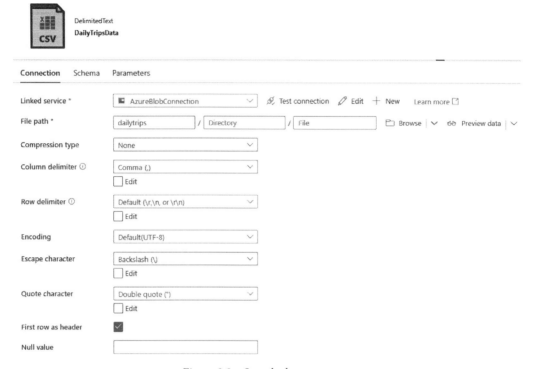

DelimitedText
DailyTripsData

| Connection | Schema | Parameters |

Linked service *   AzureBlobConnection   ⌄   🔍 Test connection   ✏ Edit   + New   Learn more 🗗

File path *   dailytrips   /   Directory   /   File   📁 Browse ⌄   👁 Preview data ⌄

Compression type   None   ⌄

Column delimiter ⓘ   Comma (,)   ⌄
                          ☐ Edit

Row delimiter ⓘ   Default (\r,\n, or \r\n)   ⌄
                          ☐ Edit

Encoding   Default(UTF-8)   ⌄

Escape character   Backslash (\)   ⌄
                          ☐ Edit

Quote character   Double quote (")   ⌄
                          ☐ Edit

First row as header   ☑

Null value

Figure 9.8 – Sample dataset screen

With the data flow created, we now have the data ingestion part taken care of. Well, actually the step is still not complete. We still have to add this copy data step to our pipeline and run it to see the results. But before that, let's learn about all the remaining batch processing components. Let's next look at the data preparation/data cleansing component.

Data preparation/data cleansing

In *Chapter 8*, *Ingesting and Transforming Data*, we explored multiple data cleansing transformations, such as handling missing data, deduping, removing outlier data, and so on. You can use the exact same transformations for this stage. As we have already explored the details in the previous chapter, we will not repeat them again here. Let's jump to the transformation step.

Transformation

Once our data is clean and prepped, we can run our transformation logic using services such as Spark, SQL, Hive, and so on. In this example, as per the certification syllabus, we will use Azure Databricks Spark. Here are the steps:

1. Create an ADB workspace – select **Azure Databricks** from the Azure portal and create a new workspace as shown in the following screenshot.

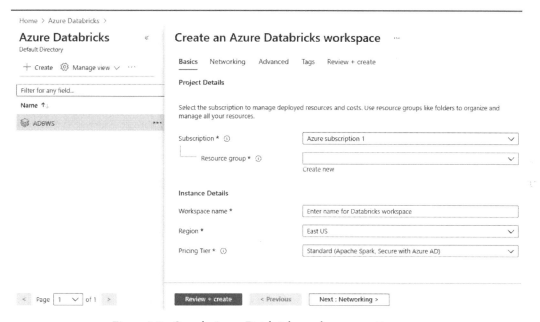

Figure 9.9 – Sample Azure Databricks workspace creation page

2. Once the workspace is created, click on the **Launch Workspace** button to launch the workspace. This will take you to the **Azure Databricks** portal.

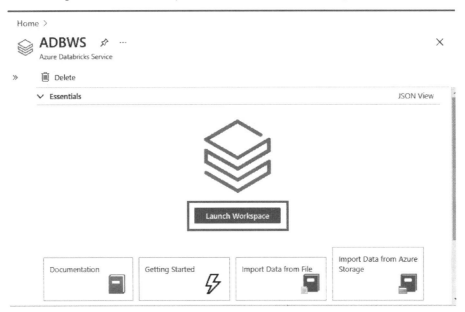

Figure 9.10 – Launching the Azure Databricks workspace

From this screen, you can create clusters, notebooks, and more. That brings us to the next step.

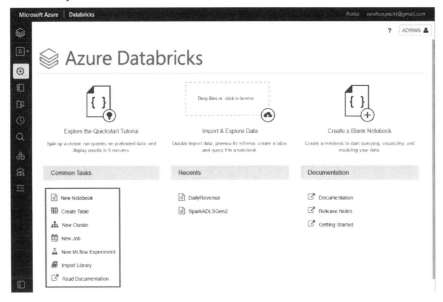

Figure 9.11 – Azure Databricks portal

3. Create an ADB cluster – click on the **New Cluster** link in the Databricks portal and enter the details.

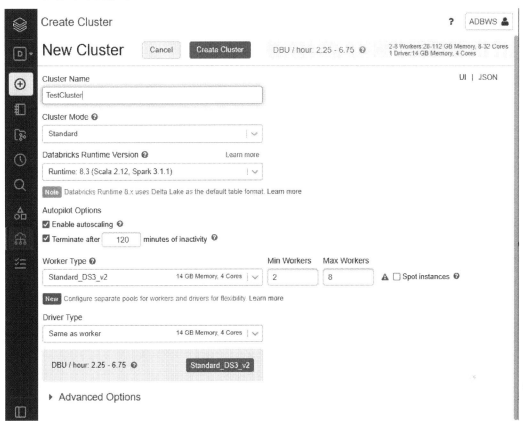

Figure 9.12 – Azure Databricks cluster creation page

This will create the cluster that will be required to run the transformations for the batch pipeline.

4. Next, click **Create** and then **Notebook** to build your transformation logic – from the Azure Databricks portal, you can choose **New Notebook**, or do it from within the side tabs as shown:

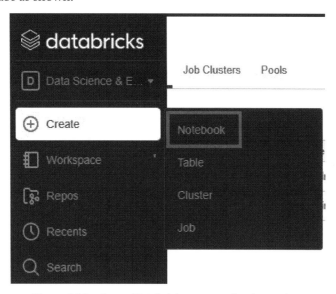

Figure 9.13 – Azure Databricks new notebook creation

Once you create the new notebook, you will get an editor as shown in the following screenshot. You can write the Spark code within the **Cmd** blocks. Azure Databricks supports the Scala, Python, SQL, and R languages.

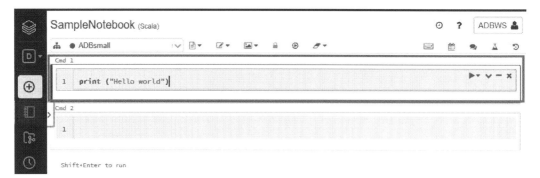

Figure 9.14 – Azure Databricks notebook

In order to generate a daily trip report, we can write a simple Scala transformation script as shown in the following steps. You will have to write these into the **Cmd** sections shown in the previous screenshot:

1. First, we need to set up the initial configs for ADB Spark to talk to ADLS Gen2:

```
spark.conf.set("fs.azure.account.auth.type." +
storageAccountName + ".dfs.core.windows.net", "OAuth")
```
```
spark.conf.set("fs.azure.account.oauth.provider.
type." + storageAccountName + ".dfs.core.windows.
net", "org.apache.hadoop.fs.azurebfs.oauth2.
ClientCredsTokenProvider")
```
```
spark.conf.set("fs.azure.account.oauth2.client.id." +
storageAccountName + ".dfs.core.windows.net", "" + appID
+ "")
```
```
spark.conf.set("fs.azure.account.oauth2.client.secret." +
storageAccountName + ".dfs.core.windows.net", "" + secret
+ "")
```
```
spark.conf.set("fs.azure.account.oauth2.client.endpoint."
+ storageAccountName + ".dfs.core.windows.net", "https://
login.microsoftonline.com/" + tenantID + "/oauth2/token")
```
```
spark.conf.set("fs.azure.
createRemoteFileSystemDuringInitialization", "true")
```
```
spark.conf.set("fs.azure.
createRemoteFileSystemDuringInitialization", "false")
```

2. Read the trip data (stored as a CSV file):

```
%scala
        .add("tripId",IntegerType)
        .add("driverId",IntegerType)
        .add("customerId",IntegerType)
        .add("cabId",IntegerType)
        .add("tripDate",IntegerType)
        .add("startLocation",StringType)
        .add("endLocation",StringType)


val tripsCSV = spark.read.format("csv")
        .option("header", "true")
        .schema(tripsSchema)
        .load("abfss:/path/to/csv")
```

3. Read the fare data (stored as Parquet files):

```scala
%scala
val faresSchema = new StructType()
        .add("tripId",IntegerType)
        .add("fare",IntegerType)
        .add("currency",StringType)

val faresParquet = spark.read.format("parquet")
            .schema(faresSchema)
            .load("abfss:/path/to/parquet")


Join them with tripId and group by startLocation:

val joinDF = tripsCSV.join(
faresParquet,tripsCSV("tripId") ===
        faresParquet("tripId"),"inner")
.groupBy("startLocation")
.sum("fare");
```

4. Join them with `tripId` and group by `startLocation`:

```scala
val joinDF = tripsCSV.join(
faresParquet,tripsCSV("tripId") ===
        faresParquet("tripId"),"inner")
.groupBy("startLocation")
.sum("fare");
```

5. Print the output table with the `City` and `Fare` columns:

```scala
import org.apache.spark.sql.functions.col;
val outputDF = joinDF.select(col("startLocation").
alias("City"),col("sum(fare)").alias("Fare"));
```

6. Finally, write the output back to ADLS Gen2 under the `transform/fares/out` folder:

```
outputDF.write.mode("overwrite").parquet("abfss:/path/to/
output")
```

Try to run the code and debug any issues within Azure Databricks before we hook it up to the ADF pipeline.

> **Tip**
>
> Azure Databricks provides a library called `dbutils` that can be used for filesystem operations such as listing files and managing secrets and data operations such as summarizing datasets and so on. Here is an example:
>
> ```
> dbutils.fs.cp("/path/to/source.txt", "/path/to/
> destination.txt")
> ```
>
> You can learn more about `dbutils` here: `https://docs.microsoft.com/en-us/azure/databricks/dev-tools/databricks-utils`.

Next, let's see how to configure ADF to call the Spark notebook that we have just created.

Configuring an ADB notebook activity in ADF

Here are the steps to add an ADB notebook into an ADF pipeline:

1. From the Azure Data Factory **Activities** tab, choose **Notebook** under **Databricks** and add it to the pipeline by dragging the icon into the worksheet area as shown in the following screenshot.

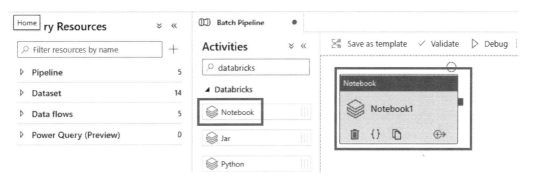

Figure 9.15 – Choosing an Azure Databricks activity in ADF

2. You have to link this **Notebook** activity to the notebook that you created in the previous step. In order to link the notebook, you will have to first get the access token from Azure Databricks. You can generate the access token from the Azure Databricks portal from the **User Settings** tab as shown in the following screenshot. Click on the **Generate New Token** button to create a new access token.

Figure 9.16 – Getting the access token from Azure Databricks

3. Now, link the previously created ADB notebook using a linked service. Similar to how we created a linked service to Azure Blob storage, we need to create one for Azure Databricks Spark too. The following screen shows the linked service configuration for Azure Databricks. You will have to fill in **Databricks Workspace URL**, the **Access token** field – with the access token that you generated in the previous step, and select whether you want to spin up a **New job cluster** or point to an **Existing interactive cluster**, and so on.

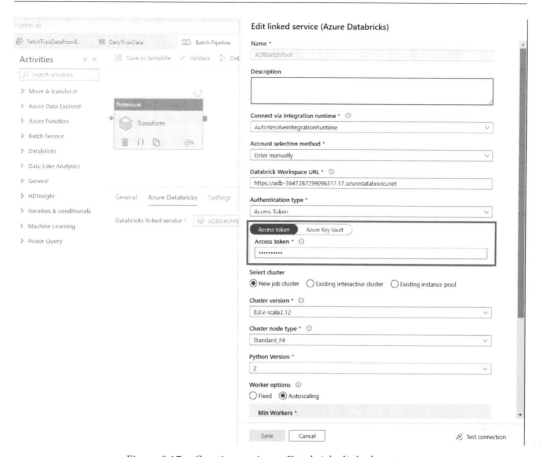

Figure 9.17 – Creating an Azure Databricks linked service

Once you have created the linked service and entered those details into the ADF notebook activity, your sample transformation stage will be complete. The final step that is pending is to import the data from this transformation stage into SQL Dedicated pool and to serve the data from there to Power BI. But before we go there, let's look at the options available for batch processing in Azure.

Batch processing technology choices

Here is a useful table reproduced from Azure that can help you decide on the technologies to use for your batch scenarios:

Capability	Azure Data Lake Analytics	Azure Synapse	HDInsight with Spark	HDInsight with Hive	HDInsight with Hive LLAP	Azure Databricks
Autoscaling	No	No	Yes	Yes	Yes	Yes
Scale-out granularity	Per job	Per cluster	Per cluster	Per cluster	Per cluster	Per cluster
In-memory caching of data	No	Yes	Yes	No	Yes	Yes
Query from external relational stores	Yes	No	Yes	No	No	Yes
Authentication	Azure AD	SQL / Azure AD	No	Azure AD[1]	Azure AD[1]	Azure AD
Auditing	Yes	Yes	No	Yes[1]	Yes[1]	Yes
Row-level security	No	Yes[2]	No	Yes[1]	Yes[1]	No
Supports firewalls	Yes	Yes	Yes	Yes[3]	Yes[3]	No
Dynamic data masking	No	Yes	No	Yes[1]	Yes[1]	No

Figure 9.18 – Comparison of batch processing technologies in Azure

You can learn more about the batch processing choices here: `https://docs.microsoft.com/en-us/azure/architecture/data-guide/technology-choices/batch-processing`.

Let's next see how to copy the data generated from the transformation stage into Synapse SQL using **PolyBase**.

Using PolyBase to ingest the data into the Analytics data store

PolyBase is a tool that enables services such as SQL Server and Synapse Dedicated SQL pool to copy and query data directly from external locations. The external sources could be Azure Storage, Oracle, Teradata, Hadoop, MongoDB, and so on. PolyBase is integrated into T-SQL, so every time we use a `COPY INTO <table> FROM` command to read data from an external storage location, PolyBase kicks in. PolyBase is one of the fastest and most scalable ways to copy data.

For the data lake scenario, we are going to use PolyBase to copy the transformed data from Azure Databricks into Synapse Dedicated SQL pool using a staging ADLS or Blob store. The steps to do this are as follows:

1. Prepare the source data in text files in ADLS or the Blob store.

2. Define an external table with the right schema in the Dedicated SQL pool instance. The format of the incoming data should match the external table schema accurately. If not, rows might get dropped.

3. If the data is coming from a non-relational source, we will have to transform it into a rows and columns format that matches the external table schema correctly.

4. Run the COPY INTO command to load the data into dedicated SQL pool external tables using PolyBase.

5. From here, you can either serve the data directly or do more processing using a Dedicated SQL pool before serving it to the BI tools.

Here is an example of how to use PolyBase:

```
CREATE EXTERNAL FILE FORMAT [Dp203ParquetFormat]
    WITH ( FORMAT_TYPE = PARQUET)


CREATE EXTERNAL DATA SOURCE [Dp203DataSource]
    WITH (
        LOCATION = 'abfss://path/to/storage/location'
    )


CREATE EXTERNAL TABLE TripExtTable
WITH (
    LOCATION = '/path/to/data/*.parquet',
    DATA_SOURCE = [Dp203DataSource],
    FILE_FORMAT = [Dp203ParquetFormat]
) AS
SELECT
    [tripId] INT,
    [driverId] INT,
. . .
    [endLocation] VARCHAR(50)
FROM
    OPENROWSET(BULK '/path/to/data/*.parquet',
FORMAT='PARQUET')
```

Now copy the data from the external table into an actual SQL table:

```
CREATE TABLE TripsProdTable
WITH
(
    CLUSTERED COLUMNSTORE INDEX,
    DISTRIBUTION = ROUND_ROBIN
)
AS
SELECT * FROM TripsExtTable
```

With the last `CREATE EXTERNAL TABLE AS SELECT (CETAS)` statement, PolyBase copies the data into Synapse SQL Dedicated pool.

> **Note**
>
> PolyBase does not support nested formats such as JSON, XML, and WinZip as of writing this book. For JSON files, you could try to flatten the data first using the techniques we saw in *Chapter 8, Ingesting and Transforming Data,* under the *Shredding JSON section*, before using PolyBase to load them into Synapse SQL.

Options for loading with PolyBase

PolyBase is also available as part of other services, such as the following:

- **Azure Data Factory** – This version of PolyBase can be used as an activity within ADF. The data copy activity can be defined as a pipeline that can be scheduled regularly. You can read more about it here: `https://docs.microsoft.com/en-us/azure/data-factory/connector-azure-sql-data-warehouse?tabs=data-factory#use-polybase-to-load-data-into-azure-synapse-analytics`.

- **Azure Databricks** – This version of PolyBase can be used to transfer data between Azure Databricks and Synapse SQL pools. You can learn more about it here: `https://docs.microsoft.com/en-us/azure/databricks/scenarios/databricks-extract-load-sql-data-warehouse`.

- **SQL Server** – This version can be used if the source is a SQL Server. The SQL **Server Integration Services** (**SSIS**) platform can be used to define the source and destination mappings and do the orchestration while using the SSIS version of PolyBase. You can learn more about it here: `https://docs.microsoft.com/en-us/sql/integration-services/sql-server-integration-services`.

You can learn more about PolyBase here: `https://docs.microsoft.com/en-us/sql/relational-databases/polybase/polybase-versioned-feature-summary`.

Let's next look at the last piece of our puzzle in the batch processing pipeline, which is to view the insights using Power BI.

Using Power BI to display the insights

Power BI is a **Business Intelligence** (**BI**) data visualization tool that is deeply integrated with Azure cloud services. It has built-in connectivity to many clouds and on-premises technologies and helps visualize and share insights from data.

The steps involved in visualizing the Synapse SQL data via Power BI are as follows:

1. Go to `powerbi.microsoft.com` and create an account. Once you have logged in, create a new workspace by clicking on the **Create a workspace** button from the **Workspaces** tab as shown in the following screenshot.

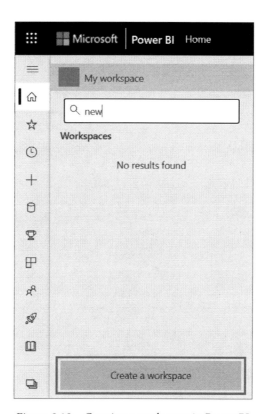

Figure 9.19 – Creating a workspace in Power BI

2. Next, go to the Synapse workspace and create a linked service to Power BI. Click on the **Manage** tab in the Synapse workspace and select **Linked services**. Then click on **+ New** and search for Power BI as shown in the following screenshot.

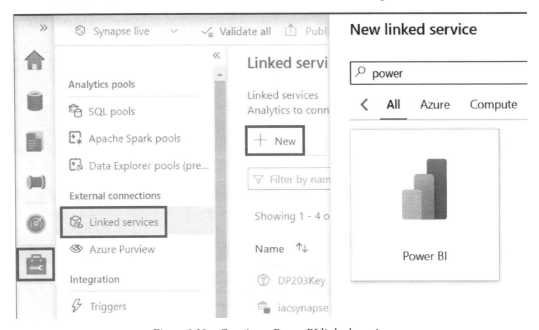

Figure 9.20 – Creating a Power BI linked service

3. On the linked service configuration screen, give a name to the linked service and select the previously created Power BI workspace for the **Workspace name** field.

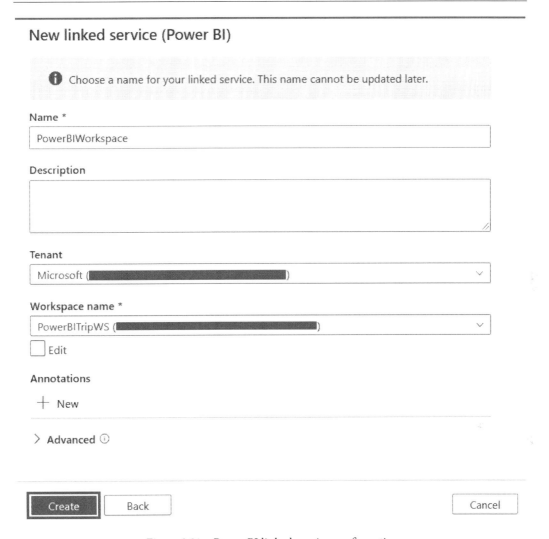

Figure 9.21 – Power BI linked service configuration

4. Once you fill in the fields and click on **Create**, a new linked service to Power BI is created.

5. Now go to the **Editor** tab in the Synapse workspace. You should see a **Power BI** section as shown in the following screenshot. Click on + **New Power BI dataset** and choose the SQL table that you want to include as your Power BI dataset.

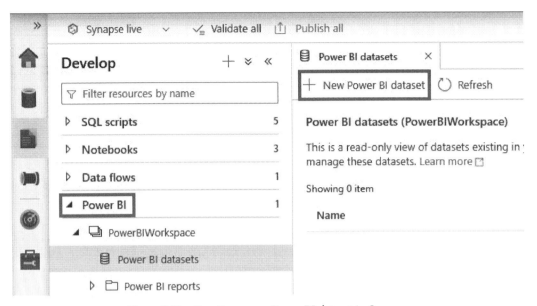

Figure 9.22 – Creating a new Power BI dataset in Synapse

6. A download screen will pop up as shown in the following screenshot. Just download the .pbids file.

Download .pbids file

Download the .pbids file below and save it to your local drive.

↓ ▬▬▬▬▬sqlpool.pbids

Figure 9.23 – Downloading the .pbids file for Power BI

7. Next, double-click on the .pbids file and it will open Power BI Desktop. If you don't have Power BI Desktop, you can install it from here: https://Power BI.microsoft.com/en-us/downloads/.

8. Once Power BI Desktop opens, choose any of the **Visualizations** and drag and drop the table fields from the right-hand **Fields** tab. Power BI will now show the graphs for your data.

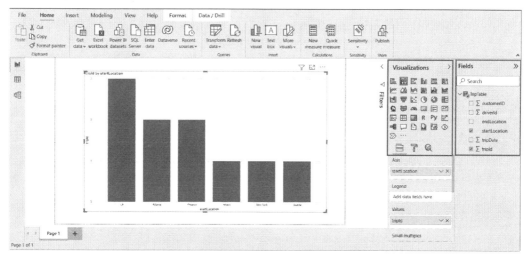

Figure 9.24 – Visualizing data from Power BI Desktop

And that's how you can connect a BI reporting tool to your Synapse SQL pool.

You can learn more about linking Synapse SQL to Power BI here: `https://docs.microsoft.com/en-us/azure/synapse-analytics/get-started-visualize-power-bi`.

Now that we have all the components required to build the pipeline, let's see how to actually link them together in Azure Data Factory and create the pipeline.

Creating data pipelines

Data pipelines are a collection of various data processing activities arranged in a particular sequence to produce the desired insights from raw data. We have already seen many examples in Azure Data Factory where we chain the activities together to produce a final desirable outcome. ADF is not the only technology available in Azure. Azure also supports Synapse pipelines (which is an implementation of ADF within Synapse) and open source technologies such as **Oozie** (available via Azure HDInsight), which can help orchestrate pipelines. If your workload only uses open source software, then Oozie could fit the bill. But if the pipeline uses other Azure or external third-party services then ADF might be a better fit as ADF provides readily available source and sink plugins for a huge list of technologies.

You can create a pipeline from the **Pipeline** tab of Azure Data Factory. All you need to do is to select the activities for your pipeline from the **Activities** tab and click and drag it into the canvas. You can link the activities using the green box (on the right side of each activity) and chain the blocks together either sequentially or parallelly to derive the required output. The following screenshot shows an example.

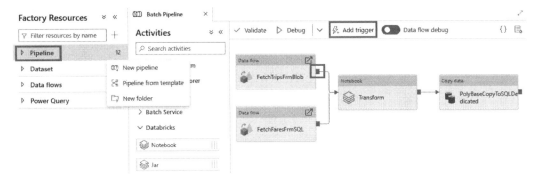

Figure 9.25 – Creating new pipelines in ADF

Once you have the pipeline stitched together, you can trigger it using the **Add trigger** button. The trigger could be one-time, event-based, or recurring.

I hope you now have an understanding of how to create and publish an end-to-end batch pipeline. Let's next look at how to integrate Jupyter and Python notebooks into a data pipeline.

Integrating Jupyter/Python notebooks into a data pipeline

Integrating Jupyter/Python notebooks into our ADF data pipeline can be done using the Spark activity in ADF. You will need an Azure HDInsight Spark cluster for this exercise.

The prerequisite for integrating Jupyter notebooks is to create linked services to Azure Storage and HDInsight from ADF and have an HDInsight Spark cluster running.

You have already seen how to create linked services, in the *Developing batch processing solutions by using Data Factory, Data Lake, Spark, Azure Synapse Pipelines, PolyBase, and Azure Databricks* section earlier in this chapter, so I'll not repeat the steps here.

Select the Spark activity from ADF and specify the HDInsight linked service that you created in the **HDInsight linked service** field under the **HDI Cluster** tab as shown in the following screenshot.

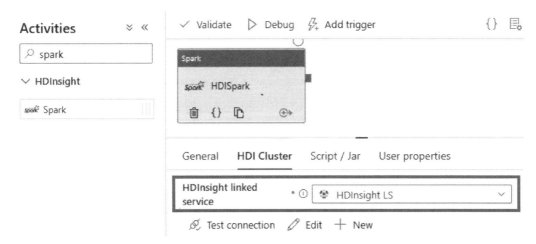

Figure 9.26 – Configuring a Spark activity in ADF

Now, start the Jupyter notebook by going to `https://<YOURHDICLUSTER>.azurehdinsight.net/jupyter` or from the HDInsight dashboard as shown in the following screenshot.

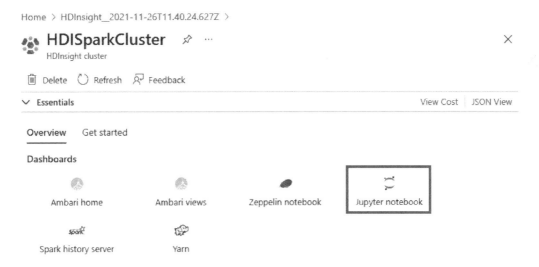

Figure 9.27 – Launching the Jupyter notebook from HDInsight

From the Jupyter launch page, you can select **PySpark** or **PySpark3** to start a Python notebook.

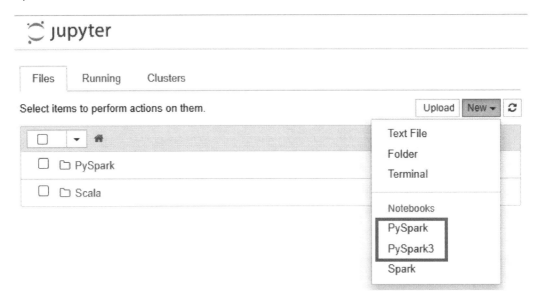

Figure 9.28 – Launching a PySpark Jupyter notebook from HDInsight

You can write your transformations in the Jupyter notebook and run it using the ADF pipelines like any other ADF activity. Now you know how to run Jupyter notebooks from data pipelines.

You can learn more about running Spark notebooks from ADF here: `https://docs.microsoft.com/en-us/azure/data-factory/v1/data-factory-spark`.

The next few sections will focus on a few advanced techniques for loading data and data preparation. Some of these topics are repeated from the previous chapters, so we will skip over them by providing references to the previous chapters and focus on the new topics that have not already been covered.

Designing and implementing incremental data loads

We covered incremental data loading in *Chapter 4, Designing the Serving Layer*. Please refer to that chapter to refresh your knowledge of incremental data loads.

Let's next see how to implement slowly changing dimensions.

Designing and developing slowly changing dimensions

We also covered **slowly changing dimensions** (**SCDs**) in detail in *Chapter 4, Designing the Serving Layer*. Please refer to that chapter to refresh your knowledge of the concepts.

Handling duplicate data

We already explored this topic in *Chapter 8, Ingesting and Transforming Data*. Please refer to that chapter to refresh your understanding of handling duplicate data.

Let's next look at how to handle missing data.

Handling missing data

We already explored this topic in *Chapter 8, Ingesting and Transforming Data*. Please refer to that chapter to refresh your understanding of handling duplicate data.

Let's next look at how to handle late-arriving data.

Handling late-arriving data

We haven't yet covered this scenario, so let's dive deeper into handling late-arriving data.

A late-arriving data scenario can be considered at three different stages in a data pipeline – during the data ingestion phase, the transformation phase, and the serving phase.

Handling late-arriving data in the ingestion/transformation stage

During the ingestion and transformation phases, the activities usually include copying data into the data lake and performing data transformations using engines such as Spark, Hive, and so on. In such scenarios, the following two methods can be used:

- Drop the data, if your application can handle some amount of data loss. This is the easiest option. You can keep a record of the last timestamp that has been processed. And if the new data has an older timestamp, you can just ignore that message and move forward.

- Rerun the pipeline from the ADF **Monitoring** tab, if your application cannot handle data loss.

Next, let's look at how to handle late-arriving data in the serving stage.

Handling late-arriving data in the serving stage

In the serving phase, data handling is usually done via a star or snowflake schema for OLAP scenarios. In such cases, there might be situations where a **dimension** arrives late (or a **fact** might arrive early). Let's look at a few common methods to handle such scenarios:

- *Drop the message*: Like in the ingestion/transformation stage, this is the easiest option, especially if the old data doesn't add much value.

- *Store the message and retry after some time*: In this technique, store the early-arriving fact rows in a staging table and try inserting this fact when in the next iteration, hoping that the dimension will have arrived by then. Repeat this process a pre-determined number of times before declaring failure.

- *Insert a dummy record in the dimension table*: In this technique, if the corresponding dimension record doesn't exist, just enter a dummy record in its place. You will have to revisit all the dummy records and update them with real values once the dimension values arrive.

- If you have enough details about the dimension, you can infer the dimension row and insert the new derived dimension row with a new surrogate key.

These are some of the ways to handle late-arriving data. Let's next look at how to **upsert** data.

Upserting data

Upsert refers to `UPDATE` or `INSERT` transactions in data stores. The data stores could be relational, key-value, or any other store that supports the concept of updating rows or blobs.

ADF supports upsert operations if the **sink** is a SQL-based store. The only additional requirement is that the **sink** activity must be preceded by an Alter Row operation. Here is an example screenshot of an ADF sink with **Allow upsert** enabled.

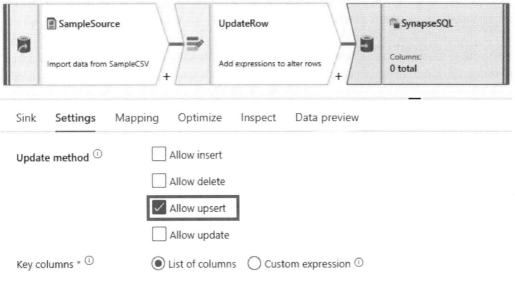

Figure 9.29 – Upsert operation in ADF

Once you have saved the preceding setup, ADF will automatically do an upsert if a row already exists in the configured sink. Let's next look at how to regress to a previous state.

Regressing to a previous state

Regressing to a previous state or rolling back to a stable state is a very commonly used technique in databases and OLTP scenarios. In OLTP scenarios, the transformation instructions are grouped together into a transaction and if any of the instructions fail or reach an inconsistent state then the entire transaction rolls back. Although databases provide such functionality, we don't have such ready-made support in Azure Data Factory or Oozie (HDInsight) today. We will have to build our own rollback stages depending on the activity. Let's look at an example of how to do a rollback of a data copy activity in ADF.

ADF provides options for checking consistency and setting limits for fault tolerance. You can enable them in the **Settings** options of a copy activity as shown in the following screenshot.

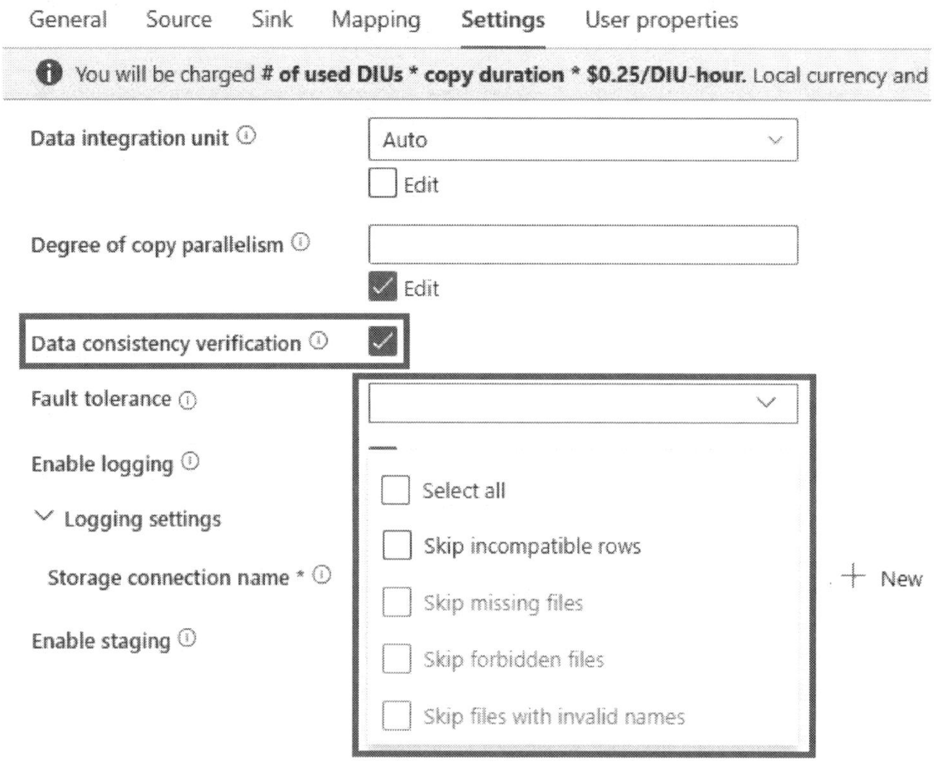

Figure 9.30 – Enabling consistency verification and fault tolerance in an ADF copy activity

If the activity fails due to consistency checks or fault tolerance beyond a level, you can define a follow-up **Delete** activity on the failure path (orange link) to completely clean up the directory as shown in the following screenshot.

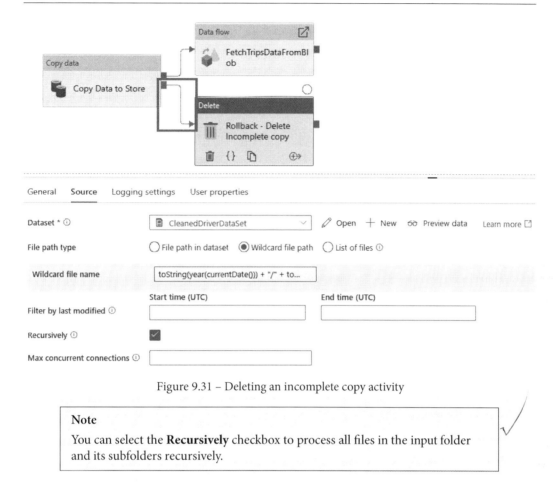

Figure 9.31 – Deleting an incomplete copy activity

> **Note**
> You can select the **Recursively** checkbox to process all files in the input folder and its subfolders recursively.

Note that the delete activity technique can be extended for other scenarios such as data insertion into tables, retrying transformations, and so on. The corresponding rollback techniques in such cases will also be different, such as deleting files, deleting rows in a table, and so on.

I hope you've got the idea of how to roll back to a previous stage using ADF. Next, we will focus on the Azure Batch service that we spoke about in the introduction of this chapter.

Introducing Azure Batch

Azure Batch is an Azure service that can be used to perform large-scale parallel batch processing. It is typically used for high-performance computing applications such as image analysis, 3D rendering, genome sequencing, optical character recognition, and so on.

Azure Batch consists of three main components:

- **Resource management**: This takes care of node management (things such as VMs and Docker containers), autoscaling, low-priority VM management, and application management. Applications are just ZIP files of all the executables, libraries, and config files required to be run for the batch job.

- **Process management**: This takes care of the job and task scheduling, retrying failed jobs, enforcing constraints on jobs, and so on. A job is a logical unit of work. A job is split into tasks that can run in parallel on the nodes from the VM or container pool.

- **Resource and process monitoring**: This takes care of all the monitoring aspects. There are several options available via the Azure portal, Application Insights, and finally logs and metrics.

Like any other Azure service, Batch can be completely provisioned using the Azure portal. Here is a sample screenshot of a Batch screen.

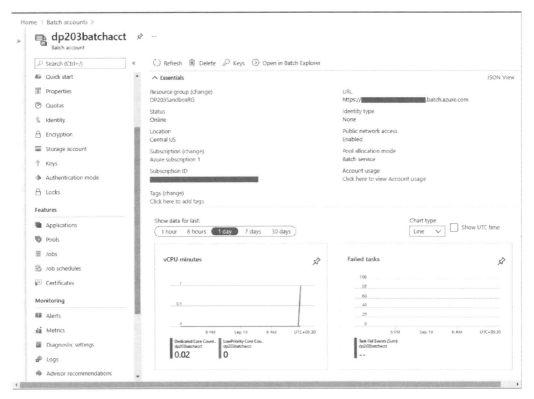

Figure 9.32 – Azure Batch portal screen

You can configure and monitor your Batch jobs directly from the portal. Let's look at how to run a Batch job using the CLI next.

Running a sample Azure Batch job

Azure Batch provides multiple approaches for running jobs. We can use the Azure portal, the Azure CLI, and even programmatic interfaces via .NET and PowerShell. Let's look at an example using the Azure CLI for this one, as we have explored the Azure portal quite a lot already.

In this example, we will learn how to create an Azure Batch account and set up a pool of VMs to execute the job. We will then learn how to run an application on the pool and download the results. You will have to replace the highlighted options within <> with your own entries. You can create a temporary ResourceGroup from the Azure portal and use it in these examples. For all other entries, such as BatchAccountName, BatchPoolName, and so on, you can just specify your own names:

1. Create a batch account as shown:

```
az batch account create -g <ResourceGroup> -n
<BatchAccountName> -l centralus
```

2. Create a storage account as shown:

```
az storage account create -g <ResourceGroup> -n
<BatchStoreAcct> -l centralus --sku Standard_LRS
```

3. Now, link the storage account to the Batch account:

```
az batch account set -g <ResourceGroup> -n
<BatchAccountName> --storage-account <BatchStoreAcct>
```

4. Next, create a pool using Ubuntu VMs to run our Batch application. This operation takes a few minutes:

```
az batch pool create \
    --id <ResourceGroup> --vm-size Standard_A1_v2 \
    --target-dedicated-nodes 2 \
    --image canonical:ubuntuserver:16.04-LTS \
    --node-agent-sku-id "batch.node.ubuntu 16.04"
```

5. You can check the status of the pool creation as shown:

```
az batch pool show --pool-id <BatchPoolName> \
    --query "allocationState"
```

6. Next, create an application that needs to be run by the Batch job:

```
az batch application create --resource-group
<ResourceGroup> --name <BatchAccountName> --application-
name sampleapp1
```

7. Next, create a job:

```
az batch job create \
    --id <BatchJobName> \
    --pool-id <BatchPoolName>
```

8. Create the tasks under the job. The tasks will start running as soon as you create them:

```
for i in {1..4}
do
    az batch task create \
    --task-id sampletask$i \
    --job-id <BatchJobName> \
    --command-line "/bin/bash -c 'printenv; sleep 30s'"
done
```

9. Monitor the jobs as shown:

```
az batch task show \
    --job-id <BatchJobName> \
    --task-id <BatchTaskName>
```

10. Download the results as shown:

```
az batch task file download \
    --job-id <BatchJobName> \
    --task-id <BatchTaskName> \
    --file-path stdout.txt \
    --destination ./stdout.txt
```

11. Finally, you can delete each of the entities as shown:

```
az batch job delete --job-id <BatchJobName>
az batch task delete –job-id <BatchJobName> --task-id
<BatchTaskName>
az batch pool delete --pool-id <BatchPoolName>
```

This example should have given you a picture of the entire life cycle of an Azure Batch job. You can learn more about Azure Batch here: `https://docs.microsoft.com/en-us/azure/batch/batch-technical-overview`.

Now that you know the basics of Azure Batch, let's next look at how to configure batch sizes.

Configuring the batch size

To configure the batch size, we will explore how to determine the batch size in Azure Batch. Batch size refers to both the size of Batch pools and the size of the VMs in those pools. The following guidelines are generic enough that they can be applied to other services such as Spark and Hive too.

Here are some of the points to consider while deciding on the batch size:

- **Application requirements**: Based on whether the application is CPU-intensive, memory-intensive, storage-intensive, or network-intensive, you will have to choose the right types of VMs and the right sizes. You can find all the supported VM sizes using the following Azure CLI command (here, `centralus` is an example):

```
az batch location list-skus –location centralus
```

- **Data profile**: If you know how your input data is spread, it will help in deciding the VM sizes that will be required. We will have to plan for the highest amount of data that will be processed by each of the VMs.

- **The number of tasks that can be run per node (VM)**: If your tasks don't need an entire VM, it will be beneficial to run multiple tasks within the same VMs.

- **Different pools for different batch loads**: If you have different types of Batch jobs that need different VM capacities, it will be efficient to have different pools for the different Batch jobs.

- **VM availability per region**: Not all VM types will be available in all regions. So, you need to consider the geolocations while planning to create your Batch pool.

- **VM quotas per Batch account**: Apart from VM availability per region, there are usually quota limitations on your Batch accounts and Azure subscriptions. Some of these quota limits are soft limits and can be raised by raising a support request. But eventually, you will hit the hard limits. So, plan your Batch pool size based on your quota limitations. You can verify your quota under the **Quotas** tab of **Batch accounts**. Here is a sample screenshot of that page.

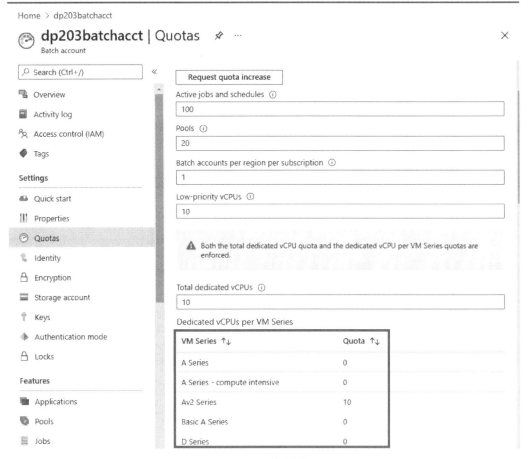

Figure 9.33 – Batch VM quotas

You can learn more about Batch VM options here: `https://docs.microsoft.com/en-us/azure/batch/batch-pool-vm-sizes`.

Let's next look at how to scale resources in Azure Batch and other batch processing services such as Spark and Synapse SQL.

Scaling resources

Scaling refers to the process of increasing or decreasing the compute, storage, or network resources to improve the performance of jobs or reduce expenses. There are two types of scaling: **Manual** and **Automatic**. As might be obvious, with manual scaling, we decide on the size beforehand. With automatic scaling, the service dynamically decides on the size of the resources based on various factors, such as the load on the cluster, the cost of running the cluster, time constraints, and more.

Let's explore the scaling options available in Azure Batch and then quickly glance at the options available in Spark and SQL too.

Azure Batch

Azure Batch provides one of the most flexible autoscale options. It lets you specify your own autoscale formula. Azure Batch will then use your formula to decide how many resources to scale up or down to.

A scaling formula can be written based on the following:

- **Time metrics**: Using application stats collected at 5-minute intervals
- **Resource metrics**: Using CPU, memory, and network bandwidth usage
- **Task metrics**: Using the number of tasks queued or completed

The Azure Batch autoscale screen itself provides sample autoscale formulas that you can adapt and enhance to your requirements. Here is a sample autoscale screen with the formula:

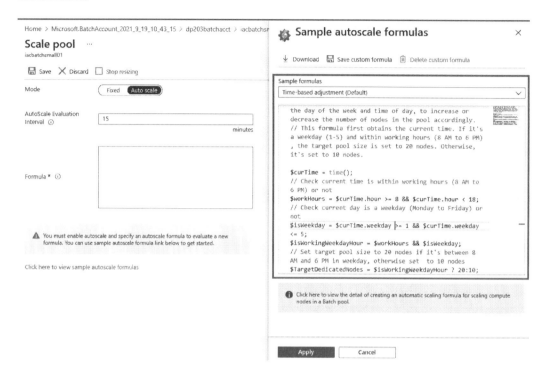

Figure 9.34 – Batch autoscale formula screen

The example in the previous screenshot is setting the number of nodes based on the time of day. You can find more such examples for Azure Batch scaling here: `https://docs.microsoft.com/en-us/azure/batch/batch-automatic-scaling`.

Let's next look at how we can set scaling options in Spark and Synapse SQL Dedicated pools.

Azure Databricks

In Azure Databricks, while creating the cluster, you can select **Enable Autoscaling** and specify the number of **Min Workers** and **Max Workers**. The cluster will automatically scale up and down between these two numbers based on the load. Unlike Azure Batch, you don't have the flexibility to provide your own scaling formula here.

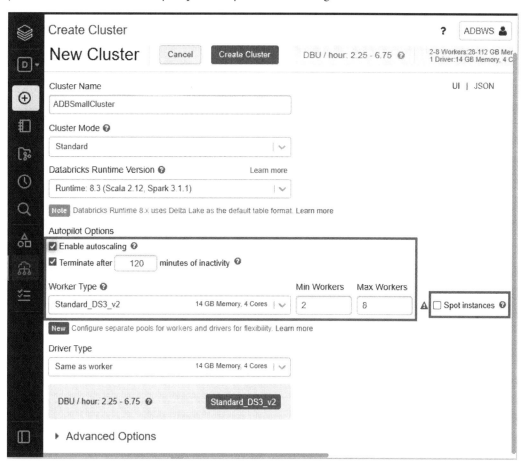

Figure 9.35 – Azure Databricks Spark autoscale option

If you would like to have a fixed-size cluster, you just have to uncheck the **Enable autoscaling** option and provide the exact worker count.

You can save on the cost of your clusters by using **Spot instances**. Spot instances are unused Azure VMs that are offered by Azure at a cheaper cost, but with no availability guarantees. If Azure needs the capacity back, it can pull back the Spot VMs with 30 seconds' notice. You can use this option if your jobs can handle interruptions, such as very large batch jobs, dev/test jobs, and so on.

Synapse Spark

Similar to Azure Databricks, Synapse Spark also provides the option to autoscale on the cluster creation screen. The following screenshot shows the screen with the **Autoscale** option.

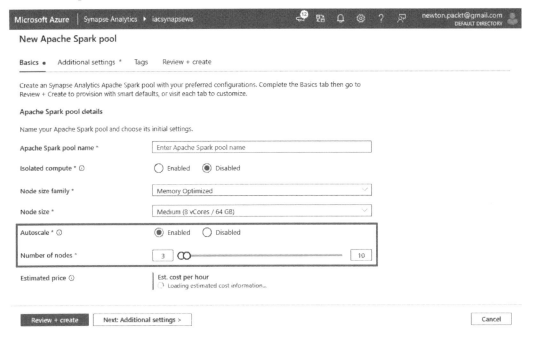

Figure 9.36 – Synapse Spark Autoscale option

Next, let's look at the option available for Synapse SQL Dedicated pools.

Synapse SQL

Synapse SQL doesn't provide the option to autoscale, but it provides the option to choose the cluster **Performance level** while creating the cluster as shown in the following screenshot. The higher the number, the better the performance.

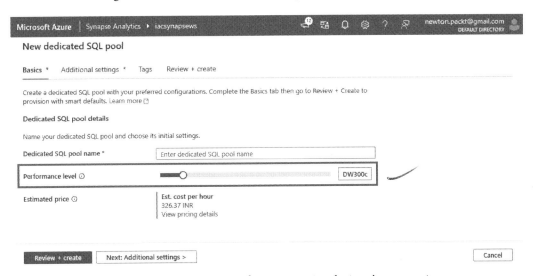

Figure 9.37 – Synapse SQL performance setting during cluster creation

Now you know how to configure scaling in Azure Batch, Azure Databricks Spark, Synapse Spark, and Synapse SQL.

Let's next look at how to configure batch retention.

Configuring batch retention

The default retention time for tasks in Azure Batch is 7 days unless the compute node is removed or lost. We can, however, set the required retention time while adding a job.

Here is an example using REST APIs. The `retentionTime` needs to be set in the request body as shown:

```
POST account.region.batch.azure.com/jobs/jobId/tasks?api-
version=2021-06-01.14.0
```

Examine the following request body:

```
{
  "id": "jobId",
  "priority": 100,
  "jobManagerTask": {
    "id": "taskId",
    "commandLine": "test.exe",
    "constraints": {
      "retentionTime": "PT1H"
    }
  }
}
```

PT1H specifies 1 hour and uses the ISO_8601 format. You can learn more about the format here: https://en.wikipedia.org/wiki/ISO_8601#Durations.

Let's next look at designing and configuring exception handling.

Designing and configuring exception handling

Azure Batch provides error codes, logs, and monitoring events to identify and handle errors. Once the errors are identified, we can handle them programmatically via APIs and .NET code.

Here are some examples of error codes returned by Batch:

Error Code	Category	User Message
AutoScalingFormulaSyntaxError	BadRequest	The specified autoscaling formula has a syntax error.
CommandLaunchFailed	UserError	Failed to launch the specified command line.
NodeBeingRebooted	Conflict	The specified node is being rebooted.
DiskFull	ServerError	There is not enough disk space on the node that was selected to run the task.

Figure 9.38 – Sample Batch error codes

You can get the complete list of error codes here: https://docs.microsoft.com/en-us/rest/api/batchservice/batch-status-and-error-codes.

Next, let's look at some common error types in Azure Batch.

Types of errors

There are four common groups of errors:

- **Application errors**: For application errors, Azure Batch writes standard output and standard error to `stdout.txt` and `stderr.txt` files in the task directory on the compute node. We can parse these files to identify the issue and take remedial measures.

- **Task errors**: A task is considered failed if it returns a non-zero exit code. The failure could happen due to multiple reasons, such as preprocessing errors, file upload errors, or command-line errors. In all such cases, the corresponding error codes will be set. And we can programmatically configure Batch to retry the tasks up to a certain number of times. For task errors, we need to check the `executionInfo` property. This property contains details of errors such as `result`, `exitCode`, `failureInfo`, and so on, which can help identify the errors.

- **Job errors**: A job is a collection of tasks. Similar to task errors, we need to check the `executionInfo` property to determine the cause of the error for the jobs.

- **Output file errors**: During file uploads, Batch writes the logs to two files, namely `fileuploadout.txt` and `fileuploaderr.txt`. These two files need to be checked in case of output file loading errors.

Let's next look at some of the common remedial actions.

Remedial actions

While the remedial action for each type of error will be unique, the following generic ones help if the jobs get stuck for a long time or there are issues with the nodes:

- Reboot the node:

```
API: POST {batchUrl}/pools/{poolId}/nodes/{nodeId}/
reboot?api-version=2021-06-01.14.0
```

- Reimage the node:

```
API: POST {batchUrl}/pools/{poolId}/nodes/{nodeId}/
reimage?api-version=2021-06-01.14.0
```

- Remove the node from the pool:

```
POST {batchUrl}/pools/{poolId}/removenodes?api-
version=2021-06-01.14.0
```

- Disable scheduling jobs on that pool:

```
API: POST {batchUrl}/pools/{poolId}/nodes/{nodeId}/
disablescheduling?api-version=2021-06-01.14.0
```

Let's next look at some of the security and compliance requirements for data pipelines in general. The concepts and ideas discussed here also apply to other technologies, such as Spark and Hive-based pipelines.

Handling security and compliance requirements

Security and compliance will always remain one of the core requirements for any cloud-based system. Azure provides a service called **Azure Policy** to enable and enforce compliance and security policies in any of the Azure services. In our case, it could be Azure Synapse, Azure Batch, VMs, VNets, and so on. Azure Policy helps enforce policies and remedial actions at scale.

Azure Policy contains pre-defined policy rules called **built-ins**. For example, one of the rules could be *Allow only VMs of a particular type to be created in my subscription*. When this policy is applied, if anyone tries to create a VM of a different SKU, the policy will fail the VM creation. It will show an error saying *Not allowed by policy* at the validation screen for the resource creation.

Azure Policy has a huge list of predetermined policies and remedial actions for different compliance use cases. You can choose the policies that are relevant to your application and apply them. Here is a sample screen of Azure policies:

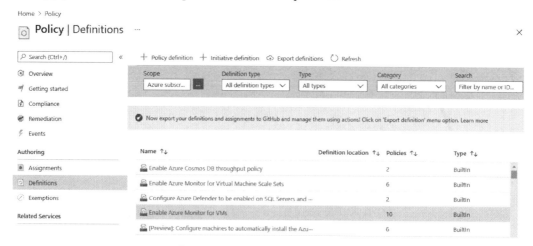

Figure 9.39 – Azure Policy examples

Here is a screenshot of the Azure Policy screen where we can apply Azure policies and Remediation methods.

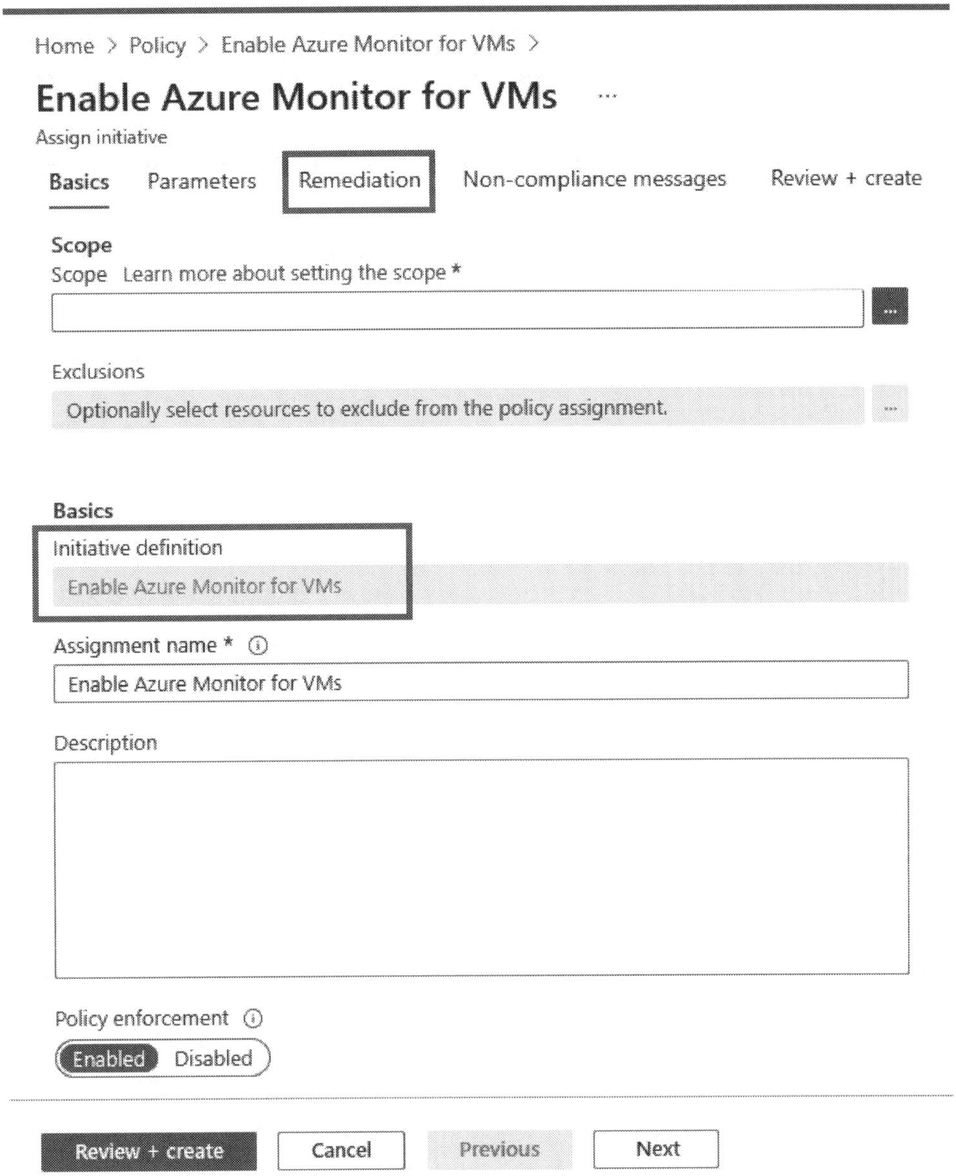

Home > Policy > Enable Azure Monitor for VMs >

Enable Azure Monitor for VMs   ···
Assign initiative

Basics   Parameters   Remediation   Non-compliance messages   Review + create

Scope

Scope   Learn more about setting the scope *

[   ] [···]

Exclusions

Optionally select resources to exclude from the policy assignment.   [···]

Basics

Initiative definition

Enable Azure Monitor for VMs

Assignment name * ⓘ

Enable Azure Monitor for VMs

Description

[   ]

Policy enforcement ⓘ

(Enabled Disabled)

[Review + create]   [Cancel]   [Previous]   [Next]

Figure 9.40 – Apply Azure policies

For example, to be **HIPAA** compliant, one of the requirements is that you need to ensure audit logging is enabled.

So, if any of your Azure services don't have audit logging enabled, then Azure Policy will flag a compliance error. You can even configure the tool to disable the service if it is not compliant.

You can learn more about the Azure Policy service here: `https://docs.microsoft.com/en-us/azure/governance/policy/overview`.

Let's next look at another recommended technique to enhance the security of batch processing systems, the Azure Security Benchmark.

The Azure Security Benchmark

Beyond Azure Policy, Azure also provides a set of recommendations to improve the security of cloud-based data, services, and workloads. This set of best practices is called the **Azure Security Benchmark**. This benchmark covers a wide range of areas, such as network security, identity management, logging, data protection, and so on. You can validate your service against this benchmark to ensure that you are following the industry standard.

Examples of **Network Security** (**NS**) benchmark rules are as follows:

- **NS-1**: Deploy Azure Batch pool(s) within a virtual network.

- **NS-2**: Connect private networks together.

- **NS-3**: Establish private network access to Azure services.

- **NS-4**: Protect applications and services from external network attacks.

Examples of identity management benchmark rules are as follows:

- **IM-1**: Standardize Azure AD as the central identity and authentication system.

- **IM-2**: Manage application identities securely and automatically.

- **IM-3**: Use Azure AD **single sign-on** (**SSO**) for application access, and so on.

You can find the comprehensive list here: `https://docs.microsoft.com/en-us/security/benchmark/azure/overview`.

Let's next look at some of the best practices for the Azure Batch service.

Best practices for Azure Batch

Here is a summary of some of the best practices to secure batch systems derived from the Azure documentation:

- **Use private endpoints**: You can use the Azure Private Link service to restrict access to the batch processing services from external networks.

- **Create pools in virtual networks**: In the Azure Batch service, you can create batch pools within a virtual network so that the nodes can communicate securely with each other.

- **Create pools without public IP addresses**: To reduce the chances of discoverability from public networks.

- Limit remote access to pool nodes by configuring firewalls.

- Encrypt data in transit by using `https://`.

- Encrypt Batch data at rest by using secret keys.

- Apply compliance and security policies described in the previous sections to your Azure Batch instance.

You can find an exhaustive list here: `https://docs.microsoft.com/en-us/azure/batch/security-best-practices`.

Summary

I hope you now have a good idea about both batch pipelines and the Azure Batch service. We learned about creating end-to-end batch pipelines by diving deep into each of the stages, such as ingestion, transformations, BI integrations, and so on. We then learned about a new service called Azure Batch and learned about batch retention, handling errors, handling autoscale, building data pipelines using Batch, and more. We also learned about some of the critical security and compliance aspects. That is a lot of information to chew on. Just try to glance through the chapter once again if you have any doubts.

We will next be focusing on how to design and develop a stream processing solution.

10

Designing and Developing a Stream Processing Solution

Welcome to the next chapter in the data transformation series. This chapter deals with stream processing solutions, also known as real-time processing systems. Similar to batch processing, stream processing is another important segment of data pipelines. This is also a very important chapter for your certification.

This chapter will focus on introducing the concepts and technologies involved in building a stream processing system. You will be learning about technologies such as **Azure Stream Analytics** (**ASA**), Azure Event Hubs, and Spark (from a streaming perspective). You will learn how to build end-to-end streaming solutions using these technologies. Additionally, you will learn about important streaming concepts such as checkpointing, windowed aggregates, replaying older stream data, handling drift, and stream management concepts such as distributing streams across partitions, scaling resources, handling errors, and upserting data.

Once you have completed this topic, you should be confident enough to build an end-to-end streaming pipeline using the technologies that are available in Azure.

As with the other chapters, I've taken the liberty of rearranging the syllabus topics for this chapter by grouping the related ones together. This helps create a good flow for the chapter. We will be covering the following topics:

- Designing a stream processing solution
- Developing a stream processing solution using ASA, Azure Databricks, and Azure Event Hubs
- Processing data using Spark Structured Streaming
- Monitoring for performance and functional regressions
- Processing time series data
- Designing and creating windowed aggregates
- Configuring checkpoints/watermarking during processing
- Replaying archived stream data
- Handling schema drifts
- Processing across partitions
- Processing within one partition
- Scaling resources
- Handling interruptions
- Designing and configuring exception handling
- Upserting data
- Designing and creating tests for data pipelines
- Optimizing pipelines for analytical or transactional purposes

Technical requirements

For this chapter, you will need the following:

- An Azure account (this could be either free or paid)
- The ability to read basic Python code (don't worry, it is very easy)

Let's get started!

Designing a stream processing solution

Stream processing systems or real-time processing systems are systems that perform data processing in near real time. Think of stock market updates, real-time traffic updates, real-time credit card fraud detection, and more. Incoming data is processed as and when it arrives with very minimal latency, usually in the range of milliseconds to seconds. In *Chapter 2, Designing a Data Storage Structure*, we learned about the Data Lake architecture, where we saw two branches of processing: one for streaming and one for batch processing. In the previous chapter, *Chapter 9, Designing and Developing a Batch Processing Solution*, we focused on the batch processing pipeline. In this chapter, we will focus on stream processing. The blue boxes in the following diagram show the streaming pipeline:

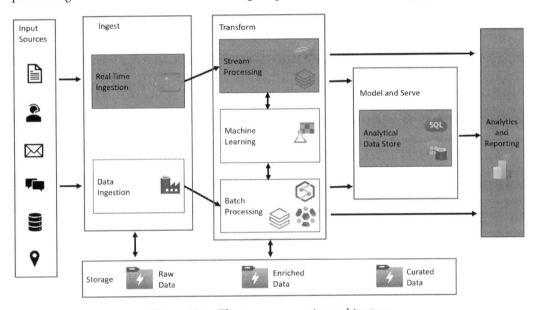

Figure 10.1 – The stream processing architecture

Stream processing systems consist of four major components:

- An **Event Ingestion service** such as **Azure Event Hubs**, **Azure IoT Hub**, **Apache Kafka** and so on. which helps to capture, store, and transmit events from multiple input sources to the stream processing services. They act as a buffer between the input sources and the data processing services. Sometimes, the event ingress rate might be too much for the stream processing systems to handle, and sometimes, it might be too little. If the event ingress rate is higher, then the ingestion service would store the events until the downstream services can process them. If the event ingress rate is lower, the ingestion service can batch them up for efficiency and send them downstream.

- **Stream processing systems** such as **ASA**, **Spark Streaming**, **Apache Storm**, **Apache Flink**, and so on which provide the ability to quickly filter, join, and aggregate the incoming events to derive insights. They are very similar to batch transformations but work on much smaller data sizes and more frequently than batch systems.

- **Analytical data stores** such as **Synapse Dedicated SQL pool**, **CosmosDB**, **HBase**, and so on, where the processed data from the stream processing systems is usually stored for BI reporting and other ad hoc queries. Some systems such as ASA can directly send data to reporting systems such as Power BI without the need for an analytical data store.

- **Reporting systems** such as **Power BI**. This is the final piece of the pipeline where we present the processed data in the form of reports for business consumption and decision-making.

Now, let's look at the services that are available in Azure to build stream processing systems. We will start with Azure Event Hubs.

Introducing Azure Event Hubs

Azure Event Hubs is a distributed ingestion service that can ingest, store, and transfer millions of events from various input sources to multiple consumers. It acts as a buffer between the event producers and the event consumers and decouples the event producers from the event consumers. This helps the downstream stream components such as ASA or Spark Streaming to asynchronously process the data. Azure Event Hubs is a fully managed PaaS service, so we don't have to worry about the upkeep of the service. Event Hubs can auto-inflate to meet the increasing requirements of the streaming system.

Here is a simplified architecture diagram of **Azure Event Hubs**:

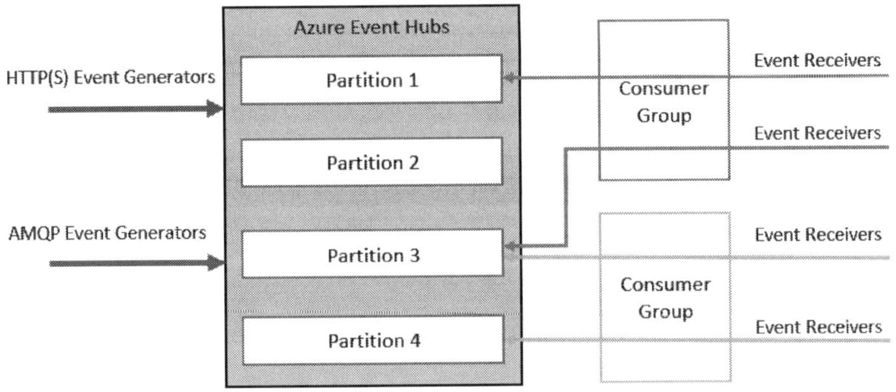

Figure 10.2 – The Azure Event Hubs architecture

As you can see from the preceding diagram, Event Hubs can take inputs via two protocols: the **Hypertext Transfer Protocol** (**HTTP**) or the **Advanced Message Queuing Protocol** (**AMQP**). It then distributes the data into partitions. The event receivers, which are part of consumer groups, can subscribe to the partitions and read the events from there. Let's take a look at what these terminologies, including partitions and consumer groups, mean.

Event Hubs partitions

Event Hubs distributes the incoming data into one or more partitions, as shown in *Figure 10.2*. Partitions help with horizontal scaling as they allow multiple consumers to read data in parallel.

Event Hubs consumer groups

A consumer group is a view of the event hub. There could be many consumer groups for each event hub, and each consumer group can have its own view of the event hub. In other words, they have access to different sets of streams or partitions. The consumers (typically, downstream applications) access the partitions via their own consumer group. The consumer group maintains state-like offsets in the stream, checkpointing information, and more. The applications within a consumer group can independently process the data without worrying about other clients.

You can learn more about Event Hubs at `https://docs.microsoft.com/en-us/azure/event-hubs/`.

Next, let's look at ASA.

Introducing ASA

ASA is Azure's primary stream processing engine. It can process large volumes of data with minimal latencies. It can be used to perform analytical functions such as filter, aggregate, join, and more to derive quick results from the incoming stream of data. ASA can be used for scenarios such as retail point-of-sale analysis, credit card fraud detection, IoT sensing and failure detection, click-stream analysis, and so on. Typically, an ASA job has three stages:

1. It reads from an ingestion service such as Event Hubs, IoT Hub, or Kafka.

2. It processes the data and generates insights.

3. Finally, it writes the data into an analytical store, such as Azure Synapse Analytics, CosmosDB, or sends the results directly to a BI reporting service. ASA can directly send the results to Power BI.

Similar to Event Hubs, ASA is also a fully managed PaaS service. So, we don't have to worry about its upgrades and patches.

You can learn more about ASA at `https://docs.microsoft.com/en-us/azure/stream-analytics/`.

Next, let's look at Spark Streaming.

Introducing Spark Streaming

In the previous chapters, we looked at Spark from a batch processing perspective, but what you might not be aware of is that you can use the same Apache Spark core APIs to build a streaming solution. Similar to ASA, Spark can also read from data ingestion services such as Azure Event Hubs, Kafka, and more, implement the data transformations, and finally, write the output to analytical databases or any other store for that matter.

Spark Streaming internally splits the incoming stream into micro-batches and processes them, so the output will be a stream of micro-batches.

You can learn more about Spark Streaming at `https://spark.apache.org/docs/latest/streaming-programming-guide.html`.

Next, let's look at how to build a stream processing solution using all the technologies that we have learned about so far.

Developing a stream processing solution using ASA, Azure Databricks, and Azure Event Hubs

In this section, we will look at two examples: one with ASA as the streaming engine and another with Spark as the streaming engine. We will use a dummy event generator to continuously generate trip events. We will configure both ASA and Azure Databricks Spark to perform real-time processing and publish the results. First, let's start with ASA.

A streaming solution using Event Hubs and ASA

In this example, we will be creating a streaming pipeline by creating an Event Hubs instance, an ASA instance, and linking them together. The pipeline will then read a sample stream of events, process the data, and display the result in Power BI:

1. First, let's create an **Event Hub** instance. From the Azure portal, search for Event Hubs and click on the **Create** button, as shown in the following screenshot:

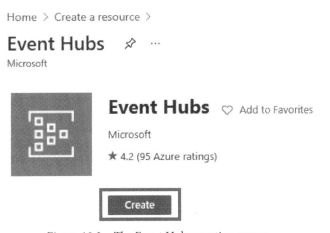

Figure 10.3 – The Event Hubs creation screen

2. This will bring up the Event Hubs **Create Namespace** screen, as shown in the following screenshot. Fill in the details including **Resource group**, **Namespace name**, **Location**, **Throughput Units**, and any other required fields:

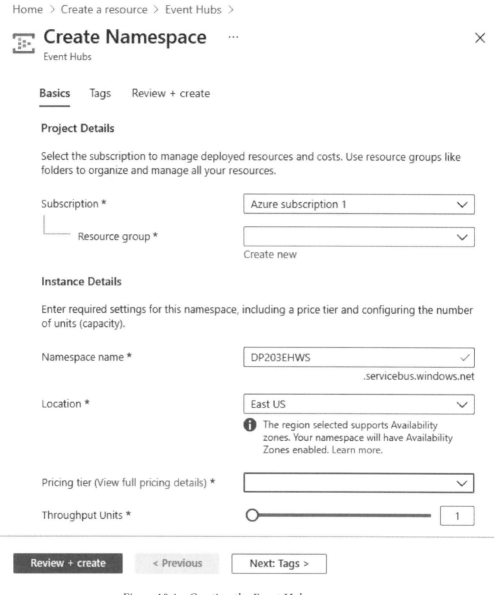

Figure 10.4 – Creating the Event Hubs namespace

3. Enter the details and click on the **Review + create** button to create the Event Hubs workspace. Once the workspace has been created, click on the **+ Event Hub** link (as shown in the following screenshot) to create a new event hub within the workspace:

Figure 10.5 – Creating an event hub from within the Event Hubs workspace

4. This will pop up a screen, as shown in the following screenshot. Enter a **Name** in the field given, select the **Partition Count** value (we will learn more about partitions later), and click on **Create**:

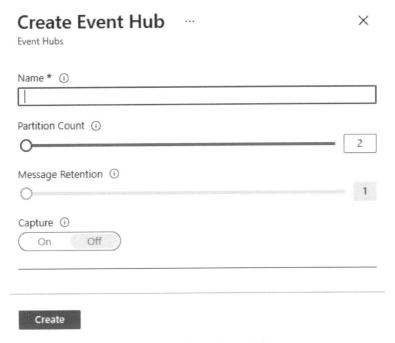

Figure 10.6 – The Create Event Hub screen

5. Now that we have an event hub, next, let's create an ASA instance. Search for `Stream Analytics jobs` in the Azure portal and select the option. On the **Stream Analytics jobs** page, click on the **+ Create** link:

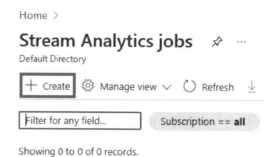

Figure 10.7 – Creating an ASA job

6. This will pop up the analytics job creation screen, as shown in the following screenshot. Fill in the details including **Job name**, **Subscription**, **Resource group**, **Location**, **Streaming units**, and any other required fields. Then, click on the **Create** button to create a new ASA job:

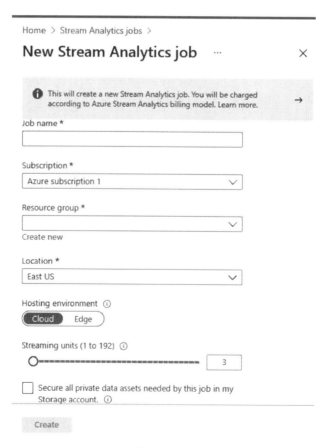

Figure 10.8 – The ASA creation screen

7. The next step is to link the input to Event Hubs. Before this step, we will need to get the connection string from Event Hubs. Go to the Event Hubs page, and click on **Shared access policies**. Click on the + **Add** button, and add a new policy, as shown in the following screenshot:

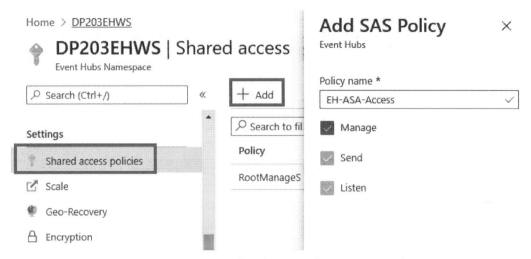

Figure 10.9 – Creating shared access policies in Event Hubs

8. Once the policy has been created, you can simply click on the policy to retrieve the **Connection string** link, as shown in the following screenshot:

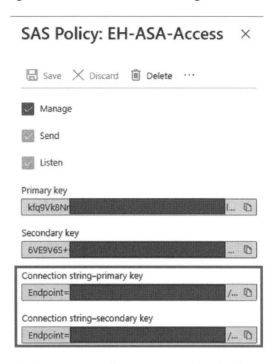

Figure 10.10 – Accessing the connection string for Event Hubs

9. Now, go back to the ASA portal and link the input (Event Hubs) and output (Power BI) to the ASA instance. Click on the **Inputs** tab and select **Event Hub** from the + **Add stream input** drop-down list. This will pop up a screen where you can select the **Event Hub** instance that you created earlier:

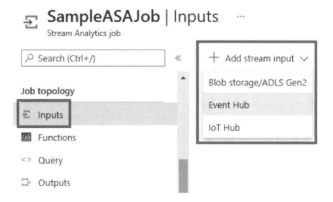

Figure 10.11 – Selecting an event hub as input for the ASA job

10. On the **Event Hub New input** screen, enter the connection string that you copied from *Figure 10.10*:

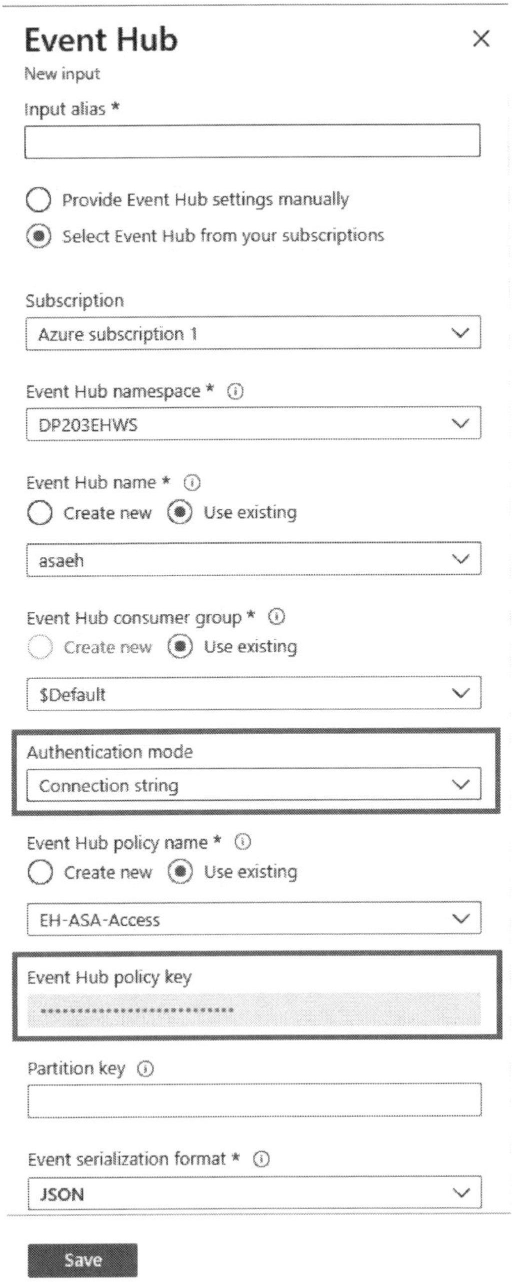

Figure 10.12 – Linking the event hub as an input in ASA

11. Similarly, click on the **Outputs** tab and select **Power BI** for the ASA output:

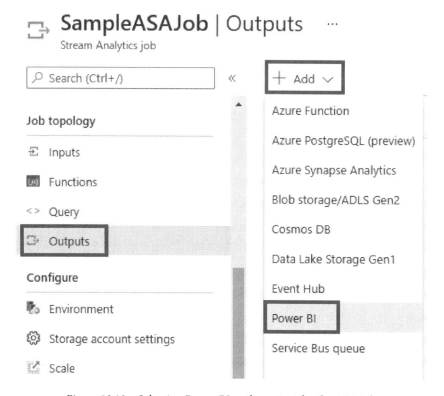

Figure 10.13 – Selecting Power BI as the output for the ASA job

12. This will pop up a screen as follows. Here, you will have to fill in your **Power BI** details:

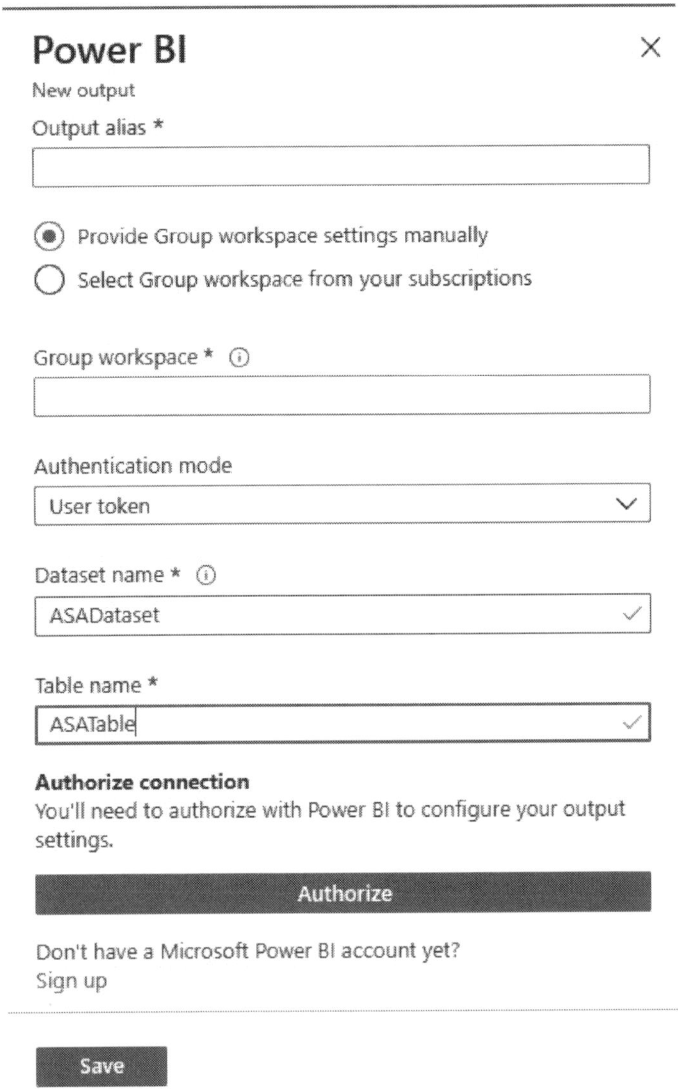

Power BI ✕

New output

Output alias *

[   ]

⦿ Provide Group workspace settings manually

◯ Select Group workspace from your subscriptions

Group workspace * ⓘ

[   ]

Authentication mode

[User token   ⌄]

Dataset name * ⓘ

[ASADataset   ✓]

Table name *

[ASATable   ✓]

Authorize connection

You'll need to authorize with Power BI to configure your output settings.

[Authorize   ]

Don't have a Microsoft Power BI account yet?
Sign up

[Save]

Figure 10.14 – Configuring the Power BI sink details for the ASA job

13. Now that we have the input and output set up and ready, run a sample event generator to generate test events. Here is a simple Python event generator module. The complete code is available in the accompanying GitHub repository.

a) Import the required Event Hub libraries:

```
from azure.eventhub.aio import EventHubProducerClient
from azure.eventhub import EventData
```

b) Instantiate a `producer` client:

```
producer = EventHubProducerClient.from_connection_string(
        conn_str=<SAS Access Connection String>,
        eventhub_name=<Event Hub Name>)
```

c) Create an event batch instance:

```
eventDataBatch = await producer.create_batch()
```

d) Create a JSON event:

```
cityList = ["San Franciso", "San Jose", "Los Angeles",…]
tripDetail = {'tripId': str(uuid.uuid4()),
        'timestamp': str(datetime.datetime.utcnow()),
        'startLocation': random.choice(cityList),
        'endLocation': random.choice(cityList),
        'distance': random.randint(10, 1000),
        'fare': random.randint(100, 1000) }
```

e) Add events to the batch:

```
eventDataBatch.add(
        EventData(json.dumps(tripDetail)))
```

f) Send the batch of events to the event hub:

```
producer.send_batch(eventDataBatch)
```

You can repeat *steps d, e, and f* in a `for` loop for as long as you need.

14. When you run the preceding code from the command line, you will be able to view the events arriving at the event hub on the Event Hubs overview page, as follows:

Figure 10.15 – The Event Hubs overview pages showing the event metrics

15. Now, let's read this data and publish the number of trips per location. On the ASA **Overview** page, you can enter the **Query** as shown in the following screenshot, and click on **Start**:

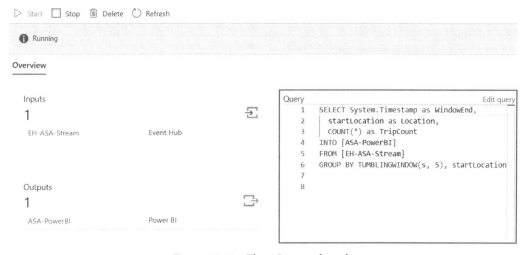

Figure 10.16 – The ASA sample code

16. Now, the ASA job will continuously read the input event hub stream, process the data, and publish it to Power BI. If you navigate to **My workspace** in your **Power BI** portal, you should see the ASA dataset that was configured earlier on the Power BI output configuration screen (*Figure 10.14*):

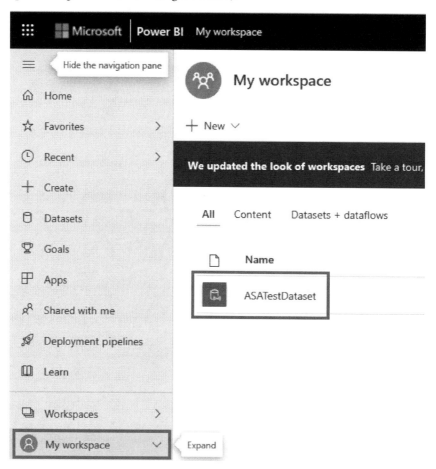

Figure 10.17 – The Power BI dataset screen

17. You can right-click on the dataset and create a report out of it, as shown in the following screenshot:

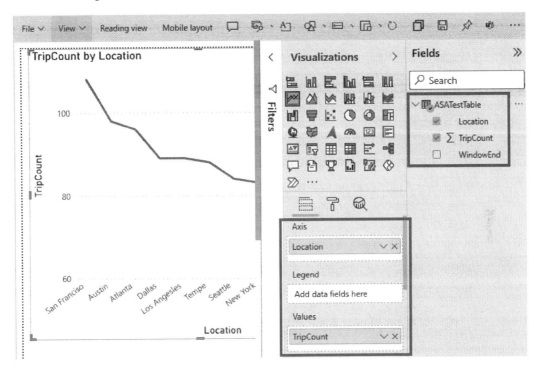

Figure 10.18 – Creating the Power BI dashboard from the ASA streaming output

Now you know how to build a streaming pipeline using Event Hubs, ASA, and Power BI.

ASA can also work with **IoT Hub** as the ingestion service. With IoT Hub, ASA can be deployed in two different modes:

- In **Cloud mode**: Here, the IoT devices send the events to an ASA job on the Azure cloud, which is very similar to the Event Hubs model.

- In **Edge mode**: Here, ASA can run directly on the IoT devices themselves, perform real-time processing, and send the events to IoT Hub.

You can find more details about ASA's Edge mode at https://docs.microsoft.com/en-us/azure/iot-edge/tutorial-deploy-stream-analytics?view=iotedge-2020-11.

Next, let's look at how to build a streaming solution using Azure Databricks Spark.

A streaming solution using Event Hubs and Spark Streaming

In this example, we will use the same event hub and data generator that we used for the ASA option. The only change is that we will use Azure Databricks Spark instead of ASA. Let's look at how to read data from Event Hubs using Databricks Spark.

Before we can connect to Event Hubs and start reading, we will have to create a Spark cluster. We learned how to create a Databricks Spark cluster in *Chapter 9, Designing and Developing a Batch Processing Solution*, in the *Developing batch processing solutions using Data Factory, Data Lake, Spark, Azure Synapse Pipelines, PolyBase, and Azure Databricks* section. Please use the same instructions to create a new Spark cluster:

1. Once the Spark cluster is up and running, open a Spark Notebook and enter the following sample code to process the stream data into the notebook.

2. Set the connection to the Event Hubs instance in the same way that we generated it in *Figure 10.10*, as shown in the following code block:

```
EHConnectionString = "<EVENT HUB CONNECTION STRING>"
EHConfig = {}
EHConfig['eventhubs.connectionString'] = sc._jvm.
org.apache.spark.eventhubs.EventHubsUtils .encrypt(
EHConnectionString )
```

3. Connect to the event hub:

```
EHStreamDF = spark.readStream.format("eventhubs")
.options(**EHConfig).load()
```

4. Next, we need to define the schema of the streaming input:

```
JsonSchema = StructType() \
.add("tripId", StringType()) \
.add("createdAt", TimestampType()) \
.add("startLocation", StringType()) \
.add("endLocation", StringType()) \
.add("distance", IntegerType()) \
.add("fare", IntegerType())
```

5. Now, let's define the stream-handling DataFrame (`EHStreamJsonDF`) to extract the key values from the incoming JSON events:

```
stringDF = EHStreamDF.selectExpr("CAST(body AS STRING)")
jsonDF= stringDF.withColumn('tripjson', from_
json(col('body'),schema=JsonSchema))
EHStreamJsonDF= jsonDF.select("tripjson.*")
```

6. Up to this point, we have ensured that the events from the event hub can be processed and acted upon directly using DataFrames. The next step is to define the transformation to be applied and actually start the streaming:

```
EHStreamJsonDF.groupBy(window('createdAt',"1
minutes"),'startLocation').count().orderBy('window')\
.writeStream.format("memory") \
.outputMode("complete") \
.option("truncate", "false") \
.option("checkpointLocation", "dbfs:/
tripsCheckpointLocation/") \
.queryName("TripsTumblingQuery").start()
```

7. In the preceding step, we are using a window of 1 minute and counting the number of trips based on `startLocation`. In the upcoming sections, we will learn about windowing, the different output modes, checkpointing, and more.

8. Once we run *Step 6*, the streaming starts and continuously looks for events from the event hub, processes them, and sends the output to a table named `TripsTumblingQuery`. If you `SELECT *` from the table, you can view the trip counts:

Table   Data Profile

	window	startLocation	count
1	▶ {"start": "2021-12-06T11:52:00.000+0000", "end": "2021-12-06T11:53:00.000+0000"}	San Franciso	4
2	▶ {"start": "2021-12-06T11:52:00.000+0000", "end": "2021-12-06T11:53:00.000+0000"}	Dallas	2
3	▶ {"start": "2021-12-06T11:52:00.000+0000", "end": "2021-12-06T11:53:00.000+0000"}	Atlanta	4
4	▶ {"start": "2021-12-06T11:52:00.000+0000", "end": "2021-12-06T11:53:00.000+0000"}	Tempe	8
5	▶ {"start": "2021-12-06T11:52:00.000+0000", "end": "2021-12-06T11:53:00.000+0000"}	San Jose	1
6	▶ {"start": "2021-12-06T11:52:00.000+0000", "end": "2021-12-06T11:53:00.000+0000"}	Denver	2

Showing all 14 rows.

Figure 10.19 – Viewing the results of the streaming query

9. You can stop the streaming, as shown in the following code block:

```
for s in spark.streams.active:
    s.stop()
```

So, this is how we can connect Azure Databricks to Event Hubs and process real-time data.

You can learn more about Azure Databricks and Event Hubs at `https://docs.microsoft.com/en-us/azure/databricks/scenarios/databricks-stream-from-eventhubs`.

Next, let's look at Spark Structured Streaming.

Processing data using Spark Structured Streaming

Structured Streaming is a feature in Apache Spark where the incoming stream is treated as an unbounded table. The incoming streaming data is continuously appended to the table. This feature makes it easy to write streaming queries, as we can now write streaming transformations in the same way we handle table-based transformations. Hence, the same Spark batch processing syntax can be applied here, too. Spark treats the Structured Streaming queries as incremental queries on an unbounded table and runs them at frequent intervals to continuously process the data.

Spark supports three writing modes for the output of Structured Streaming:

- **Complete mode**: In this mode, the entire output (also known as the result table) is written to the sink. The sink could be a blob store, a data warehouse, or a BI tool.

- **Append mode**: In this mode, only the new rows from the last time are written to the sink.

- **Update mode**: In this mode, only the rows that have changed are updated; the other rows will not be updated.

In the previous section, when we used Azure Databricks Spark to process the stream, we had already used the concept of Spark Structured Streaming. Every time we use the `writestream` or `readstream` methods, Spark uses Structured Streaming. Let's look at another example in which we continuously write the streaming trips data and query it like a regular table:

```
EHStreamJsonDF.selectExpr(
                        "tripId"\
                    ,"timestamp"\
                    ,"startLocation"\
                    ,"endLocation"\
                    ,"distance"\
                    ,"fare")\
.writeStream.format("delta")\
.outputMode("append")\
.option("checkpointLocation", "dbfs:/
TripsCheckpointLocation/")\
.start("dbfs:/TripsEventHubDelta")
```

In the preceding query, we are specifying the column names to be extracted as part of `selectExpr`, the format to be written as **delta**, the output mode as `append`, the checkpoint location as `dbfs:/TripsCheckpointLocation`, and finally, the sink location to be written as `dbfs:/TripsEventHubDelta` within the `start()` method. **Delta** is an open source storage layer that can be run on top of data lakes. It enhances the data lake to support features such as ACID transactions, updates, deletes, unified batch, interactive and streaming systems via Spark. We will learn more about Delta in the *Compacting small files* section of *Chapter 14, Optimizing and Troubleshooting Data Storage and Data Processing*.

Now you can query the data like a regular table, as follows:

```
%sql
CREATE TABLE IF NOT EXISTS TripsAggTumbling
    USING DELTA LOCATION "dbfs:/TripsEventHubDelta/"
SELECT * FROM TripsAggTumbling
```

This is how we can use Spark Structured Streaming to handle streaming data. You can learn more about Structured Streaming at `https://docs.microsoft.com/en-us/azure/databricks/getting-started/spark/streaming`.

Next, let's look at how to monitor the streaming performance.

Monitoring for performance and functional regressions

Let's explore the monitoring options available in Event Hubs, ASA, and Spark for streaming scenarios.

Monitoring in Event Hubs

The Event Hubs **Metric** tab provides metrics that can be used for monitoring. Here is a sample screenshot of the metric options that are available:

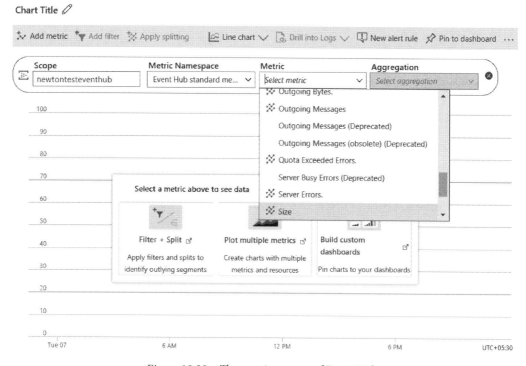

Figure 10.20 – The metrics screen of Event Hubs

We can get useful metrics such as the number of **Incoming Messages**, the number of **Outgoing Messages**, **Server Errors**, CPU and memory utilization, and more. You can use all of these metrics to plot graphs and dashboards as required.

Next, let's look at the monitoring options in ASA.

Monitoring in ASA

The ASA **Overview** page provides high-level monitoring metrics, as shown in the following screenshot:

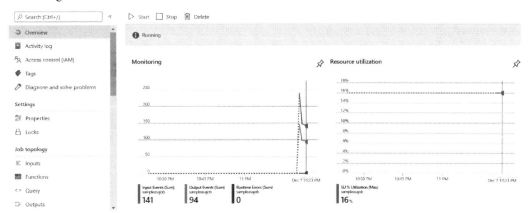

Figure 10.21 – The ASA Overview page with metrics

Similar to the Event Hubs metric page, ASA also provides a rich set of metrics that can be used for monitoring. Here is a sample screenshot of the ASA Metric tab:

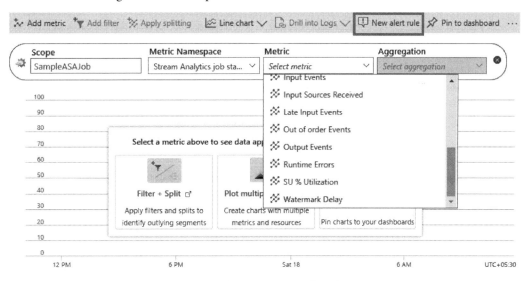

Figure 10.22 – The ASA Metric tab with metrics

As you can see from the preceding screenshot, it provides useful information such as **SU % Utilization**, **Runtime Errors**, **Watermark Delay**, and more. We can even configure alerts on top of these metrics. Let's look at an example of how to configure an alert to trigger if SU% crosses 80%.

Configuring alerts in ASA

Let's examine how to configure an alert for high SU% usage.

Select the **New alert rule** link in *Figure 10.22*. This will take you to a page that lists all the signals available to build the alert on. Select the **SU % Utilization** option, as shown in the following screenshot:

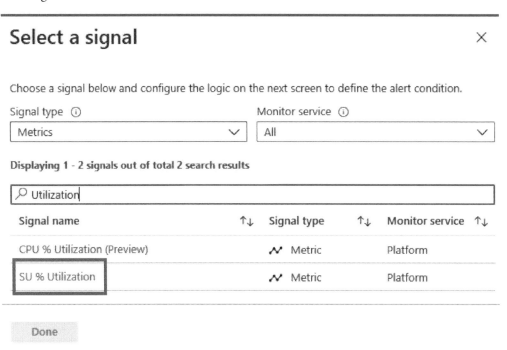

Figure 10.23 – Selecting the signal name to set up the alert

On the page that opens, you can configure the alert logic to set the threshold to 80%. This is shown in the following screenshot:

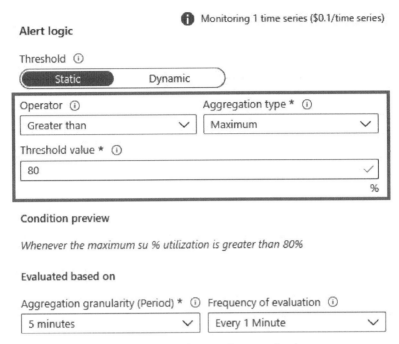

Figure 10.24 – Configuring the ASA alert logic

Once we have defined the alert logic, we have to define an *action group* (not shown in the preceding screenshot) to determine what should be done when the preceding condition matches. We could link it to an automation runbook, trigger an Azure function to perform an action, trigger a Webhook, or simply send notifications using emails.

The process of creating alerts is similar to other technologies such as Event Hubs, Synapse SQL, and more.

Next, let's look at the monitoring options available in Spark Streaming.

Monitoring in Spark Streaming

Azure Databricks Spark notebooks provide built-in graphs that continuously display metrics such as **Input rate**, **Processing rate**, **Batch Duration**, and more. Here is an example screenshot:

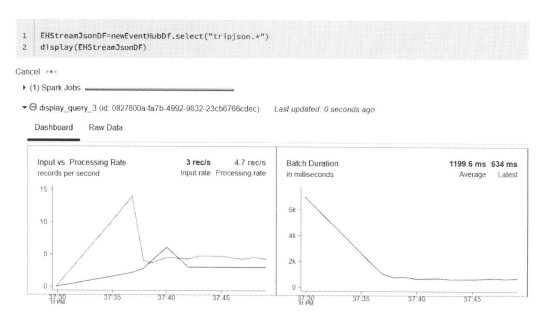

Figure 10.25 – Spark Streaming metrics from within a Spark notebook

These graphs can be used to monitor the progress of the Spark Streaming jobs.

That is how we can monitor streaming jobs. Let us next look at how to processing time series data.

Processing time series data

Time series data is nothing but data recorded continuously over time. Examples of time series data could include stock prices recorded over time, IoT sensor values, which show the health of machinery over time, and more. Time series data is mostly used to analyze historic trends and identify any abnormalities in data such as credit card fraud, real-time alerting, and forecasting. Time series data will always be appended heavily with very rare updates.

Time series data is a perfect candidate for real-time processing. The stream processing solutions that we discussed earlier in this chapter, in the *Developing a stream processing solution using ASA, Azure Databricks, and Azure Event Hubs* section, would perfectly work for time series data. Let's look at some of the important concepts of time series data.

Types of timestamps

The central aspect of any time series data is the time attribute. There are two types of time in time series data:

- **Event time**: This indicates the actual time when the event occurred.

- **Processing time**: The time when the event is processed by a data processing system.

It is important to consider the event time while processing events rather than the processing time, as the latter might be delayed due to processing speed, network delays, and other issues in the stream processing pipeline.

Windowed aggregates

Since time series events are unbounded events, or in other words, since they don't have a well-defined end time, it is necessary to process the events in small batches (that is, windows of time). There are different windowing mechanisms available such as tumbling windows, hopping windows, sliding windows, and more. We will explore these windowing techniques, in detail, in the next section.

Checkpointing or watermarking

Checkpointing or watermarking refers to the process of keeping track of the last event or timestamp that was processed by the stream processing system. This helps ensure that we start from the previously stopped place and don't miss out on processing any events after outages, system upgrades, processing delays, and more. We will learn how we can achieve this in the *Configuring checkpoints/watermarking during processing* section of this chapter.

Replaying data from a previous timestamp

We might be required to reprocess older events in the case of machine failures or errors in processing logic. In such cases, tools such as Event Hubs provide features that allow you to replay the events again from a previous offset location.

You can learn more about time series data at `https://docs.microsoft.com/en-us/azure/architecture/data-guide/scenarios/time-series`.

Next, let's take a look at each of the concepts, in detail, starting with the different windowed aggregate options.

Designing and creating windowed aggregates

In this section, let's explore the different windowed aggregates that are available in ASA. ASA supports the following five types of windows:

- Tumbling windows
- Hopping windows
- Sliding windows
- Session windows
- Snapshot windows

Let's look at each of them in detail. We will be using the following sample event schema in our examples.

```
eventSchema = StructType()
    .add("tripId", StringType())
    .add("createdAt", TimestampType())
    .add("startLocation", StringType())
    .add("endLocation", StringType())
    .add("distance", IntegerType())
    .add("fare", IntegerType())
```

Let us start with Tumbling windows.

Tumbling windows

Tumbling windows are non-overlapping time windows. All the windows are of the same size. Here is a depiction of how they look:

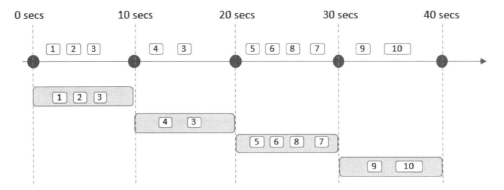

Figure 10.26 – An example of a tumbling window

Here is the syntax of how to use a tumbling window:

```
{TUMBLINGWINDOW | TUMBLING} ( timeunit  , windowsize,
[offsetsize] )
```

```
{TUMBLINGWINDOW | TUMBLING} ( Duration( timeunit  , windowsize
), [Offset(timeunit  , offsetsize)] )
```

Here is sample code to use a tumbling window in ASA. It calculates the number of trips grouped by `tripLocation`, in 10-second-wide tumbling windows:

```
SELECT System.Timestamp() AS WindowEnd, tripLocation, COUNT(*)
INTO [Output]
FROM [Input] TIMESTAMP BY createdAt
GROUP BY tripLocation, TumblingWindow(Duration(second, 10),
Offset(millisecond, -1))
```

Next, let's look at hopping windows.

Hopping windows

Hopping windows are just overlapping tumbling windows. Each window will have a fixed size overlap with the previous window. Here is a depiction of how it looks:

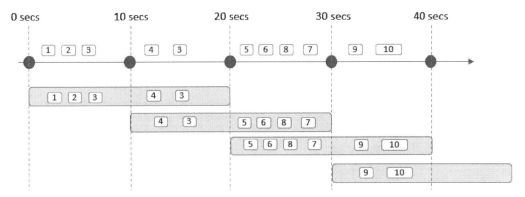

Figure 10.27 – An example of a hopping window

Here is the syntax for a hopping window:

```
{HOPPINGWINDOW | HOPPING} ( timeunit  , windowsize , hopsize,
[offsetsize] )
```

```
{HOPPINGWINDOW | HOPPING} ( Duration( timeunit  , windowsize
) , Hop (timeunit  , windowsize ), [Offset(timeunit  ,
offsetsize)])
```

If `windowsize` and `hopsize` have the same `timeunit`, you can use the first syntax.

Here is an example of a hopping window. Every 10 seconds, fetch the trip count per `tripLocation` for the last 20 seconds. Here, the window size is 20 seconds, and the hop size is 10 seconds:

```
SELECT System.Timestamp() AS WindowEnd, tripLocation, COUNT(*)
INTO [Output]
FROM [Input]  TIMESTAMP BY createdAt
GROUP BY tripLocation, HoppingWindow(Duration(second, 20),
Hop(second, 10), Offset(millisecond, -1))
```

Next, let's look at sliding windows.

Sliding windows

Sliding windows have a fixed size, but the window only moves forward when either event is added or removed. Otherwise, they don't emit any results:

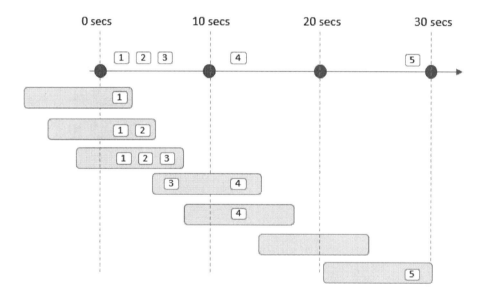

Figure 10.28 – An example of a sliding window

Here is the syntax for the sliding window:

```
{SLIDINGWINDOW | SLIDING} ( timeunit, windowsize )
{SLIDINGWINDOW | SLIDING} ( Duration( timeunit, windowsize ) )
```

Here is an example of a sliding window. For every 10 seconds, alert if a location appears more than 5 times:

```
SELECT System.Timestamp() AS WindowEnd, tripLocation, COUNT(*)
INTO [Output]
FROM [Input] TIMESTAMP BY createdAt
GROUP BY tripLocation, SlidingWindow(second, 10)
HAVING COUNT(*) > 5
```

Next, let's look at session windows.

Session windows

Session windows don't have fixed sizes. We need to specify a maximum window size and timeout duration for session windows. The session window tries to grab as many events as possible within the maximum window size. On the other hand, if there are no events, it waits for the timeout duration and closes the window. Here is a depiction of how it looks:

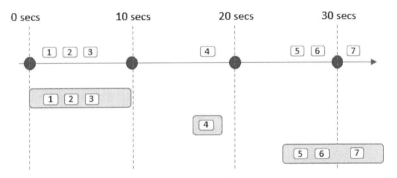

Figure 10.29 – An example of a session window

Here is the syntax for the session window:

```
{SESSIONWINDOW | SESSION} (timeunit, timeoutSize,
maxDurationSize) [OVER (PARTITION BY partitionKey)]
{SESSIONWINDOW | SESSION} (Timeout(timeunit , timeoutSize),
MaxDuration(timeunit, maxDurationSize)) [OVER (PARTITION BY
partitionKey)]
```

Here is an example of a session window. Find the number of trips that occur within 5 seconds of each other:

```
SELECT System.Timestamp() AS WindowEnd, tripId, COUNT(*)
INTO [Output]
```

```
FROM [Input] TIMESTAMP BY createdAt
GROUP BY tripId, SessionWindow(second, 5, 10)
```

Next, let's take a look at snapshot windows.

Snapshot windows

A snapshot window is not really a windowing technique. It is simply used to get a snapshot of the events at a particular time:

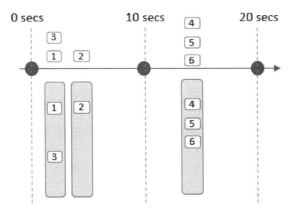

Figure 10.30 – An example of a snapshot window

Here is how we can use a snapshot window:

```
SELECT tripId, COUNT(*)
INTO [Output]
FROM [Input] TIMESTAMP BY createdAt
GROUP BY tripId, System.Timestamp()
```

These are all the windowing options that we have in ASA. You can learn more about the ASA windowing functions at https://docs.microsoft.com/en-us/azure/stream-analytics/stream-analytics-window-functions.

The next important concept for handling time series data is checkpointing or watermarking. Let's dive into that topic next.

Configuring checkpoints/watermarking during processing

Let's look at the checkpointing options available in ASA, Event Hubs, and Spark.

Checkpointing in ASA

ASA does internal checkpointing periodically. Users do not need to do explicit checkpointing. The checkpointing process is used for job recoveries during system upgrades, job retries, node failures, and more.

During node failures or OS upgrades, ASA automatically restores the failed node state on a new node and continues processing.

> **Note**
>
> During ASA service upgrades (not OS upgrades), the checkpoints are not maintained, and the stream corresponding to the downtime needs to be replayed.

Next, let's look at how to checkpoint in Event Hubs.

Checkpointing in Event Hubs

Checkpointing or watermarking in Event Hubs refers to the process of marking the offset within a stream or partition to indicate the point up to where the processing is complete. Checkpointing in Event Hubs is the responsibility of the event consumer process. Checkpointing is a relatively expensive operation, so it is usually better to checkpoint after a batch of event processing. The main idea of checkpointing is to have a restart point in the event that the event hub fails or undergoes service upgrades.

Here is sample code of how to perform checkpointing in Event Hubs using the `BlobCheckpoint` store. All the entries within < > are user-provided values:

```
Import asyncio
from azure.eventhub.aio import EventHubConsumerClient
from azure.eventhub.extensions.checkpointstoreblobaio import
BlobCheckpointStore
async def on_event(partition_context, event):
    # Process the event
    # Checkpoint after processing
    await partition_context.update_checkpoint(event)
async def main():
    storeChkPoint = BlobCheckpointStore.from_connection_string(
        <STORE_CONN_STRING>,
        <STORE_CONTAINER_NAME>
    )
```

```
    ehClient = EventHubConsumerClient.from_connection_string(
        <EVENTHUB_CONN_STRING>,
        <CONSUMER_GROUP_NAME>,
        eventhub_name=<EVENTHUB_NAME>,
        checkpoint_store= storeChkPoint
    )
    async with ehClient:
        await ehClient.receive(on_event)
if __name__ == '__main__':
    loop = asyncio.get_event_loop()
    loop.run_until_complete(main())
```

Next, let's look at checkpointing in Spark.

Checkpointing in Spark

The Structured Streaming feature of Spark delivers end-to-end exactly-once semantics. In other words, it ensures that an event is delivered exactly once. Spark uses checkpointing and write-ahead logs to accomplish this. In our Structured Streaming example earlier, we learned how to configure the checkpointing location in the Spark queries. Here is another simple example:

```
EHStreamJsonDF.writeStream.format("delta")\
.outputMode("append")\
.option("checkpointLocation", "dbfs:/
TripsCheckpointLocation/")\
.start("dbfs:/TripsEventHubDelta")
```

Spark Structured Streaming takes care of checkpointing internally. This is so that the user does not need to worry about manually checkpointing the input stream.

Now that we have learned how to checkpoint data, let's look at how to replay old data in the case of failures, restarts, upgrades, and more.

Replaying archived stream data

Event Hubs stores up to 7 days of data, which can be replayed using the EventHub consumer client libraries. Here is a simple Python example:

```
Consumer_client = EventHubConsumerClient.from_connection_
string(
```

```
    conn_str=CONNECTION_STR,
    consumer_group='$Default',
    eventhub_name=EVENTHUB_NAME,
)
consumer_client.receive(
    on_event=on_event,
    partition_id="0",
    starting_position="-1" # "-1" is the start of the
partition.
)
```

You can specify offsets or timestamps for the starting_position value.

You can learn more about the Python EventHub APIs at https://azuresdkdocs.
blob.core.windows.net/$web/python/azure-eventhub/latest/azure.
eventhub.html.

Let's take a look at some of the common data transformations that are possible using
streaming analytics.

Transformations using streaming analytics

One of the common themes that you might notice in streaming queries is that if there
is any kind of transformation involved, there will always be windowed aggregation that
has to be specified. Let's take the example of counting the number of distinct entries in
a time frame.

The COUNT and DISTINCT transformations

This type of transformation can be used to count the number of distinct events that have
occurred in a time window. Here is an example to count the number of unique trips in the
last 10 seconds:

```
SELECT
    COUNT(DISTINCT tripId) AS TripCount,
    System.TIMESTAMP() AS Time
INTO [Output]
FROM [Input] TIMESTAMP BY createdAt
GROUP BY TumblingWindow(second, 10)
```

Next, let's look at an example where we can cast the type of input in a different format.

CAST transformations

The CAST transformation can be used to convert the data type on the fly. Here is an example to convert the fare into a FLOAT and calculate the total fare every 10 minutes:

```
SELECT tripId, SUM(CAST(fare AS FLOAT)) AS TenSecondFares
INTO [Output]
FROM [Input] TIMESTAMP BY createdAt
GROUP BY tripId, TumblingWindow(second, 10)
```

Next, let's look at how to compare entries using LIKE.

LIKE transformations

We can use this transformation to perform string matching using patterns. In the following example, we try to match all the startLocation from San Francisco:

```
SELECT *
INTO [Output]
FROM [Input] TIMESTAMP BY timestamp
WHERE startLocation LIKE 'S%F'
```

These are just a few sample transformations. You can find a more detailed list at https://docs.microsoft.com/en-us/azure/stream-analytics/ stream-analytics-stream-analytics-query-patterns.

Next, let's look at how to handle schema drifts in a streaming solution.

Handling schema drifts

A schema drift refers to the changes in schema over time due to changes happening in the event sources. This could be due to newer columns or fields getting older, columns getting deleted, and more.

Handling schema drifts using Event Hubs

If an event publisher needs to share schema details with the consumer, they have to serialize the schema along with the data, using formats such as Apache Avro, and send it across Event Hubs. Here, the schema has to be sent with every event, which is not a very efficient approach.

If you are dealing with statically defined schemas on the consumer side, any schema changes on the producer side would spell trouble.

Event Hubs provides a feature called **Azure Schema Registry** to handle schema evolution and schema drift. It provides a central repository to share the schemas between event publishers and consumers. Let's examine how to create and use Azure Schema Registry.

Registering a schema with schema registry

Here is an example of how to register a schema:

1. Import the necessary libraries:

```
From azure.schemaregistry import SchemaRegistryClient
from azure.identity import DefaultAzureCredential
```

2. Define your schema:

```
sampleSchema = """
{"namespace": "com.azure.sampleschema.avro",
 "type": "record",
 "name": "Trip",
 "fields": [
     {"name": "tripId", "type": "string"},
     {"name": "startLocation", "type": "string"},
     {"name": "endLocation", "type": "string"}
 ]
}"""
```

3. Create the Schema Registry client:

```
azureCredential = DefaultAzureCredential()
schema_registry_client = SchemaRegistryClient(
fully_qualified_namespace=<SCHEMA-NAMESPACE>.servicebus.
windows.net,
credential=azureCredential)
```

4. Register the schema:

```
With schema_registry_client:
    schema_properties = schema_registry_client.register_
schema(
```

```
        <SCHEMA_GROUPNAME>,
        <SCHEMA_NAME>,
        sampleSchema,
        "Avro")
```

5. Get the schema ID:

```
        schema_id = schema_properties.id
```

Next, let's see how to retrieve the schema.

Retrieving a schema from Schema Registry

Here are the high-level steps to retrieve the schema:

1. Import the necessary libraries:

```
from azure.identity import DefaultAzureCredential
from azure.schemaregistry import SchemaRegistryClient
```

2. Create the Schema Registry client:

```
azureCredential = DefaultAzureCredential()
schema_registry_client = SchemaRegistryClient(
fully_qualified_namespace=<SCHEMA-NAMESPACE>.servicebus.
windows.net,
credential=azureCredential)
```

3. Retrieve the schema:

```
With schema_registry_client:
    schema = schema_registry_client.get_schema(schema_id)
    definition = schema.definition
    properties = schema.properties
```

Once you have the schema, you can define your events and start reading the data in the correct format.

You can learn more about Event Hubs Schema Registry at https://docs.microsoft.com/en-us/azure/event-hubs/schema-registry-overview.

Next, let's look at how to handle schema drifts in Spark.

Handling schema drifts in Spark

Azure Databricks Delta Lake provides a feature called Schema Evolution to take care of schema changes over time. It automatically adapts to the new schema when new columns get added. Schema Evolution can be enabled by adding the `.option('mergeSchema', 'true')` option to the `writeStream` streaming command.

Here is a simple example:

```
StreamDF.writeStream.format("delta")\
.option("mergeSchema", "true") \
.outputMode("append")\
.option("checkpointLocation", "dbfs:/CheckpointLocation/")\
.start("dbfs:/StreamData")
```

Once the `mergeSchema` option has been specified, Spark takes care of handling newer columns in the stream automatically.

Next, let's look at the partitioning of events in Event Hubs.

Processing across partitions

Before we look at how to process data across partitions, first, let's understand partitions.

What are partitions?

Event Hubs can distribute incoming events into multiple streams so that they can be accessed, in parallel, by the consumers. These parallel streams are called partitions. Each partition stores the actual event data and metadata of the event such as its offset in the partition, its server-side timestamp when the event was accepted, its number in the stream sequence, and more. Partitioning helps in scaling real-time processing, as it increases the parallelism by providing multiple input streams for downstream processing engines. Additionally, it improves availability by redirecting the events to other healthy partitions if some of the partitions fail.

You can learn more about Event Hubs partitions at `https://docs.microsoft.com/en-in/azure/event-hubs/event-hubs-scalability`.

Now, let's look at how to send data across partitions and how to process data across partitions.

Processing data across partitions

Client libraries to access Event Hubs are available in different languages such as C#, Python, Java, and more. In this section, we will use the Python library for our examples.

Event Hubs provides the `EventHubConsumerClient` class as part of the Python client libraries to consume the data from the event hub. `EventHubConsumerClient` can be used to read events from all the partitions with load balancing and checkpointing. We have already used this class in the checkpointing example in the *Checkpointing in Event Hubs* section. The same example will work for reading across partitions. Here, we will provide the important steps again for convenience.

Note that all the entries within the angular brackets, < >, are user-provided values:

1. Instantiate the checkpoint store:

```
storeChkPoint = BlobCheckpointStore.from_connection_
string(
        <STORE_CONN_STRING>,
        <STORE_CONTAINER_NAME>
    )
```

2. Instantiate the `EventHubConsumerClient` class:

```
ehClient = EventHubConsumerClient.from_connection_string(
        <EVENTHUB_CONN_STRING>,
        <CONSUMER_GROUP_NAME>,
        eventhub_name=<EVENTHUB_NAME>,
        checkpoint_store= storeChkPoint # This enables
load balancing across partitions
    )
```

3. Define an `on_event` method to process the event when it arrives:

```
Def on_event(partition_context, event):
    # Process the event
    partition_context.update_checkpoint(event)
```

4. Call the `on_event` method when an event arrives:

```
With ehClient:
    ehClient.receive(
        on_event=on_event,
        starting_position="-1",   # To start from the
beginning of the partition.
    )
```

When we don't specify a specific partition while instantiating the `EventHubConsumerClient` class, it will automatically read from across all the partitions in the specified consumer group. You can learn more about the Event Hubs Python libraries at `https://azuresdkdocs.blob.core.windows.net/$web/python/azure-eventhub/latest/azure.eventhub.html`.

Next, let's look at the details of how to process the data within a partition.

Processing within one partition

Similar to the previous example, where we learned how to process across partitions, we can use the `EventHubConsumerClient` class to process data within single partitions, too. All we have to do is specify the partition ID in the `client.receive` call, as demonstrated in the following code snippet. The rest of the code will remain the same as the previous example:

```
With client:
    client.receive(
        on_event=on_event,
        partition_id='0', # To read only partition 0
    )
```

This is how we can programmatically process the data from specific Event Hubs partitions.

Next, let's look at how to scale resources for stream processing.

Scaling resources

Let's look at how to scale resources in Event Hubs, ASA, and Azure Databricks Spark.

Scaling in Event Hubs

There are two ways in which Event Hubs supports scaling:

- **Partitioning**: We have already learned how partitioning can help scale our Event Hubs instance by increasing the parallelism with which the event consumers can process data. Partitioning helps reduce contention if there are too many producers and consumers, which, in turn, makes it more efficient.

- **Auto-inflate**: This is an automatic scale-up feature of Event Hubs. As the usage increases, EventHub adds more throughput units to your Event Hubs instance, thereby increasing its capacity. You can enable this feature if you have already saturated your quota using the partitioning technique that we explored earlier, in the *Processing across partitions* section.

Next, let's explore the concept of throughput units.

What are throughput units?

Throughput units are units of capacity that can be purchased in Event Hubs. A single throughput unit allows the following:

- Ingress of up to 1 MB per second or 1,000 events per second

- Egress of up to 2 MB per second or 4,096 events per second

> **Note**
> In the Event Hubs Premium tier, the throughput units are called processing units.

Here is how you can enable the auto-inflate feature in Event Hubs:

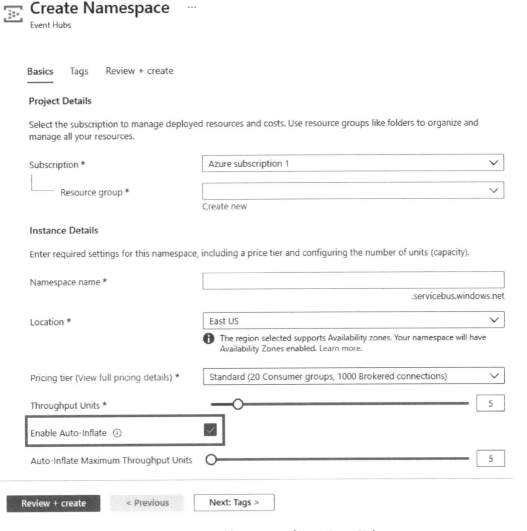

Figure 10.31 – Enabling Auto-inflate in Event Hubs

You can learn more about Event Hubs' scalability at `https://docs.microsoft.com/en-in/azure/event-hubs/event-hubs-scalability`.

Next, let's look at how to scale the processing engine, ASA.

Scaling in ASA

You can scale your ASA clusters directly from the Azure portal. Just click on the **Scale** tab on the ASA home page, and configure the **Streaming units** toggle, as shown in the following screenshot:

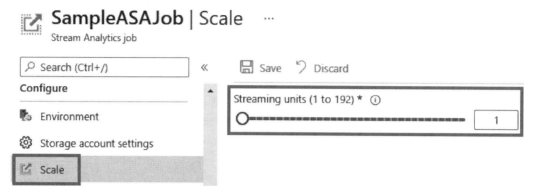

Figure 10.32 – Scaling an ASA job

Streaming units are a measure of the streaming capacity. Scaling units doesn't have an absolute capacity configuration like in the case of Event Hubs throughput units. In general, the higher the number of streaming units, the higher the capacity. You will have to do some trial-and-error runs to identify the sweet spot.

> **Tip**
>
> For ASA queries that are not using the PARTITION BY transformation, the recommendation is to start with six SUs and then modify the numbers iteratively by running your jobs and monitoring the SU% utilization metric.

You can learn about streaming unit optimization at https://docs.microsoft.com/en-us/azure/stream-analytics/stream-analytics-streaming-unit-consumption.

You can learn more about scaling ASA at https://docs.microsoft.com/en-us/azure/stream-analytics/scale-cluster.

ASA doesn't have an internal autoscale mechanism. However, you can simulate one using services such as **Azure Automation**. This is an external service that can be used to monitor the ASA metrics and trigger a scale up or scale down externally.

If you are interested in learning more, you can refer to `https://docs.microsoft.com/en-us/azure/stream-analytics/stream-analytics-autoscale`.

Next, let's look at how to scale Azure Databricks Spark.

Scaling in Azure Databricks Spark Streaming

We learned how to configure autoscaling for Azure Databricks in *Chapter 9*, *Designing and Developing a Batch Processing Solution*, in the *Scaling resources* section. Please refer to that section to refresh your memory regarding how to configure autoscaling for Spark.

Next, let's look at how to handle interruptions.

Handling interruptions

Interruptions to stream processing might occur due to various reasons such as network connectivity issues, background service upgrades, intermittent bugs, and more. Event Hubs and ASA provide options to handle such interruptions natively using the concept of Azure **Availability zones**. Availability zones are physically isolated locations in Azure that help applications become resilient to local failures and outages. Azure lists the regions that are paired together to form availability zones.

Services that support availability zones deploy their applications to all the locations within the availability zone to improve fault tolerance. Additionally, they ensure that service upgrades are always done one after the other for the availability zone locations. Therefore, they ensure that at no point will all the locations suffer an outage due to service upgrade bugs. Both Event Hubs and ASA support availability zones. Let's look at how to enable this feature for both Event Hubs and ASA.

Handling interruptions in Event Hubs

When Event Hubs is deployed to regions that are part of the availability zones, both the metadata and events are replicated to all the locations in that availability zone. In order to use availability zones, all you need to do is to select a region that supports the availability zone for the **Location** field, as shown in the following screenshot:

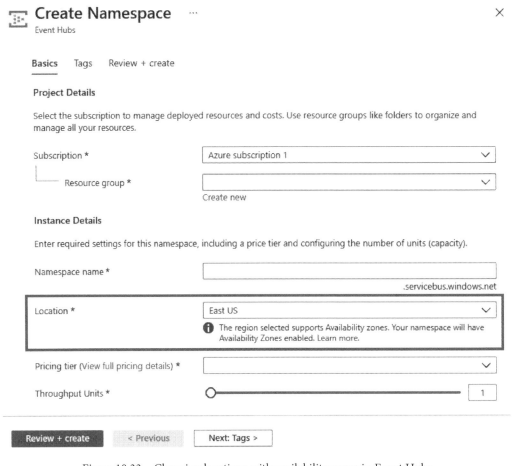

Figure 10.33 – Choosing locations with availability zones in Event Hubs

Once you have chosen the availability zone-supported region and clicked on **Review + create**, the Event Hubs instance is created in all the locations of the availability zone.

Here are a few other points to make the Event Hubs instance more resilient:

- Try to build back off and retry logic into your applications. This is so that transient errors can be caught, and the stream processing can be retried. If your application is built using the Event Hubs SDKs, then the retry logic is already built in.

- If the application doesn't need strictly ordered messages, you can send the events without specifying a partition. This will ensure that Event Hubs load balances the events across all partitions. If a partition fails, the Event Hubs instance will distribute the event to other partitions, thereby improving availability.

You can learn more about Event Hubs availability zones at `https://docs. microsoft.com/en-in/azure/event-hubs/event-hubs-geo-dr`.

Next, let's look at how to handle interruptions in ASA.

Handling interruptions in ASA

Similar to Event Hubs, ASA also deploys to availability zones (or Azure-paired regions) by default. Additionally, ASA ensures that service updates always happen in separate batches between the locations of the availability zones. There is no configuration required from the users.

> **Note**
> At the time of writing, the Central India region does not have a paired region for ASA.

You can learn more about availability zones and interruption handling in ASA at `https://docs.microsoft.com/en-us/azure/stream-analytics/ stream-analytics-job-reliability`.

Next, let's look at how to design and configure exception handling.

Designing and configuring exception handling

Event Hubs' exceptions provide very clear information regarding the reason for errors. All EventHub issues throw an `EventHubsException` exception object.

The `EventHubsException` exception object contains the following information:

- `IsTransient`: This indicates whether the exceptions can be retried.
- `Reason`: This indicates the actual reason for the exception. Some example reasons could include timeouts, exceeding quota limits, exceeding message sizes, client connection disconnects, and more.

Here is a simple example of how to catch exceptions in .NET:

```
try
{
    // Process Events
}
catch (EventHubsException ex) where
(ex.Reason == EventHubsException.FailureReason.
MessageSizeExceeded)
{
    // Take action for the oversize messages
}
```

You can learn more about exception handling at `https://docs.microsoft.com/en-us/azure/event-hubs/exceptions-dotnet`.

Next, let's look at upserting data using Synapse Analytics.

Upserting data

Upserting refers to the `INSERT` or `UPDATE` activity in a database or any analytical data store that supports it. We have already seen `UPSERT` as part of the batch activity, in the *Upserting data* section of *Chapter 9, Designing and Developing a Batch Processing Solution*. ASA supports `UPSERT` with CosmosDB. **CosmosDB** is a fully managed, globally distributed No-SQL database. We will learn more about CosmosDB in *Chapter 14, Optimizing and Troubleshooting Data Storage and Data Processing*, in the *Implementing HTAP using Synapse Link and CosmosDB* section.

ASA has two different behaviors based on the compatibility level that is set. ASA supports three different compatibility levels. You can think of compatibility levels as API versions. As and when ASA evolved, the compatibility levels increased. **1.0** was the first compatibility version, and **1.2** is the latest compatibility version. The main change in version **1.2** is the support for the AMQP messaging protocol.

You can set the compatibility level, as shown in the following screenshot:

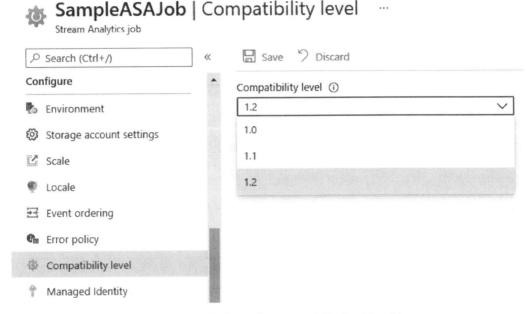

Figure 10.34 – Updating the compatibility level in ASA

With the compatibility levels of **1.0** and **1.1**, ASA does a property level insert or update within the document. It enables partial updates to the document as a PATCH operation.

With a compatibility level of **1.2** onward, ASA does an insert or replace document operation. First, ASA does an insert. If that fails due to a document ID conflict, then it does an update.

> **Note**
>
> Upserts work in CosmosDB when the document ID is set. If it has not been set, the update scenarios will throw an error.

You can learn more about **ASA – CosmosDB Upserts** at https://docs.microsoft.com/en-us/azure/stream-analytics/stream-analytics-documentdb-output#upserts-from-stream-analytics.

Next, let's look at how to create tests for data pipelines.

Designing and creating tests for data pipelines

This section has already been covered in *Chapter 9, Designing and Developing a Batch Processing Solution*, in the *Designing and creating tests for data pipelines* section. Please refer to that section for details.

Optimizing pipelines for analytical or transactional purposes

We will be covering this topic in *Chapter 14, Optimizing and Troubleshooting Data Storage and Data Processing*, under the *Optimizing pipelines for analytical or transactional purposes* section, as that entire chapter deals with optimizations.

Summary

That brings us to the end of this chapter. This is one of the important chapters both from a syllabus perspective and a data engineering perspective. Batch and streaming solutions are fundamental to building a good big data processing system.

So, let's recap what we learned in this chapter. We started with designs for streaming systems using Event Hubs, ASA, and Spark Streaming. We learned how to monitor such systems using the monitoring options available within each of those services. Then, we learned about time series data and important concepts such as windowed aggregates, checkpointing, replaying archived data, handling schema drifts, how to scale using partitions, and adding processing units. Additionally, we explored the upsert feature, and towards the end, we learned about error handling and interruption handling.

You should now be comfortable with creating streaming solutions in Azure. As always, please go through the follow-up links that have been provided to learn more, and try the examples yourself to understand the nitty-gritty details of these technologies.

In the next chapter, we will learn how to manage batches and pipelines.

11

Managing Batches and Pipelines

Welcome to Chapter 11! This is one of the smaller and easier chapters and will be a breeze to read through. In this chapter, we will be focusing on four broad categories: triggering Batch jobs, handling failures in Batch jobs, managing pipelines, and configuring version control for our pipelines. Once you have completed this chapter, you should be able to comfortably set up and manage Batch pipelines using Azure Batch, **Azure Data Factory** (**ADF**), or Synapse pipelines.

In this chapter, we will cover the following topics:

- Triggering Batches

- Handling failed Batch loads

- Validating Batch loads

- Managing data pipelines in Data Factory/Synapse pipelines

- Scheduling data pipelines in Data Factory/Synapse pipelines

- Managing Spark jobs in a pipeline

- Implementing version control for pipeline artifacts

Technical requirements

For this chapter, you will need the following:

- An Azure account (free or paid)

- An active Synapse workspace

- An active Azure Data Factory workspace

Let's get started!

Triggering batches

We learned about Azure Batch in *Chapter 9, Designing and Developing a Batch Processing Solution*, in the *Introducing Azure Batch* section. In this section, we will learn how to trigger those Batch jobs using **Azure Functions**. Azure Functions is a serverless service provided by Azure that helps build cloud applications with minimal code, without you having to worry about hosting and maintaining the technology that runs the code. Azure takes care of all the hosting complexities such as deployments, upgrades, security patches, scaling, and more. Even though the name says serverless, it has servers running in the background. It just means that you don't have to maintain those servers – Azure does it for you.

For our requirement of triggering a Batch job, we will be using the **Trigger** functionality of Azure Functions. A Trigger defines when and how to invoke an Azure function. Azure Functions supports a wide variety of triggers, such as timer trigger, HTTP trigger, Azure Blob trigger, Azure EventHub trigger, and so on.

> **Note**
>
> An Azure function can have only one trigger associated with it. If you need multiple ways to trigger a function, you will have to define different functions for it.

For our example, we will define a blob trigger and define an Azure function that can call our Batch job:

1. From the Azure portal, search for *Function App* and create a new function app. Once created, click on the **+ Create** button to create a new function, as shown in the following screenshot:

Figure 11.1 – Creating a new Azure Function App

2. The **Create function** screen will look as shown in the following image. Select the **Azure Blob Storage trigger** option from the **Select a template** section and configure the required details, such as the function name (**New Function**), **Path**, and so on:

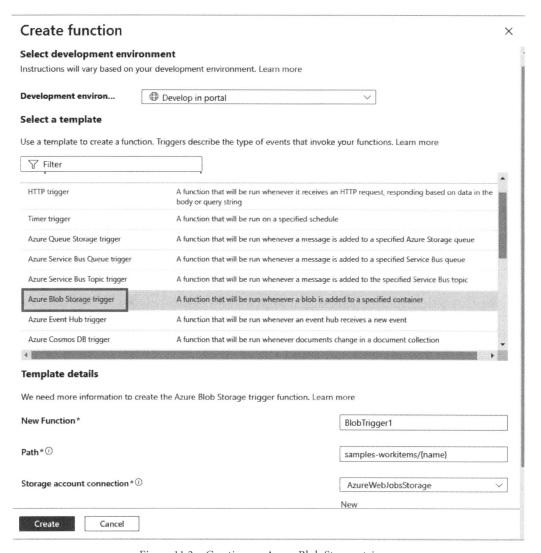

Figure 11.2 – Creating an Azure Blob Storage trigger

3. Click on the **Create** button to create the function that you will use as the trigger.

4. Now that we have the trigger, we need to define what to do when the trigger fires. Go to the **Code + Test** tab and add your business logic there. The business logic code could be in C#, Java, Python, or PowerShell:

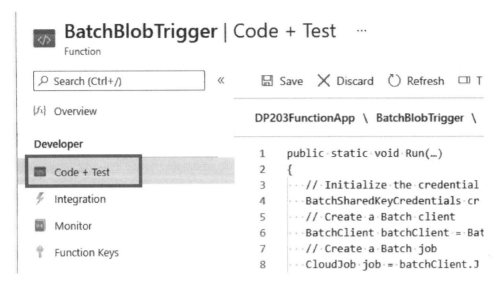

Figure 11.3 – Entering code for the Trigger function

In our example, we will use snippets of C# code to demonstrate the flow. We must add the business logic inside a Run() method. Here is a sample code reference block:

```
public static void Run(…)
{
    // Initialize the credentials
    BatchSharedKeyCredentials cred = new
BatchSharedKeyCredentials(…);
    // Create a Batch client
    BatchClient batchClient = BatchClient.Open(cred))
    // Create a Batch job
    CloudJob job = batchClient.JobOperations.GetJob(<JOB_ID>);
    // Add your business logic
    // Add tasks to the job.
    CloudTask task = new CloudTask(<TASK_ID>, <COMMAND>);
    batchClient.JobOperations.AddTask(<JOB_ID>, task);
}
```

Now, every time we add or update a file in the blob storage in the **Path** field, the preceding function will get called, which will start a Batch job.

You can refer to the complete sample C# job by going to this book's GitHub repository: `https://github.com/Azure-Samples/batch-functions-tutorial`.

Next, let's learn how to handle failed jobs in Azure Batch.

Handling failed Batch loads

An Azure Batch job can fail due to four types of errors:

- Pool errors
- Node errors
- Job errors
- Task errors

Let's look at some of the common errors in each group and ways to handle them.

Pool errors

Pool errors occur mostly due to infrastructure issues, quota issues, or timeout issues. Here are some sample pool errors:

- **Insufficient quota**: If there is not enough of a quota for your Batch account, pool creation could fail. The mitigation is to request an increase in quota. You can check the quota limits here: `https://docs.microsoft.com/en-us/azure/batch/batch-quota-limit`.

- **Insufficient resources in your VNet**: If your **virtual network** (**VNet**) doesn't have enough resources, such as available IP addresses, **Network Security Groups** (**NSGs**), VMs, and so on, the pool creation process may fail. The mitigation is to look for these errors and request higher resource allocation or move to a different VNet that has enough capacity.

- **Short timeouts**: Some of the operations, such as pool resizing, may take more than 15 minutes, which is the default that's set by Azure Batch. In such cases, increasing your timeout using the following API could help:

```
POST {batchUrl}/pools?timeout={timeout}&api-
version=2021-06-01.14.0
```

Next, let's look at some of the common node errors.

Node errors

Node errors could be due to hardware issues or due to failures in the job setup activities, such as the startup scripts, download scripts, and so on. Here are some sample node errors:

- **Start task failures**: If you have configured a start task for your job and it fails, then the node becomes unusable. You can look for the errors in the `TaskExecutionResult` and `TaskFailureInformation` fields in the response of the following API:

  ```
  GET {batchUrl}/pools/{poolId}/nodes/{nodeId}?api-
  version=2021-06-01.14.0
  ```

  Once you have identified the error, you will have to take corrective actions, such as fixing the user's start scripts.

- **Application download failures**: If Batch is unable to download your application package, then it will throw a node error. The `ComputeNodeError` property in the response of the previously shown GET API will list such application download failures. Check for file permissions, correct locations, and so on to fix such issues.

- **Nodes going into a bad state**: This could happen due to infrastructure failures, network issues, bad OS/security upgrades, the disk being full, and so on.

  In such cases, the `ComputeNodeError` property in the response of the GET API will indicate the error. Based on the error, you will have to take corrective actions, such as spinning up new nodes, fixing network issues, cleaning up the disk, and so on.

You can learn more about handling pool and node errors here: `https://docs.microsoft.com/en-us/azure/batch/batch-pool-node-error-checking`.

Next, let's look at job errors.

Job errors

Jobs can fail due to multiple reasons. Let's look at a few of them:

- Job constraints such as setting `maxWallClockTime` can result in job failures.
- Errors in job preparation or job release tasks. These are tasks that are run before the first task and after the last task of the job. Any failures in these can cause the job to fail.

In all such cases, the `JobExecutionInformation` and `JobSchedulingError` properties in the response of the following API will contain the error's details:

```
GET {batchUrl}/jobs/{jobId}?api-version=2021-06-01.14.0
```

Based on the actual error that's identified by the preceding API response, we should be able to fix the issue. Now, let's look at task errors.

Task errors

Task failures can happen in the following cases:

- The `tasks` command fails and returns a non-zero exit code.

- Resource file download issues, such as if the task is unable to download the resource files from the source folders.

- Output files upload issues, such as if the task is unable to upload the output file to the destination folders.

In all such cases, you can check the `TaskExecutionInformation` property in the response of the following REST API to get the details of the task error:

```
GET {batchUrl}/jobs/{jobId}/tasks/{taskId}?api-
version=2021-06-01.14.0
```

For the file output issues, the Batch tasks also write the `Fileuploadout.txt` and `fileuploaderr.txt` files on the node. These files can also provide valuable information about the errors.

You can learn more about handling job and task errors here: `https://docs.microsoft.com/en-us/azure/batch/batch-job-task-error-checking`.

In the next section, we will look at the options that are available for validating Azure Batch loads.

Validating Batch loads

Batch jobs are usually run as part of **Azure Data Factory** (**ADF**). ADF provides functionalities for validating the outcome of jobs. Let's learn how to use the Validation activity in ADF to check the correctness of Batch loads:

1. The **Validation** activity of ADF can be used to check for a file's existence before proceeding with the rest of the activities in the pipeline. The validation pipeline will look similar to the following:

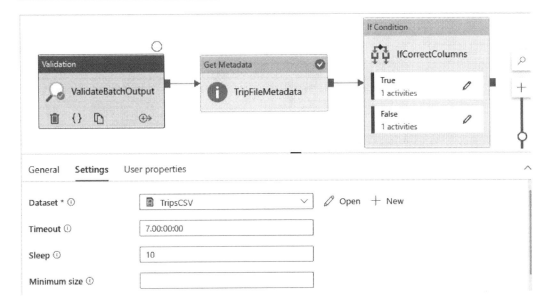

Figure 11.4 – ADF Validation activity

2. Once we have validated that the files exist, we can use the **Get Metadata** activity to get more information about the output files. In the following screenshot, we output **Column count**, which we'll check later using an **If Condition** activity to decide if the output files are any good:

Figure 11.5 – Configuring the Get Metadata activity to publish the Column count

3. Once we get the metadata, we must use the **If Condition** activity to decide on if we want to continue processing the pipeline or not based on the metadata from the previous stage:

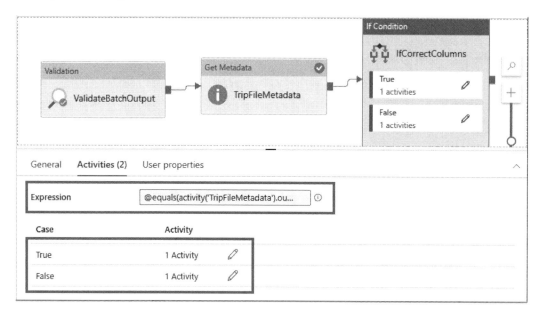

Figure 11.6 – Using the metadata from the Get Metadata activity to make a decision

The condition could be something as follows, where we check if the number of columns is equal to the expected column count. In this example, I'm expecting five columns:

```
@equals(activity('TripFileMetadata').output.columnCount, 5)
```

You can perform similar validation checks using a combination of ADF activities for Batch and other technologies.

Now, let's learn how to schedule data pipelines in ADF and Synapse Pipelines.

Scheduling data pipelines in Data Factory/ Synapse pipelines

Scheduling pipelines refers to the process of defining when and how a pipeline needs to be started. The process is the same between ADF and Synapse pipelines. ADF and Synapse pipelines have a button named **Add Trigger** in the **Pipelines** tab that can be used to schedule the pipelines, as shown in the following screenshot:

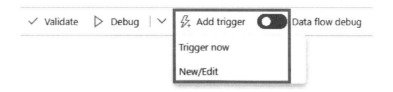

Figure 11.7 – Adding a trigger from ADF/Synapse pipelines

The following screenshot shows the details that are required to configure a **Schedule** trigger:

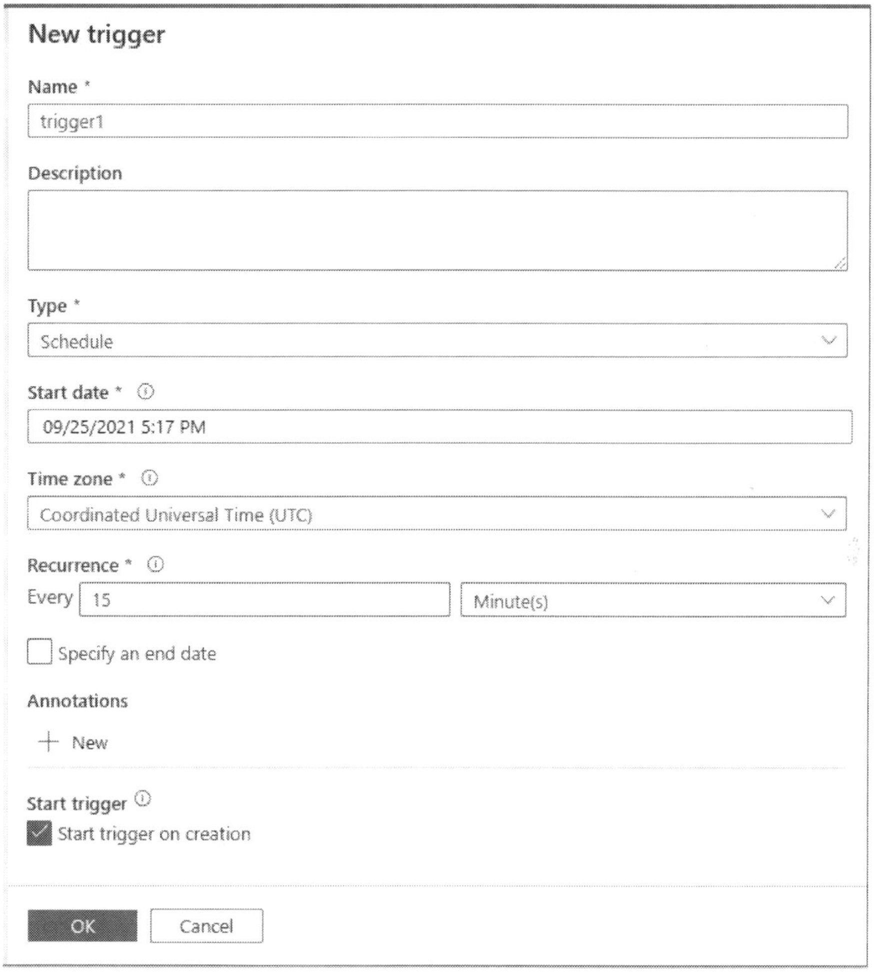

New trigger

Name *

trigger1

Description

Type *

Schedule

Start date * ⓘ

09/25/2021 5:17 PM

Time zone * ⓘ

Coordinated Universal Time (UTC)

Recurrence * ⓘ

Every 15

Minute(s)

☐ Specify an end date

Annotations

\+ New

Start trigger ⓘ

☑ Start trigger on creation

OK   Cancel

Figure 11.8 – Defining the trigger in ADF

ADF and Synapse pipeline services support four types of triggers:

- **Schedule trigger**: This triggers a pipeline once or regularly based on the wall clock time.

- **Tumbling window trigger**: This triggers a pipeline based on periodic intervals while maintaining state; that is, the trigger understands which window of data was processed last and restarts from there.

- **Event-based trigger**: This triggers a pipeline based on store events such as files being created in Blob or ADLS.

- **Custom trigger**: This triggers pipelines based on events from **Azure Event Grid**. ADF can listen to topics in Azure Event Grid and trigger pipelines based on certain messages or events occurring in the Event Grid topic.

Once the trigger has been set up, you can see the pipelines being triggered automatically from the **Monitoring** tab of ADF or Synapse pipelines.

You can learn more about triggers and scheduling pipelines here: `https://docs.microsoft.com/en-us/azure/data-factory/concepts-pipeline-execution-triggers`.

Now, let's learn to manage and monitor data pipelines in ADF and Synapse pipelines.

Managing data pipelines in Data Factory/ Synapse pipelines

ADF and Synapse pipelines provide two tabs called **Manage** and **Monitor**, which can help us manage and monitor the pipelines, respectively.

In the **Manage** tab, you can add, edit, and delete linked services, integration runtimes, triggers, configure Git, and more, as shown in the following screenshot:

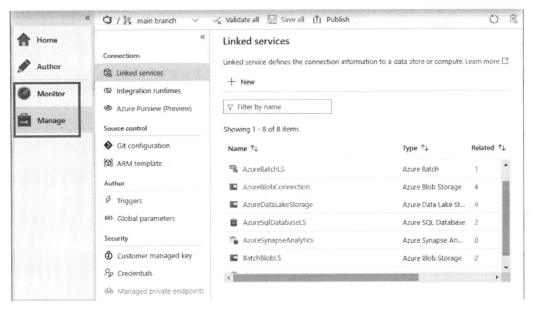

Figure 11.9 – The Manage screen of ADF

We have already learned about linked services throughout this book. Now, let's explore the topic of integration runtimes in ADF and Synapse pipelines.

Integration runtimes

An **integration runtime** (**IR**) refers to the compute infrastructure that's used by ADF and Synapse Pipelines to run data pipelines and data flows. These are the actual machines or VMs that run the job behind the scenes.

The IR takes care of running data flows, copying data across public and private networks, dispatching activities to services such as Azure HDInsight and Azure Databricks, and executing **SQL Server Integration Services** (**SSIS**).

You can create IRs from the **Manage** tab of ADF and Synapse pipelines by clicking on the **+ New** button, as shown in the following screenshot:

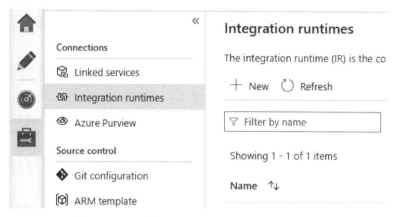

Figure 11.10 – Creating a new integration runtime

ADF provides support for three types of IRs:

- **Azure Integration Runtime**: This is the default option and supports connecting data stores and compute services across public endpoints. Use this option to copy data between Azure-hosted services. Azure IR also supports connecting data stores using private links.

- **Self-Hosted Integration Runtime**: Use this option when you need to copy data between on-premises clusters and Azure services. You will need machines or VMs on the on-premises private network to install a self-hosted IR.

- **Azure – SSIS Integration Runtime**: The SSIS IRs are used for SSIS lift and shift uses cases.

You can learn more about IRs here: `https://docs.microsoft.com/en-us/ azure/data-factory/create-azure-integration-runtime?tabs=data-factory`.

Next, let's look at the monitoring options in ADF.

ADF monitoring

Pipelines can be triggered manually or automatically (using triggers). Once they're triggered, we can monitor them from the **Monitor** tab, as shown in the following screenshot:

Figure 11.11 – Monitoring ADF pipelines

You can **Cancel** any in-progress runs and **Rerun** any failed pipelines from the **Monitor** tab. You can click on each of those runs to look at the details of each flow, as shown in the following screenshot. Click on the spectacles icon for statistics about the run, such as how many stages were there, how many lines were processed, how long each stage took, and so on:

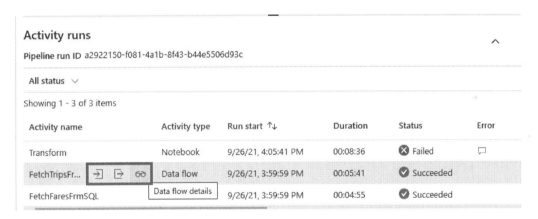

Figure 11.12 – Data flow details in the Activity runs tab

Synapse pipelines also provides similar **Manage** and **Monitor** screens, so we will not be repeating them here.

Next, let's learn how to manage Spark jobs in an ADF pipeline.

Managing Spark jobs in a pipeline

Managing Spark jobs in a pipeline involves two aspects:

- **Managing the attributes of the pipeline's runtime that launches the Spark activity**: Managing the Spark activity pipeline attributes is no different than managing any other activities in a pipeline. The **Managing** and **Monitoring** pages we saw in *Figure 11.9*, *Figure 11.11*, and *Figure 11.12* are the same for any Spark activity as well. You can use the options provided on these screens to manage your Spark activity.

- **Managing Spark jobs and configurations**: This involves understanding how Spark works, being able to tune the jobs, and so on. We have a complete chapter dedicated to optimizing Synapse SQL and Spark jobs towards the end of this book. You can refer to *Chapter 14, Optimizing and Troubleshooting Data Storage and Data Processing*, to learn more about managing and tuning Spark jobs.

In this section, we'll learn how to add an Apache Spark job (via HDInsight) to our pipeline so that you get an idea of the parameters that can be configured while setting up a Spark job using ADF and HDInsight. This is slightly different than adding Databricks Notebooks to the ADF pipeline. Here are the steps:

1. We must create a **Linked service** for an **HDInsight** cluster from the **Manage** tab of ADF. The following screenshot shows how to create this linked service. You can use **AutoResolveIntegrationRuntime** as your HDInsight cluster since they are also hosted on Azure. Specify the other details, such as an existing **Hdi Cluster** name or an **On-demand HDInsight** cluster, as well as the **Azure Storage linked service** name associated with the storage account for that HDI cluster to create the linked service:

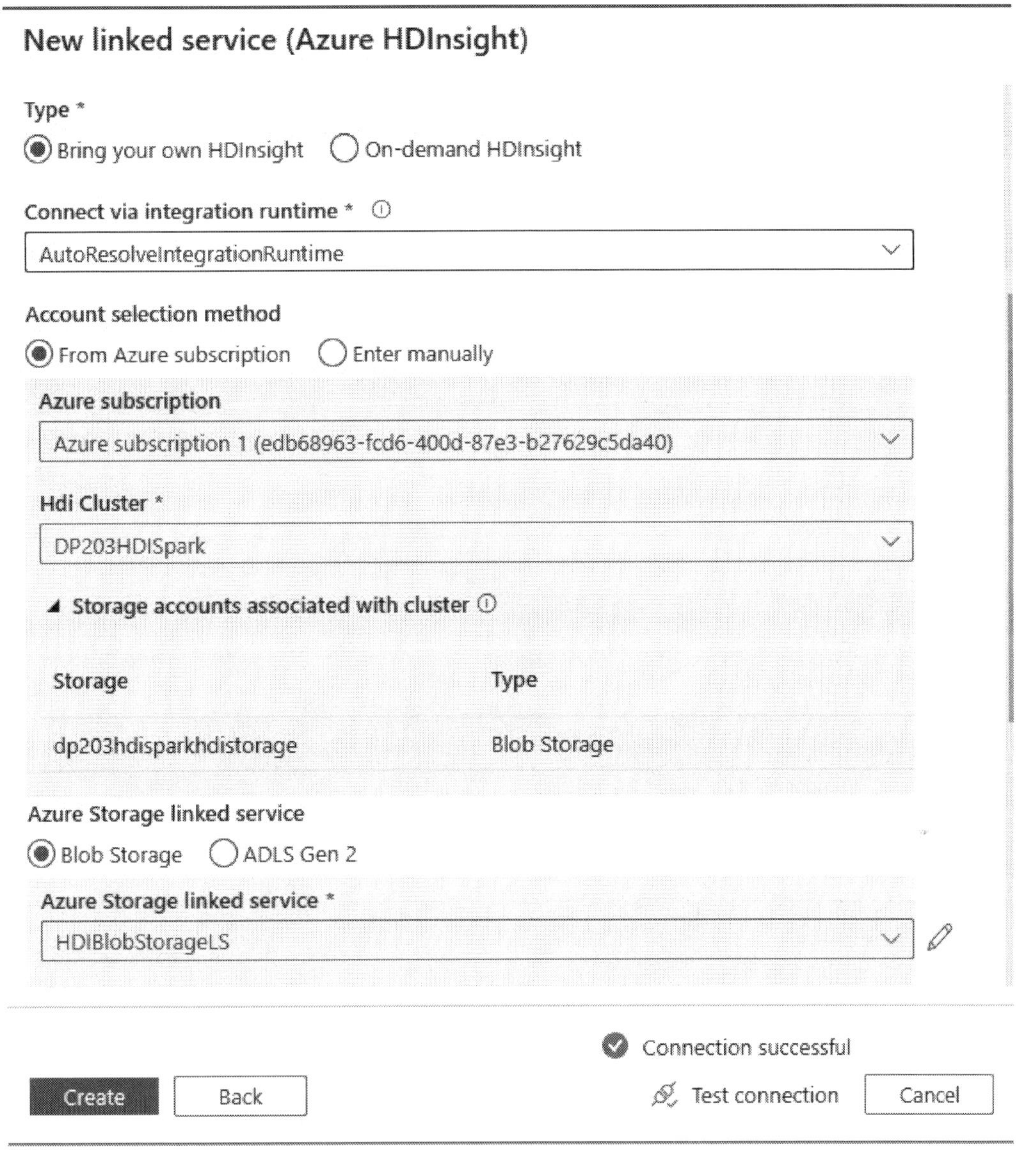

New linked service (Azure HDInsight)

Type *

(●) Bring your own HDInsight   (○) On-demand HDInsight

Connect via integration runtime *   ⓘ

| AutoResolveIntegrationRuntime | ∨ |

Account selection method

(●) From Azure subscription   (○) Enter manually

Azure subscription

| Azure subscription 1 (edb68963-fcd6-400d-87e3-b27629c5da40) | ∨ |

Hdi Cluster *

| DP203HDISpark | ∨ |

▲ **Storage accounts associated with cluster** ⓘ

Storage	Type
dp203hdisparkhdistorage	Blob Storage

Azure Storage linked service

(●) Blob Storage   (○) ADLS Gen 2

Azure Storage linked service *

| HDIBlobStorageLS | ∨ | ✎ |

(✓) Connection successful

| Create | | Back | | | ⌀ Test connection | Cancel |

Figure 11.13 – Creating an HDInsight linked service

2. Next, select the **Spark** activity from the ADF activity tab and select the linked service that we created in the previous step for the **HDInsight linked service** field:

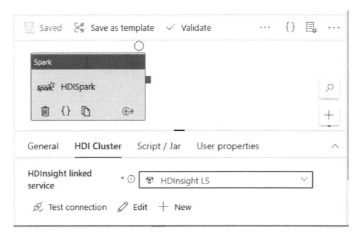

Figure 11.14 – Configuring the HDInsight Spark cluster inside the ADF pipeline

3. In the **Script/Jar** tab, provide the link to the actual Spark driver job file. In this case, we will point it to a `wordcount` script, which was uploaded into the Blob storage:

Figure 11.15 – Creating a pipeline with Spark

4. Now, if we just trigger this pipeline using the **Add Trigger** button, the entire Spark pipeline will run.

That should have given you a good understanding of managing Spark in pipelines. Next, let's learn how to implement version control in ADF.

Implementing version control for pipeline artifacts

By default, ADF and Synapse pipelines save pipeline details in their internal stores. These internal stores don't provide options for collaboration, version control, or any other benefits provided by the source control systems. Every time you click on the **Publish All** button, your latest changes are saved within the service. To overcome this shortcoming, both ADF and Synapse pipelines provide options to integrate with source control systems such as Git. Let's explore how to configure version control for our pipeline artifacts.

Configuring source control in ADF

ADF provides a **Set up code repository** button at the top of the home screen, as shown in the following screenshot. You can use this button to start the Git configuration process:

Figure 11.16 – The Set up code repository button on the ADF home screen

You can also reach the **Git Configuration** page from the **Manage** tab (the toolkit icon), as shown in the following screenshot. This screenshot shows Synapse pipelines, but ADF has a very similar page:

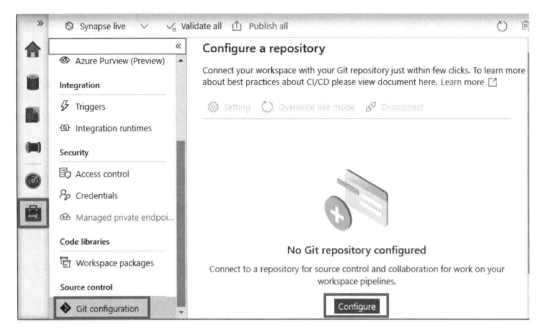

Figure 11.17 – Launching Git configuration from Synapse's Manage tab

Both ADF and Synapse pipelines support the **Azure DevOps** version of Git and external **GitHub** accounts. Let's learn how to integrate both these source control systems into ADF and Synapse.

Integrating with Azure DevOps

Let's look at the configuration for Azure DevOps. You will need to have an existing Azure DevOps account. If you don't have one, you can easily create one:

1. Just search for **Azure DevOps Organizations** from the Azure portal. Click on the **My Azure DevOps Organizations** button on the Azure DevOps screen, as shown in the following screenshot, and set one up. Alternatively, you could also directly visit `https://azure.microsoft.com/en-us/services/devops/` to get started with Azure DevOps:

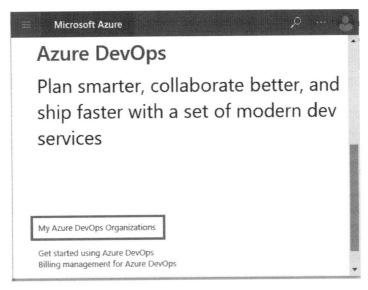

Figure 11.18 – Creating a new DevOps organization

Once you have created a new Azure DevOps organization, you can create new Git repositories under it.

2. Now, go back to the Azure Data Factory **Git Configuration** screen and click on the **Configure** button (*Figure 11.17*). here, you will be able to choose between Azure DevOps and GitHub. If you choose Azure DevOps, you will see the **Configure a repository** screen, as shown in the following screenshot. Here, you must provide an **Azure DevOps organization name**, **Project name**, **Repository name**, **Collaboration branch**, **Publish branch**, **Root folder**, and so on:

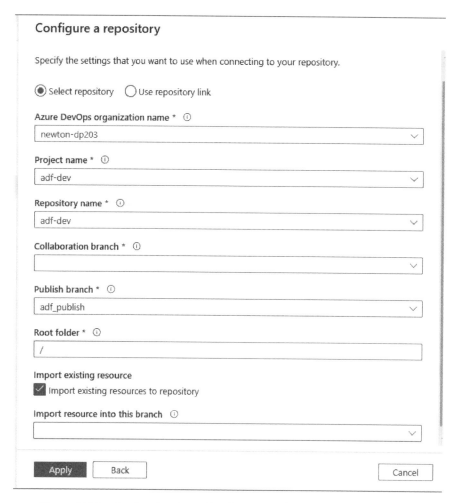

Figure 11.19 – Configuring Azure DevOps Git as the source control for ADF

3. Fill in the details and click **Apply** to configure the Azure DevOps Git repository. From now on, every time you click **Publish** it will save the changes to the git repository specified by you.

Now, let's look at the GitHub configuration details.

Integrating with GitHub

The configuration screen for GitHub is also very similar. You will have to specify attributes such as **Repository name**, **Collaboration branch**, **Publish branch**, **Root folder**, and so on, as shown in the following screenshot:

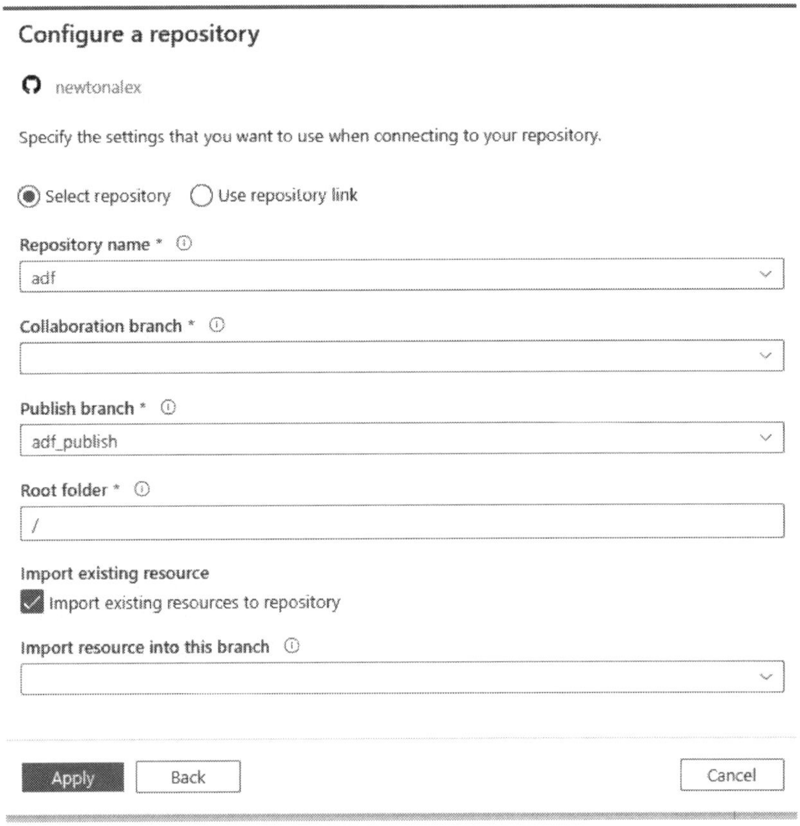

Configure a repository

newtonalex

Specify the settings that you want to use when connecting to your repository.

● Select repository   ○ Use repository link

Repository name *

adf

Collaboration branch *

Publish branch *

adf_publish

Root folder *

/

Import existing resource

☑ Import existing resources to repository

Import resource into this branch

Apply   Back   Cancel

Figure 11.20 – Configuring GitHub as the source control for ADF

> **Note**
>
> In both these cases, ADF creates a new branch called `adf_publish`, which it will use as the source to publish to the ADF service. You will not be able to make changes to this branch directly, but you can merge your changes via pull requests.

Once you have configured the Azure DevOps or GitHub version of Git, every time you click on **Publish**, the pipeline artifacts will be stored in the Git repository.

Now that you know how to configure version control for pipeline artifacts, let's summarize this chapter.

Summary

With that, we have come to the end of this small chapter. We started by learning how to trigger Batch loads, how to handle errors and validate Batch jobs, and then moved on to ADF and Synapse pipelines. We learned about setting up triggers, managing and monitoring pipelines, running Spark pipelines, and configuring version control in ADF and Synapse Pipelines. With all this knowledge, you should now be confident in creating and managing pipelines using ADF, Synapse Pipelines, and Azure Batch.

This chapter marks the end of the *Designing and Developing Data Processing* section, which accounts for about 25-30% of the certification goals. From the next chapter onward, we will next move on to the *Designing and Implementing Data Security* section, where we will be focusing on the security aspects of data processing.

Part 4:
Design and
Implement Data
Security (10-15%)

This part focuses on data security and compliance. Security and compliance are integral components of any cloud system. Different countries and governments have different compliance requirements. Even though Azure provides very high levels of security, the compliance aspect depends on the individual components. We need to ensure that the technologies we choose satisfy the compliance requirements of the countries or companies that you work with.

This section comprises the following chapter:

- *Chapter 12, Designing Security for Data Policies and Standards*

12
Designing Security for Data Policies and Standards

Welcome to the next section of the syllabus, *Design and Implement Data Security*. This section accounts for about 10–15% of the questions in the certification. According to the syllabus, this section is supposed to have two chapters: one focusing on the design aspects, and another focusing on implementation aspects. But, to ensure a better flow of topics and to avoid too many context switches, I've merged both the design and implementation details into this single chapter. Once you have completed this chapter, you should be able to recognize sensitive information and be able to design and implement various sensitive information-handling techniques such as data masking, row and column level security, implementing role-based access and access-controlled lists, enabling encryption and more. You will also be aware of the good practices for handling keys, secrets, and certificates, and understand the low-level implementation details of handling secure data in Spark. Overall, you will be able to take care of the design and implementation of the data security and privacy aspects of your data lake.

We will be covering the following topics in this chapter:

- Designing and implementing data encryption for data at rest and in transit
- Designing and implementing data auditing strategies
- Designing and implementing data masking strategies
- Designing and implementing Azure role-based access control and POSIX-like access control lists for Data Lake Storage Gen2
- Designing and implementing row-level and column-level security
- Designing and implementing data retention policies
- Designing and implementing purging data based on business requirements
- Managing identities, keys, and secrets across different data platform technologies
- Implementing secure endpoints (private and public)
- Implementing resource tokens in Azure Databricks
- Loading DataFrames with sensitive information
- Writing encrypted data to tables or Parquet files
- Designing for data privacy and managing sensitive information

Technical requirements

For this chapter, you will need the following:

- An Azure account (free or paid)

Let's get started!

Introducing the security and privacy requirements

How do you go about designing for the security and privacy of data? Well, let's take an example and try to walk through some scenarios. Let's consider our faithful **Imaginary Airport Cabs (IAC)** example that we used in our previous chapters. We have already seen that the cab company gets a lot of trips, customers, and driver information streaming in. We have also learned how to store the data in the data lake and SQL stores. Now, let's get a little deeper into the storage topic and figure out how to safeguard confidential and private information.

Let's consider the following requirements from the IAC security team:

- Data needs to be stored and transferred securely as we are dealing with cloud systems, and no one other than the IAC employees should have access to the data.

- Changes to data and any activity on the data should be recorded for compliance reasons.

- Not everyone should have access to all the data. It should be on a need-to-know basis.

- Maintain customer privacy at all costs.

- Older data should be safely deleted after one month.

These look like pretty standard requirements for any company. Now, let's get into each of the topics in this chapter and learn how they help accomplish the preceding requirements.

Designing and implementing data encryption for data at rest and in transit

The usual questions from anyone who wants to store data on a public cloud would be as follows:

- How safe is my data?

- Can the employees of the cloud company access my data?

- Can any outsiders access my data?

Such concerns are usually addressed by cloud companies like Azure using encryption at rest and in transit. This also happens to be the first requirement of our example requirements for IAC. Let's look at encryption at rest in detail.

Encryption at rest

Encryption at rest is the process of encrypting data before writing it to disks and decrypting the data when requested by applications. Encryption at rest protects data from physical disk theft, retrieval of data from lost disks, unauthorized data access by malicious cloud company employees, and so on. Unless someone has the decryption key or possesses insanely powerful supercomputing resources (the kind that governments might have – although, even with the current supercomputers, it is extremely difficult if the encryption key is strong and big enough), the data cannot be retrieved. It will just appear as gibberish if anyone tries to directly copy the data from the disks.

This form of security has become a fundamental requirement for any data stored on the cloud, and Azure does a good job of providing encryption-at-rest options for most of its storage solutions. In this topic, we will look at the encryption-at-rest options available in Azure Storage and Azure Synapse SQL.

Encryption at rest and in transit is usually required for compliance with various regulations. So, it is not just about customer concerns; it might be required by law too. You can learn about the various regulations and the levels of compliance provided by the various Microsoft services here: `https://docs.microsoft.com/en-us/compliance/regulatory/offering-home`.

Let's now learn how Azure Storage and Synapse SQL pools provide encryption at rest.

Encryption at rest in Azure Storage

Azure Storage provides encryption at rest by default. It secures your data without you even requesting it. In fact, you cannot disable Azure Storage encryption. Azure Storage uses its own keys to encrypt data. It also provides the option for customers to use their own encryption keys. This provides additional control to the user. Such user-provided keys are called **Customer-Managed Keys (CMKs)**. You can enable CMKs from the Azure Storage screen, as shown here:

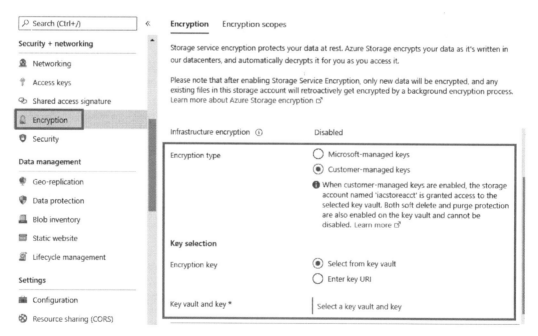

Figure 12.1 – Enabling CMKs in Azure Storage

One of the requirements for the CMK is that the customer's key needs to be safely stored in **Azure Key Vault**. Think of Azure Key Vault as an online version of a physical vault. You can store all your passwords, secret keys, access keys, and so on in Key Vault and applications can access these keys securely during runtime. This method ensures that secrets and passwords need not be stored as part of the code base. We will learn more about Key Vault later in this chapter.

You can learn more about CMKs here: `https://docs.microsoft.com/en-us/azure/storage/common/customer-managed-keys-overview`.

Encryption using CMKs would address IAC's concerns about the secure storage of data. Let's look next at how Synapse SQL encrypts data files.

Encryption at rest in Azure Synapse SQL

This section applies to Azure SQL technologies in general. In Azure Synapse SQL, encryption at rest is accomplished using a feature called **Transparent Data Encryption (TDE)**. In TDE, the encryption happens in real time at the page level. Pages are encrypted before writing to disk and decrypted before reading back into memory. Unlike Azure Storage, TDE must be manually enabled for Azure Synapse SQL. But for other SQL technologies such as Azure SQL, it is enabled by default.

You can enable TDE in Azure Synapse SQL from the **SQL pool** screen under the **Transparent data encryption** tab:

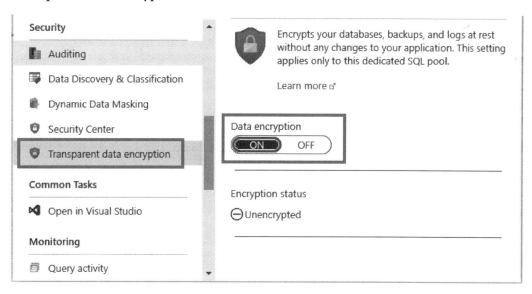

Figure 12.2 – Enabling TDE using the Azure portal

You can also enable TDE by executing the following statement as an admin user on the Azure Synapse SQL terminal:

```
ALTER DATABASE <TABLENAME> SET ENCRYPTION ON;
```

> **Note**
> TDE encrypts the database and secures against data theft by encrypting the backup and snapshot files too.

You can learn more about TDE here: `https://docs.microsoft.com/en-us/ azure/synapse-analytics/sql-data-warehouse/sql-data-warehouse- encryption-tde-tsql`.

Azure Synapse SQL also provides the option for customers to bring in their own encryption keys. If you need to configure a **Customer Managed Key** (**CMK**), you should enable double encryption using a CMK during the creation of a Synapse workspace itself, as shown in the following screenshot.

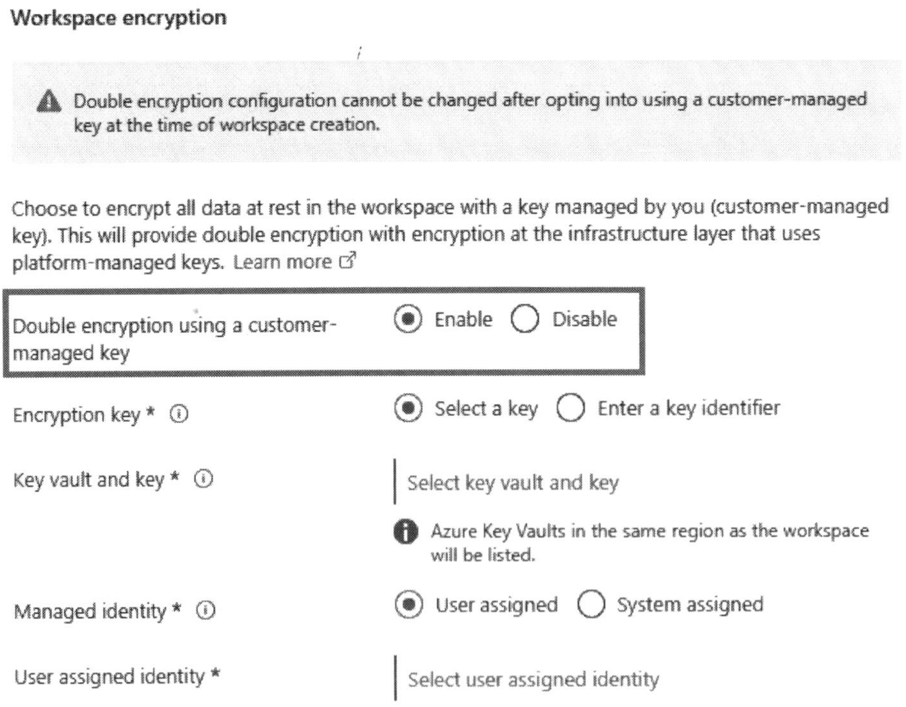

Figure 12.3 – Configuring a CMK in Azure Synapse SQL

You can learn more about CMKs with TDE here: `https://docs.microsoft.com/en-us/azure/azure-sql/database/transparent-data-encryption-tde-overview?tabs=azure-portal#customer-managed-transparent-data-encryption---bring-your-own-key`.

Let's look at the Always Encrypted feature of Azure SQL next.

Always Encrypted

Always Encrypted is a feature provided by Azure SQL and SQL Server databases to encrypt selected database columns using client drivers. The Always Encrypted client driver fetches the encryption key from a secure location such as Azure Key Vault to encrypt or decrypt the specified column data. Since the encryption key is never available to the database engine, the database administrators cannot access the data; only the data owners who have access to the encryption keys will be able to access the data.

There are two types of keys used for Always Encrypted:

- Column encryption key – The key that is used to encrypt/decrypt a column
- Column master key – The protection key to encrypt column encryption keys

Here is sample code to encrypt the two columns **Email** and **SSN** of a Customer table:

```
CREATE COLUMN MASTER KEY CMK
WITH (
     KEY_STORE_PROVIDER_NAME = 'AZURE_KEY_VAULT',
     KEY_PATH = 'KeyVault/key/path'
   );
-----------------------------------------------
CREATE COLUMN ENCRYPTION KEY CEK
WITH VALUES (
    COLUMN_MASTER_KEY = CMK,
    ALGORITHM = 'RSA_OAEP',
    ENCRYPTED_VALUE = 0x020002134……
);
-----------------------------------------------
CREATE TABLE Customer (
    [name] VARCHAR(30),
    [email] VARCHAR(10)
        COLLATE  Latin1_General_BIN2 ENCRYPTED WITH (COLUMN_
ENCRYPTION_KEY = CEK,
```

```
        ENCRYPTION_TYPE = RANDOMIZED,
        ALGORITHM = 'AEAD_AES_256_CBC_HMAC_SHA_256'),
[phone] VARCHAR (12),
[SSN] VARCHAR (11)
        COLLATE  Latin1_General_BIN2 ENCRYPTED WITH (COLUMN_
ENCRYPTION_KEY = CEK,
        ENCRYPTION_TYPE = DETERMINISTIC ,
        ALGORITHM = 'AEAD_AES_256_CBC_HMAC_SHA_256'),
);
```

The DETERMINISTIC option specified for email ensures the client driver always generates the same encrypted value for the given plain text. The RANDOMIZED option, on the other hand, generates a different encrypted value each time.

> **Tip**
> If you plan to use the encrypted column in JOINs, INDEXES, AGGREGATES, and so on, use the Deterministic type and not a random type.

There are four database permissions that are needed for Always Encrypted.

- ALTER ANY COLUMN MASTER KEY – For creating and deleting column master keys

- *ALTER ANY COLUMN ENCRYPTION KEY* – For creating and deleting column encryption keys

- VIEW ANY COLUMN MASTER KEY DEFINITION – To read column master keys to query encrypted columns

- VIEW ANY COLUMN ENCRYPTION KEY DEFINITION – To read column master keys to query encrypted columns

> **Note**
> Since the encryption and decryption are done using a client driver, server-side operations such as SELECT INTO, UPDATE, and BULK INSERT will not work with Always Encrypted columns.

You can learn more about Always Encrypted here: `https://docs.microsoft.com/en-us/sql/relational-databases/security/encryption/always-encrypted-database-engine?view=sql-server-ver15`.

Next, let's look at encryption in transit.

Encryption in transit

Another important security concept is encryption in transit. This refers to encrypting the data that is being sent over a wire or, in other words, any data that is being moved from one place to another. Examples of data movement could be data being read by an application, data getting replicated to a different zone, or data being downloaded from the cloud. Safeguarding the data during transfer is as important as keeping it safe while storing.

Encryption in transit is usually accomplished via two protocols, **Secure Sockets Layer (SSL)** or **Transport Layer Security (TLS)**. SSL support is being discontinued for some Azure services, so TLS is the preferred network protocol to encrypt data during transit.

Let's learn how Azure Storage and Synapse SQL pools provide encryption in transit.

Enabling encryption in transit for Azure Storage

Let's look at how to enable TLS in Azure Storage.

You can go to the Blob or ADLS Gen2 storage home page and select the **Configuration** tab under **Settings**. On the configuration page, you will be able to configure the minimum TLS version. The recommendation is to go with TLS version 1.2. Here is a screenshot of the TLS version page.

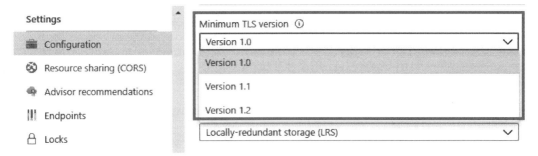

Figure 12.4 – Enabling TLS in Azure Storage

This is how we can enable TLS for Azure Storage. Next, let's look at how to configure TLS in a Synapse SQL pool.

Enabling encryption in transit for Azure Synapse SQL

Azure Synapse SQL automatically secures data in transit using TLS protocols. In fact, Synapse SQL enforces encryption of all the connections irrespective of the setting of `Encrypt` or `TrustServerCertificate` in the connection string. So, we don't need to do any additional configurations from our side.

You can learn more about information protection in Azure Synapse SQL and other Azure SQL variants here: `https://docs.microsoft.com/en-us/azure/azure-sql/database/security-overview`.

Apart from encryption, the other ways to secure data while in transit is to set up dedicated **Virtual Private Networks** (**VPNs**) or to use **Azure ExpressRoute**.

You can find more information about **VPNs** here: `https://docs.microsoft.com/en-us/azure/vpn-gateway/`.

ExpressRoute provides a private connection from your on-premises network to the Azure cloud. It uses connectivity providers for the connection and doesn't use the public internet. As such, the connections are fast, reliable, and secure.

You can find more about Azure ExpressRoute here: `https://docs.microsoft.com/en-us/azure/expressroute/`.

Let's look next at data auditing strategies.

Designing and implementing a data auditing strategy

This was the second requirement of our example IAC requirements – to keep track of the activities on the data store for compliance purposes. Data auditing is the process of keeping track of the activities that were performed on a service. This is usually done via logs and metrics. Let's look at how Azure Storage supports data auditing.

Storage auditing

Azure Storage supports audit logging via **Storage Analytics logging**. This is now called **classic monitoring**. There is a newer version of logging available under **Azure Monitor**. Azure Monitor storage support was in preview mode at the time of writing this book. Let's look at both ways of enabling audit logging. Storage Analytics logging can be enabled as shown in the following screenshot:

Using a classic diagnostic setting

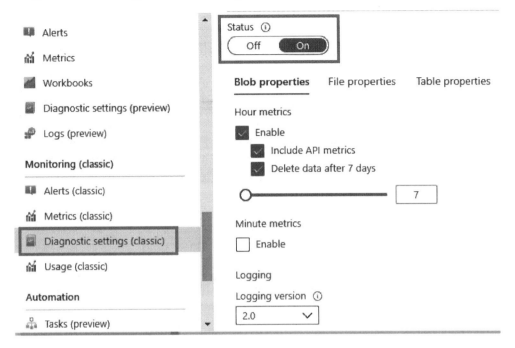

Figure 12.5 – Enabling metrics logging for auditing in the Azure storage

Once enabled, the logs will get stored in a container called $logs under your storage account. You can use any data explorer or data processing tools to view and analyze the data under this folder.

> **Important Note**
>
> It might take up to an hour for the logs to appear under the $logs container. Storage Analytics doesn't immediately flush the logs. It does it at regular intervals or when it has enough data to flush the data to the blob.

You can learn more about Azure Storage Analytics logging here: https://docs. microsoft.com/en-us/azure/storage/common/storage-analytics-logging.

Next, let's look at how to achieve this using Azure Monitor.

Using Azure Monitor

Azure Monitor is Azure's full-stack monitoring service. It is enabled by default for most Azure services. It collects certain default metrics and logs for every service and can be configured to collect more detailed logs and metrics as required. In the case of Azure Storage, Azure Monitor starts collecting metrics and logs once we enable **Diagnostic settings** on the Azure Storage screen in the Azure portal, as shown in the following screenshot:

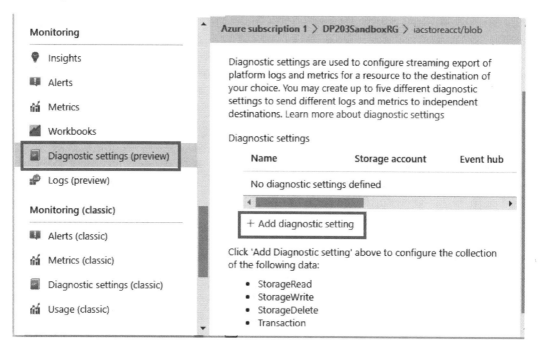

Figure 12.6 – Azure Monitoring – Diagnostic settings

Click on the + **Add diagnostic setting** link to configure the diagnostic setting, as shown in the following screenshot:

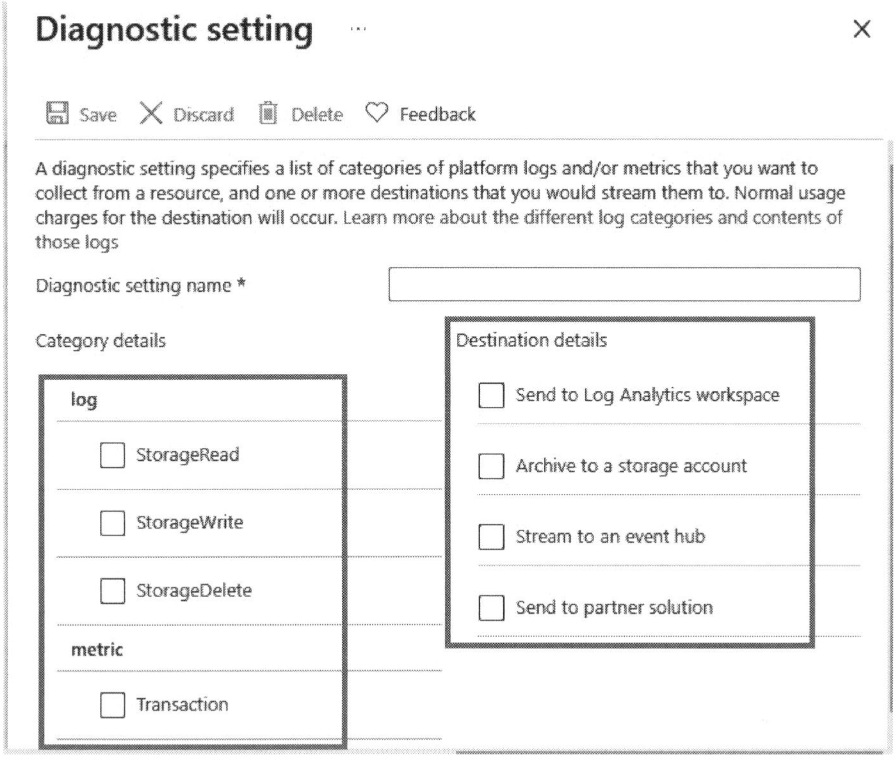

Figure 12.7 – Configuring a diagnostic setting using Azure monitoring

On the **Diagnostic setting** screen, you can specify which logs and metrics you want to record and which location/tool to send them to. Azure Monitor will start recording and sending the logs and metrics from then on to the configured service. You can also select the destination where you want to send the logs to. Remember that there will be a cost associated with storing the logs in any of these destinations, similar to the cost of storing any other data in them.

You can learn more about Azure monitoring for storage here: `https://docs.microsoft.com/en-us/azure/storage/blobs/monitor-blob-storage`.

Let's look next at auditing in SQL.

SQL auditing

Azure Synapse SQL provides the option to track all database events and activities via its **Auditing** feature. You can easily enable Auditing from the **Azure SQL Auditing** tab on the SQL pool portal page. An example is shown in the next screenshot. It provides multiple storage options, such as Azure **Storage**, **Log Analytics**, and **Event Hub** as the destination of the audit logs. You can configure the destination according to your business needs. For example, if you want to do some real-time analysis of audit logs, then you can send them to **Event Hub**. If you want to store it for compliance purposes, you can choose to store it in **Azure Blob storage**. If you want to do some ad hoc querying and analysis, then use **Log Analytics**. We will learn more about Log Analytics later in this chapter.

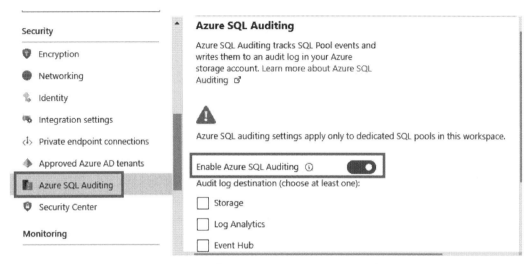

Figure 12.8 – Configuring Azure Synapse SQL Auditing

You can learn more about SQL Auditing here: `https://docs.microsoft.com/en-us/azure/azure-sql/database/auditing-overview`.

Let's look next at data masking strategies.

Designing and implementing a data masking strategy

Data masking is a technique used in SQL technologies to hide sensitive data in SQL query results from non-privileged users. For example, the credit card info of a customer might be masked as XXXX-XXXX-XXXX-1234 instead of showing the complete number while querying a customer table in Synapse SQL. The data itself is not changed in the tables, but the queries and views modify the data dynamically to mask sensitive information.

This feature helps enforce the following two requirements of IAC:

- Not everyone should have access to all the data – it should be on a need-to-know basis.

- Maintain customer privacy at all costs.

You can easily create a data mask in Azure Synapse SQL (and in Azure SQL too) using a feature called **Dynamic Data Masking** (**DDM**). The following screenshot shows how this can be done in Azure Synapse SQL:

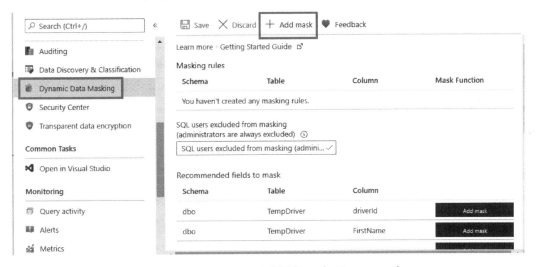

Figure 12.9 – Setting up DDM from the Azure portal

From the previous screen, you can click on the + **Add mask** link to create a new mask. For example, if you want to create an email mask, you just need to select the **Email** option from the drop-down list, as shown in the following screenshot:

Figure 12.10 – Creating an email mask

The previous screenshot also shows other options that you can use, such as **Credit card value**, **Number**, and **Custom string**.

You can also set up DDM using T-SQL in Azure Synapse SQL, as shown here:

```
ALTER TABLE dbo.DimCustomer
ALTER COLUMN emailId ADD MASKED WITH (FUNCTION = 'email()');
```

> **Note**
>
> DDM does not encrypt the column. It only masks the values during queries.

You can learn more about DDM here: `https://docs.microsoft.com/en-us/azure/azure-sql/database/dynamic-data-masking-overview`.

Let's look next at Azure RBAC and ACL policies, which also deal with a similar requirement of restricting access to data.

Designing and implementing Azure role-based access control and a POSIX-like access control list for Data Lake Storage Gen2

This section also deals with restricting data access to unauthorized users and satisfies the following requirement of our sample IAC requirements:

Not everyone should have access to all the data. It should be on a need-to-know basis.

Azure uses and recommends the *principle of least privilege*, which means assigning the least possible privilege required to accomplish a task. Let's see how RBAC and ACLs help to achieve this goal.

Restricting access using Azure RBAC

Azure Role-Based Access Control (**Azure RBAC**) is an authorization system that controls who can access what resources in Azure. Azure RBAC works hand in hand with Azure AAD. Let's try to understand the basics of RBAC before getting into the details.

RBAC has three components:

- **Security principal**: This could be any **user**, **group**, or **managed identity** (service accounts whose life cycle is completely managed by Azure) created within AAD. You can think of the service principal as the "who" part of the authorization. It is the entity that we are requesting permission for. It could be real people or service accounts that are used to run services automatically without human intervention.

- **Role**: Think of the examples of admin roles or read-only guest roles that you have used to log in to any system. An admin role would have had complete access to create, read, write, delete, and so on, while a guest account might have just had read-only access. A role basically defines what actions can be performed by a user. Azure has a huge list of predefined roles, such as **Owner**, **Contributor**, and **Reader**, with the right list of permissions already assigned. So, you can just choose to use one of them instead of creating a new role.

- **Scope**: Scope refers to all the resources where the role needs to be applied. Do you want the rules to apply only to a resource group? Only to a container in storage? Multiple containers? And so on.

In order to define an RBAC rule, we need to define all three of the above and assign a role and scope to the security principal.

Now, let's look at how to accomplish this for a data lake. From the Azure Storage home page, select **Access Control (IAM)**. There, you can add role assignments, as shown in the following screenshot. You can select the role from the **Role** field, the security principal from the **Assign access to** field, and finally, the scope, in this case, would be the Storage account itself:

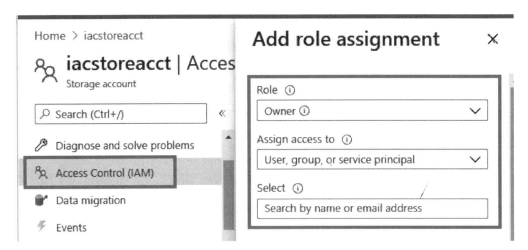

Figure 12.11 – Configuring the RBAC role assignment in ADLS Gen2

You can learn more about Azure RBAC here: `https://docs.microsoft.com/
en-us/azure/role-based-access-control/`.

Let's look next at **Access Control Lists (ACLs)**.

Restricting access using ACLs

While Azure RBAC provides coarse-grained access such as who can read/write data in an
account, ACLs provide more fine-grained access such as who can read data from a specific
directory or a file. RBAC and ACL complement each other to provide a wide spectrum of
access control.

Each directory and file in Azure Storage has an ACL. You can assign any of (or all of) the
read, **write**, and **execute** permissions to individual security principals (users) or groups to
provide them with the required access to the file or directory. ACLs are enabled by default
for ADLS Gen2.

Here is how we can assign ACLs in ADLS Gen2. Just right-click on the file or folder name
and select **Manage ACL**:

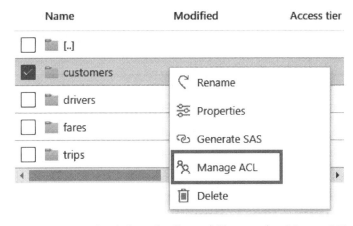

Figure 12.12 – Right-click on the files or folders to select Manage ACL

On the **Manage ACL** screen, you can assign **Read**, **Write**, and **Execute** access to the principals under **Security principal**, as shown in the following screenshot:

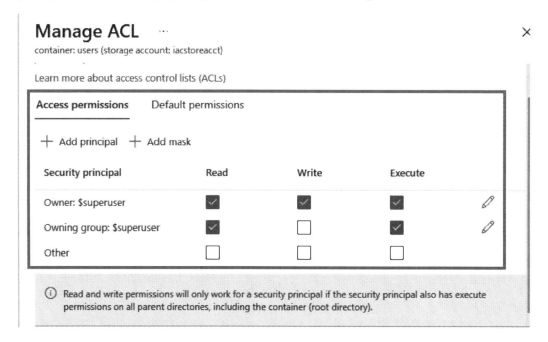

Figure 12.13 – Configuring the ACL in ADLS Gen2

You can configure the right access level for users according to your requirements. Let's next see the order in which Azure evaluates RBAC and ACLs.

How does Azure decide between RBAC and ACLs if there are conflicting rules?

Here is a flow chart reproduced from Azure that shows how the authorization decision is made between RBAC and ACL:

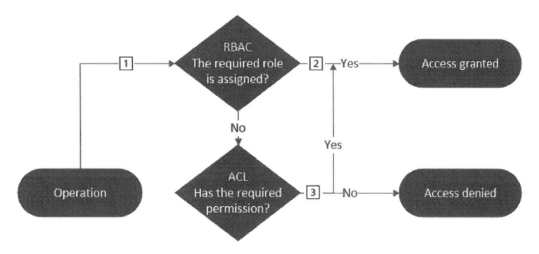

Figure 12.14 – RBAC and ACL evaluation sequence

In case of conflicts, Azure gives precedence to **RBAC**. So be aware of this priority rule while designing the security/compliance aspects of your data lake.

Let's next learn about some of the limitations of RBAC and ACLs.

Limitations of RBAC and ACL

Here are some other restrictions on RBAC and ACL that you should be aware of while designing for security and privacy requirements:

- Azure RBAC allows 2,000 role assignments per subscription.

- ACL allows up to 32 ACL entries per file and directory. This number is a bit restricting, so ensure that you don't end up adding too many individual users; instead, create groups and add only groups to ACLs.

You can learn more about ACLs here: `https://docs.microsoft.com/en-us/ azure/storage/blobs/data-lake-storage-access-control`.

Azure also supports two other authentication methods, called **Shared Key** authorization and **Shared Access Signature** (**SAS**) authorization. Shared Key authorization involves sharing an Access key, which basically gives admin-like access to the resource to anyone possessing the key. SASs are slightly better because you can define what actions are allowed with the SAS key.

If you use Shared Key or SAS authorization methods, they will override both RBAC and ACLs. The recommendation is to use AAD RBAC and ACLs wherever possible. We will learn more about SAS keys later in this chapter.

Let's next learn about row- and column-level security in Azure Synapse SQL. Since this also deals with restricting access to data, I've grouped it together with the RBAC and ACL sections.

Designing and implementing row-level and column-level security

Azure Synapse SQL (and Azure SQL) provide some very useful fine-grained security at the level of rows and columns in a table. Let's learn how to use these features for restricting data access, starting with row-level security.

Designing row-level security

Row-level security restricts access to certain table rows to unauthorized users. On a high level, you can think of this as similar to using `WHERE` conditions in a `SELECT` statement. Row-level security is achieved by creating security policies. We will look at an example of how to create such a rule in the next few pages. These rules reside in the database itself. Hence, irrespective of how the data is accessed, either via queries, views, or any other methods, the data access restriction will be enforced.

Let's look at an example using our IAC scenario again. Let's imagine that the IAC company is trying to launch their service at a bunch of new locations, but they want to keep the details under wrap as they don't want the news to be leaked. So, they define two sets of users, one called `HiPriv_User` that has access to all the rows and one called `LowPriv_Users` that doesn't have access to all the rows. Let's see how to implement this example in Azure Synapse SQL. Start a Synapse dedicated pool and open an editor from the Synapse workspace:

1. Create a new schema to store our row access policy:

    ```
    CREATE SCHEMA Security;
    ```

2. Create a T-SQL function that has the logic to decide who has access to the pre-launch data. In this case, we can assume that all the `tripId >= 900` are the pre-launch locations:

```
CREATE FUNCTION Security.tvf_securitypredicate(@
tripId AS int)
    RETURNS TABLE
WITH SCHEMABINDING
AS   RETURN SELECT 1 AS tvf_securitypredicate_result
WHERE   @tripId < 900 OR USER_NAME() = 'HiPriv_User';
```

3. Create a security policy using the previously defined function:

```
CREATE SECURITY POLICY PrivFilter
ADD FILTER PREDICATE Security.tvf_
securitypredicate(tripId)
ON dbo.TripTable WITH (STATE = ON);
```

4. Now, test it out with `HiPriv_User`:

```
EXECUTE AS USER = 'HiPriv_User';
SELECT * from dbo.TripTable
```

5. When executed as `HiPriv_User`, all the rows, including the pre-launch rows with `ID >= 900`, show up, as shown in the following screenshot:

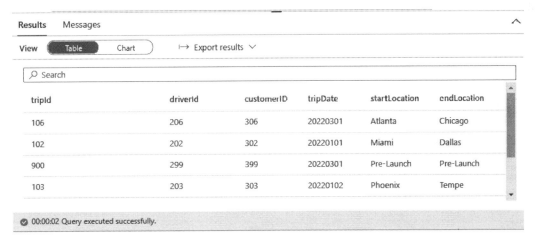

Figure 12.15 – All rows including pre-launch show up

6. Now, let's test it out with `LowPriv_User`:

```
EXECUTE AS USER = <LowPriv_User>;
SELECT * from dbo.TripTable
```

7. When executed as `LowPriv_User`, the pre-launch lines are hidden, as shown in the following screenshot:

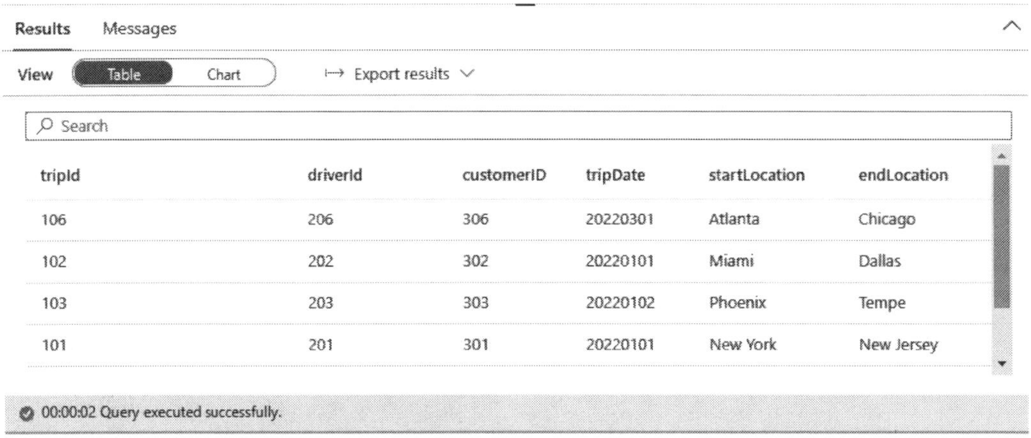
Results Messages
View Table Chart
Export results
Search
tripId driverId customerID tripDate startLocation endLocation
106 206 306 20220301 Atlanta Chicago
102 202 302 20220101 Miami Dallas
103 203 303 20220102 Phoenix Tempe
101 201 301 20220101 New York New Jersey
00:00:02 Query executed successfully.

Figure 12.16 – Row-level security blocking the pre-launch location rows

I hope that you've got a good idea of the row-level security concept. Now, let's look next at column-level security.

Designing column-level security

Column-level security is similar to the data masking feature that we saw earlier in this chapter in the *Designing and implementing a data masking strategy* section. But instead of just masking the values of the column, here we restrict the column access completely to unauthorized users. In the case of column-level security also, the rules reside in the database itself. Hence, irrespective of how the data is accessed – say, via queries, views, or any other method – the data access restriction will be enforced.

Here is an example of how to implement column restrictions.

Let's consider our IAC example, the `DimCustomer` dimension table. Here is the definition of the table:

```
CREATE TABLE dbo.DimCustomer
(
    [customerId] INT NOT NULL,
```

```
    [name] VARCHAR(40) NOT NULL,
    [emailId] VARCHAR(40),
    [phoneNum] VARCHAR(40),
    [city] VARCHAR(40)
)
```

In order to restrict access, you need to use the GRANT command, as shown here:

```
GRANT SELECT ON dbo.DimCustomer (customerId, name, city) TO
LowPriv_User;
```

Here, we just give LowPriv_User access to the customerId, name, and city columns. LowPriv_User will not have access to the emailId or phoneNum columns. If you run the following query as LowPriv_User, you will get an error:

```
SELECT * FROM Customer;
-- The SELECT permission was denied on the column 'emailId'
of the object 'DimCustomer', database 'DedicatedSmall',
schema 'dbo'. The SELECT permission was denied on the
column 'phoneNum' of the object 'DimCustomer', database
'DedicatedSmall', schema 'dbo'.
```

The row and column restriction features are particularly useful when only a very small subset of the data in the table is sensitive. This avoids the need to split the table and store the sensitive data separately.

You can learn more about column-level security here: https://docs.microsoft.com/en-us/azure/synapse-analytics/sql-data-warehouse/column-level-security.

Let's look next at data retention policies.

Designing and implementing a data retention policy

The last requirement for IAC was to securely delete the data so that it doesn't get into the hands of any malicious users.

Older data should be safely deleted after a period of time.

This section on data retention and the next section on data purging explain some of the techniques that can be used to achieve regular and secure cleanup of data.

In *Chapter 2, Designing a Data Storage Structure*, under the *Designing a data archiving solution* section, we learned about data life cycle management. We can use the same service to design our data retention policies too. The data life cycle management screen has options to either move data to Cool or Archive tiers or delete the blob itself. Let's look at a screenshot from *Chapter 2, Designing a Data Storage Structure*, again for convenience:

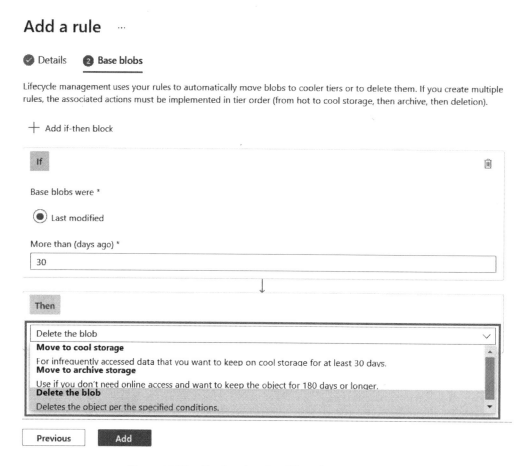

Figure 12.17 – Configuring data life cycle management

Based on our requirements, we can configure entire batches of data to be deleted after a specified time.

You can learn more about data life cycle management in Azure Data Lake Storage here: `https://docs.microsoft.com/en-us/azure/storage/blobs/lifecycle-management-overview`.

Let's look next at the other options available to purge data from data lake stores and SQL-based stores.

Designing to purge data based on business requirements

Data purging is another overlapping concept with data retention. Data purging refers to the process of safely deleting data as per business requirements. Let's look at the options available in Azure Data Lake Storage and Azure Synapse SQL.

Purging data in Azure Data Lake Storage Gen2

There are two ways in which we can achieve scheduled data deletion or data purging. One is the same as data retention, using life cycle management in Azure Storage. The second technique is to use Azure Data Factory. Whenever we delete data in Azure, it ensures that the storage locations are overwritten so that the deleted data cannot be retrieved by a malicious user. You can refer to Microsoft's data protection policy here: `https://docs.microsoft.com/en-us/azure/security/fundamentals/protection-customer-data`.

We can periodically or conditionally delete files from Azure Storage using the **Delete Activity** in ADF. We have already seen the Delete activity as part of the *Regressing to a previous stage* section in *Chapter 9, Designing and Developing a Batch Processing Solution*. Let's look at it again here with a different example. Here, we have set up the Delete activity to delete all files older than 30 days:

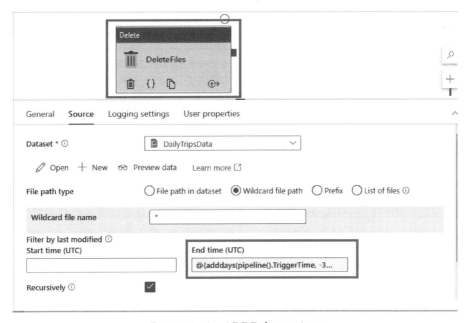

Figure 12.18 – ADF Delete options

In the **End time (UTC)** section, we have added the following line to select all files older than 30 days – @{adddays(pipeline().TriggerTime, -30)}. This takes care of deleting all data in the configured folder that is older than 30 days.

You can learn more about the ADF Delete activity here: https://azure.microsoft.com/en-in/blog/clean-up-files-by-built-in-delete-activity-in-azure-data-factory/.

Let's look next at how to purge data in SQL.

Purging data in Azure Synapse SQL

Purging in Synapse SQL is done using the TRUNCATE command. Here is an example of how that can be done where dbo.DimCustomer is a table name:

```
TRUNCATE TABLE dbo.DimCustomer;
```

Let's next look at how to create and manage keys, secrets, and managed identities.

Managing identities, keys, and secrets across different data platform technologies

There are mainly two technologies used in Azure for managing identities, keys, secrets, certificates, and basically anything confidential. They are **Azure Active Directory (AAD)** and **Azure Key Vault**. We looked briefly into Azure Key Vault earlier in this chapter in the *Encryption at rest in Azure Storage* section. Let's look into both of these services in detail here.

Azure Active Directory

AAD is Azure's identity and access management service. It supports managing users, groups, **service principals**, and so on. You can think of service principals as the service accounts used to run applications automatically. These service principals are also called **AAD applications**.

Let's now see an example of creating users in AAD:

1. From the Azure portal, search for *AAD* or *Azure Active Directory*, and select that service.

2. Once inside, you can click on the **Users** tab under the **Manage** category, and then select the **+ Add** link, as shown in the following screenshot:

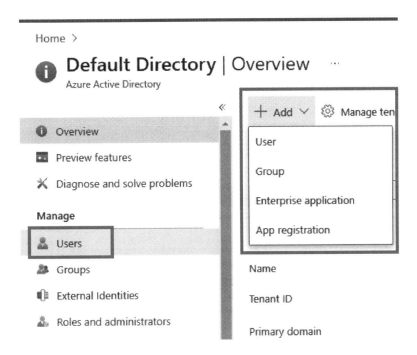

Figure 12.19 – Creating a new user in AAD

3. That opens up the **New user** screen, where you can add the details of the user and click on the **Create** button to create a new user, as shown in the following screenshot:

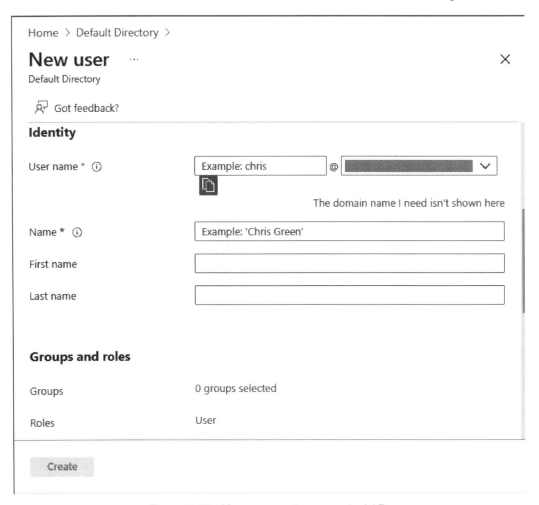

Figure 12.20 – New user creation screen in AAD

4. To manage users, you can go to the **Users** tab where you should be able to see the list of users under your AAD tenant. You can select users and perform operations such as edit, delete, and so on.

Creating groups and apps is similar to creating new users, so we will not be going into the details of it. Next, let's look at another important concept that services and resources (such as VMs, SQL databases, Synapse SQL, and so on) in Azure use to authenticate themselves to AAD.

Managed identities

Azure AAD supports another important feature called **managed identities**. These are identities that are assigned to instances of Azure services such as VMs, Synapse, SQL databases, and so on. The life cycle of these identities is automatically managed by AAD; hence, they are called managed identities. For example, when we create a new Synapse workspace, it has a managed identity automatically created in AAD, and when the workspace is deleted, the managed identity is automatically deleted. This managed identity can be used by the Azure Synapse instance to authenticate itself with AAD, instead of the application owners having to store secrets inside the application or having separate code sections to authenticate each and every service to AAD. You can find the managed identity ID on your application overview page. An example for Synapse is shown in the following screenshot:

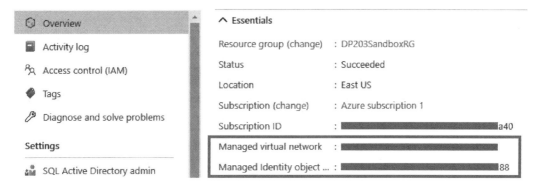

Figure 12.21 – A managed identity for Synapse

You can learn more about AAD here: `https://docs.microsoft.com/en-us/azure/active-directory/`.

Next, let's learn about storing keys, secrets, and certificates securely using Azure Key Vault.

Azure Key Vault

Azure Key Vault is another very commonly used service in Azure that is used to store keys, secrets, and certificates securely. A key vault is just like a real-world vault used to store confidential things. Azure Key Vault is a digital version of a vault that encrypts and decrypts information using 256-bit AES encryption. It provides the following functionalities:

- **Key Management**: Helps in creating and managing encryption keys
- **Secrets Management**: Helps in creating and storing secrets, passwords, URIs with keys, and so on that can be accessed by authorized applications and users using Key Vault links

- **Certificate Management**: Helps to create and manage SSL and TLS certificates for Azure resources

Key Vault simplifies secret management. It eliminates the need to store secrets in code. It is a centralized service, so every time we need to change a secret or an encryption key, we just have to update it in Key Vault. It also supports rotating certificates and keys without human intervention. If you have any kind of secrets in your applications, it is highly recommended to use Azure Key Vault.

Let's look at how to generate some keys and secrets using Key Vault:

1. From the Azure portal, search for Key Vault and select that service.

2. Once inside, select the **Keys** tab and then select the **+ Generate/Import** link, as shown in the following screenshot:

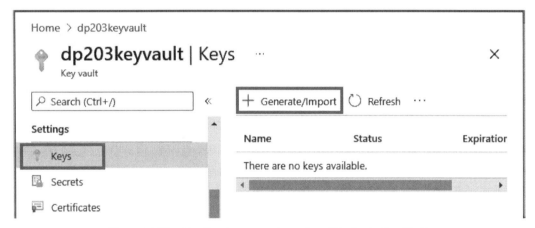

Figure 12.22 – Creating keys, secrets, and certificates in Key Vault

3. When you click on the +**Generate/Import** link, you will get the **Create a key** screen, as shown in the following screenshot:

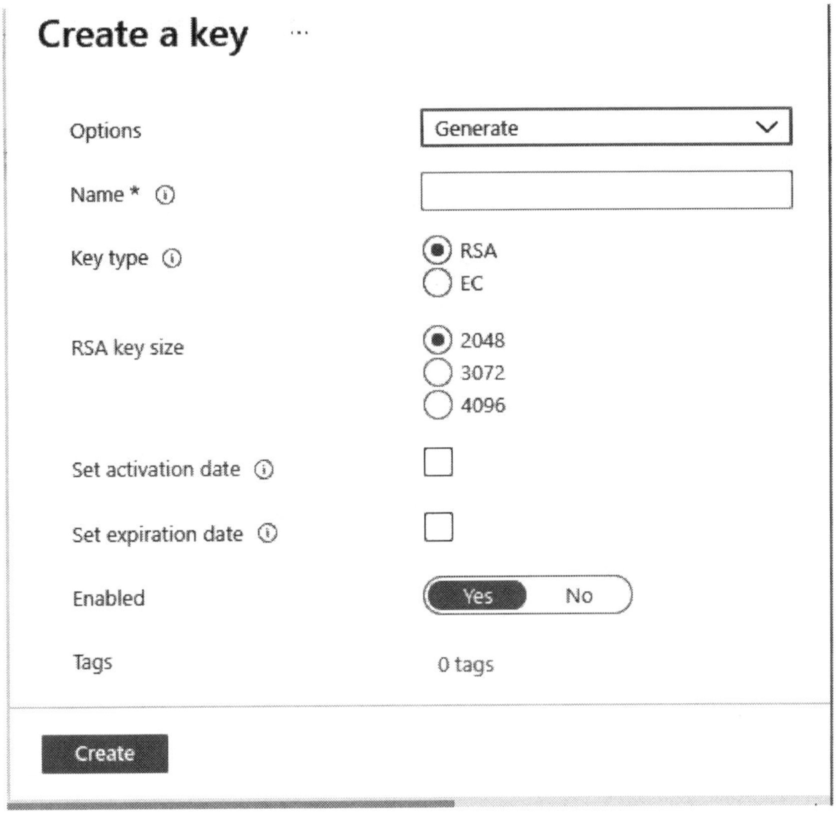

Create a key   ...

Options	Generate ▾
Name * ⓘ	
Key type ⓘ	◉ RSA ◯ EC
RSA key size	◉ 2048 ◯ 3072 ◯ 4096
Set activation date ⓘ	☐
Set expiration date ⓘ	☐
Enabled	Yes No
Tags	0 tags

Create

Figure 12.23 – Creating new encryption keys in Key Vault

4. Just enter the details and click on **Create** to create a new encryption key. You can use this encryption key to encrypt your storage accounts or databases.

5. Similar to keys, you can also create secrets. You just have to select the **Secrets** tab on the Azure Key Vault page and click on **+ Generate/Import**; you will see the following screen:

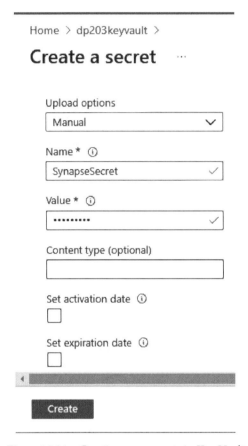

Figure 12.24 – Creating new secrets in Key Vault

6. Once you enter the details and click on **Create**, a new secret will get created.

Next, let's see how to use the secrets stored in Key Vault in other services such as Azure Synapse Analytics.

In order to use Key Vault in Synapse Analytics, we have to first add the Key Vault itself as one of the **linked services**. We have already looked at many examples of adding a linked service, so you should be familiar with the process already. Once we have Key Vault registered as one of the linked services, anytime we add any other linked service, we will have the option to use secrets directly from Azure Key Vault. The following screenshot shows an example of creating a new linked service to Azure MySQL Database. You can see the option to use an **Azure Key Vault** secret instead of manually entering the **Connection string** details:

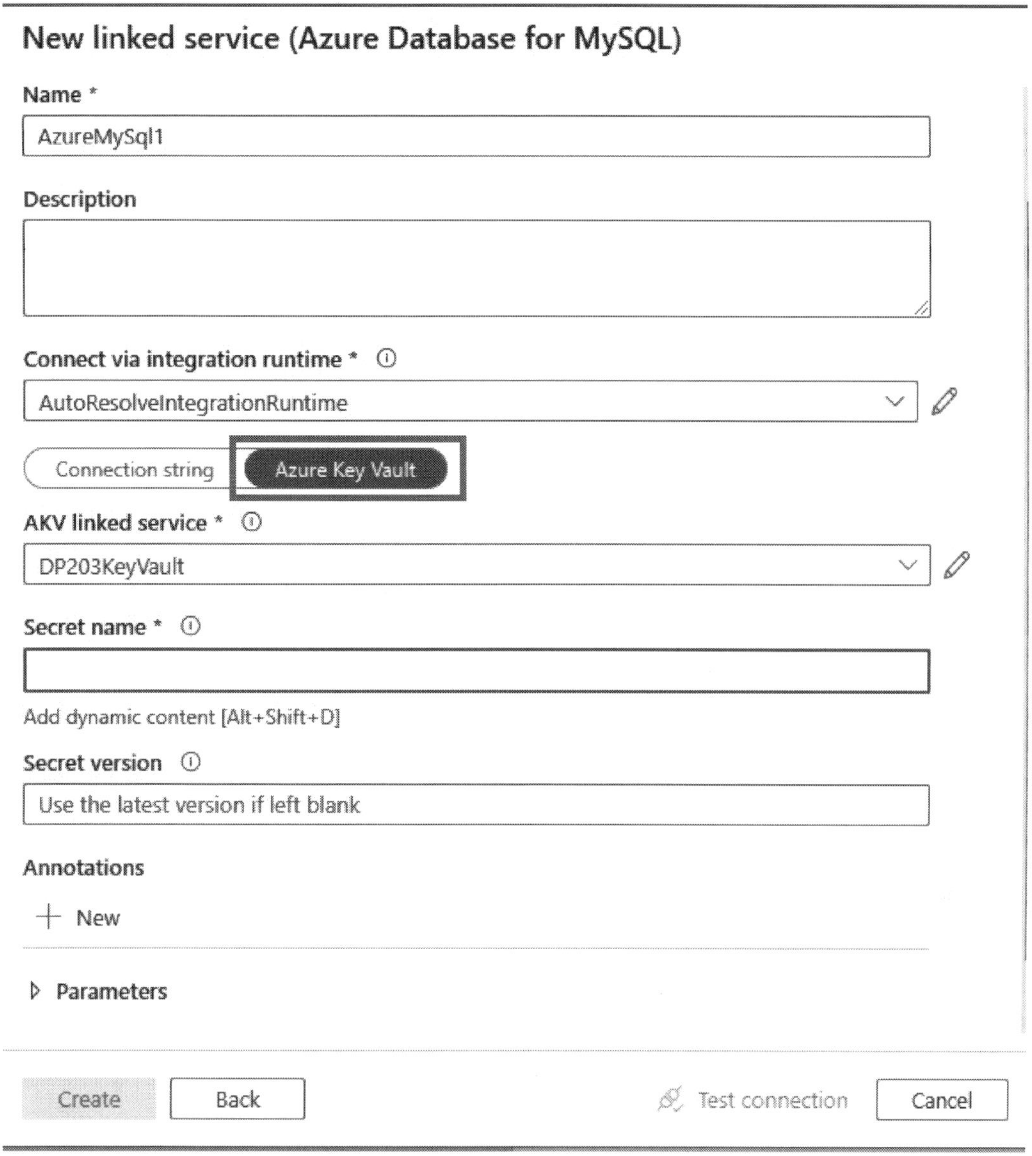

New linked service (Azure Database for MySQL)

Name *

AzureMySql1

Description

Connect via integration runtime * ⓘ

AutoResolveIntegrationRuntime ∨ ✎

Connection string   **Azure Key Vault**

AKV linked service * ⓘ

DP203KeyVault ∨ ✎

Secret name * ⓘ

Add dynamic content [Alt+Shift+D]

Secret version ⓘ

Use the latest version if left blank

Annotations

+ New

▷ **Parameters**

Create   Back   ✐ Test connection   Cancel

Figure 12.25 – Accessing keys from inside Synapse Analytics

Azure Key Vault can be accessed using the command line too:

- You can also set a new password using the CLI, as shown here:

```
az keyvault secret set --vault-name "<KEYVAULT-NAME>"
--name "SamplePassword" --value "SecretValue"
```

- You can access your passwords using the following URL:

```
https://<KEYVAULT-NAME>.vault.azure.net/secrets/
SamplePassword
```

- You can view the password using the following:

```
az keyvault secret show --name " SamplePassword "
--vault-name "< KEYVAULT-NAME>" --query "value"
```

You can learn more about Azure Key Vault here: `https://docs.microsoft.com/en-in/azure/key-vault/`.

I hope this has given you a fairly good understanding of the components involved in managing identities, keys, and secrets in Azure.

Let's learn a bit more about the Azure Storage SAS keys that we introduced in the RBAC section of this chapter as this is important from a certification perspective.

Access keys and Shared Access keys in Azure Storage

Azure Storage generates two 512-bit storage **access keys** when we create a new storage account. These keys can be used to access the data in the storage accounts. When these keys are used to authenticate access, it Is called the **Shared Access key authentication** method.

You can view the access keys from the Storage portal. Select the **Security + networking** tab and select the **Access Keys** option under that.

Access keys are like root passwords. They give complete access to all the resources in a storage account. So, if we need to give restricted access to someone or some application, we can either use the Azure RBAC option that we discussed earlier in this chapter or use a **Shared Access Signature (SAS)**. A SAS is a URI that grants restricted access for a specific period, to specific IP addresses, specific permissions, and so on. Unlike access keys, SAS keys will not have permissions to modify or delete accounts.

There are three types of SAS keys:

- **Service SAS**: This type of SAS key provides access to just one of the storage services, such as Blobs, Tables, Files, or Queues. Service SAS keys are signed using Storage access keys.

- **Account SAS**: This type of SAS key provides access to multiple storage services such as Blobs, Tables, Files, and Queues. Account SAS keys provide access to read, write, and delete operations on multiple services like blob containers, tables, queues, and files. Account SAS keys are signed using Storage access keys.

- **User Delegation SAS**: If a SAS key is signed by AAD, the SAS is called a User Delegation SAS. This is the SAS approach recommended by Azure. But this option works only for Blob storage and not other storage options such as tables, queues, or file services.

> **Note**
> Since access keys are used to sign Shared Access keys like service SAS, and account SAS, these keys will get invalidated when you regenerate new access keys for storage.

You can learn more about SAS keys and how to generate them here: `https://docs.microsoft.com/en-us/rest/api/storageservices/authorize-with-shared-key`.

Let's look next at how to use private and public endpoints.

Implementing secure endpoints (private and public)

A **public endpoint** refers to the default way of creating Azure services (such as Azure Storage, Azure Synapse, and Azure SQL), where the service can be accessed from a public IP address. So, any service that you create in Azure without configuring a **Virtual Network** (**VNet**) would fall under the public endpoint category.

On the other hand, (as you would have guessed by now), private endpoints are more secure setups involving private IP addresses. A **private endpoint** is part of a bigger service called the **Private Link** service. The Private Link service makes your Azure service available only on certain private IP addresses within your VNets. No one from outside your VNets will even be aware of the existence of such a service. The private endpoint technically refers to the network interface that uses the private IP from your VNet, and the Private Link service refers to the overall service that comprises the private endpoints and the private network (link) over which the traffic traverses. When you establish a private link to your Azure service, all the data to that service traverses through Microsoft's backbone network without being exposed to the public internet.

Let's look at how to create a private link to one of our existing Synapse workspaces:

1. Create a VNet. From the Azure portal, select **Virtual networks** and click on the **Create virtual network** option. You will get a screen like the one shown in the following figure. Fill in the details on this screen:

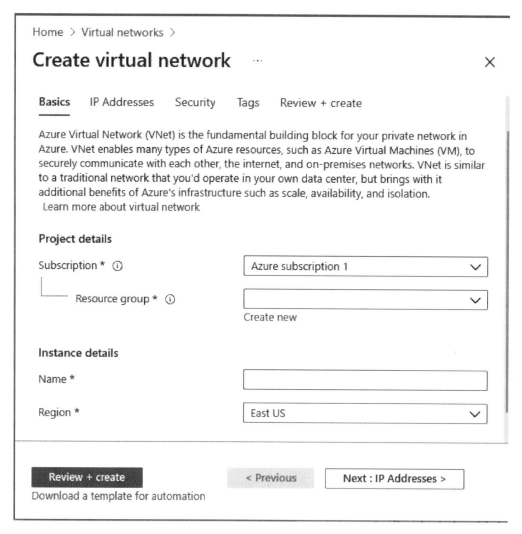

Figure 12.26 – Creating a new VNet

2. On the **IP Addresses** tab, you will have the ability to specify your IP address range and subnets, as shown in the following screenshot:

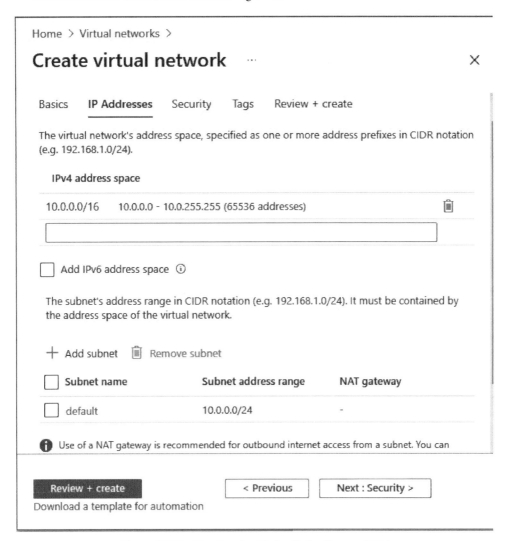

Figure 12.27 – Configuring IP details for the new VNet

3. Fill in the rest of the tabs and click on **Review + create** to create the new VNet.

4. Next, we will have to open the **Private Link Service** page from the Azure portal. Just search for `Private Link` and you will see the service at the top.

5. On the **Private Link Center** page, select the **Private endpoints** tab and click on **+Add**:

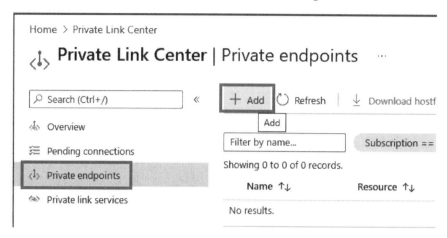

Figure 12.28 – Creating a private endpoint from Private Link Center

6. On the next page, you can select in which resource you want the endpoint to be created:

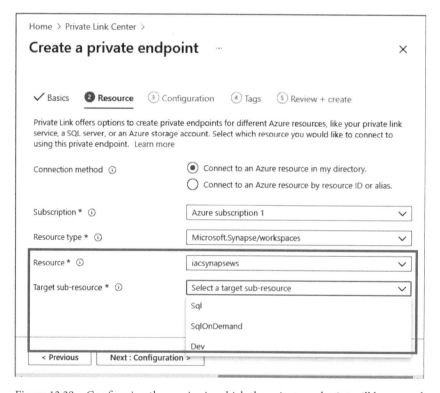

Figure 12.29 – Configuring the service in which the private endpoint will be created

7. On the **Configuration** tab, you will be able to provide the VNet details:

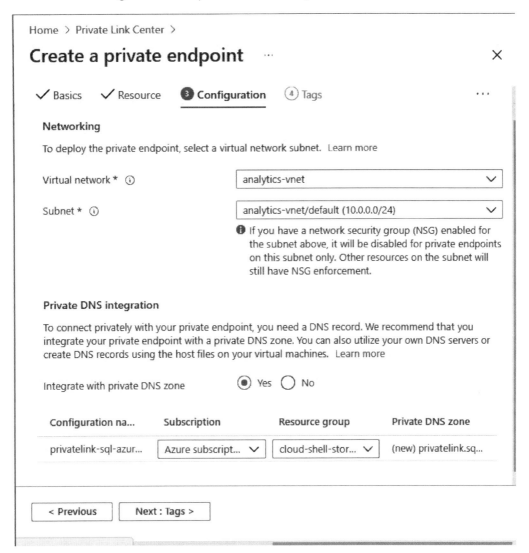

Figure 12.30 – Configuring the VNet for the private endpoint

8. Once the preceding details are entered and you have clicked on the **Review + create** button on the final screen, the private endpoint will be created.

From now on, the Synapse workspace can be accessed only within the **analytics-vnet** that was specified in the example.

You can learn more about private endpoints here: `https://docs.microsoft.com/en-us/azure/private-link/create-private-endpoint-portal`.

Now that you know how to create a private endpoint, there is another easy way to do so using a **managed virtual network** and **managed endpoints**. When you create a Synapse workspace, under the **Networking** tab, there is a **Managed virtual network** option, as shown in the following screenshot:

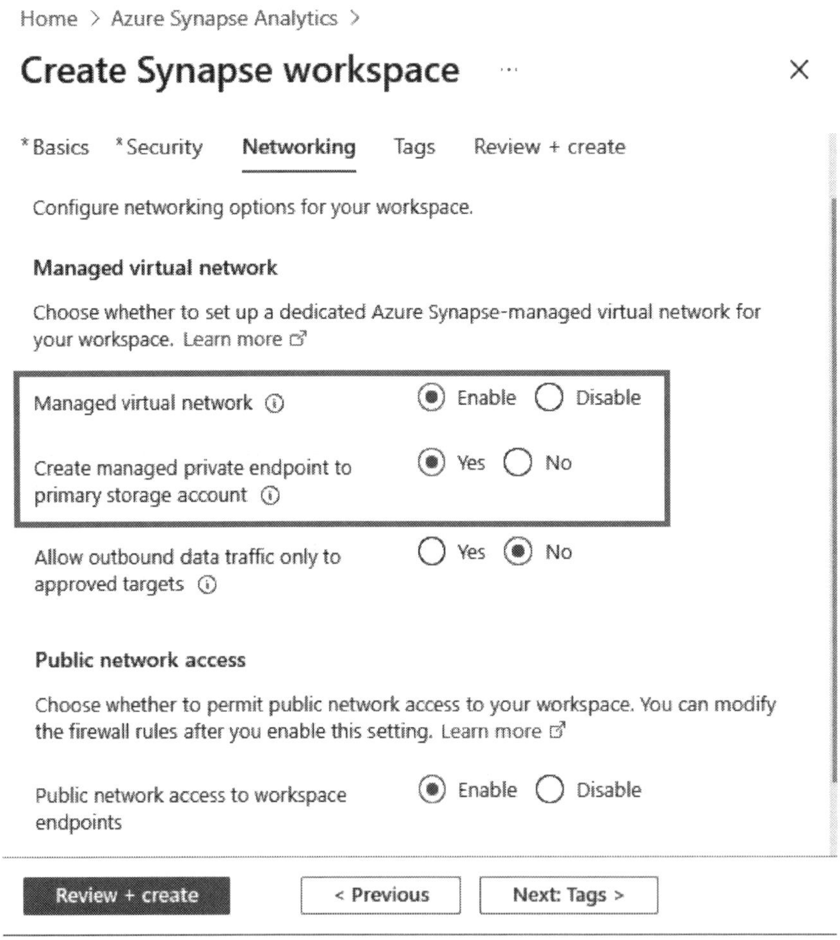

Figure 12.31 – Creating a managed virtual network while creating a Synapse workspace

When you enable **Managed virtual network**, Synapse takes care of creating the VNet, creating the private endpoints, creating the right firewall rules, creating the right subnets, and so on. This is a very convenient and less error-prone way to create private endpoints. A managed private VNet and endpoints are no different than manually created ones. It is just that the life cycle of managed VNets and endpoints are taken care of by the host service, which in our case is Synapse.

Let's look next at using access tokens in Azure Databricks.

Implementing resource tokens in Azure Databricks

Azure Databricks provides access tokens called **Personal Access Tokens (PATs)** that can be used to authenticate Azure Databricks APIs.

The following example shows how to create a new Azure Databricks PAT:

1. Select **User Settings** from the **Settings** tab.

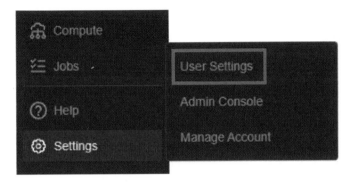

Figure 12.32 – Accessing User Settings in Azure Databricks

2. Click on the **Generate New Token** button.

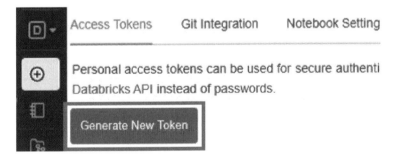

Figure 12.33 – The Generate New Token button in Azure Databricks

3. Fill in the **Comment** and **Lifetime** fields required for the token:

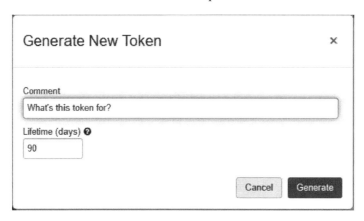

Figure 12.34 – Creating a new Azure Databricks PAT

> **Note**
>
> When you click on **Generate**, it will pop up a screen with the token. You will have to copy and store it safely at that time. You will not be able to copy that token again once that screen is closed. If you lose the token, you will have to delete it and generate a new one.

4. You can also create a PAT using APIs, as shown here. For example, the following request is for a token that will be valid for 1 day (86,400 seconds):

```
curl --netrc --request POST \
https://<databricks-instance>/api/2.0/token/create \
--data '{ "comment": "ADB PAT token", "lifetime_seconds":
86400 }'
```

5. Once you have a PAT, you can use it in the APIs, as shown in the following code block:

```
export DATABRICKS_TOKEN=<INSERT YOUR TOKEN>
curl -X GET --header "Authorization: Bearer $DATABRICKS_
TOKEN"
https://<ADB-INSTANCE>.azuredatabricks.net/api/2.0/
clusters/list
```

> **Note**
>
> The maximum number of PATs per Azure Databricks workspace is 600.

You can learn more about PATs here: `https://docs.microsoft.com/en-us/azure/databricks/administration-guide/access-control/tokens`.

Similar to the PATs of Azure Databricks, regular AAD tokens can also be used for authorization. If you are interested, you can read about it here: `https://docs.microsoft.com/en-us/azure/databricks/dev-tools/api/latest/aad/service-prin-aad-token`.

Let's look next at how to handle sensitive information within Spark DataFrames.

Loading a DataFrame with sensitive information

Earlier in this chapter, we learned about techniques such as data masking, and row- and column-level security for Azure Synapse SQL. Spark, at the time of writing this book, didn't have such techniques to handle sensitive information. In this section, we will look at an example of how to best emulate handling sensitive information such as **Personally Identifiable Information** (PII) using encryption and decryption:

1. Let's create a simple table that contains PII information such as **social security numbers (SSNs)** using PySpark:

```
from pyspark.sql.types import StructType,StructField,
StringType, IntegerType
cols = StructType([ \
    StructField("Name",StringType(),True), \
    StructField("SSN",StringType(),True), \
    StructField("email",StringType(),True)
  ])
data = [("Adam Smith","111-11-1111","james@james.com"),
    ("Brenda Harman","222-22-2222","brenda@brenda.com"),
    ("Carmen Pinto","333-33-3333", "carmen@carmen.com")
  ]
piidf = spark.createDataFrame(data=data,schema=cols)
display(piidf)
```

The output will be something like the following:

	Name	▲	SSN	▲	email	▲
1	Adam Smith		111-11-1111		james@james.com	
2	Brenda Harman		222-22-2222		brenda@brenda.com	
3	Carmen Pinto		333-33-3333		carmen@carmen.com	

Figure 12.35 – Sample table with PII

2. Next, let's import the Fernet encryption library, which provides the ability to encrypt and decrypt text. You can download the Fernet library from https://cryptography.io/en/latest/fernet/:

```
from cryptography.fernet import Fernet
encryptionKey = Fernet.generate_key()
```

3. Define the **User Defined Function (UDF)** encrypt:

```
def encryptUdf(plaintext, KEY):
    from cryptography.fernet import Fernet
    f = Fernet(KEY)
    encryptedtext = f.encrypt(bytes(plaintext, 'utf-8'))
    return str(encryptedtext.decode('ascii'))
encrypt = udf(encryptUdf, StringType())
```

4. Define the UDF decrypt:

```
def decryptUdf(encryptedtext, KEY):
    from cryptography.fernet import Fernet
    f = Fernet(KEY)
    plaintext=f.decrypt( encryptedtext.encode()).decode()
    return plaintext
decrypt = udf(decryptUdf, StringType())
```

5. Encrypt the SSN column DataFrame:

```
df = piidf.withColumn("SSN", encrypt("SSN",
lit(encryptionKey)))
display(encrypteddf)
```

The output will now be encrypted.

	Name ▲	SSN
1	Adam Smith	gAAAAABhYbAciaaO-twCsrR2cRSxv8i5HSQcQl5nLDQPGXrDabn5UW5a5hGNkzooEEilPqmqrnlvxq8niDF1
2	Brenda Harman	gAAAAABhYbAdEYKEYdqSKyr3DG87EvVre2SMXK2_dfB2zZM4pt1Wlm2DKB-Yl1kinKsdSVP4Fz_EshH7HdU6EHyvj5JU1OGBDA==
3	Carmen Pinto	gAAAAABhYbAcMjc-lj0rkAcMbB5t4A3dLouJxVKj4o_DbxTLnPENuaM6JsnKRMwnqKhZs3mNzdxjHgrxXDqQUfugDYdmg==

Figure 12.36 – Output with PII information encrypted

6. Now, we can go ahead and save it as a table:

```
df.write.format("delta").mode("overwrite").
option("overwriteSchema", "true").
saveAsTable("PIIEncryptedTable")
```

7. Alternatively, you can also write the encrypted file to Parquet, as shown here:

```
encrypted.write.mode("overwrite").parquet("abfss://path/
to/store")
```

8. From now on, only whoever has the encryption key will be able to decrypt and see the PII information. If you have the encryption key, you could decrypt the column, as shown here:

```
decrypted = encrypteddf.withColumn("SSN",
decrypt("SSN",lit(encryptionKey)))
```

```
display(decrypted)
```

▶ 🖿 decrypted: pyspark.sql.dataframe.DataFrame = [Name: string, SSN: string

	Name ▲	SSN ▲	email ▲
1	Adam Smith	111-11-1111	james@james.com
2	Brenda Harman	222-22-2222	brenda@brenda.com
3	Carmen Pinto	333-33-3333	carmen@carmen.com

Figure 12.37 – Decrypted table with PII again

I hope you've now got an idea of how to perform column-level encryption and decryption using DataFrames. This technique would work fine with both Synapse Spark and Databricks Spark.

Next, let's see how to write encrypted data into tables and files.

Writing encrypted data to tables or Parquet files

We actually just saw how to write encrypted data into tables and Parquet files in the previous example. Here it is again, writing to tables:

```
df.write.format("delta").mode("overwrite").
option("overwriteSchema", "true").
saveAsTable("PIIEncryptedTable")
```

Here it is writing to Parquet files:

```
encrypted.write.mode("overwrite").parquet("abfss://path/to/
store")
```

Let's look next at some guidelines for managing sensitive information.

Designing for data privacy and managing sensitive information

Any organization that handles sensitive information is usually bound by its country or state laws and other compliance regulations to keep the data secure and confidential. Aside from legal reasons, keeping sensitive data protected is very important for the reputation of an organization and to reduce the risk of identity theft for its customers. Azure security standards recommend the following techniques to keep sensitive data safe:

- **Identifying and classifying sensitive data** – The very first step is to analyze and identify all the sensitive data in your data stores. Some might be straightforward, such as SQL tables or structured files, and some might be not so straightforward, such as PII data being logged in log files. Azure also provides tools that can help with the identification and classification of data. For example, the Synapse SQL portal provides a feature for **Data Discovery and Classification**, which automatically suggests sensitive columns. Here is a sample screenshot of the **Data Discovery and Classification** page:

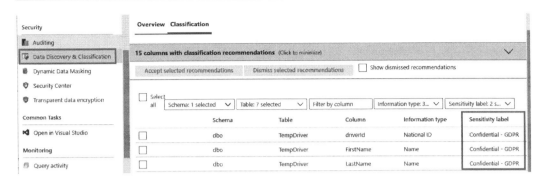

Figure 12.38 – Data Discovery and Classification

- **Protecting the sensitive data** – Once we have cataloged all the sensitive data in our data stores, the next step is to take the necessary steps to protect it. This includes all the techniques we discussed in this chapter and in the storage chapters, such as separating the sensitive data into different accounts, partitions, or folders, restricting access using RBAC and ACLs, encrypting data at rest, encrypting data in transit, data masking, and row- and column-level security.

- **Monitoring and auditing the consumption of sensitive data** – The best security policy is to not trust anyone, not even the folks who officially have access to the sensitive data. So, adding strong monitoring capabilities and enabling audit trails helps in actively and passively tracking down any malicious data access.

Let's also briefly look at the other services available in Azure to help with security and threat management.

Microsoft Defender

In order to further strengthen your Azure application's security and threat management ability, Azure provides a service called **Microsoft Defender**. Microsoft Defender provides the tools and services required to continuously monitor, alert, and mitigate threats to Azure services. Microsoft Defender is natively integrated into most Azure services, so it can be enabled easily without requiring major changes to your applications.

Microsoft Defender for Storage

Microsoft Defender for Storage can help identify threats such as anonymous access, malicious content, compromised credentials, privilege abuse, and so on.

You can learn more about Microsoft Defender for Storage here: `https://docs.microsoft.com/en-us/azure/defender-for-cloud/defender-for-storage-introduction`.

Microsoft Defender for SQL

Microsoft Defender for SQL can help identify threats such as SQL injection, brute-force attacks, and privilege abuse.

You can learn more about Microsoft Defender for SQL here: `https://docs.microsoft.com/en-us/azure/defender-for-cloud/defender-for-sql-introduction`.

That brings us to the end of this section. You can find more information about handling sensitive information and data protection guidelines at the following links:

- `https://docs.microsoft.com/en-us/security/benchmark/azure/security-control-data-protection`
- `https://docs.microsoft.com/en-us/security/benchmark/azure/security-controls-v2-data-protection`

Summary

With that, we have come to the end of this chapter. This chapter is one of the lengthiest chapters but luckily not so complicated. We started with designing the security requirements of our IAC example and then used that as our guide to explore the various security and compliance topics. We learned about encryption at rest and transit, enabling auditing for Azure Data Lake Storage and Synapse SQL, implementing data masking, RBAC and ACL rules, row- and column-level security, and had a recap on data retention and purging. After that, we continued with topics such as AAD and Key Vault to manage keys, secrets, and certificates, learned about secure endpoints, and details of tokens and encryption in Spark. Finally, we wrapped it up with concepts to be followed to design data privacy. You have now covered more or less all the important topics in handling security and privacy. You should now be able to design and implement a complete security and privacy solution on top of Azure Data Lake.

We will be exploring monitoring and optimization techniques for data storage and data processing in the next chapter.

Part 5: Monitor and Optimize Data Storage and Data Processing (10-15%)

This part covers the final, but important, aspect of how we monitor, manage, and optimize our data pipelines.

This section comprises the following chapters:

- *Chapter 13, Monitoring Data Storage and Data Processing*
- *Chapter 14, Optimizing and Troubleshooting Data Storage and Data Processing*

13
Monitoring Data Storage and Data Processing

Welcome to the next chapter. We are now in the final leg of our certification training. This is the last section of the certification: *Monitoring and Optimizing Data Storage and Data Processing*. This section contains two chapters—the current one, *Monitoring Data Storage and Data Processing*, and the next chapter, *Optimizing and Troubleshooting Data Storage and Data Processing*. As this chapter's title suggests, we will be focusing on the monitoring aspect of data storage and pipelines. Once you complete this chapter, you should be able to set up monitoring for any of your Azure data services, set up custom logs, process logs using tools such as Azure Log Analytics, and understand how to read Spark **directed acyclic graphs (DAGs)**. As with the previous chapters, I've taken the liberty of reordering the topic sequence to make reading more comfortable, without too many context switches.

In this chapter, we will cover the following topics:

- Implementing logging used by Azure Monitor
- Configuring monitoring services
- Understanding custom logging options
- Interpreting Azure Monitor metrics and logs
- Measuring the performance of data movement
- Monitoring data pipeline performance
- Monitoring and updating statistics about data across a system
- Measuring query performance
- Interpreting a Spark DAG
- Monitoring cluster performance
- Scheduling and monitoring pipeline tests

Technical requirements

For this chapter, you will need the following:

- An Azure account (free or paid)
- An active **Azure Data Factory** (**ADF**) workspace

Let's get started!

Implementing logging used by Azure Monitor

Azure Monitor is the service we use to monitor infrastructure, services, and applications. Azure Monitor records two types of data: **metrics** and **logs**. Metrics are numerical values that describe an entity or an aspect of a system at different instances of time—for example, the number of **gigabytes** (**GBs**) of data stored in a storage account at any point in time, the current number of active pipelines in ADF, and so on. Metrics are stored in time-series databases and can be easily aggregated for alerting, reporting, and auditing purposes.

Logs, on the other hand, are usually text details of what is happening in the system. Unlike metrics, which are recorded at regular intervals, logs are usually event-driven. For example, a user logging in to a system, a web app receiving a **REpresentational State Transfer** (**REST**) request, and triggering a pipeline in ADF could all generate logs.

Since Azure Monitor is an independent service, it can aggregate logs from multiple different services and multiple instances of the same service in Azure to give a global perspective of what is happening with all our Azure services.

Here is an architecture diagram reproduced from the Azure documentation that shows the core components of Azure Monitor and the sources and destinations for the metrics and logs data:

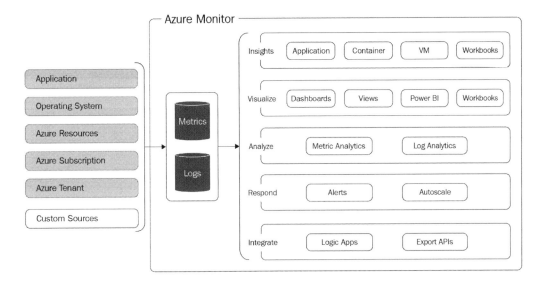

Figure 13.1 – Azure Monitor architecture

Let's look at a simple example of how to add *Activity logs* into Azure Monitor. In order to get started, we need to understand a sub-service of Azure Monitor called **Log Analytics workspaces**. A Log Analytics workspace is a component of Azure Monitor that specializes in processing and exploring log messages. You can access Log Analytics from the **Logs** tab of any Azure service or the **Logs** tab of Azure Monitor's menu. Log Analytics supports a powerful query language called **Kusto Query Language** (**KQL**) that can be used to perform analysis on log data. We will be seeing some examples of KQL in this chapter.

> **Note**
>
> Log Analytics is one of the options to store logs, and it might incur additional charges based on the storage cost and the number of Kusto queries run. You can also choose to store logs on regular Azure storage options such as Blob and Data Lake or use services such as Event Hubs to do real-time processing of logs.

Let's look at the steps required to log data to a Log Analytics workspace.

1. First, we need to create a new Log Analytics workspace. Just search for `Log Analytics workspaces` in the Azure portal and click on the result. Click the **+ Create** button on the Log Analytics home page. You should see a screen like the one shown next. Fill in the details such as the **Resource group**, **Name**, and **Region** fields for the Log Analytics instance, and then click on **Review + Create** to create a new Log Analytics workspace:

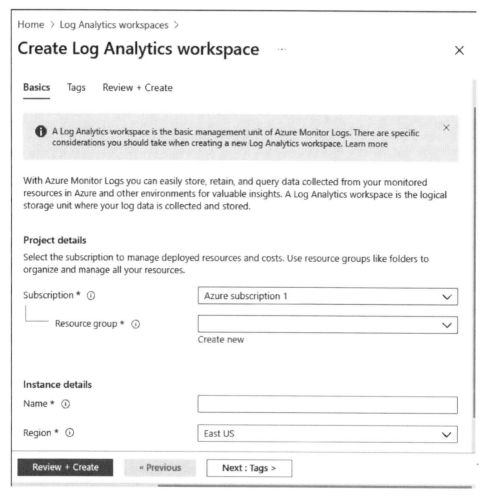

Figure 13.2 – Creating a Log Analytics workspace

2. Next, select the Azure **Monitor** service from the Azure portal and click on the **Activity log** tab, as illustrated in the following screenshot:

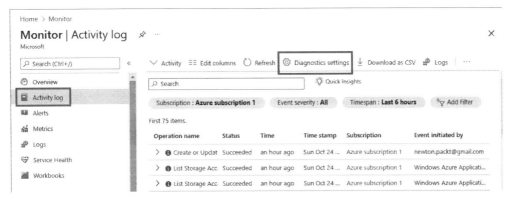

Figure 13.3 – Azure Monitor Activity log screen

3. Click on the **Diagnostics settings** button and select all the logs that you want to send to the Log Analytics workspace (the workspace you created in *Step 1*), as illustrated in the following screenshot:

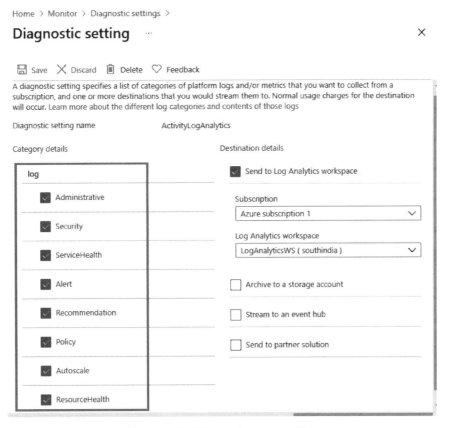

Figure 13.4 – Diagnostic screen setting

4. After a few minutes, you will see an `AzureActivity` table created in the Log Analytics workspace, as shown in the following screenshot:

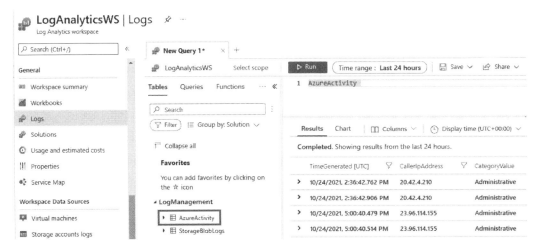

Figure 13.5 – AzureActivity table in the Log Analytics workspace

5. From now on, all the Activity logs will start getting populated into this `AzureActivity` table. You can query the table using KQL to gain insights into the log.

You can learn more about sending logs to a Log Analytics workspace here: `https://docs.microsoft.com/en-us/azure/azure-monitor/essentials/quick-collect-activity-log-portal`

Next, let's look at how to configure monitoring for Azure resources.

Configuring monitoring services

Azure Monitor is enabled as soon as we create an Azure resource. By default, the basic metrics and logs are recorded without requiring any configuration changes from the user side, but we can perform additional configurations such as sending the logs to Log Analytics, as we saw in the previous section. We can configure monitoring at multiple levels, as outlined here:

- **Application monitoring**—Metrics and logs about the applications that you have written on top of Azure services.

- **Operating system (OS) monitoring**—OS-level metrics and logs, such as CPU usage, memory usage, disk usage, and so on.

- **Azure resource monitoring**—Metrics and logs from Azure services such as Azure Storage, Synapse Analytics, Event Hubs, and more.

- **Subscription-level monitoring**—Metrics and logs of Azure subscriptions, such as how many people are using a particular account, what is the account usage, and so on.

- **Tenant-level monitoring**—Metrics and logs of tenant-level services such as **Azure Active Directory (Azure AD)**.

For resource, subscription-level, and tenant-level monitoring, the data is mostly already generated and we just need to enable the diagnostic setting, as shown in *Figure 13.4*, to move that data into any of the following three log destinations:

- Log Analytics workspace

- Event Hubs

- Storage account

But for applications and guest OS monitoring, we will have to install the **Azure Monitor agent (AMA)** or the Log Analytics agent to start collecting metrics and logs. The AMA or Azure Monitor agent can be installed in multiple ways. Here is an easy way to install it via **virtual machine (VM)** extensions on a Linux server. You can log in to the Azure **command-line interface (CLI)** and run the following command:

```
az vm extension set \
  --resource-group <YOUR_RESOURCE_GROUP> \
  --vm-name <VM_NAME> \
  --name OmsAgentForLinux \
  --publisher Microsoft.EnterpriseCloud.Monitoring \
  --protected-settings '{"workspaceKey":"<YOUR_WORKSPACE_
KEY>"}' \
  --settings '{"workspaceId":"<YOUR_WORKSPACE_ID>"}'
```

For other ways to install monitoring clients, please refer to the following link: https://docs.microsoft.com/en-us/azure/azure-monitor/agents/log-analytics-agent#installation-options.

Let's now focus on the options available for monitoring Azure resources, as this is important from a certification perspective. Let's take the example of Azure storage.

Metrics such as **Ingress**, **Egress**, **Blob Capacity**, and so on that indicate the status of operations within Azure Storage is directly available in the **Metrics** tab of Azure Storage. You can filter, create new graphs, and create new alerts using all the metrics available on this page, as shown in the following screenshot:

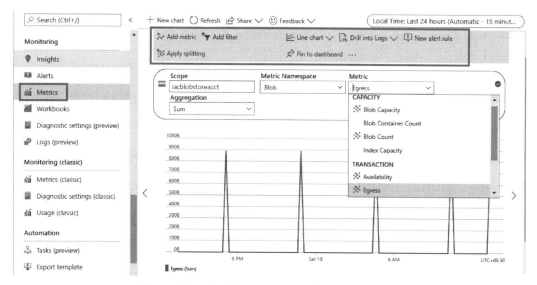

Figure 13.6 – Configuring metrics for Azure Storage

But if you need to find the status of the storage service itself, such as the *availability* of the Blob storage account, then we will have to look at Azure Monitor. From Azure Monitor, select **Storage accounts**. You should be able to see details such as overall **Transactions**, **Transactions Timeline**, and so on, as shown in the following screenshot:

Figure 13.7 – Storage metrics from Azure Monitor

If you click on any of the storage account links and select the **Insights** tab, it shows details for **Failures**, **Performance**, **Availability**, and **Capacity**, as shown in the following screenshot:

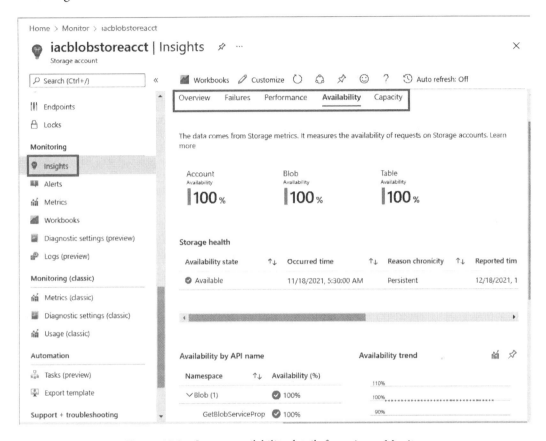

Figure 13.8 – Storage availability details from Azure Monitor

This is how you can use the monitoring features available within the service and with Azure Monitor to get a complete picture of the health of your service.

Let's next learn about the custom logging options available in Azure Monitor.

Understanding custom logging options

The **Custom logs** option in Azure Monitor helps to collect text-based logs that are not part of the standard logs collected by Azure Monitor, such as the system logs, event logs in Windows, and similar ones in Linux. In order to configure custom logs, the host machine must have the Log Analytics agent or the newer AMA installed on it. We just saw how to install the agents in the previous section.

Once we have ensured that the agents are in place, it is a very easy process to set up custom logs. Here are the steps:

1. In the Log Analytics workspace, select the **Custom logs** section and click on the + **Add custom log** option, as illustrated in the following screenshot:

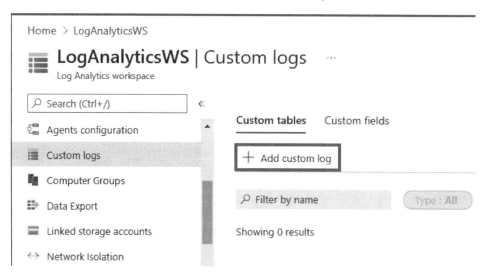

Figure 13.9 – Setting up a new custom log using Log Analytics

2. In the wizard that follows, upload a sample log file so that the tool can parse it and understand the log format. Here is an example of a sample log file:

```
samplelog - Notepad
File  Edit  Format  View  Help
2021-12-01 10:20:05 200, Success, LIST API Success
2021-12-01 10:20:10 302, Error, Could not connect to API Gateway
2021-12-01 10:20:11 303, Error, Ping test failed
```

Figure 13.10 – Sample log file

3. Browse to the location of the sample file and upload it, as shown in the following screenshot:

Figure 13.11 – Uploading a sample log file to the custom log wizard

4. Click on **Next**, and on the next screen, you will see your sample log lines displayed, as shown in the following screenshot:

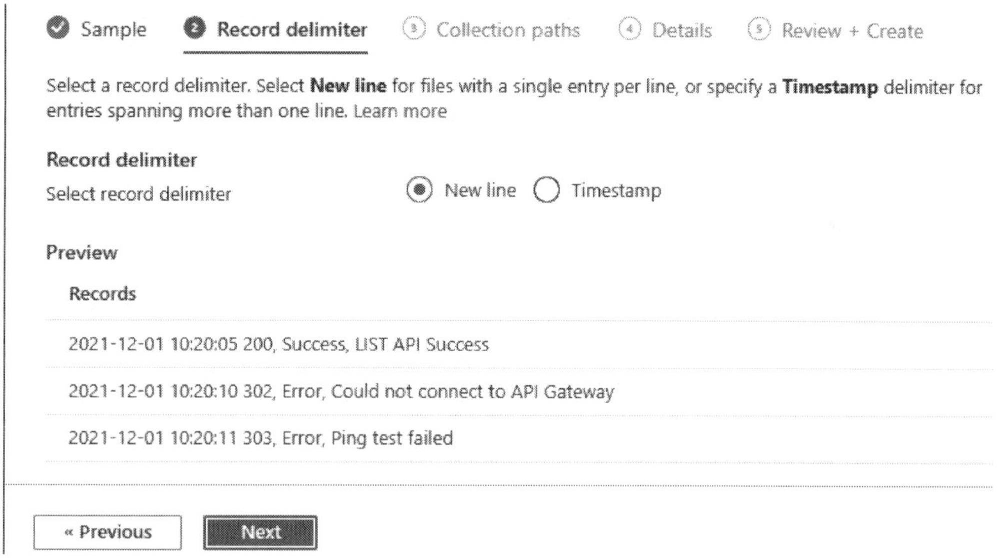

Figure 13.12 – Sample log lines being displayed in the wizard

5. In the next tab, enter the OS type and the path of the log files, as illustrated in the following screenshot:

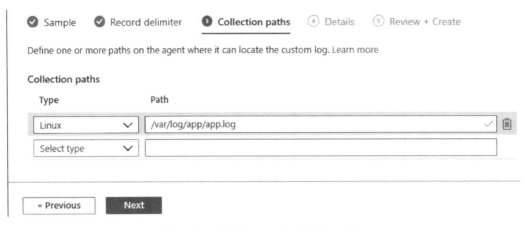

Figure 13.13 – Configuring the log paths

6. In the **Details** tab, enter a **Custom log name** value and a description for your custom log, as shown in the following screenshot, and click **Next**:

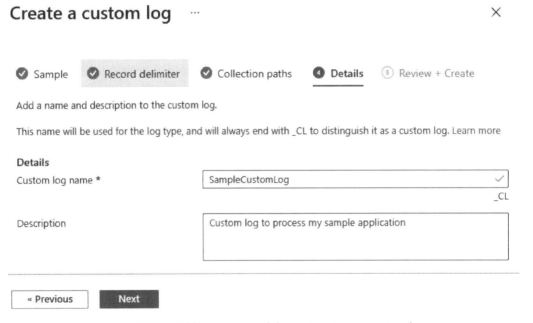

Figure 13.14 – Adding a name and description to your custom log

7. Finally, in the **Review + Create** tab, review the entries, and click on the **Create** button to create a custom log. It's as easy as that.

Note that custom logs have the following restrictions:

- Only the following pre-defined set of timestamp formats are allowed:

```
YYYY-MM-DD HH:MM:SS
M/D/YYYY HH:MM:SS AM/PM
Mon DD, YYYY HH:MM:SS
yyMMdd HH:mm:ss
ddMMyy HH:mm:ss
MMM d hh:mm:ss
dd/MMM/yyyy:HH:mm:ss zzz
yyyy-MM-ddTHH:mm:ssK
```

- No log rotations are allowed.
- Only **American Standard Code for Information Interchange** (**ASCII**) or **Unicode Transformation Format 8** (**UTF-8**) support is provided.
- Time zone conversion is not available for Linux.

You can learn more about custom logs here: `https://docs.microsoft.com/en-us/azure/azure-monitor/agents/data-sources-custom-logs`.

Let's next learn how to interpret Azure Monitor metrics and logs.

Interpreting Azure Monitor metrics and logs

As we have seen in the introduction to Azure Monitoring, metrics and logs form the two main sources of data for monitoring. Let's explore how to view, interpret, and experiment with these two types of monitoring data.

Interpreting Azure Monitor metrics

The metrics data collected from Azure resources is usually displayed on the overview page of the resource itself, and more details are available under the **Metrics** tab. Here is an example again of how it looks for a storage account:

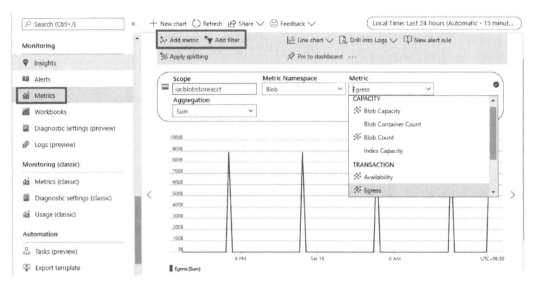

Figure 13.15 – Metrics data for a storage account

For each of the metrics, you can aggregate based on Sum, Avg, Min, and Max. The tool also provides the flexibility to overlay with additional metrics using the **Add metric** option, filter out unwanted data using the **Add filter** option, and so on. You can access the data for up to 30 days using this metrics explorer.

Let's next see how to interpret logs.

Interpreting Azure Monitor logs

We already learned how to send logs to Log Analytics. Let's now explore how to read and experiment with logs in Log Analytics. Once you start sending logs to Log Analytics, you will be able to see the tables for the Azure resource you configured. In the following screenshot, you will see `AzureActivity` and `StorageBlobLogs` tables. These tables will get populated with logs continuously:

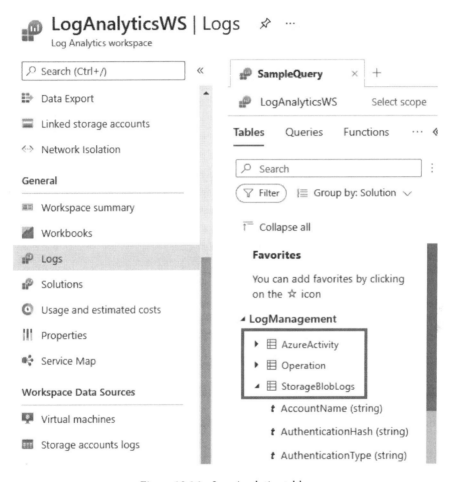

Figure 13.16 – Log Analytics tables

Once we have the log data in the tables, we can use the KQL query language provided by Azure Monitor to query the tables, as we do in **Structured Query Language (SQL)**. KQL queries can be directly typed into the query block, as shown in the following screenshot:

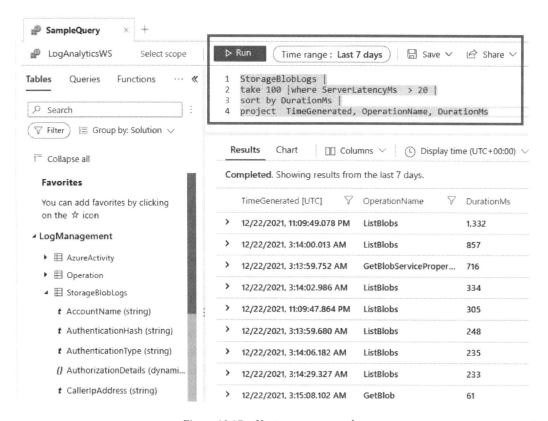

Figure 13.17 – Kusto query example

A Kusto query consists of a sequence of statements that can be delimited by semicolons. You start with a source of data such as a table and then use pipes (|) to transform the data from one step to another. For example, consider the previous screenshot. We start with the StorageBlobLogs table—just specifying the name of the table will list the contents of the table. We then pipe that data to take 100. Now, the 100 entries are piped through the next statement, where ServerLatencyMs > 20, which filters the rows whose latency is higher than 20 **milliseconds (ms)**. We then sort it in descending order and print out a table that contains three columns: TimeGenerated, OperationName, and DurationMs, for how long the operation took.

As you see, Kusto—or KQL—is a very intuitive language that is a mix of SQL and Linux pipes (|). Once you get a hang of it, you can generate very powerful insights by using log data in Log Analytics.

You can learn more about KQL here: `https://docs.microsoft.com/en-us/azure/data-explorer/kusto/query/`.

Now that we have learned about configuring and interpreting metrics and logs for Azure services, let's explore how to measure the performance of data movements within such services. We will learn how to check the performance of data movements while using ADF.

Measuring the performance of data movement

ADF provides a rich set of performance metrics under its Monitoring tab. In the following example, we have a sample Copy Data activity as part of a pipeline called **FetchDataFromBlob**, which copies data from Blob storage into **Azure Data Lake Storage Gen2 (ADLS Gen2)**. If you click on the **Pipeline runs** tab under the **Monitoring** tab, you will see the details of each of the pipelines. If you click on any of the steps, you will see diagnostic details:

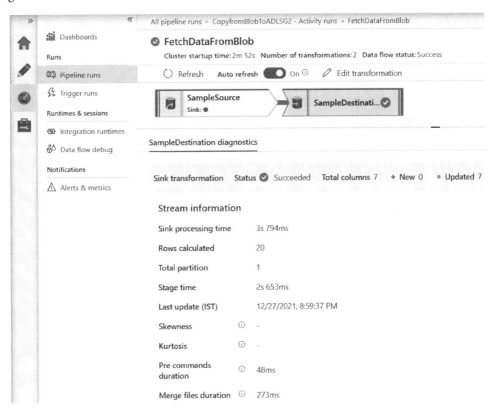

Figure 13.18 – Data movement performance details

This is how you can monitor the performance of data movement. You can learn more about **Copy Data** monitoring here: `https://docs.microsoft.com/en-us/azure/data-factory/copy-activity-monitoring`.

Let's next look at how to monitor overall pipeline performance.

Monitoring data pipeline performance

Similar to the data movement metrics we saw in the previous section, ADF provides metrics for overall pipelines too. In the **Pipeline runs** page under the **Monitoring** tab, if you hover over the pipeline runs, a small **Consumption** icon appears, as shown in the following screenshot:

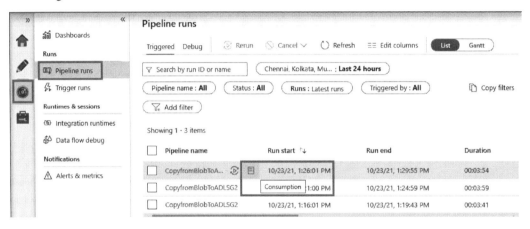

Figure 13.19 – Consumption icon in the Pipeline runs screen

If you click on that icon, ADF shows the pipeline consumption details. Here is a sample screen:

Pipeline run consumption   ✕

	Quantity	Unit
Pipeline orchestration		
Activity Runs	1	Activity runs
Data flow		
General purpose	0.5001	vCore-hour
Compute optimized	0.0000	vCore-hour
Memory optimized	0.0000	vCore-hour

Learn more ⟶

Pricing calculator ⟶

Figure 13.20 – Pipeline resource consumption details screen

You can also get additional metrics about each of the runs from the **Gantt** chart section. You can change the view from **List** to **Gantt**, as shown in the following screenshot:

Figure 13.21 – Additional pipeline details in the Gantt chart page

> **Note**
>
> ADF only maintains pipeline execution details and metrics for 45 days. If you need to analyze the pipeline data for more than 45 days, you will have to send the data to Log Analytics and then use Kusto queries to get the performance details.

This is how we can keep track of pipeline performance. Let's next see how to monitor and update statistics about data.

Monitoring and updating statistics about data across a system

Statistics is an important concept in query optimization. Generating statistics is the process of collecting metadata about your data—such as the number of rows, the size of tables, and so on—which can be used as additional inputs by the SQL engine to optimize query plans. For example, if two tables have to be joined and one table is very small, the SQL engine can use this statistical information to pick a query plan that works best for such highly skewed tables. The Synapse SQL pool engine uses something known as **cost-based optimizers** (**CBOs**). These optimizers choose the least expensive query plan from a set of query plans that can be generated for a given SQL script.

Let's look at how to create statistics for both Synapse dedicated and serverless pools.

Creating statistics for Synapse dedicated pools

You can enable statistics in Synapse SQL dedicated pools using the following command:

```
ALTER DATABASE [DW_NAME] SET AUTO_CREATE_STATISTICS ON
```

Once AUTO_CREATE_STATISTICS is ON, any SELECT, INSERT-SELECT, CTAS, UPDATE, DELETE, or EXPLAIN statements will automatically trigger the creation of statistics for the columns involved in the query, if not already present.

> **Note**
>
> Automatic creation of statistics is not available for temporary or external tables.

You can create statistics on demand using the following command:

```
CREATE STATISTICS [statistics_name]
    ON [schema_name].[table_name]([column_name])
    WITH SAMPLE 40 PERCENT;
```

In the preceding example, we are using a 40% sample. If you do not provide a sample value, the default is 20%. You can also do a full scan instead of sampling by using the following command:

```
CREATE STATISTICS [statistics_name]
    ON [schema_name].[table_name]([column_name])
    WITH FULLSCAN;
```

> **Tip**
> As a general guideline, for less than 1 billion rows, use default sampling (20%). With more than 1 billion rows, use sampling of 2 to 10%.

Let's next look at updating existing statistics in Synapse dedicated pools.

Updating statistics for Synapse dedicated pools

Similar to creating statistics, you can also periodically update statistics. You can use the following command to achieve this:

```
UPDATE STATISTICS [schema_name].[table_name]([stat_name]);
```

It is a good practice to update statistics after every fresh data load.

For more information on statistics in Synapse SQL pools, you can refer to the following link: https://docs.microsoft.com/en-us/azure/synapse-analytics/sql/develop-tables-statistics#statistics-in-dedicated-sql-pool.

Next, let's look at how to create statistics for Synapse serverless pools.

Creating statistics for Synapse serverless pools

The concept of statistics is the same for dedicated and serverless pools. In the case of serverless pools, the auto-creation of statistics is turned on by default for Parquet files but not for **comma-separated values (CSV)** files. Since we deal with external tables in serverless pools, we will have to create statistics for external tables. The command for external tables is shown here:

```
CREATE STATISTICS [statistics_name]
ON { external_table } ( column )
    WITH
        { FULLSCAN
```

```
      | [ SAMPLE number PERCENT ] }
    , { NORECOMPUTE }
```

> **Note**
>
> Only single-column statistics are possible on external tables, while others allow multi-column statistics.

Let's next look at how to update existing statistics for serverless pools.

Updating statistics for Synapse serverless pools

In order to update statistics for Synapse serverless pools, you will have to first drop the existing statistics and then recreate them. The following command shows how to drop the old table:

```
DROP STATISTICS [OLD_STATISTICS_TABLE_NAME]
```

And then, we can recreate the statistics afresh by following the commands shown here:

```
CREATE STATISTICS [statistics_name]
    on [NEW_STATISTICS_TABLE_NAME] (STATENAME)
    WITH FULLSCAN, NORECOMPUTE
```

> **Note**
>
> Statistics collection might cause a slight performance degradation if statistics are missing for the columns in a query. But once statistics are generated, future queries will be much faster.

If you would like to learn more about generating statistics, you can refer to the following link: https://docs.microsoft.com/en-us/azure/synapse-analytics/sql/develop-tables-statistics#statistics-in-serverless-sql-pool.

Let's next look at how to measure query performance.

Measuring query performance

Query performance is a very interesting topic in databases and analytical engines such as Spark and Hive. You will find tons of books and articles written on these topics. In this section, I'll try to give an overview of how to monitor query performance in Synapse dedicated SQL pools and Spark. In the next chapter, we will focus on how to actually optimize the queries. I've provided links for further reading in each section so that you can learn more about the techniques if you wish.

For measuring the performance of any SQL-based queries, it is recommended to set up the **Transaction Processing Performance Council H** or **DS** (**TPC-H** or **TPC-DS**) benchmarking suites and run them on a regular basis to identify any regressions in the platform. TPC-H and TPC-DS are industry-standard benchmarking test suites. If you are interested in learning more about them, please follow these links:

- You can learn more about TPC-H here: `http://www.tpc.org/tpch/`.
- You can learn more about TPC-DS here: `http://www.tpc.org/tpcds/`.

Let's next look at how we can monitor Synapse SQL pool performance.

Monitoring Synapse SQL pool performance

The Synapse SQL **Metrics** page itself has quite a lot of metrics that can be easily used to identify any performance regressions. Here is a sample screenshot of the Synapse SQL **Metrics** section:

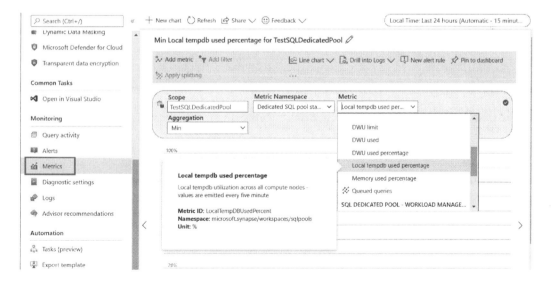

Figure 13.22 – Query monitoring screen of Synapse SQL pool

The **Metrics** tab in Synapse SQL provides metrics for **Data Warehouse Unit (DWU)** usage, memory usage, and so on, but it doesn't provide details about query performance or query wait times. We will have to use one of the following two approaches to get such query performance details.

Querying system tables

Synapse SQL pool provides the following system tables that can be used to monitor query performance:

- `sys.dm_pdw_exec_requests`—This contains all current and recently active requests in Azure Synapse Analytics. It contains details such as `total_elapsed_time`, `submit_time`, `start_time`, `end_time`, `command`, `result_cache_hit`, and so on.

- `sys.dm_pdw_waits`—This contains details of the wait states in a query, including locks and waits on transmission queues.

You can find details on all such system tables with monitoring and management information here:

`https://docs.microsoft.com/en-us/sql/relational-databases/system-dynamic-management-views/sql-and-parallel-data-warehouse-dynamic-management-views`

Next, let's look at how to get performance details using a feature called Query Store.

Using Query Store

Azure SQL and Synapse SQL support a feature called **Query Store** that can be used for both query performance monitoring and performance tuning. It is supported in Synapse SQL pool and other flavors of SQL in Azure. **Query Store** is used to store the history of queries, plans, and runtime statistics. This historical data can then be used to aid in query optimization, identifying query regressions, monitoring trends in resource utilization such as CPU and memory for queries, identifying wait time patterns in query plans, and so on.

Query Store is not enabled by default for Synapse SQL pool. You can enable **Query Store** using the following **Transact-SQL (T-SQL)** command:

```
ALTER DATABASE <database_name> SET QUERY_STORE = ON;
```

Query Store in Synapse SQL stores the following three main components:

- **Query details**—Details such as query parameters, compilation times, compilation counts, and so on. Here are the specific tables that contain **Query Store** query details:

  `sys.query_store_query`

  `sys.query_store_query_text`

- **Plan details**—Query plan details such as the query **identifier** (**ID**), query hash, query text, and so on. Here is the specific table that contains **Query Store** plan details:

  `sys.query_store_plan`

- **Runtime statistics**—Runtime details of queries such as the time taken, CPU time, average duration, row counts, and so on. Here are the specific tables that contain runtime statistics:

  `sys.query_store_runtime_stats`

  `sys.query_store_runtime_stats_interval`

Here is a sample of the `sys.query_store_runtime_stats` table so that you have an idea of how it looks:

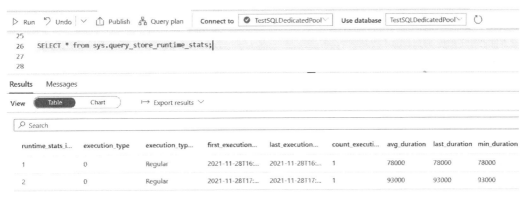

Figure 13.23 – Sample Query Store runtime statistics

Wait statistics are not yet available for Azure Synapse SQL, as of writing this book. However, they are available in other Azure SQL flavors, such as Azure SQL Database.

You can learn more about **Query Store** here: `https://docs.microsoft.com/en-us/sql/relational-databases/performance/monitoring-performance-by-using-the-query-store`.

Let's next look at the options available for monitoring the performance of Spark.

Spark query performance monitoring

Spark performance monitoring can be done directly via the Spark **user interface** (**UI**). The Spark UI, along with the **Spark History server**, provides job-specific and stage-specific metrics that can be used to determine if jobs are slowing down compared to previous runs. The techniques we explored in *Chapter 9, Designing and Developing a Batch Processing Solution*, under the *Debugging Spark jobs by using the Spark UI* section, will be the same for analyzing performance regression in Spark jobs. Since we have already covered the details in that chapter, we'll not repeat them here. Please glance through *Chapter 9, Designing and Developing a Batch Processing Solution*, if you have any doubts regarding using the Spark UI.

Once slow queries are identified via the Spark UI, we can use query optimization techniques to speed up queries. We will explore these techniques in the next chapter.

In the meantime, let's explore another topic that is related to performance tuning: interpreting Spark DAGs.

Interpreting a Spark DAG

A DAG is just a regular graph with nodes and edges but with no cycles or loops. In order to understand a Spark DAG, we first have to understand where a DAG comes into the picture during the execution of a Spark job.

When a user submits a Spark job, the Spark driver first identifies all the tasks involved in accomplishing the job. It then figures out which of these tasks can be run in parallel and which tasks depend on other tasks. Based on this information, it converts the Spark job into a graph of tasks. The nodes at the same level indicate jobs that can be run in parallel, and the nodes at different levels indicate tasks that need to be run after the previous nodes. This graph is acyclic, as denoted by A in DAG. This DAG is then converted into a physical execution plan. In the physical execution plan, nodes that are at the same level are segregated into stages. Once all the tasks and stages are complete, the Spark job is termed as completed.

Let's look at what a DAG looks like. You can access a Spark DAG from the Spark UI. Just click on any of the job links and then click on the **DAG Visualization** link.

Here is a DAG for a simple word count problem:

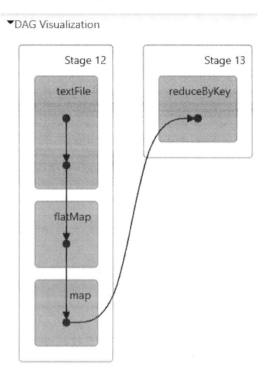

Figure 13.24 – DAG with multiple stages

In the first stage, we see that the word count has three steps and a reduce step in the next stage. Ignore the stage numbers, as Spark assigns consecutive numbers for all jobs that are run in that Spark session. So, if you have run any other job before this job, the number gets sequentially incremented. Here is some further information about each task:

- The textFile task corresponds to the reading of the file from the storage.

- The flatMap task corresponds to the splitting of the words.

- The map task corresponds to the formation of (word, 1) pairs.

- The reduceByKey task corresponds to the aggregation of all the (word, 1) pairs together to get the sum of each distinct word.

You can get more details about each step by clicking on the **Stage** boxes. Here is an example of a detailed view of **Stage 12** from the previous screenshot:

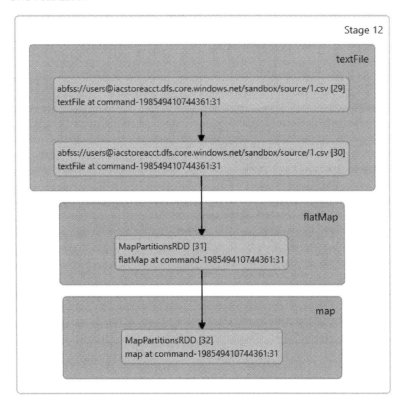

Figure 13.25 – Detailed view of the stage

The main advantage of learning to read Spark DAGs is that they help you identify bottlenecks in your Spark queries. You can identify how much data movement is happening between stages (also known as **data shuffle**), if there are too many sequential stages, if there are slow stages in the critical path, and so on.

You can learn more about Spark DAGs here: `https://spark.apache.org/docs/3.0.0/web-ui.html`.

Now that we have learned a bit about query performance monitoring and analyzing Spark DAGs, let's also look at how to monitor overall cluster performance.

Monitoring cluster performance

Since services such as Synapse and ADF are **platform-as-a-service (PaaS)** services where you will not have explicit control over the clusters, the one place where we can control each and every aspect of a cluster is the **Azure HDInsight** service. In HDInsight, you can create your own Hadoop, Spark, Hive, HBase, and other clusters and control every aspect of the cluster. You can use Log Analytics to monitor cluster performance, as with the other examples we saw earlier in the chapter. You can learn more about using Log Analytics in HDInsight here: `https://docs.microsoft.com/en-us/azure/hdinsight/hdinsight-hadoop-oms-log-analytics-tutorial`.

Apart from the Log Analytics approach, there are four main areas of the HDInsight portal that help monitor cluster performance. Let's look at them.

Monitoring overall cluster performance

The HDInsight **Ambari** dashboard is the first place to check for cluster health. If you see very high heap usage, disk usage, or network latencies, then these might be indicators of non-optimal cluster usage. Here is a sample screenshot of the **Ambari** dashboard:

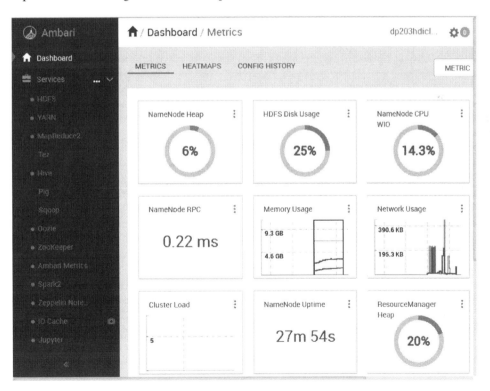

Figure 13.26 – HDInsight Ambari dashboard home page

But these overall cluster details will not be enough to isolate node-level or query-level performance issues. For this, we will have to look into the next monitoring option available, which is a per-node monitor.

Monitoring per-node performance

From the **Ambari** dashboard home page, if you select the **Hosts** tab, you will be able to see the per-host performance level, as illustrated in the following screenshot:

Figure 13.27 – Per-host metrics in Ambari

If you click on each of the hostnames, it will show even more details of the host, as shown in the following screenshot:

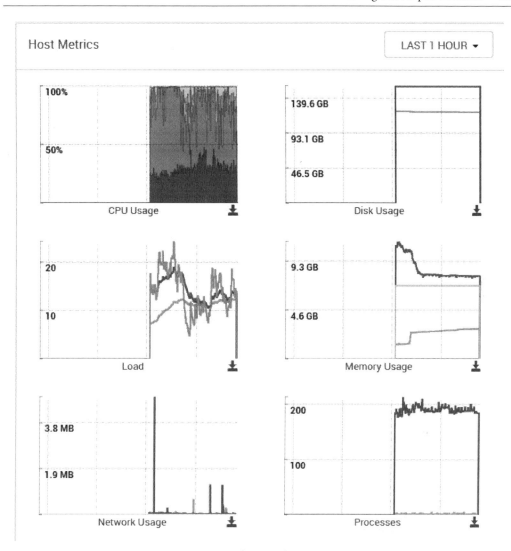

Figure 13.28 – Ambari per-host metrics page

If you want to drill down deeper to the query level, then we can look at **Yet Another Resource Negotiator** (**YARN**) queues.

Monitoring YARN queue/scheduler performance

From the **Resource Manager** page in **Ambari**, select the **Application Queues** option. This will show all the applications and metrics related to the applications. On the left-hand side, you will have the **Scheduler** link, as illustrated in the following screenshot. Select that to see the status of the YARN queues:

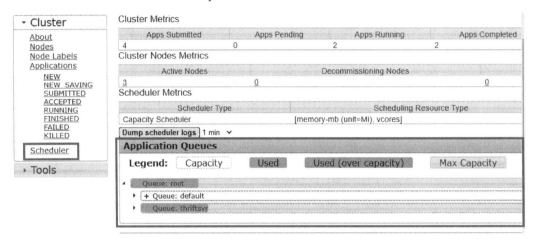

Figure 13.29 – Checking the YARN queues' status

Based on the color of the queue, you should be able to distinguish if a queue is underused or overused.

There is one more aspect of clusters that usually results in slower performance, and that is storage throttling.

Monitoring storage throttling

If you get a `429 Too many requests` error code in your applications, you might be encountering throttling from the storage. Either check your storage account to increase the limit or try to distribute your application processing over multiple storage accounts to overcome this problem.

You can learn more about throttling here: `https://docs.microsoft.com/en-us/azure/azure-resource-manager/management/request-limits-and-throttling`.

Hope you got a good idea of how to monitor cluster performance. Now, let's look at how to schedule and monitor ADF pipeline **continuous integration/continuous deployment (CI/CD)**.

Scheduling and monitoring pipeline tests

In *Chapter 11*, *Managing Batches and Pipelines*, we briefly introduced Azure DevOps for version control. **Azure DevOps** provides another feature called **Azure Pipelines**, which can be used to create CI/CD pipelines to deploy ADF. If you are not aware of CI/CD, it is a method of continuously testing and deploying applications to the production environment in an automated manner. In this section, we will look into how to create, schedule, and monitor a CI/CD pipeline.

> **Note**
>
> As of writing this book, Azure DevOps Pipelines support for Synapse Pipelines was not available. It is only available for ADF.

Here are the high-level steps to create a CI/CD pipeline using Azure pipelines:

1. Select **Azure DevOps** from the Azure portal. On the **Azure DevOps** page, select **Releases** under **Pipelines** and click the **New Pipeline** button. This will take you to a new screen, shown in the following screenshot. Choose the **Empty job** option:

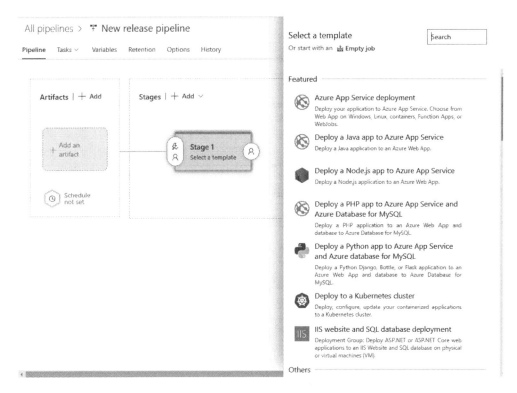

Figure 13.30 – Azure pipeline creation wizard

2. Next, click on the **Add an artifact** option and update your ADF source repository details, as shown in the following screenshot:

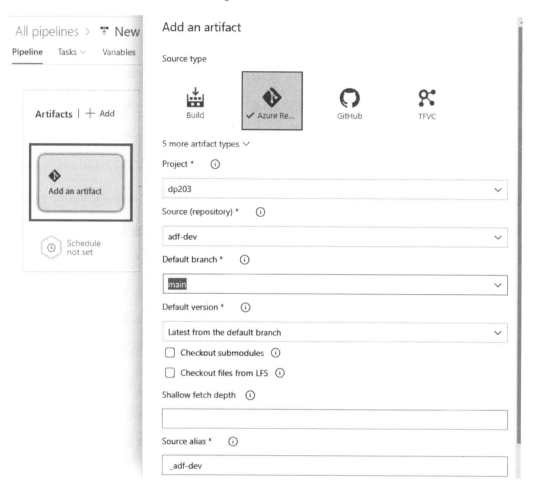

Figure 13.31 – Updating artifact information in Azure Pipelines

3. Once added, click on the **View Tasks** link on the next page, then click on the + symbol. From the task list, choose the **ARM template deployment** task, as illustrated in the following screenshot:

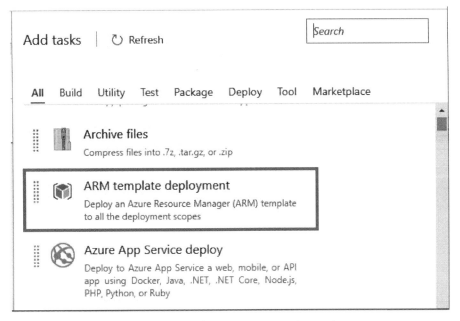

Figure 13.32 – Choosing Azure Pipeline tasks

4. This will bring up the **Azure Resource Manager** (**ARM**) template configuration page, as shown in the following screenshot:

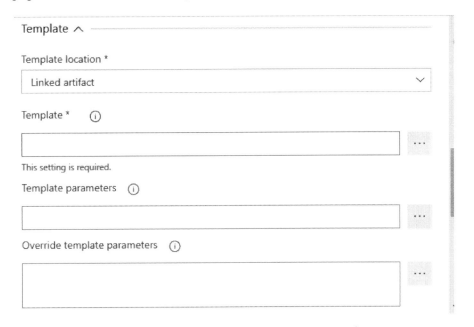

Figure 13.33 – ARM template and template parameters specification page

5. For the **Template** textbox, browse to the file named `ARMTemplateForFactory.json` in your `ADF` folder of the `adf_publish` branch.

6. For the **Template parameters** textbox, choose the `ARMTemplateParametersForFactory.json` file in your `ADF` folder of the `adf_publish` branch.

7. Once you are done filling up the details, save the page.

8. Finally, click on the **Create Release** button at the top to create a CI/CD pipeline.

Now that we have a pipeline to deploy CI/CD, it can be scheduled in multiple ways. Some examples are provided here:

- **CI triggers**—To trigger a pipeline when a user pushes a change to the `git` branch

- **Pull request (PR) triggers**—When a PR is raised or changes are submitted to the PR

- **Scheduled triggers**—Time-based scheduling

- **Pipeline completion triggers**—Triggering based on the completion of previous pipelines

You can learn more about implementing triggers here: `https://docs.microsoft.com/en-us/azure/devops/pipelines/build/triggers?view=azure-devops`.

Once we have the triggers set up, the pipelines continue to get tested and deployed. We can monitor the progress from the **Releases** tab of Azure DevOps. Here is a sample image of the **Pipelines** screen with a summary of the pipelines that were run:

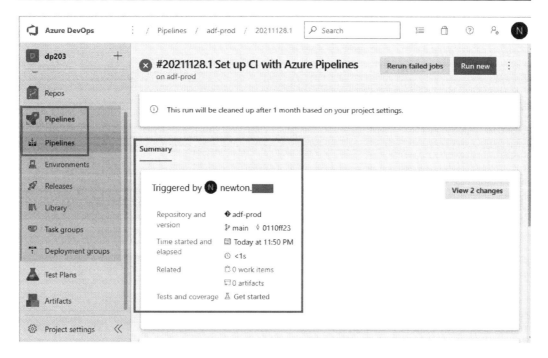

Figure 13.34 – Release pipelines CI/CD monitoring

Azure DevOps and Pipelines are a huge topic of their own and we will not be able to do them justice in a small section here, so I'm providing follow-up links to understand more about ADF CI/CD, Azure pipelines, and adding tests to pipelines.

You can learn more about ADF CI/CD here: `https://docs.microsoft.com/en-us/azure/data-factory/continuous-integration-delivery`.

Summary

This chapter introduced a lot of new technologies and techniques, and I hope you got a grasp of them. Even though the number of technologies involved is high, the weightage of this chapter with respect to the certification is relatively low, so you may have noticed that I've kept the topics slightly at a higher level and have provided further links for you to read more on the topics.

In this chapter, we started by introducing Azure Monitor and Log Analytics. We learned how to send log data to Log Analytics, how to define custom logging options, and how to interpret metrics and logs data. After that, we focused on measuring the performance of data movements, pipelines, SQL queries, and Spark queries. We also learned how to interpret Spark DAGs, before moving on to monitoring cluster performance and cluster pipeline tests. You should now be able to set up a monitoring solution for your data pipelines and be able to tell if your data movement, pipeline setups, cluster setups, and query runs are performing optimally.

In the next chapter, we will be focusing on query optimization and troubleshooting techniques.

14

Optimizing and Troubleshooting Data Storage and Data Processing

Welcome to the final chapter in the *Monitoring and Optimizing Data Storage and Data Processing* section of the syllabus. The only chapter left after this is the *revision* and *sample questions* for the certification. Congratulations on reaching this far; you are now just a hop away from acquiring your certification.

In this chapter, we will be focusing on the optimization and troubleshooting techniques for data storage and data processing technologies. We will start with the topics for optimizing Spark and Synapse SQL queries using techniques such as compacting small files, handling UDFs, data skews, shuffles, indexing, cache management, and more. We will also look into techniques for troubleshooting Spark and Synapse pipelines and general guidelines for optimizing any analytical pipeline. Once you complete this chapter, you will have the knowledge to debug performance issues or troubleshoot failures in pipelines and Spark jobs.

We will be covering the following topics in this chapter:

- Compacting small files
- Rewriting **user-defined functions** (**UDFs**)
- Handling skews in data
- Handling data spills
- Tuning shuffle partitions
- Finding shuffling in a pipeline
- Optimizing resource management
- Tuning queries by using indexers
- Tuning queries by using cache
- Optimizing pipelines for analytical or transactional purposes
- Optimizing pipelines for descriptive versus analytical workloads
- Troubleshooting a failed Spark job
- Troubleshooting a failed pipeline run

Technical requirements

For this chapter, you will need the following:

- An Azure account (free or paid)
- An active Azure Data Factory or Synapse workspace
- An active Azure Databricks workspace

Let's get started!

Compacting small files

Small files are the nightmares of big data processing systems. Analytical engines such as Spark, Synapse SQL, and Hive, and cloud storage systems such as Blob and ADLS Gen2, are all inherently optimized for big files. Hence, to make our data pipelines efficient, it is better to merge or compact the small files into bigger ones. This can be achieved in Azure using **Azure Data Factory** and **Synapse Pipelines**. Let's look at an example using Azure Data Factory to concatenate a bunch of small CSV files in a directory into one big file. The steps for Synapse pipelines will be very similar:

1. From the Azure Data Factory portal, select the **Copy Data** activity as shown in the following screenshot. In the **Source** tab, either choose an existing source dataset or create a new one, pointing to the data storage where the small files are present. Next, choose the **Wildcard file path** option for **File Path type**. In the **Wildcard Paths** field, provide a folder path ending with a *. This will ensure that the **Copy data** activity considers all the files in that folder. In the following screenshot, all the small files are present in the folder named sandbox/driver/in.

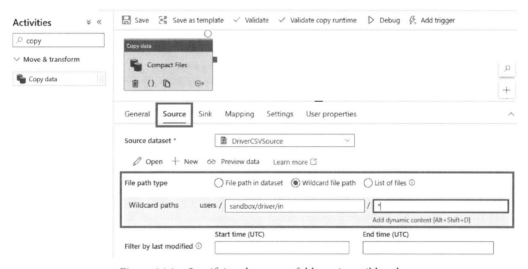

Figure 14.1 – Specifying the source folder using wildcards

2.   Next, in the **Sink** tab, select your destination dataset, and, for **Copy behavior**, select the **Merge files** option, as shown in the following screenshot:

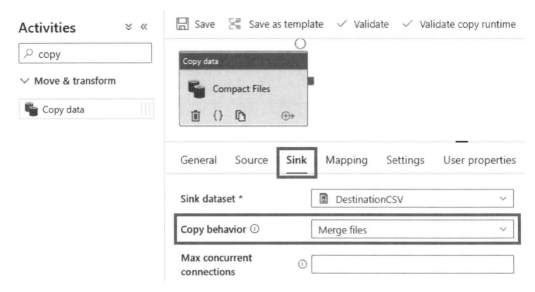

Figure 14.2 – Selecting the Merge files copy behavior in Copy Activity of ADF

Now, if you run this pipeline, the files in the source folder (CSV files in our case) will get merged into a file called Output.csv in the destination folder that is defined in the DestinationCSV dataset.

You can learn more about the merge option of Copy Activity in ADF here: https://docs.microsoft.com/en-us/azure/data-factory/connector-file-system?tabs=data-factory#copy-activity-properties.

Another way to compact small files is the incremental copy method that we have already explored in *Chapter 4*, *Designing the Serving Layer*, under the *Designing for incremental loading* section. In this option, we incrementally update tables with small incoming changes. This would also qualify as a compaction option as we are incrementally merging small files into a big one via SQL tables.

There is a third way of compacting small files using **Azure Databricks Spark** and **Synapse Spark**. Spark provides a feature called **bin packing**, via its specialized storage layer called **Delta Lake** (note the spelling, not Data Lake).

A Delta Lake is an *open source storage layer* that runs on top of Data Lakes. It enhances the Data Lake to support features including the following:

- **ACID Transactions**: Similar to what is available in databases and data warehouses, Delta Lake enables ACID transactions on top of Data Lakes.

- **Unified Batch**, **Interactive**, and **Streaming System**: Tables defined in Delta Lakes can serve as the source for batch processing systems, interactive systems such as notebooks, and streaming systems.

- **Updates and Deletes**: This feature supports updates, deletes, and merges to tables. This enables automatic support for **Slowly Changing Dimensions** (**SCDs**), streaming **upserts**, and any other operations that require the ability to update or merge data.

A Delta Lake engine is enabled by default in Azure Databricks and Synapse Spark. So, all you need to do is just attach your Spark notebook to any Databricks or Synapse Spark cluster and run the Delta commands. Let's look at some sample commands of how to read, write, and create tables in Delta Lake:

- We can write to Azure Blob storage in delta format as shown. abfss in the following code refers to the Azure storage protocol: **Azure Blob File System [Secure]**:

```
df.write.mode("overwrite").format("delta").save("abfss://
path/to/delta/files")
```

- Load data from the delta file, as shown here:

```
Val df: DataFrame = spark.read.format("delta").
load(abfss://path/to/delta/files)
```

- Create a table using delta, as shown here:

```
Spark.sql("CREATE TABLE CUSTOMER USING DELTA LOCATION
"abfss://path/to/delta/files")
```

As you may have noticed, working with Delta Lake is very similar to working with file formats such as Parquet, JSON, or CSV.

You can learn more about Delta Lake here: https://docs.microsoft.com/en-us/azure/databricks/delta/.

Now let's look at how to enable bin packing. Bin packing is the feature provided by Delta Lake to compact small files into bigger ones to improve the performance of read queries. We can run bin packing on a folder using the OPTIMIZE command, as shown in the following code block.

```
Spark.sql("OPTIMIZE delta.' abfss://path/to/delta/files'")
```

This will merge the small files in the folder into optimal large files.

The third option is to enable Optimize by default while creating the tables using the following properties:

- `delta.autoOptimize.optimizeWrite = true`
- `delta.autoOptimize.autoCompact = true`

Here is an example of how to use the `optimize` properties while creating a table:

```
CREATE TABLE Customer (
id INT,
name STRING,
location STRING
) TBLPROPERTIES (
delta.autoOptimize.optimizeWrite = true,
delta.autoOptimize.autoCompact = true
)
```

You can learn more about Azure Databricks bin packing here: `https://docs.microsoft.com/en-us/azure/databricks/delta/optimizations/file-mgmt`.

Now you know three different ways to compact small files. Next, let's look at using user-defined functions.

Rewriting user-defined functions (UDFs)

User-defined functions are custom functions that can be defined in databases and in certain analytical and streaming engines such as Spark and Azure Stream Analytics. An example of a UDF could be a custom function to check whether a given value is a valid email address.

The DP-203 syllabus just mentions the topic as *Rewriting user-defined functions*. In a literal sense, this is just dropping a UDF and recreating a new one, as we do for SQL or Spark tables. However, I believe the syllabus committee might have referred to rewriting normal repetitive scripts as UDFs to make them efficient from a development perspective. Note that UDFs can also decrease runtime performance if not designed correctly. Let's look at the ways to create UDFs in SQL, Spark, and Streaming.

Writing UDFs in Synapse SQL Pool

You can create a user-defined function in Synapse SQL using the CREATE FUNCTION command in Synapse SQL. Here is an example of using the CREATE FUNCTION command to create a simple email validation UDF. The script checks for the email pattern and, if not valid, returns the string "Not Available":

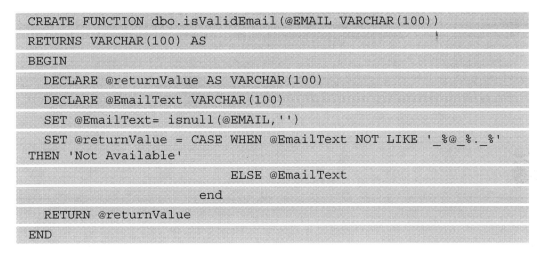

```
CREATE FUNCTION dbo.isValidEmail(@EMAIL VARCHAR(100))
RETURNS VARCHAR(100) AS
BEGIN
   DECLARE @returnValue AS VARCHAR(100)
   DECLARE @EmailText VARCHAR(100)
   SET @EmailText= isnull(@EMAIL,'')
   SET @returnValue = CASE WHEN @EmailText NOT LIKE '_%@_%._%'
THEN 'Not Available'
                           ELSE @EmailText
                    end
   RETURN @returnValue
END
```

Now that we have the UDF, let's see how to use it in a query. Let's say you have a sample table with some valid and invalid email IDs.

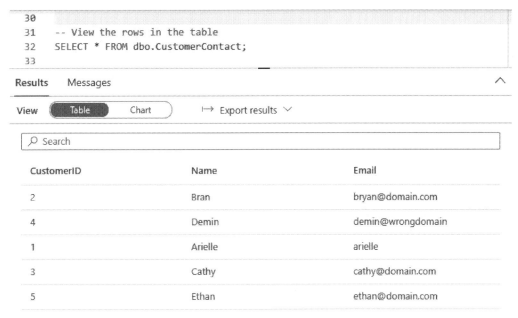

```
30
31    -- View the rows in the table
32    SELECT * FROM dbo.CustomerContact;
33
```

Results   Messages

View (Table   Chart)   ↦ Export results ∨

🔍 Search

CustomerID	Name	Email
2	Bran	bryan@domain.com
4	Demin	demin@wrongdomain
1	Arielle	arielle
3	Cathy	cathy@domain.com
5	Ethan	ethan@domain.com

Figure 14.3 – Sample table with valid and invalid email IDs

We want to mark the rows with invalid email IDs as **Not Available**. We can accomplish this using the following query.

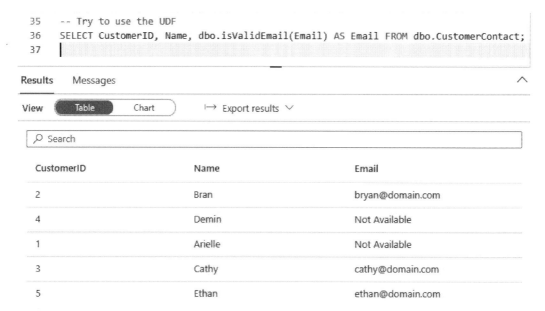

```
35    -- Try to use the UDF
36    SELECT CustomerID, Name, dbo.isValidEmail(Email) AS Email FROM dbo.CustomerContact;
37
```

Results   Messages

View (**Table**   Chart)   ⊢→ Export results ∨

🔍 Search

CustomerID	Name	Email
2	Bran	bryan@domain.com
4	Demin	Not Available
1	Arielle	Not Available
3	Cathy	cathy@domain.com
5	Ethan	ethan@domain.com

Figure 14.4 – Using UDFs in a query

As expected, the rows with invalid emails got substituted with the **Not Available** string.

You can learn more about UDFs in Synapse SQL here: `https://docs.microsoft.com/en-us/sql/t-sql/statements/create-function-sql-data-warehouse`.

Next, let's look at how to write UDFs in Spark.

Writing UDFs in Spark

Spark also supports the UDF feature. In Spark, UDFs are just like any regular functions. Here is a simple example of registering a UDF in Spark:

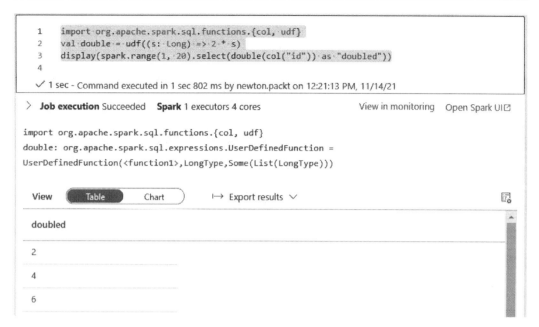

Figure 14.5 – Simple Spark UDF example

The sample script just doubles any values given to it. You can define UDFs to reduce the repetition of code.

You can learn more about Spark UDFs here: `https://spark.apache.org/docs/latest/sql-ref-functions-udf-scalar.html`.

Next, let's look at writing UDFs in Azure Stream Analytics.

Writing UDFs in Stream Analytics

Azure Stream Analytics supports simple UDFs via **JavaScript**. The UDFs are stateless and can only return single (scalar) values. Unlike SQL and Spark examples, in Stream Analytics, we have to register the UDF from the portal before using it. Let's see an example:

1. Here is a UDF definition for extracting `customer.id` from an input JSON blob:

```
function main(arg) {
    var customer = JSON.parse(arg);
    return customer.id;
}
```

2. Next, we need to register the UDF. From the Stream Analytics job page, select **Functions** under **Job topology**. Click on the **+ Add** link and select **Javascript UDF**, as shown in the following screenshot:

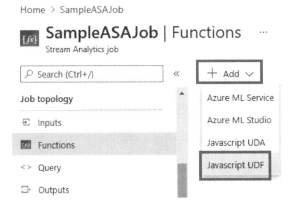

Figure 14.6 – Adding UDFs in Azure Stream Analytics

3. Once you click on the **Javascript UDF** option, this will reveal a screen as shown in the following screenshot, where you can fill in the UDF code and provide a name for the UDF in the **Function alias** field. Click on **Save** to register the new UDF.

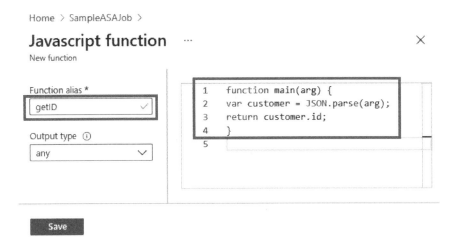

Figure 14.7 – Defining the UDF in the ASA portal

4. Once the UDF is registered, you can call it in your streaming queries, as shown here:

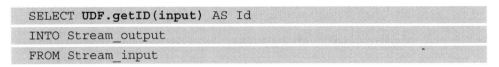

```
SELECT UDF.getID(input) AS Id
INTO Stream_output
FROM Stream_input
```

You can learn more about the Stream Analytics UDF here: `https://docs.microsoft.com/en-us/azure/stream-analytics/functions-overview`.

Now you know how to define UDFs in SQL, Spark, and Streaming. Let's next look at handling data skews.

Handling skews in data

A data skew refers to an extreme, uneven distribution of data in a dataset. Let's take an example of the number of trips per month of our **Imaginary Airport Cab (IAC)** example. Let's assume the data distribution as shown in the following graph:

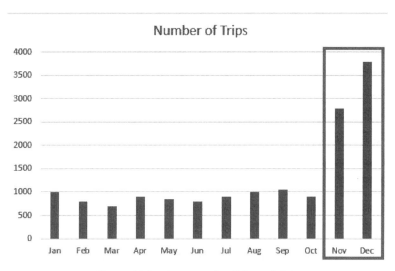

Figure 14.8 – An example of skewed data

As you can see from the graph, the trip numbers for November and December are quite high compared to the other months. Such an uneven distribution of data is referred to as a **data skew**. Now, if we were to distribute the monthly data to individual compute nodes, the nodes that are processing the data for November and December are going to take a lot more time than the ones processing the other months. And if we were generating an annual report, then all the other stages would have to wait for the November and December stages to complete. Such wait times are inefficient for job performance. To make the processing more efficient, we will have to find a way to assign similar amounts of processing data to each of the compute nodes. We will explore a few options recommended by Azure for handling such data skews.

Skews can be fixed either at the storage level or the compute level. Based on where we fix the issue, there are different options available.

Fixing skews at the storage level

Here are a few techniques for fixing skews at the storage level:

- Find a better distribution/partition strategy that would balance the compute time evenly. In our example of the monthly trip count, we could explore partitioning the data into smaller chunks at the weekly level or try to partition along a different dimension, such as ZIP codes altogether, and see whether that helps.

- Add a second distribution key. If the primary key is not splitting the data evenly, and if the option of moving to a new distribution key is not possible, you could add a secondary partition key. For example, after the data is split into months, you can further split them into, say, states of the country within each month. That way, if you are in the USA, you get 50 more splits, which could be more evenly distributed.

- Randomize the data and use the round-robin technique to distribute the data evenly into partitions. If you are not able to find an optimal distribution key, then you can resort to round-robin distribution. This will ensure that the data is evenly distributed.

Note that it might not always be possible to recreate tables or distributions. So, some pre-planning is very important when we first decide on the partition strategy. However, if we end up in a situation where the partitioning strategies are not helping, we might still have one more option left to improve our skew handling. This option is to trust our compute engine to produce an intelligent query plan that is aware of the data skew. Let's look at how to achieve that next.

Fixing skews at the compute level

Here are a few techniques for fixing skews at the compute level:

- *Improving the query plan by enabling statistics*. We have already seen how to enable statistics in *Chapter 13, Monitoring Data Storage and Data Processing,* in the *Monitoring and updating statistics about data across a system* section. Once we enable statistics, query engines such as the Synapse SQL engine, which uses a cost-based optimizer, will utilize statistics to generate the most optimal plan based on the cost associated with each plan. The optimizer can identify data skews and automatically apply the appropriate optimizations in place to handle skew.

- *Ignore the outlier data if not significant*. This is probably the simplest of the options, but might not be applicable to all situations. If the data that is skewed is not very important, then you can safely ignore it.

While we are on the topic of handling skews at the compute level, Synapse Spark has a very helpful feature that helps identify data skews in each stage of the Spark job. If you go to the **Apache Spark applications** tab under the **Monitoring** section of a Synapse workspace, you can see the skew details. See the following screenshot:

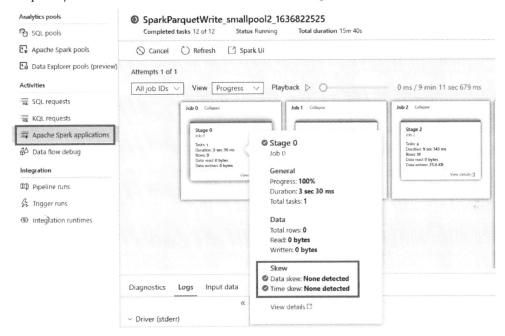

Figure 14.9 – Synapse Spark notifying data skews in Spark stages

This Synapse Spark feature makes it very easy for anyone to identify skews in their datasets.

Now you know the basic techniques for handling data skews. Let's next look at handling data spills.

Handling data spills

Data spill refers to the process where a compute engine such as SQL or Spark, while executing a query, is unable to hold the required data in memory and writes (spills) to disk. This results in increased query execution time due to the expensive disk reads and writes. Spills can occur for any of the following reasons:

- The data partition size is too big.

- The compute resource size is small, especially the memory.

- The exploded data size during merges, unions, and so on exceeds the memory limits of the compute node.

Solutions for handling data spills would be as follows:

- Increase the compute capacity, especially the memory if possible. This will incur higher costs, but is the easiest of the options.

- Reduce the data partition sizes, and repartition if necessary. This is more effort-intensive as repartitioning takes time and effort. If you are not able to afford the higher compute resources, then reducing the data partition sizes is the best option.

- Remove skews in data. Sometimes, it is the data profile that causes the spills. If the data is skewed, it might cause spills in the partitions with the higher data size. We already looked at the options for handling data skews in the previous section. You could try to use those options.

These are the general techniques for handling spills. However, to fix data spills, we need to first identify the spills. Let's see how to identify spills in Synapse SQL and Spark.

Identifying data spills in Synapse SQL

The primary indicator in Synapse SQL that indicates excessive data spills is **TempDB** running out of space. If you notice your Synapse SQL queries failing due to TempDB issues, it might be an indicator of a data spill.

Azure provides the following query to monitor memory usage and TempDB usage for Synapse SQL queries. As the query is big and will not be easy for anyone to read and reproduce from a textbook, I'm just providing the links here:

- Query to monitor SQL query memory usage: `https://docs.microsoft.com/en-us/azure/synapse-analytics/sql-data-warehouse/sql-data-warehouse-manage-monitor#monitor-memory`

- Query to monitor SQL query TempDB usage: `https://docs.microsoft.com/en-us/azure/synapse-analytics/sql-data-warehouse/sql-data-warehouse-manage-monitor#monitor-tempdb`

Next, let's look at how to identify spills in Spark.

Identifying data spills in Spark

Identifying spills in Spark is relatively straightforward as Spark publishes metrics for spills. You can check the spills in the **Tasks summary** screen from Spark UI.

Duration	GC Time	Spill (Disk)
76.0 ms		124 B / 4
76.0 ms		122 B / 4

Figure 14.10 – Identifying Spark spills from the Tasks summary metrics

The last column **Spill (Disk)** indicates the bytes of data written to disk. That is how we can identify data spills in Spark. Next, let's look at a Spark technique to tune shuffle partitions.

Tuning shuffle partitions

Spark uses a technique called **shuffle** to move data between its executors or nodes while performing operations such as `join, union, groupby`, and `reduceby`. The shuffle operation is very expensive as it involves the movement of data between nodes. Hence, it is usually preferable to reduce the amount of shuffle involved in a Spark query. The number of partition splits that Spark performs while shuffling data is determined by the following configuration:

```
spark.conf.set("spark.sql.shuffle.partitions",200)
```

`200` is the default value and you can tune it to a number that suits your query the best. If you have too much data and too few partitions, this might result in longer tasks. But, on the other hand, if you have too little data and too many shuffle partitions, the overhead of shuffle tasks will degrade performance. So, you will have to run your query multiple times with different shuffle partition numbers to arrive at an optimum number.

You can learn more about Spark performance tuning and shuffle partitions here: `https://spark.apache.org/docs/latest/sql-performance-tuning.html`.

Next, let's look at how to identify shuffles in pipelines in order to tune the queries.

Finding shuffling in a pipeline

As we learned in the previous section, shuffling data is a very expensive operation and we should try to reduce it as much as possible. In this section, we will learn how to identify shuffles in the query execution path for both Synapse SQL and Spark.

Identifying shuffles in a SQL query plan

To identify shuffles, print the query plan using the EXPLAIN statement. Here is an example.

Consider a Synapse SQL table, DimDriver, as shown in the following screenshot:

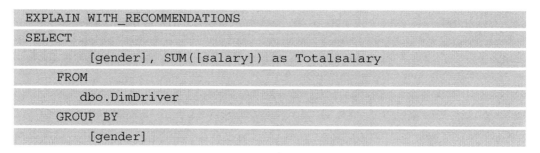

29   SELECT * FROM dbo.DimDriver;

Results   Messages

View   (Table   Chart)   ↦ Export results ∨

🔍 Search

driverId	firstName	middleName	lastName	city	gender	salary
211	Brandon		Rhodes	New York	Male	3000
213	Dennis		Li	Florida	Male	2500
210	Alicia		Yang	New York	Female	2000
215	Maile		Green	Florida	Female	4000
212	Cathy		Mayor	California	Female	3000
214	Jeremey		Stilton	Arizona	Male	2500

Figure 14.11 – Sample DimDriver table

Here is a sample EXPLAIN statement:

```
EXPLAIN WITH_RECOMMENDATIONS
SELECT
        [gender], SUM([salary]) as Totalsalary
    FROM
        dbo.DimDriver
    GROUP BY
        [gender]
```

This will generate a plan similar to the one shown in the following screenshot. The query prints an XML plan. I've copied and pasted the plan into a text editor to make it easier to read the XML.

```xml
<?xml version="1.0" encoding="utf-8"?>
<dsql_query number_nodes="1" number_distributions="60" number_distributions_per_node="60">
    <sql>SELECT [gender], SUM([salary]) as Totalsalary FROM dbo.DimDriver GROUP BY [gender]
    </sql>
    <materialized view candidates>
    <dsql_operations total_cost="0.01056" total_number_operations="5">
        <dsql_operation operation_type="RND_ID">
        <dsql_operation operation_type="ON">
        <dsql_operation operation_type="SHUFFLE_MOVE">
            <operation_cost cost="0.01056" accumulative_cost="0.01056" average_rowsize="44"
            output_rows="31.6228" GroupNumber="8"/>
            <source_statement>SELECT [T1_1].[gender] AS [gender], [T1_1].[col] AS [col] FROM
            (SELECT SUM([T2_1].[salary]) AS [col], [T2_1].[gender] AS [gender] FROM
            [dp203dedicatedsql].[dbo].[DimDriver] AS T2_1 GROUP BY [T2_1].[gender]) AS T1_1
            OPTION (MAXDOP 1, MIN_GRANT_PERCENT = [MIN_GRANT], DISTRIBUTED_MOVE(N''))
            </source_statement>
            <destination_table>[TEMP_ID_5]</destination_table>
            <shuffle_columns>gender;</shuffle_columns>
        </dsql_operation>
        <dsql_operation operation_type="RETURN">
        <dsql_operation operation_type="ON">
    </dsql_operations>
</dsql_query>
```

Figure 14.12 – Sample query plan from Synapse SQL

In the query plan, look for the keyword **SHUFFLE_MOVE** to identify the shuffle stages. The shuffle move section will have the cost details, the number of rows involved, the exact query causing the shuffle, and more. You can use this information to rewrite your queries to avoid shuffling.

> **Tip**
> Read a query plan from the bottom up to understand the plan easily.

Next, let's learn to identify shuffle stages in Spark.

Identifying shuffles in a Spark query plan

Similar to SQL, we can use the EXPLAIN command to print the plans in Spark. Here is a simple example to generate two sets of numbers, partition them, and then join them. This will cause lot of data movement:

```scala
val jump2Numbers = spark.range(0, 100000,2)
val jump5Numbers = spark.range(0, 200000, 5)
val ds1 = jump2Numbers.repartition(3)
val ds2 = jump5Numbers.repartition(5)
val joined = ds1.join(ds2)
joined.explain
```

The `joined.explain` request will print a plan similar to the sample shown as follows:

```
== Physical Plan ==
BroadcastNestedLoopJoin BuildRight, Inner
:- Exchange RoundRobinPartitioning(3), [id=#216]
:  +- *(1) Range (0, 100000, step=2, splits=4)
+- BroadcastExchange IdentityBroadcastMode, [id=#219]
   +- Exchange RoundRobinPartitioning(5), [id=#218]
      +- *(2) Range (0, 200000, step=5, splits=4)
```

Just search for the Exchange keyword to identify the shuffle stages.

Alternatively, you can identify the shuffle stage from the Spark DAG. In the previous chapter, we saw how to view the Spark DAG from the Spark UI screen. In the DAG, look for sections named **Exchange**. These are the shuffle sections. Here is an example Spark DAG containing two **Exchange** stages:

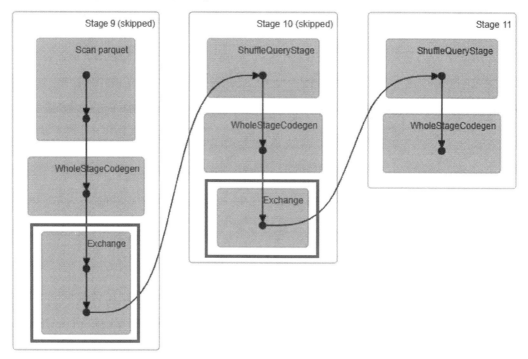

Figure 14.13 – Exchange stages (Shuffle stages) in a Spark job

If there are very expensive shuffle sections, consider enabling the statistics and checking whether the engine generates a better plan. If not, you will have to rewrite the query to reduce the shuffles as much as possible.

Next, let's look at optimizing resource management for cloud-based analytic pipelines.

Optimizing resource management

Optimizing resource management in this context refers to how to reduce your billing expenses while using Azure analytic services. Here are some of the general techniques that can help.

Optimizing Synapse SQL pools

Here are a few suggestions for Synapse dedicated SQL pools:

- Since the storage and compute are decoupled, you can pause your SQL pool compute when not in use. This will not impact your data but will save you some costs.

- Use the right size of compute units. In the SQL pool, the compute units are defined in terms of **Data Warehouse Units** (**DWUs**). You can start with the smallest DWU and then gradually increase to higher DWUs to strike the right balance between cost and performance.

- Manually scale out or scale in the compute resources based on the load. You can also automate the scale-out and in using Azure Functions.

You can learn more about resource management optimizations for the SQL pool here: `https://docs.microsoft.com/en-us/azure/synapse-analytics/ sql-data-warehouse/sql-data-warehouse-manage-compute-overview`.

Optimizing Spark

Here are a few suggestions for Spark in both Synapse Spark and Azure Databricks Spark:

- Choose **autoscale** options in Azure Databricks or Synapse Spark while setting up the cluster. This will eliminate the need to manage the resources manually.

- Select the **auto-terminate** option in Azure Databricks and Synapse Spark so that the cluster automatically shuts down if not used for a configured period of time.

- You can choose **spot instances** where available to reduce the overall cluster cost. These are nodes that are cheap but might get pulled out if there are higher priority jobs that need the nodes.

- Choose the right type of cluster nodes based on memory-intensive, CPU-intensive, or network-intensive jobs. Always select nodes that have more memory than the maximum memory required by your jobs.

These are some of the ways to optimize your resource usage. Next, let's look at how to tune queries using indexers.

Tuning queries by using indexers

Indexing is another common optimization technology used in database systems, data warehouses, and analytical engines such as Spark. Let's look at the indexing options and tuning guidelines for both Synapse SQL and Spark.

Indexing in Synapse SQL

If you remember, we learned about the different types of indexing in *Chapter 5, Implementing Physical Data Storage Structures*, in the *Implementing different table geometries with Azure Synapse Analytics pools* section. I'll recap the different types of indexers we have along with tips for tuning Synapse SQL here again.

There are three primary types of indexing available in Synapse SQL:

- **Clustered Columnstore Index**: This is the default index option for Synapse SQL. If you don't specify any indexing options, the table will automatically get indexed using this method. Use this index for large tables > 100 million rows. It provides very high levels of data compression and good overall performance.

- **Clustered Index**: This type of indexing is better if you have very specific filter conditions that return only a few rows, for example, if you have a WHERE clause that returns only 100 rows from a million rows. Typically, this type of indexing is good for < 100 million rows.

- **Heap Index**: This index is suitable for temporary staging tables to quickly load data. They are also good for small lookup tables and tables with transient data.

> **Tip**
> If the index performance degrades over time due to incremental loads or schema drift, try to rebuild your indexes.
>
> You can also build a secondary non-clustered index on top of your clustered index tables to speed up filtering.

You can learn more about indexing in Synapse SQL here: `https://docs.microsoft.com/en-us/azure/synapse-analytics/sql-data-warehouse/sql-data-warehouse-tables-index#index-types`.

Next, let's look at the indexing options available for Spark.

Indexing in the Synapse Spark pool using Hyperspace

Spark doesn't have any inbuilt indexing options as of the time of writing this book, although there is an external indexing system developed by Microsoft. Microsoft has introduced a project called **Hyperspace** that helps to create indexes that can be seamlessly integrated into Spark to speed up query performance. Hyperspace supports common data formats such as CSV, JSON, and Parquet.

Hyperspace provides a simple set of APIs that can be used to create and manage the indexes. Let's now look at an example of how to use Hyperspace within Spark. In this example, we load two tables, one containing trips data and another containing driver data. We then run a join query to see how Hyperspace indexing kicks in. Let's look at the steps involved:

1. Load your data into a DataFrame:

```
val tripsParquetPath = "abfss://path/to/trips/parquet/
files"

val driverParquetPath = "abfss://path/to/driver/parquet/
files"

val tripsDF: DataFrame = spark.read.
parquet(tripsParquetPath)

val driverDF: DataFrame = spark.read.
parquet(driverParquetPath)
```

2. Create the Hyperspace index:

```
import com.microsoft.hyperspace._

import com.microsoft.hyperspace.index._

val hs: Hyperspace = Hyperspace()

hs.createIndex(tripsDF, IndexConfig("TripIndex",
indexedColumns = Seq("driverId"), includedColumns =
Seq("tripId")))

hs.createIndex(driverDF, IndexConfig("DriverIndex",
indexedColumns = Seq("driverId"), includedColumns =
Seq("name")))
```

3. Enable the `Hyperspace` index and reload the DataFrames from the same file location again:

```
spark.enableHyperspace

val tripIndexDF: DataFrame = spark.read.
parquet(tripsParquetPath)

val driverIndexDF: DataFrame = spark.read.
parquet(driverParquetPath)
```

4.   Run a query with `join`:

```
val filterJoin: DataFrame = tripIndexDF.
join( driverIndexDF, tripIndexDF("driverId") ===
driverIndexDF("driverId")).select( tripIndexDF("tripId"),
driverIndexDF("name"))
```

5.   Check how the Hyperspace index was included in your query plan by using the `explain` command:

```
spark.conf.set("spark.hyperspace.explain.displayMode",
"html")
```

```
hs.explain(filterJoin)(displayHTML(_))
```

6.   Here is a sample of what a query plan with the Hyperspace index would look like:

```
=============================================================
Plan with indexes:
=============================================================
Project [tripId#859, name#874]
+- BroadcastHashJoin [driverId#860], [driverId#873], Inner, BuildRight, false
   :- Filter isnotnull(driverId#860)
   :  +- ColumnarToRow
   :     +- FileScan Hyperspace(Type: CI, Name: TripIndex, LogVersion: 25) [driverId#860,tripId#859] Batched: true,
DataFilters: [isnotnull(driverId#860)], Format: Parquet, Location:
InMemoryFileIndex[abfss://sandbox@dp203teststorage.dfs.core.windows.net/synapse/workspaces/dp203t..., PartitionFilters: [],
PushedFilters: [IsNotNull(driverId)], ReadSchema: struct
   +- BroadcastExchange HashedRelationBroadcastMode(List(input[0, string, false]),false), [id=#857]
      +- *(1) Filter isnotnull(driverId#873)
         +- *(1) ColumnarToRow
            +- FileScan Hyperspace(Type: CI, Name: DriverIndex, LogVersion: 25) [driverId#873,name#874] Batched: true,
DataFilters: [isnotnull(driverId#873)], Format: Parquet, Location:
InMemoryFileIndex[abfss://sandbox@dp203teststorage.dfs.core.windows.net/synapse/workspaces/dp203t..., PartitionFilters: [],
PushedFilters: [IsNotNull(driverId)], ReadSchema: struct


=============================================================
Plan without indexes:
=============================================================
Project [tripId#859, name#874]
+- BroadcastHashJoin [driverId#860], [driverId#873], Inner, BuildRight, false
   :- Filter isnotnull(driverId#860)
   :  +- ColumnarToRow
   :     +- FileScan parquet [tripId#859,driverId#860] Batched: true, DataFilters: [isnotnull(driverId#860)], Format:
Parquet, Location: InMemoryFileIndex[abfss://sandbox@dp203teststorage.dfs.core.windows.net/hyperspace/trips],
PartitionFilters: [], PushedFilters: [IsNotNull(driverId)], ReadSchema: struct
   +- BroadcastExchange HashedRelationBroadcastMode(List(input[0, string, false]),false), [id=#810]
      +- *(1) Filter isnotnull(driverId#873)
         +- *(1) ColumnarToRow
            +- FileScan parquet [driverId#873,name#874] Batched: true, DataFilters: [isnotnull(driverId#873)], Format:
Parquet, Location: InMemoryFileIndex[abfss://sandbox@dp203teststorage.dfs.core.windows.net/hyperspace/driver],
PartitionFilters: [], PushedFilters: [IsNotNull(driverId)], ReadSchema: struct
```

Figure 14.14 – Query plan using Hyperspace indexes

Notice that `FileScan` is reading the Hyperspace index file instead of the original Parquet file.

That is how easy it is to use Hyperspace within Spark. You can learn more about Hyperspace indexing for Spark here: `https://docs.microsoft.com/en-us/azure/synapse-analytics/spark/apache-spark-performance-hyperspace`.

Next, let's look at how to tune queries using cache.

Tuning queries by using cache

Caching is a well-known method for improving read performance in databases. Synapse SQL supports a feature called **Result set caching**. As the name implies, this enables the results to be cached and reused if the query doesn't change. Once result set caching is enabled, the subsequent query executions directly fetch the results from the cache instead of recomputing the results. The result set cache is only used under the following conditions:

- The query being considered is an exact match.
- There are no changes to the underlying data or schema.
- The user has the right set of permissions to the tables referenced in the query.

You can enable result set caching at the database level in Synapse SQL using the following SQL statement:

```
ALTER DATABASE [database_name]
SET RESULT_SET_CACHING ON;
```

You can also turn result set caching on from within a session by using the following command:

```
SET RESULT_SET_CACHING { ON | OFF };
```

> **Note**
>
> The maximum size of the result set cache is 1 TB per database. Synapse SQL automatically evicts the old data when the maximum size is reached or if the results are invalidated due to data or schema changes.

You can learn more about result set caching here: `https://docs.microsoft.com/en-us/azure/synapse-analytics/sql-data-warehouse/performance-tuning-result-set-caching`.

Similar to Synapse SQL, Synapse Spark and Azure Databricks Spark also support caching, but these are at much smaller scopes like caching a RDD or a Dataframe. Spark provides methods including `cache()` and `persist()`, which can be used to cache intermediate results of RDDs, DataFrames, or datasets. Here is a simple example to cache the inputs of a DataFrame created from a CSV file:

```
df = spark.read.csv("path/to/csv/file")
cached_df = df.cache()
```

Once you cache the DataFrame, the data is kept in memory and offers you faster query performance. You can learn more about Spark caching options here: `https://docs.microsoft.com/en-us/azure/synapse-analytics/spark/apache-spark-performance#use-the-cache`.

Let's next look at how to optimize pipelines for both analytical and transactional use cases.

Optimizing pipelines for analytical or transactional purposes

You have surely heard the terms **OLAP** and **OLTP** if you have been working in the data domain. Cloud data systems can be broadly classified as either **Online Transaction Processing (OLTP)** or **Online Analytical Processing (OLAP)** systems. Let's understand each of these at a high level.

OLTP systems

OLTP systems, as the name suggests, are built to efficiently process, store, and query transactions. They usually have transaction data flowing into a central ACID-compliant database. The databases contain normalized data that adheres to strict schemas. The data sizes are usually smaller, in the range of gigabytes or terabytes. Predominantly RDBMS-based systems, such as Azure SQL and MySQL, are used for the main database.

OLAP systems

On the other hand, OLAP systems are usually big data systems that typically have a warehouse or key value-based store as the central technology to perform analytical processing. The tasks could be data exploration, generating insights from historical data, predicting outcomes, and so on. The data in an OLAP system arrives from various sources that don't usually adhere to any schemas or formats. They usually contain large amounts of data in the range of terabytes, petabytes, and above. The storage technology used is usually column-based storage such as Azure Synapse SQL Pool, HBase, and CosmosDB Analytical storage, which have better read performance.

We can optimize the pipelines for either OLAP or OLTP, but how do we optimize for both? Enter **Hybrid Transactional Analytical Processing (HTAP)** systems. These are a new breed of data systems that can handle both transactional and analytical processing. They combine row- and column-based storage to provide a hybrid functionality. These systems remove the requirement for maintaining two sets of pipelines, one for transactional processing and the other for analytical processing. Having the flexibility to perform both transactional and analytical systems simultaneously opens up a new realm of opportunities, such as real-time recommendations during transactions, real-time leaderboards, and the ability to perform ad hoc queries without impacting the transaction systems.

Let's now look at how to build an HTAP system using Azure technologies.

Implementing HTAP using Synapse Link and CosmosDB

HTAP is accomplished in Azure using **Azure Synapse** and **Azure CosmosDB** via **Azure Synapse Link**. We already know about Azure Synapse, so let's look into CosmosDB and Synapse Link here.

Introducing CosmosDB

CosmosDB is a fully managed globally distributed NoSQL database that supports various API formats, including **SQL**, **MongoDB**, **Cassandra**, **Gremlin**, and **Key-Values**. It is extremely fast and seamlessly scales across geographies. You can enable multi-region writes across the globe with just a few simple clicks. CosmosDB is suitable for use cases such as retail platforms for order processing, cataloging, gaming applications that need low latency with the ability to handle spurts in traffic, telemetry, and logging applications to generate quick insights.

CosmosDB internally stores the operational data in a row-based transactional store, which is good for OLTP workloads. However, it also provides support to enable a secondary column-based analytical store that is persisted separately from the transaction store, which is good for analytical workloads. So, it provides the best of both the OLTP and OLAP environments. Hence, CosmosDB is perfectly suited for the HTAP workloads. Since the row store and column store are separate from each other, there is no performance impact on running transactional workloads and analytical workloads simultaneously. The data from the transactional store is automatically synced to the columnar store in almost real time.

Introducing Azure Synapse Link

Synapse Link, as the name suggests, links Synapse and CosmosDB to provide cloud-native HTAP capability. We can use any of the Synapse compute engines, be it Synapse Serverless SQL Pool or the Spark pool, to access the CosmosDB operational data and run analytics without impacting the transactional processing on Cosmos DB. This is significant because it completely eliminates the need for ETL jobs, which were required earlier. Prior to the availability of Synapse Link, we had to run ETL pipelines to get the transactional data into an analytical store such as a data warehouse before we could run any analysis or BI on the data. Now, we can directly query the data from the CosmosDB analytical store for BI.

Here is the Synapse link architecture reproduced from the Azure documentation:

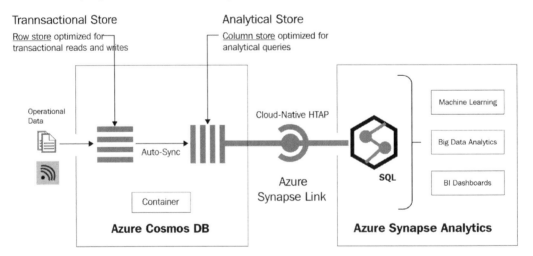

Figure 14.15 – Azure Synapse Link for CosmosDB architecture

> **Note**
>
> Accessing the Azure Cosmos DB analytics store with Azure Synapse Dedicated SQL pool was not supported as of the time of writing this book. Only the Serverless SQL pool was supported.

Let's now look at the steps to create a Synapse link and set up an HTAP system:

1. Let's first create a CosmosDB instance. Search for `CosmosDB` in the Azure portal and select it. In the CosmosDB portal, select the + **Create** button to create a new CosmosDB instance, as shown:

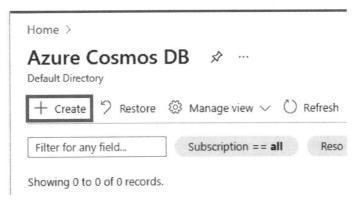

Figure 14.16 – Creating a new CosmosDB instance

2. When you click **+ Create**, it will show the different API options available in CosmosDB. Select **Core SQL**. Once this is selected, you will see a screen as shown in the following screenshot. Just complete the details, including **Resource Group**, **Account Name**, **Location**, and other required fields and click on **Review + create** to create the new CosmosDB instance.

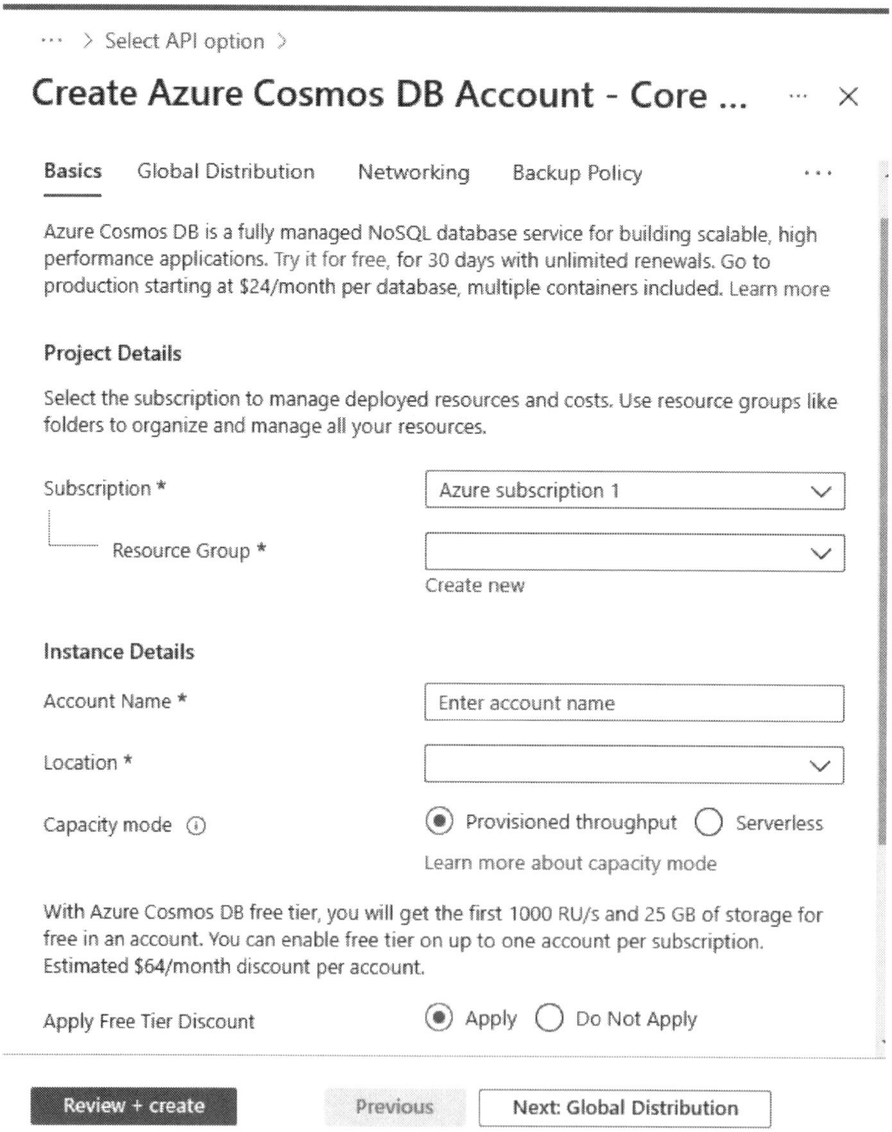

Figure 14.17 – CosmosDB create screen

3. Once you create the CosmosDB instance, it will prompt you to create a container and add a sample dataset. Go ahead and add them.

4. Now, go to the **Azure Synapse Link** tab under **Integrations**. Click on the **Enable** button to enable Synapse Link, as shown in the following screenshot:

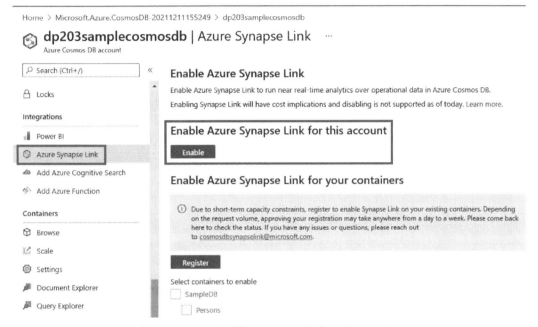

Figure 14.18 – Enabling Synapse Link in CosmosDB

5. Next, go to the **Data Explorer** tab, click on **New Container**, and complete the details in the form that pops up as shown in the following screenshot. Select **On** for the **Analytical store** option at the bottom of the screen. This should set up the CosmosDB for Synapse link.

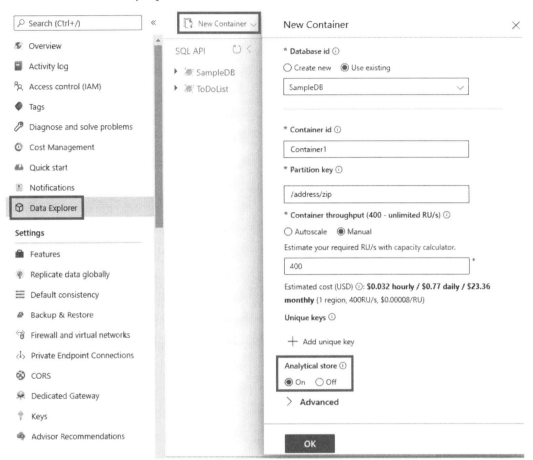

Figure 14.19 – Configuring a new container with Analytical store on

6. Now, we have to set up Synapse to talk to CosmosDB. We have to first set up a linked service to CosmosDB from the Synapse workspace. From the Synapse portal, go to the **Manage** tab and then select **Linked Services**. Click on the **+ New** button and select **Azure CosmosDB (SQL API)**, as shown in the following screenshot:

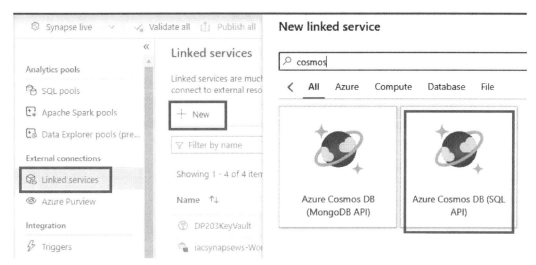

Figure 14.20 – Creating a linked service to Cosmos DB

7. On the screen that will pop up (not shown here), complete the details of the CosmosDB that we created earlier and create the linked service.

8. When you click on the newly created linked service, it should show the details of the CosmosDB linked service along with the **Connection string** details, as shown in the following screenshot:

Figure 14.21 – CosmosDB linked service details

9. Now the Synapse link setup is complete. Go to the Synapse workspace, select the **Data** tab, and you should now be able to see an **Azure Cosmos DB** entry there. We can explore the data in CosmosDB by clicking on the container names under the Azure Cosmos DB entry and selecting **Load to DataFrame**, as shown in the following screenshot:

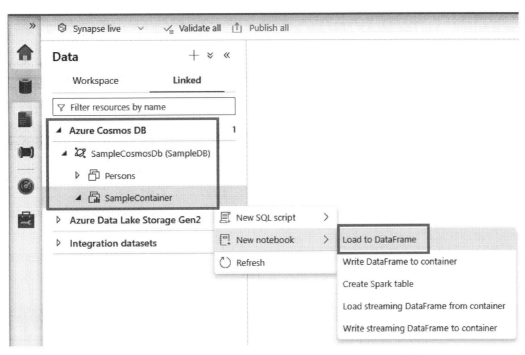

Figure 14.22 – Loading CosmosDB data using the Synapse link

10. You can query the CosmosDB data from the Spark notebook using OLAP, as shown:

```
df = spark.read.format("cosmos.olap")\
    .option("spark.synapse.linkedService", "<Linked
Service Name>")\
    .option("spark.cosmos.container", "<CosmosDB
Container Name>")\
    .load()
```

For OLTP queries, change `format` to `cosmos.oltp` instead of `cosmos.olap`.

11. Now you know how to implement an HTAP system and query from it.

You can learn more about HTAP and the Azure Synapse link here: `https://docs.microsoft.com/en-us/azure/cosmos-db/synapse-link`.

Let's next look at how to optimize pipelines for descriptive and analytics workloads.

Optimizing pipelines for descriptive versus analytical workloads

Data analytics is categorized into four different types:

- **Descriptive Analytics**: The type of analytics that deals with the analysis of what happened and when it happened. Most BI reports, such as sales reports and trip reports, that display current and historical data points fall under this category. The analytics tasks would usually be counts, aggregates, filters, and so on.

- **Diagnostic Analytics**: This type of analytics also does the why part, along with the what and when. Examples include **Root Cause Analysis** (**RCA**). Apart from identifying what happened, we also delve deeper into the logs or metrics to identify why something happened. For example, you could be looking at why a certain cab route is having a dip in revenue, or why a particular type of VM is failing sooner than others by looking into the load on those machines.

- **Predictive Analytics**: As the name suggests, this type of analytics refers to the prediction of what will happen. This is usually associated with machine learning. We use historical datasets and trends to predict what could happen next. This could be for predicting sales during holiday seasons, predicting the peak hour rush for cabs, and so on.

- **Prescriptive Analytics**: This final type of analytics is the most advanced version, where, based on predictions, the system also recommends remediate action. For example, based on the peak sales prediction, the system might recommend stocking up more on certain retail items or, based on the peak hour rush, recommend moving more cabs to a particular region.

The topic of this section says optimizing pipelines for descriptive versus analytical, but in essence, all the previously listed categories are just different types of analytical workloads. I'm taking an educated guess that the syllabus committee might have meant optimizing a data warehouse-centric system versus a data pipeline-based system that can feed data into other services, such as machine learning.

Descriptive analytics almost always includes a data warehouse system such as a Synapse SQL pool to host the final data that can be served to BI tools. And analytics in a generic sense usually involves big data analytical compute engines such as Spark, Hive, and Flink to process large amounts of data from a variety of sources. The data generated would then be used by various systems, including BI, machine learning, and ad hoc queries. So, let's look at the optimization techniques for pipelines involving data warehouses such as Synapse SQL and technologies such as Spark.

Common optimizations for descriptive and analytical pipelines

The optimization techniques we have learned throughout this book will all be applicable to both descriptive and general analytical pipelines. For example, the following techniques are common irrespective of SQL Pool-centric (descriptive) or Spark-centric (analytical) approaches.

Optimizations at the storage level:

- Divide the data clearly into zones: Raw, Transformation, and Serving zones.

- Define a good directory structure, organized around dates.

- Partition data based on access to different directories and different storage tiers.

- Choose the right data format – Parquet with a Snappy comparison works well for Spark.

- Configure the data life cycle, purging old data or moving it to archive tiers.

Optimizations at the compute level:

- Use caching.

- Use indexing when available.

- Handle data spills.

- Handle data skews.

- Tune your queries by reading the query plans.

Next, let's look at the specific optimizations for descriptive and analytical pipelines.

Specific optimizations for descriptive and analytical pipelines

For Synapse SQL, consider the following optimizations:

- Maintain statistics to improve performance while using Synapse SQL's cost-based optimizer.

- Use PolyBase to load data faster.

- Use hash distribution for large tables.

- Use temporary heap tables for transient data.

- Do not over-partition as Synapse SQL already partitions the data into 60 sub-partitions.

- Minimize transaction sizes.

- Reduce query result sizes.

- Use the Result set cache if necessary.

- Use the smallest possible column size.

- Use a larger resource class (larger memory size) to improve query performance.

- Use a smaller resource class (smaller memory size) to increase concurrency.

You can learn more about optimizing a Synapse SQL pipeline here:

- `https://docs.microsoft.com/en-us/azure/synapse-analytics/sql/best-practices-dedicated-sql-pool`.

- `https://docs.microsoft.com/en-us/azure/synapse-analytics/sql-data-warehouse/cheat-sheet#index-your-table`.

And for Spark, consider the following optimizations:

- Choose the right data abstraction – DataFrames and datasets usually work better than RDDs.

- Choose the right data format – Parquet with a Snappy compression usually works fine for the majority of Spark use cases.

- Use cache – either the inbuilt ones in Spark, such as `.cache()` and `.persist()`, or external caching libraries.

- Use indexers – use Hyperspace to speed up queries.

- Tune your queries – reduce shuffles in the query plan, choose the right kind of merges, and so on.

- Optimize job execution – choosing the right container sizes so that the jobs don't run out of memory. This can usually be done by observing the logs for the details of previous runs.

You can learn more about optimizing Spark pipelines here: `https://docs.microsoft.com/en-us/azure/synapse-analytics/spark/apache-spark-performance`.

Let's next look at how to troubleshoot a failed Spark job.

Troubleshooting a failed Spark job

There are two aspects to troubleshooting a failed Spark job in a cloud environment: environmental issues and job issues. Let's look at both of these factors in detail.

Debugging environmental issues

Here are some of the steps involved in checking environmental issues:

1. Check the health of Azure services in the region where your Spark clusters are running by using this link: `https://status.azure.com/en-us/status`.

2. Next, check whether your Spark cluster itself is fine. You can do this for your HDInsight clusters by checking the Ambari home page. We saw how to check Ambari for the status in *Chapter 13, Monitoring Data Storage and Data Processing*, in the *Monitoring overall cluster performance* section. Here is the Ambari screen home page again for your reference:

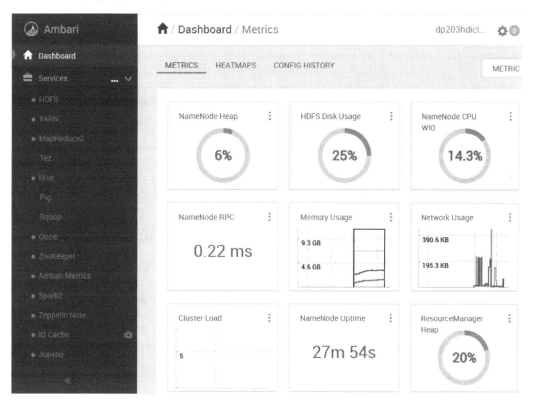

Figure 14.23 – Ambari home page showing the status of the cluster

3. Check to see whether any service is down or whether any of the resources are
    running hot with metrics, such as a very high CPU or very high memory usage.

Next, let's look at how to debug job issues.

Debugging job issues

If the cloud environment and the Spark clusters are healthy, we have to next check
for job-specific issues. There are three main log files you need to check for any
job-related issues:

- **Driver Logs**: You can access the driver log from the **Compute** tab, as shown, in
  Azure Databricks:

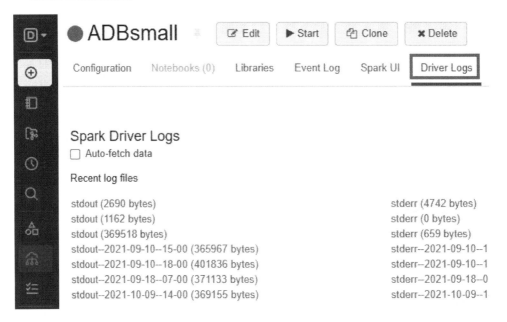

Figure 14.24 – Driver Logs location

- **Tasks** logs: You can access the task logs from the **Stages** tab of Spark UI.

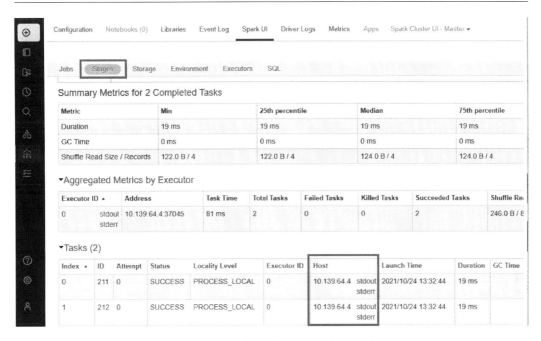

Figure 14.25 – Task log location in the Spark UI

- **Executors** log: The executor logs are also available from both the **Stages** tab, as shown in the preceding screenshot, and from the **Executors** tab, as shown in the following screenshot:

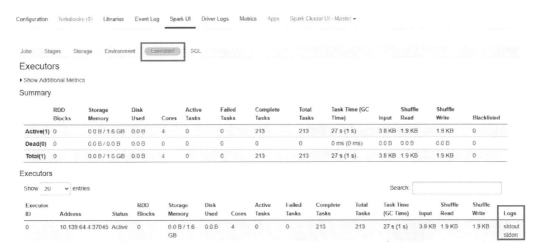

Figure 14.26 – Executor log location in the Spark UI

Start with the driver log, and then proceed to the task logs, followed by the executor logs, to identify any errors or warnings that might be causing the job to fail.

You can learn more about debugging Spark jobs here: `https://docs.microsoft.com/en-us/azure/hdinsight/spark/apache-troubleshoot-spark`.

Next, let's look at how to troubleshoot a failed pipeline run.

Troubleshooting a failed pipeline run

Azure Data Factory and Synapse pipelines provide detailed error messages when pipelines fail. Here are three easy steps to debugging a failed pipeline:

- **Check Datasets**: Click on **Linked Services** and then click on the **Test connection** link to ensure that the linked services are working fine and that nothing has changed on the source. Here is an example of how to use **Test connection** on the **Edit linked service** page.

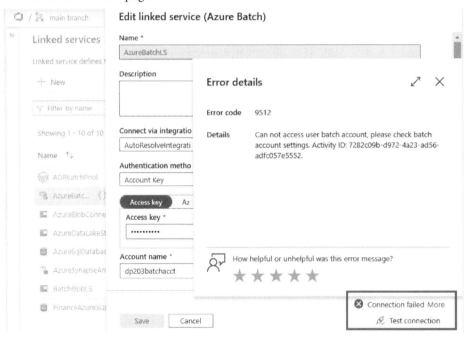

Figure 14.27 – Using Test connection for linked services

- **Use data previews to check your transformations**: Turn the **Data flow debug** mode on and check the data previews for each of your pipeline activities, starting from the data source. This will help narrow down the issue. Here is an example of how to use **Data preview**:

Figure 14.28 – Using the Data preview option to see whether the data is getting populated correctly

- If the issues persist, run the pipeline and click on the error message tag to see what the error code is. Here is an example:

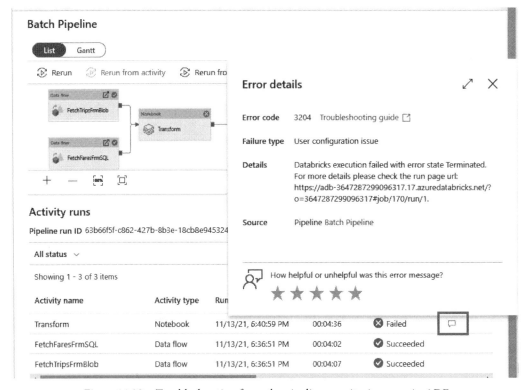

Figure 14.29 – Troubleshooting from the pipeline monitoring page in ADF

The following troubleshooting guide has the details of all the error codes and recommendations on how to fix the issues: `https://docs.microsoft.com/en-us/azure/data-factory/data-factory-troubleshoot-guide`.

Here is an example of a sample error code and recommendation from the Azure Data Factory troubleshooting guide:

```
Error code: 2105
Message: An invalid json is provided for property
'%propertyName;'. Encountered an error while trying to parse:
'%message;'.
Cause: The value for the property is invalid or isn't in the
expected format.
Recommendation: Refer to the documentation for the property and
verify that the value provided includes the correct format and
type.
```

Debugging is a skill that comes with practice. Use the guidelines in this chapter as a starting point and practice with as many examples as possible to become an expert.

With that, we have come to the end of this chapter.

Summary

Like the last chapter, this chapter also introduced a lot of new concepts. Some of these concepts will take a long time to master, such as **Spark debugging**, **optimizing shuffle partitions**, and **identifying and reducing data spills**. These topics could be separate books on their own. I've tried my best to give you an overview of these topics with follow-up links. Please go through the links to learn more about them.

Let's recap what we learned in this chapter. We started with data compaction as small files are very inefficient in big data analytics. We then learned about UDFs, and how to handle data skews and data spills in both SQL and Spark. We then explored shuffle partitions in Spark. We learned about using indexers and cache to speed up our query performance. We also learned about HTAP, which was a new concept that merges OLAP and OLTP processing. We then explored the general resource management tips for descriptive and analytical platforms. And finally, we wrapped things up by looking at the guidelines for debugging Spark jobs and pipeline failures.

You should now know the different optimizations and query tuning techniques. This should help you with both certification and becoming a good Azure data engineer.

You have now completed all the topics listed in the syllabus for DP-203 certification. Congratulations to you for your persistence in reaching the end!

The next chapter will cover sample questions to help you prepare for the exam.

Part 6:
Practice Exercises

This part focuses on where we put everything we have learned into practice. We will explore a bunch of real-world problems and learn how to use the information we learned in the previous chapters. This will help you prepare for both the exam and real-world problems.

This section comprises the following chapter:

- *Chapter 15, Sample Questions with Solutions*

15

Sample Questions with Solutions

This is the last chapter of the book – hurray! This chapter will provide sample questions and tips for attending the **DP-203 certification**. Once you complete this chapter, you should be familiar with the types of questions that appear in the certification along with some techniques for handling them. After you have read this chapter, I'd recommend you go back and read all the important concepts again and look carefully at the notes, tips, and *Further reading* sections provided in the previous chapters.

This chapter will cover the following topics:

- Exploring the question formats
- Sample questions from the *Design and Implement Data Storage* section
- Sample questions from the *Design and Develop Data Processing* section
- Sample questions from the *Design and Implement Data Security* section
- Sample questions from the *Monitor and Optimize Data Storage and Data Processing* section

Let's get started!

Exploring the question formats

Azure certification teams regularly update their questions and question formats, so there is no fixed pattern, but the following types of questions are common:

- Case study-based questions
- Scenario-based questions
- Direct questions
- Ordering sequence questions
- Code segment questions

There could be about 40-60 questions and the questions are usually distributed according to the weightage given to the topics in the syllabus.

- Design and Implement Data Storage (40-45%)
- Design and Develop Data Processing (25-30%)
- Design and Implement Data Security (10-15%)
- Monitor and Optimize Data Storage and Data Processing (10-15%)

The sequence of the questions will be random. Let's look at an example for each of the common types of questions.

Case study-based questions

Let's start with a data lake case study question.

Case study – data lake

In a case study question, a use case will be described in detail with multiple inputs such as business requirements and technical requirements. You will have to carefully read the question and understand the requirements before answering the question.

> **Note**
> In the actual exam, the title of the question will *NOT* have a category such as **Data Lake**. I've just added it here so that it is easy for you to locate the questions directly from the table of contents. This is true for all the question headings in this chapter.

Background

Let's assume you are a data architect in a retail company that has both online and bricks and mortar outlets all over the world. You have been asked to design their data processing solution. The leadership team wants to see a unified dashboard of daily, monthly, and yearly revenue reports in a graphical format, from across all their geographic locations and the online store.

The company has analysts who are SQL experts.

For simplicity, let's assume that the retail outlets are in friendly countries, so there is no limitation in terms of moving data across the countries.

Technical details

The online transaction data gets collected into Azure SQL instances that are geographically spread out. The overall size is about 10 GB per day.

The bricks and mortar point of sale transactions are getting collected in local country-specific SQL Server databases with different schemas. The size is about 20 GB per day.

The store details are stored as JSON files in Azure Data Lake Gen2.

The inventory data is available as CSV files in Azure Data Lake Gen2. The size is about 500 MB per day.

> **Tip**
>
> The trick is to identify key terminologies such as file formats, streaming, or batching (based on the frequency of reports), the size of the data, security restrictions – if any, and technologies to be used, such as SQL in this case (as the analysts are SQL experts). Once we have all this data, the decision-making process becomes a bit simpler.

Question 1

Choose the right storage solution to collect and store all the different types of data.

[Options: Azure Synapse SQL pool, Azure Data Lake Gen2, Azure Files, Event Hubs]

Solution

Azure Data Lake Gen2

Explanation

- ADLS Gen2 can handle multiple different types of formats and can store petabytes of data. Hence, it would suit our use case.

- Azure Synapse SQL pool is for storing processed data in SQL tables.

- Azure Files are file sharing storage services that can be accessed via **Server Message Block** (**SMB**) or **Network File System** (**NFS**) protocols. They are used to share application settings, as extended on-premises file servers, and so on.

- Event Hubs is used for streaming real-time events and not an actual analytical data store.

Question 2

Choose the mechanism to copy data over into your common storage.

[Choices: PolyBase, Azure Data Factory, Azure Databricks, Azure Stream Analytics]

Solution

Azure Data Factory

Explanation

- ADF provides connectors to read data from a huge variety of sources, both on the cloud and on-premises. Hence, it will be a good fit for this situation.

- PolyBase is mostly used for converting data from different formats to standard SQL table formats and copying them into Synapse SQL pool.

- Azure Databricks can be used for batch and Spark stream processing, not for storing large volumes of data.

- Azure Stream Analytics is used for stream processing, not for storing large volumes of data.

Question 3

Choose storage to store the daily, monthly, and yearly data for the analysts to query and generate reports using SQL.

[Choices: Azure Databricks, Azure Queues, Synapse SQL pool, Azure Data Factory]

Solution

Synapse SQL pool

Explanation

- Synapse SQL pool is a data warehouse solution that perfectly fits the requirements for storing data to generate reports and find insights. The daily, monthly, and yearly data is usually the data that is cleaned, filtered, joined, aggregated from various sources, and stored in pre-defined schemas for easy analysis. Since Synapse SQL pools are natively SQL-based, it works well for analysts of the company who are SQL experts.

- Azure Databricks is used for batch and stream processing, not for storing large volumes of data. Hence, it wouldn't fit the bill for our use case.

- Azure Queues storage is a messaging service that can hold millions of messages and that can be processed asynchronously. Hence, it wouldn't fit the bill for our use case.

- Azure Data Factory is used to copy/move data, do basic transformations, and orchestrate pipelines. It cannot be used for storing data.

> **Tip**
> If you find terminologies that you are not aware of, use the principle of negation to find the most suitable answer. In this case, if you didn't know what Azure Queues does, you can try to establish whether any of the other options is a good solution and then go with it. Or, if you are not sure, try to eliminate the obviously wrong answers and take an educated guess.

Question 4

Visualize the insights generated in a graphical format.

[Choices: Azure Data Factory, Synapse Serverless SQL pool, Power BI, Azure Databricks]

Solution

Power BI

Explanation

- Power BI can generate insights from various sources of data, such as Synapse SQL pools, Azure Stream Analytics, Azure SQL, and Cosmos DB. It provides a very rich set of tools to graphically display the data.

- ADF provides connectors to read data from a huge variety of sources and orchestration support. Hence, it will not be a good fit for this situation.

- Synapse SQL pool is a data warehouse solution that can be used to process data and store it, to be used by business intelligence tools such as Power BI.

- Azure Databricks can be used for visualizing data patterns, but not usually for generating and visualizing graphical insights.

These were examples of case study-based questions. Let's next look at scenario-based questions.

Scenario-based questions

In a scenario-based question, you will be presented with a scenario and asked to derive a solution to the problem in the scenario. Let's look at an example.

Shared access signature

You are the security engineer for a company. One of the developers has mistakenly checked in the storage access key as part of a test file into a Git repository. You are planning to immediately regenerate new access keys. Which of the following existing authorization keys will have to be regenerated? [Select all applicable answers]

1. AAD security groups
2. User delegation shared access signature keys
3. Account shared access signature keys
4. Service shared access signature keys

Solution

1. Account shared access signature keys
2. Service shared access signature keys

Explanation

- Both account shared access signature keys and service shared access signature keys are signed using the storage access keys. So, if the access keys are regenerated, it will invalidate the account **shared access signature** (**SAS**) and service SAS keys.

- AAD security groups are independent of the storage access keys, and so will not be impacted.

- User delegation shared access signature keys are signed using AAD credentials, so they will also not be impacted.

Let's next look at direct questions.

Direct questions

These are just simple direct questions. Let's look at an example.

ADF transformation

You are designing the data processing pipeline for a cab company using Azure Data Factory. The company has two fleets of cars: *electric* and *gas*. You have to branch the pipeline based on the type of car. Which transformation would you use?

[Options: Join, Split, Conditional Split, New Branch]

Solution

Conditional Split

Explanation

- **Conditional Split** – This is used to split the input data into multiple streams based on a condition. In our use case, the condition could be the type of car.
- **Join** – Used to merge two inputs into one based on a `Join` condition, so will not work for our use case.
- **Split** – There is no such transformation in ADF.
- **New Branch** – To replicate the current source as is to perform a different set of transformations on the same source of data. Hence, this will also not work for our use case.

These are usually straightforward questions and there might not be any twists. Let's next look at an ordering sequence question.

Ordering sequence questions

In this type of question, you will be given a bunch of statements in a random order. You will have to choose the right set of instructions and arrange them in the right sequential order. Let's look at an example.

ASA setup steps

You have been appointed as a technical consultant for the **Department of Motor Vehicles** (**DMV**). You have been asked to analyze the data coming in from sensors on roads to identify traffic congestion in real time and display it on a graphical dashboard. Since the DMV doesn't have many technical people, they expect the solution to be code-free or with minimal code. You have decided to go ahead with Event Hubs, ASA, and a Power BI-based solution.

Here are the options you have to set up the system. Arrange the five actions that you should perform in the right sequence.

- A – Configure Power BI as the output for the ASA job.
- B – Start the ASA job.
- C – Build the Power BI dashboard to visualize the traffic data on a map.
- D – Configure Azure Blob storage to store the data coming in from the sensors.
- E – Build the ASA query to aggregate the data based on locality.
- F – Copy the aggregated data into Synapse SQL pool.
- G – Configure Event Hubs as the input for the ASA job.

Solution

- G – Configure Event Hubs as the input for the ASA job.
- A – Configure Power BI as the output for the ASA job.
- E – Build the ASA query to aggregate the data based on locality.
- B – Start the ASA job.
- C – Build the Power BI dashboard to visualize the traffic data on a map.

Explanation

The incorrect options are as follows:

- D – Configure Azure Blob storage to store the data coming in from the sensors.

We don't need to configure Blob storage as Event Hubs can stream the data directly to ASA. There was no requirement to store the events for any long-term processing.

- F – Copy the aggregated data into Synapse SQL pool.

ASA can directly publish the data to Power BI. Hence, we don't need the Synapse SQL pool in between.

> **Tip**
> Ordering questions are tricky because unless you have tried the process yourself, you might not remember the sequence in which you will have to perform the tasks. So, do try out the concepts hands-on at least once before your certification.

Let's next look at coding questions.

Code segment questions

In code questions, you might be asked to fill in the missing sections of the code or to identify the right set of the code from multiple choices. Let's look at an example.

Column security

Let's assume that you have a `Customer` table with sensitive information in it. You want to hide the **Social Security Number** (**SSN**) details from `LowPrivUser`. Here is the table definition:

```
CREATE TABLE Customer
(
    CustomerID VARCHAR (20),
    Name VARCHAR (200),
    SSN VARCHAR (9) NOT NULL,
    Phone VARCHAR (12) NULL,
);
```

Complete the following code snippet:

```
GRANT _____ Customer (CustomerID, Name, Phone) TO
LowPrivUser';
```

[Options: ALTER ON, SELECT ON, MASK ON, ENCRYPT ON]

Solution

SELECT ON

Explanation

- **SELECT ON** – Gives permission to run the `SELECT` queries only on `CustomerID`, `Name`, and `Phone`, which is what is required in this use case.

- **ALTER ON** – Gives permission to change the table itself – this is not what is asked in the question.

- **MASK ON** – Invalid syntax; there is no syntax called `MASK ON`.

- **ENCRYPT ON** – Invalid syntax; there is no syntax called `ENCRYPT ON`.

> **Tip**
> Coding questions also need practice. So please try out simple code snippets from the book and Azure websites before your certification.

The preceding five examples cover the most common types of questions in Azure certification.

> **Note**
> During the exam, except possibly for the case study questions, the title of the question will not specify whether it is a scenario, direct, ordering-based, or code-based problem. Once you read the question, it will usually be obvious to you.

Let's now look at a few more sample questions from each of the sections in the syllabus, starting with data storage.

Sample questions from the Design and Implement Data Storage section

Let's look at a random mix of questions from data storage-related topics.

Case study – data lake

The case study questions will have a detailed description of the case followed by the questions.

Background

You have been hired to build a ticket scanning system for a country's railways department. Millions of passengers will be traveling on the trains every day. It has been observed that some passengers misuse their tickets by sharing them with others or using them for more rides than allowed. The railway officers want a real-time system to track such fraud occurrences.

Technical details

- A ticket is considered fraudulent it if is used more than 10 times a day.

- Build a real-time alerting system to generate alerts whenever such fraud happens.

- Generate a monthly fraud report of the number of incidents and the train stations where it happens.

You need to build a data pipeline. Recommend the services that can be used to build such a fraud detection system.

Question 1

You recommend the following components to be used:

- Azure Blob storage to consume the data

- Azure Stream Analytics to process the fraud alerts

- Power BI to display the monthly report

[Options: Correct/ Incorrect]

Solution

Incorrect

Explanation

We cannot use Azure Blob storage to consume real-time data. It is used to store different formats of data for analytical processing or long-term storage.

Question 2

You recommend a system to use:

- IOT Hub to consume the data

- Azure Stream Analytics to process the fraud alerts

- Azure Databricks to store the monthly data and generate the reports

- Power BI to display the monthly report

[Options: Correct/ Incorrect]

Solution

Incorrect

Explanation

We cannot use Azure Databricks to store the monthly data. It is not a storage service; it is a compute service.

Question 3

You recommend a system to use:

- IOT Hub to consume the data

- Azure Stream Analytics to process the fraud alerts

- Azure Synapse SQL pool to store the monthly data and generate the reports

- Power BI to display the monthly report

[Options: Correct/ Incorrect]

Solution

Correct

Explanation

IOT Hub can be used to consume real-time data and feed it to Azure Stream Analytics. Stream Analytics can perform real-time fraud detection and store the aggregated results in Synapse SQL pool. Synapse SQL pool can store petabytes of data for longer durations to generate reports. Power BI can graphically display both the real-time alerts and monthly reports. So, this is the right set of options.

Let's look at a data visualization question next.

Data visualization

You have data from various data sources in JSON and CSV formats that has been copied over into Azure Data Lake Gen2. You need to graphically visualize the data. What tool would you use?

- Power BI
- Azure Databricks/Synapse Spark
- Azure Data Factory
- Azure Storage Explorer

Solution

Azure Databricks/Synapse Spark

Explanation

- Azure Databricks Spark or Synapse Spark provides graphing options that can be used to sample and visualize data.
- Power BI is not used to visualize raw data. It is used to visualize insights derived from processed data.
- Azure Data Factory provides options to preview the data, but not many options for graphically visualizing it.
- Storage Explorer helps explore the filesystem but doesn't have the ability to visualize the data graphically.

> **Tip**
>
> Look for the nuances in the question. The moment we see *graphically visualize*, we tend to select Power BI. But Azure Databricks Spark has built-in graphing tools that can help visualize the data.
>
> Power BI is used to build and display insights from processed data.

Let's look at a data partition question next.

Data partitioning

You have a table as follows in Azure SQL:

```
CREATE TABLE Books {
    BookID VARCHAR(20) NOT NULL,
    CategoryID VARCHAR (20) NOT NULL,
    BookName VARCHAR (100),
    AuthorID VARCHAR (20),
    ISBN VARCHAR (40)
}
```

Assume there are 100 million entries in this table. CategoryID has about 25 entries and 60% of the books align to about 20 categories. You need to optimize the performance of this table for queries that aggregate on CategoryID. What partitioning technique would you use and what key would you choose?

- Vertical partitioning with CategoryID
- Horizontal partitioning with BookID
- Vertical partitioning with BookID
- Horizontal partitioning with CategoryID

Solution

Horizontal partitioning with CategoryID

Explanation

- Horizontal partitioning with CategoryID is the right choice as we need to horizontally partition (shard) the data based on categoryID, which has a fairly good distribution. This can speed up the processing by distributing the data evenly across the partitions.

- Vertical partitioning with CategoryID – Splitting the table vertically will not optimize as we will have to scan through the entire database to aggregate the categories. Vertical partitioning is effective when we need to speed up queries only based on a few columns.

- Horizontal partitioning with BookID – Horizontal partitioning (sharding) is fine, but the key we are looking to optimize is the categories. So BookID will not create the optimal partitions.

- Vertical partitioning with BookID – For the same reason as vertical partitioning with CategoryID, vertical partitions will not be efficient as we need to access all the rows.

Let's look at a Synapse SQL pool design question next.

Synapse SQL pool table design – 1

You are the architect of a cab company. You are designing the schema to store trip information. You have a large fact table that has a billion rows. You have dimension tables in the range of 500–600 MB and you have daily car health data in the range of 50 GB. The car health data needs to be loaded into a staging table as quickly as possible. What distributions would you choose for each of these types of data?

- A – Fact table
- B – Dimension tables
- C – Staging table

[Options: Round Robin, Hash, Replicated]

Solution

- A – Fact table – Hash
- B – Dimension tables – Replicated
- C – Staging table – Round Robin

Explanation

- **Replicated** – Use replication to copy small tables to all the nodes so that the processing is much faster without much network traffic.

- **Hash** – Use hash distribution for fact tables that contain millions or billions of rows/are several GBs in size. For small tables, hash distribution will not be very performant.

- **Round Robin** – Use round robin for staging tables where you want to quickly load the data.

Let's look at another Synapse SQL pool design question next.

Synapse SQL pool table design – 2

You are a data engineer for an online bookstore. The bookstore processes hundreds of millions of transactions every month. It has a Catalog table of about 100 MB. Choose the optimal distribution for the Catalog table and complete the following script:

```
CREATE TABLE Catalogue (
    BookID VARCHAR 50,
    BookName VARCHAR 100,
    ISBN: VARCHAR 100,
    FORMAT: VARCHAR 20
) WITH
    CLUSTERED COLUMNSTORE INDEX,
    DISTRIBUTION = _____
)
```

[Options: ROUND-ROBIN, REPLICATE, HASH, PARTITION]

Solution

```
Replicate
```

Explanation

- Replicate distribution copies the data to all the compute nodes. Hence, the processing will be much faster in the case of smaller tables.

- **Hash** – Use hash distribution for fact tables that contain millions of rows or are several GBs in size. For small tables, hash distribution will not be very performant.

- **Round Robin** – Use round robin for staging tables where you want to quickly load the data.

- **Partition** – This is used for data partitioning, which is not our use case.

Let's look at a slowly changing dimension question next.

Slowly changing dimensions

Identify the type of SCD by looking at this table definition:

```
CREATE TABLE DimCustomer (
    SurrogateID IDENTITY,
    CustomerID VARCHAR(20),
```

```
    Name VARCHAR(100),
    Email VARCHAR(100),
    StartDate DATE,
    EndDate DATE,
    IsActive INT
)
```

[Options: SCD Type 1, SCD Type 2, SCD Type 3]

Solution

SCD Type 2

Explanation

SCD Type 2 keeps track of all the previous records using the `StartDate`, `EndDate`, and, optionally, an `IsActive` or a `VersionNumber` field.

Let's look at a storage tier-based question next.

Storage tiers

You are a data engineer working with an ad serving company. There are three types of data the company wants to store in Azure Blob storage. Select the storage tiers that you should recommend for each of the following scenarios.

- A – Auditing data for the last 5 years for yearly financial reporting
- B – Data to generate monthly customer expenditure reports
- C – Media files to be displayed in online ads

[Options: Hot, Cold, Archive]

Solution

A – Archive

B – Cold

C – Hot

Explanation

- Auditing data is accessed rarely and the use case says yearly financial reporting. So, this is a good candidate for the archive tier. The archive tier requires the data to be stored for at least 180 days.

- Monthly customer expenditure data is not used frequently, so it is a good candidate for cold storage. Cold storage requires the data to be stored for at least 30 days.

- Media files to be displayed in ads will be used every time the ad is displayed. Hence, this needs to be on the hot tier.

Let's look at a disaster recovery question next.

Disaster recovery

You work in a stock trading company that stores most of its data on ADLS Gen2 and the company wants to ensure that the business continues uninterrupted even when an entire data center goes down. Select the disaster recovery option(s) that you should choose for such a requirement:

- **Geo-Redundant Storage (GRS)**

- **Zone-Redundant Storage (ZRS)**

- **Geo-Zone-Redundant Storage (GZRS)**

- **Locally Redundant Storage (LRS)**

- **Geo-Replication**

Solution

- **Geo-Redundant Storage (GRS)** or **Geo-Zone-Redundant Storage (GZRS)**

Explanation

- Both **Geo-Redundant Storage (GRS)** and **Geo-Zone-Redundant Storage (GZRS)** can ensure that the data will be available even if entire data centers or regions go down. The difference between GRS and GZRS is that in GRS, the data is synchronously copied three times within the primary region using the LRS technique, but in GZRS, the data is synchronously copied three times within the primary region using ZRS. With GRS and GZRS, the data in the secondary region will not be available for simultaneous read or write access. If you need simultaneous read access in the secondary regions, you could use the **Read-Access – Geo-Redundant Storage (RA-GRS)** or **Read-Access Geo-Zone-Redundant Storage (RA-GZRS)** options.

- LRS – LRS provides only local redundancy, but doesn't guarantee data availability if entire data centers or regions go down.

- ZRS – ZRS provides zone-level redundancy but doesn't hold up if the entire data center or region goes down.

- Geo-replication – This is an Azure SQL replication feature that replicates the entire SQL server to another region and provides read-only access in the secondary region.

> **Tip**
>
> If you notice any options that you are not aware of, don't panic. Just look at the ones you are aware of and check whether any of those could be the answer. For example, in the preceding question, if you had not read about geo-replication, it would have still been okay because the answer was among the choices that you already knew.

Synapse SQL external tables

Fill in the missing code segment to read Parquet data from an ADLS Gen2 location into Synapse Serverless SQL:

```
IF NOT EXISTS (SELECT * FROM sys.external_file_formats
WHERE name = 'SynapseParquetFormat')
    CREATE _____ [SynapseParquetFormat]
    WITH (FORMAT_TYPE = PARQUET)
IF NOT EXISTS (SELECT * FROM sys.external_data_sources
WHERE name = 'sample_acct')
    CREATE _____ [sample_acct]
    WITH (
        LOCATION   = 'https://sample_acct.dfs.core.windows.net/
users',
    )
CREATE _____ TripsExtTable (
    [TripID] varchar(50),
    [DriverID] varchar(50),
    . . .
    )
    WITH (
    LOCATION = 'path/to/*.parquet',
```

```
    DATA_SOURCE = [sample_acct],
    FILE_FORMAT = [SynapseParquetFormat]
    )
GO
```

[Options: TABLE, EXTERNAL TABLE, EXTERNAL FILE FORMAT, EXTERNAL DATA SOURCE, VIEW, FUNCTION]

You can reuse the options provided above for more than one blank if needed.

Solution

EXTERNAL FILE FORMAT, EXTERNAL DATA SOURCE, EXTERNAL TABLE

Explanation

- The correct keywords are EXTERNAL FILE FORMAT, EXTERNAL DATA SOURCE, and EXTERNAL TABLE in the order in which they appear in the question.

- You cannot use TABLE as this is not an internal table. We are reading external Parquet data as an external table.

- You cannot use VIEW as views are logical projections of existing tables.

- You cannot use FUNCTION as this is not a UDF.

Let's next look at some sample questions from the data processing section.

Sample questions from the Design and Develop Data Processing section

This section focuses on the data processing section of the syllabus. Let's start with a data lake-based question.

Data lake design

You are working in a marketing firm. The firm provides social media sentiment analysis to its customers. It captures data from various social media websites, Twitter feeds, product reviews, and other online forums.

Technical requirements:

- The input data includes files in CSV, JSON, image, video, and plain text formats.
- The data is expected to have inconsistencies such as duplicate entries and missing fields.
- The overall data size would be about 5 petabytes every month.
- The engineering team are experts in Scala and Python and would like a Notebook experience.
- Engineers must be able to visualize the data for debugging purposes.
- The reports have to be generated on a daily basis.
- The reports should have charts with the ability to filter and sort data directly in the reports.

You need to build a data pipeline to accomplish the preceding requirements. What are the components you would select for the following zones of your data lake?

Landing zone:

[Options: Azure Data Lake Gen2, Azure Blob storage, Azure Synapse SQL, Azure Data Factory]

Transformation zone:

[Options: Synapse SQL pool, Azure Databricks Spark, Azure Stream Analytics]

Serving zone:

[Options: Synapse SQL pool, Azure Data Lake Gen2, Azure Stream Analytics]

Reporting:

[Azure Databricks Spark, Power BI, the Azure portal]

Solution

- **Landing zone**: Azure Blob storage
- **Transformation zone**: Azure Databricks Spark
- **Serving zone**: Synapse SQL pool
- **Reporting**: Power BI

Explanation

Landing zone:

- Since the input contains a wide variety of data formats, including images and videos, it is better to store them in Azure Blob storage.

- Azure Data Lake Gen2 provides a hierarchical namespace and is usually a good storage choice for data lakes. But since this use case includes images and videos, it is not recommended here.

- Synapse SQL pool is a data warehouse solution that can be used to process data and store it to be used by business intelligence tools such as Power BI.

- Azure Data Factory provides connectors to read data from a huge variety of sources and orchestration support. Hence, it will not be a good fit for this situation.

Transformation zone:

- Since the requirement includes cleaning up the incoming data, visualizing the data, and transforming the different formats into a standard schema that can be consumed by reports, Azure Databricks would fit the bill. Azure Databricks also supports Notebooks with Scala and Python support.

- Synapse SQL pool can be used to store the processed data generated by Azure Databricks, but would not be a good fit for Scala and Python support.

- Azure Stream Analytics is used for real-time processing. Hence, it will not work for our use case.

Serving zone:

- Synapse SQL pool, being a data warehouse that can support petabytes of data, would be a perfect choice here.

- Azure Data Lake Gen2 provides a hierarchical namespace and is usually a good storage choice for data lake landing zones, but not for the serving zone. Serving zones need to be able to serve the results quickly to BI systems, so usually SQL-based or key-value-based services work the best.

- Azure Stream Analytics is used for real-time data processing. Hence, it will not work for our use case.

Reporting:

- Power BI is a graphical business intelligence tool that can help visualize data insights. It provides a rich set of graphs and data filtering, aggregating, and sorting options.

- The Azure portal is the starting page for all Azure services. It is the control center for all services that provides options for creating, deleting, managing, and monitoring the services.

Let's next look at an ASA windowed aggregates question.

ASA windows

You are working for a credit card company. You have been asked to design a system to detect credit card transaction fraud. One of the scenarios is to check whether a credit card has been used more than 3 times within the last 10 mins. The system is already configured to use Azure Event Hubs and Azure Stream Analytics. You have decided to use the windowed aggregation feature of ASA. Which of the following solutions would work? (Select one or more)

- A – Use a tumbling window with a size of 10 mins and check whether the count for the same credit card > 3.

- B – Use a sliding window with a size of 10 mins and check whether the count for the same credit card > 3.

- C – Use a hopping window with a size of 10 mins and a hop of 3 mins and check whether the count for the same credit card > 3.

- D – Use a session window with a size of 10 mins and check whether the count for the same credit card > 3.

Solution

B – Sliding Window

Explanation

- A sliding window has a fixed size, but the window moves forward only when events are either added or removed. Otherwise, it won't emit any results. This will work perfectly as the window is of a fixed size and is moving after considering each and every event in progressive windows of 10 mins. This is a typical use case for a sliding window: *For every 10 seconds, alert if an event appears more than 5 times.*

- A tumbling window calculates the number of events in fixed-size non-overlapping windows, so it might miss out on counting the events across window boundaries. Here's a typical use case: *Find the number of events grouped by card number, in 10-second-wide tumbling windows.*

- A hopping window calculates the count of events at every X interval, for the previous Y window width duration. If the overlap window is not big enough, this will also miss counting the events across window boundaries. Here's a typical use case: *Every 10 seconds, fetch the transaction count for the last 20 seconds.*

- Session windows don't have fixed sizes. We need to specify a maximum window size and a timeout duration for session windows. The session window tries to grab as many events as possible within the max window size. Since this is not a fixed-size window, it will not work for our use case. Here's a typical use case: *Find the number of trips that occur within 5 seconds of each other.*

Let's next look at a Spark transformation question.

Spark transformation

You work for a cab company that is storing trip data in Parquet format and fare data in CSV format. You are required to generate a report to list all the trips aggregated using the `City` field. The report should contain all fields from both files.

Trip file format (Parquet):

`tripId, driverId, City, StartTime, EndTime`

Fare file format (CSV):

`tripId, Fare`

Fill in the blanks of the following code snippet to achieve the preceding objective:

```scala
%%scala
val fromcsv = spark.read.options(Map("inferSchema"-
>"true","header"->"true"))
.csv("abfss://path/to/csv/*")
val fromparquet = spark.read.options(Map("inferSchema"-
>"true"))
.parquet("abfss:// abfss://path/to/parquet/*")
val joinDF = fromcsv._____(fromparquet,fromcsv("tripId") ===
fromparquet("tripId"),"inner")._____("City")
```

[Options: `join`, `orderBy`, `select`, `groupBy`]

Solution

`Join`, `groupBy`

Explanation

- `join()` – To join two tables based on the provided conditions
- `groupBy()` – Used to aggregate values based on some column values, such as `City` in this case
- `select()` – To select the data from a subset of columns
- `orderBy()` – To sort the rows by a particular column

Let's next look at an ADF integration runtime-based question.

ADF – integration runtimes

You are working as a data engineer for a tax consulting firm. The firm processes thousands of tax forms for its customers every day. Your firm is growing and has decided to move to the cloud, but they want to be in a hybrid mode as they already have invested in a good set of on-premises servers for data processing. You plan to use ADF to copy data over nightly. Which of the following integration runtimes would you suggest?

- A – Azure integration runtime
- B – Self-Hosted integration runtime
- C – Azure – SSIS integration runtime

Solution

B – Self-Hosted Integration Runtime: Since this is an on-premises to the cloud use case, the self-hosted integration would be ideal. Also, since they have their local compute available, it would become much easier to set up the IR on the local servers.

Explanation

Azure Integration Runtime – This is the default option and supports connecting data stores and compute services across public endpoints. Use this option to copy data between Azure-hosted services.

Self-Hosted Integration Runtime – Use the self-hosted IR when you need to copy data between on-premises clusters and Azure services. You will need machines or VMs on the on-premises private network to install a self-hosted integration runtime.

Azure – SSIS Integration Runtime – The SSIS IRs are used for **SQL Server Integration Services (SSIS)** lift and shift use cases.

Let's next look at a question on ADF triggers.

ADF triggers

Choose the right kind of trigger for your ADF pipelines:

- A – Trigger when a file gets deleted in Azure Blob storage
- B – To handle custom events in Event Grid
- C – Trigger a pipeline every Monday and Wednesday at 9:00 A.M. EST
- D – Trigger a pipeline daily at 9:00 A.M. EST but wait for the previous run to complete

[Options: Storage event trigger, Custom event trigger, Tumbling window trigger, Schedule trigger]

Solution

- A – Storage event trigger
- B – Custom event trigger
- C – Schedule trigger
- D – Tumbling window trigger

Explanation

- **Schedule trigger** – These are triggers that get fired on fixed schedules. You specify the start date, recurrence, and end date, and ADF takes care of firing the pipeline at the mentioned date and time.
- **Tumbling window trigger** – These are stateful scheduled triggers that are aware of the previous pipeline runs and offer retry capabilities.
- **Storage event trigger** – These are triggers that get fired on Blob storage events such as creating or deleting a file.
- **Custom trigger** – These are triggers that work on custom events mainly for Event Grid.

Let's next look at a question from the data security section.

Sample questions from the Design and Implement Data Security section

This section contains sample questions from the data security section of the syllabus. Let's start with a Synapse SQL encryption-based question.

TDE/Always Encrypted

You have configured active geo-replication on an Azure Synapse SQL instance. You are worried that the data might be accessible from the replicated instances or backup files and need to safeguard it. Which security solution do you configure?

- Enable Always Encrypted
- Enable **Transport Layer Security (TLS)**
- Enable **Transparent Data Encryption (TDE)**
- Enable row-level security

Solution

Enable **Transparent Data Encryption (TDE)**

Explanation

- TDE encrypts the complete database, including offline access files such as backup files and log files.
- Always Encrypted is used to encrypt specific columns of database tables, not the complete database or the offline files.
- TLS is for encrypting data in motion. It doesn't deal with encrypting databases.
- Row-level security is for hiding selected rows from non-privileged database users. It doesn't encrypt the database itself.

Let's next look at an Azure SQL/Synapse SQL auditing question.

Auditing Azure SQL/Synapse SQL

You work for a financial institution that stores all transactions in an Azure SQL database. You are required to keep track of all the delete activities on the SQL server. Which of the following activities should you perform? (Select one or more correct options)

- Create alerts using Azure SQL Metrics.
- Enable auditing.
- Configure Log Analytics as the destination for the audit logs.
- Build custom metrics for delete events.

Solution

- Enable auditing.
- Configure Log Analytics as the destination for the audit logs.

Explanation

- Enabling auditing will track all the events in the database, including delete activities.
- Configuring the destination as Log Analytics or Storage (Blob) will suffice the requirement to keep track of the activities. Log Analytics provides the advantage of Kusto queries, which can be run to analyze the audit logs. In the case of Blob storage, we will have to write custom code to analyze the audit logs.
- Building custom metrics is not required as the audit function will automatically keep track of all deletions.
- Creating alerts is not required as the requirement is to only keep track of the delete activities, not to alert.

Let's next look at a **Dynamic Data Masking (DDM)** question.

Dynamic data masking

You need to partially mask the numbers of an SSN column. Only the last four digits should be visible. Which of the following solutions would work?

- A – ALTER TABLE [dbo].[Customer] ALTER COLUMN SSN ADD MASKED WITH FUNCTION ='PARTIAL(4, "xxx-xx-", 4)');
- B – ALTER TABLE [dbo].[Customer] ALTER COLUMN SSN ADD MASKED WITH FUNCTION = 'PARTIAL(4, "xxx-xx-", 0)');

- C – `ALTER TABLE [dbo].[Customer] ALTER COLUMN SSN ADD MASKED WITH (FUNCTION = 'PARTIAL(0,"xxx-xx-", 4)');`

- D – `ALTER TABLE [dbo].[Customer] ALTER COLUMN SSN ADD MASKED WITH FUNCTION = 'PARTIAL("xxx-xx-")');`

Solution

C – `ALTER TABLE [dbo].[Customer] ALTER COLUMN SSN ADD MASKED WITH FUNCTION ='PARTIAL(0, 'xxx-xx-', 4)');`

Explanation

The syntax for partial masking is `partial(prefix, [padding], suffix)`.

Let's next look at an RBAC-based question.

RBAC – POSIX

Let's assume that you are part of the engineering AAD security group in your company. The sales team has a directory with the following details:

Container	Owner	Permission (POSIX)
/Sales	Sales AAD security group	740

Figure 15.1 – Sample sales directory with owner and permission information

Will you be able to read the files under the `/Sales` directory?

Solution

No

Explanation

In POSIX representation, there are numbers to indicate the permissions for `Owner`, `Owner Group`, and `Others`.

In our question, the 740 would expand into:

Owner: 7 (Read – 4, Write – 2, Execute – 1. Total: 4+2+1 = 7) // Can Read, Write, and Execute

`Owner Group`: 4 (Read – 4, Write – 0, Execute – 0. Total: 4+0+0 = 4) // Can Read, but not Write or Execute

`Others`: 0 (Read – 0, Write – 0, Execute – 0. Total: 0+0+0 = 0) // Cannot Read, Write, or Execute

So, the answer to the question would be *No*. Since you are part of the engineering security group, you would fall under the `Other` category, which doesn't have any permissions.

Let's next look at a row-level security question.

Row-level security

You are building a learning management system and you want to ensure that a teacher can see only the students in their class with any `SELECT` queries. Here is the `STUDENT` table:

```
CREATE TABLE StudentTable {
    StudentId VARCHAR (20),
    StudentName VARCHAR(40),
    TeacherName sysname,
    Grade VARCHAR (3)
}
```

Fill in the missing sections of the following row-level security script:

1. Step 1:

    ```
    CREATE _____ Security.TeacherPredicate (@TeacherName AS
    sysname)
    RETURNS TABLE
    AS RETURN SELECT 1
    WHERE @TeacherName = USER_NAME()
    ```

    [Options: FUNCTION, TABLE, VIEW]

2. Step 2:

    ```
    CREATE _____ PrivFilter
    ADD FILTER PREDICATE Security.TeacherPredicate
    (TeacherName)
    ON StudentTable WITH (STATE = ON);
    ```

    [Options: SECURITY POLICY, TABLE, VIEW]

Solution

- Step 1: `FUNCTION`
- Step 2: `SECURITY POLICY`

Explanation

- Step 1: You must create a `FUNCTION` that can be applied as a `FILTER PREDICATE`, not a `TABLE` or a `VIEW`.
- Step 2: You must create a `SECURITY POLICY` that can be applied on the table, not a `TABLE` or a `VIEW`.

Let's next look at a few sample questions from the monitoring and optimization section.

Sample questions from the Monitor and Optimize Data Storage and Data Processing section

This section contains sample questions from the monitoring and optimization section of the syllabus. Let's start with a Blob storage monitoring question.

Blob storage monitoring

You have been hired as an external consultant to evaluate Azure Blob storage. Your team has been using Blob storage for a month now. You want to find the usage and availability of the Blob storage.

Question 1:

You can find the Blob storage usage from the **Storage Metrics** tab.

[Options: Yes/No]

Question 2:

You can find the Blob availability metrics from the **Storage Metrics** tab.

[Options: Yes/No]

Question 3:

You can find the Blob availability metrics from the **Azure Monitor** -> **Storage Accounts** –> **Insights** tab.

[Options: Yes/No]

Solution

1. **Question 1**: **Yes**
2. **Question 2**: **No**
3. **Question 3**: **Yes**

Explanation

You can find the Blob storage usage from the **Metrics** tab on the Storage portal page. But it doesn't have the store availability metrics. To look at the availability, you will have to go to Azure Monitor and click on the **Insights** tab under **Storage accounts**.

T-SQL optimization

You are running a few T-SQL queries and realize that the queries are taking much longer than before. You want to analyze why the queries are taking longer. Which of the following solutions will work? (Select one or more).

- A – Create a diagnostic setting for Synapse SQL pool to send the `ExecRequests` and `Waits` logs to Log Analytics and analyze the diagnostics table using Kusto to get the details of the running query and the query waits.

- B – Run a T-SQL query against the `sys.dm_pdw_exec_requests` and `sys.dm_pdw_waits` table to get the details of the running query and the query waits.

- C – Go to the Synapse SQL Metrics dashboard and look at the query execution and query wait metrics.

Solution

B

Explanation

The diagnostic setting for Synapse SQL pool didn't provide the options for `ExecRequests` and `Waits` as of writing this book.

`sys.dm_pdw_exec_requests` – Contains all the current and recently active requests in Azure Synapse Analytics.

`sys.dm_pdw_waits` – Contains details of the wait states in a query, including locks and waits on transmission queues.

The SQL Metrics dashboard doesn't provide the query performance details.

Let's next look at an ADF monitoring question.

ADF monitoring

There are two sub-questions for this question. Select all the statements that apply.

Question 1:

How would you monitor ADF pipeline performance for the last month?

- A – Use the ADF pipeline **activity** dashboard.
- B – Create a diagnostic setting, route the pipeline data to Log Analytics, and use Kusto to analyze the performance data.

[Options: A, B]

Question 2:

How would you monitor ADF pipeline performance for the last 3 months?

- A – Use the ADF pipeline **activity** dashboard.
- B – Create a diagnostic setting, route the pipeline data to Log Analytics, and use Kusto to analyze the performance data.

[Options: A, B]

Solution

Question 1:

A and **B**

Question 2:

Only A

Explanation

The ADF activity dashboard only keeps 45 days of data. Beyond that, we need to use Azure Monitoring and Log Analytics.

Let's next look at an ASA alert-related question.

Setting up alerts in ASA

Select the four steps required to set up an alert to fire if SU % goes above 80%. Arrange the steps in the right order:

- A – Configure diagnostic settings.
- B – Define the actions to be done when the alert is triggered.
- C – Select the signal as SU % utilization.
- D – Redirect logs to Log Analytics and use Kusto to check for Threshold > 80%
- E – Select the scope as your Azure Stream Analytics job.
- F – Set the alert logic as `Greater Than` Threshold value `80`%.

Solution

E, C, F, B

Explanation

The steps involved in setting up an ASA alert for SU % utilization are as follows:

- Select the scope as your Azure Stream Analytics job.
- Select the signal as SU % utilization.
- Set the alert logic as `Greater Than` Threshold value `80`%.
- Define the actions to be done when the alert is triggered.

Diagnostic settings and Log Analytics are not required. The required SU % utilization metric is already available as part of ASA metrics.

That was the last of our sample questions!

Summary

With that, we have come to the end of the book. I hope you enjoyed reading it as much as I enjoyed writing it. The questions provided in this chapter are just samples but should give you a good idea of how the questions will be in the certification exam. One last piece of advice before you take the test: please try and get familiar with all the concepts hands-on. The Azure certification tests look for practical experience, so do try to create the resources, run sample jobs, set up alerts, tune your queries, and so on, to boost your confidence levels.

Wishing you all the very best for your certification!

Index

S

`Packt.com`

Subscribe to our online digital library for full access to over 7,000 books and videos, as well as industry leading tools to help you plan your personal development and advance your career. For more information, please visit our website.

Why subscribe?

- Spend less time learning and more time coding with practical eBooks and Videos from over 4,000 industry professionals

- Improve your learning with Skill Plans built especially for you

- Get a free eBook or video every month

- Fully searchable for easy access to vital information

- Copy and paste, print, and bookmark content

Did you know that Packt offers eBook versions of every book published, with PDF and ePub files available? You can upgrade to the eBook version at `packt.com` and as a print book customer, you are entitled to a discount on the eBook copy. Get in touch with us at `customercare@packtpub.com` for more details.

At `www.packt.com`, you can also read a collection of free technical articles, sign up for a range of free newsletters, and receive exclusive discounts and offers on Packt books and eBooks.

Other Books You May Enjoy

If you enjoyed this book, you may be interested in these other books by Packt:

Azure Data Scientist Associate Certification Guide

Andreas Botsikas , Michael Hlobil

ISBN: 978-1-80056-500-5

- Create a working environment for data science workloads on Azure
- Run data experiments using Azure Machine Learning services
- Create training and inference pipelines using the designer or code
- Discover the best model for your dataset using Automated ML
- Use hyperparameter tuning to optimize trained models
- Deploy, use, and monitor models in production
- Interpret the predictions of a trained model

Data Engineering with Apache Spark, Delta Lake, and Lakehouse

Manoj Kukreja

ISBN: 978-1-80107-774-3

- Discover the challenges you may face in the data engineering world

- Add ACID transactions to Apache Spark using Delta Lake

- Understand effective design strategies to build enterprise-grade data lakes

- Explore architectural and design patterns for building efficient data ingestion pipelines

- Orchestrate a data pipeline for preprocessing data using Apache Spark and Delta Lake APIs

- Automate deployment and monitoring of data pipelines in production

- Get to grips with securing, monitoring, and managing data pipelines models efficiently

Packt is searching for authors like you

If you're interested in becoming an author for Packt, please visit `authors.packtpub.com` and apply today. We have worked with thousands of developers and tech professionals, just like you, to help them share their insight with the global tech community. You can make a general application, apply for a specific hot topic that we are recruiting an author for, or submit your own idea.

Share Your Thoughts

Now you've finished *DP-203: Azure Data Engineer Associate Certification Guide*, we'd love to hear your thoughts! Scan the QR code below to go straight to the Amazon review page for this book and share your feedback or leave a review on the site that you purchased it from.

`https://packt.link/r/1-801-81606-9`

Your review is important to us and the tech community and will help us make sure we're delivering excellent quality content.

Made in the USA
Coppell, TX
19 December 2023

26261326R10315